COMPARATIVE EUROPEAN POLITICS, THIRD EDITION

This is a clear, comprehensive and authoritative introduction to the institutional regimes of countries in Western Europe written by an outstanding group of political scientists. Completely revised and updated throughout, *Comparative European Politics*, third edition:

- Provides a complete coverage of individual countries or group of countries, as well as the European Union, allowing readers to draw sophisticated comparisons between countries.
- Is written to a common template so that each chapter explores political parties, elections and electoral rules, parliaments, local, regional and state governments, and the relations between domestic institutions and the European Union.

Josep M. Colomer is Professor of Political Science and Chair of Comparative European Politics at the University of Bristol. He is the author, among other books, of *Great Empires, Small Nations* (2007), *Political Institutions* (2001) and editor of the *Handbook of Electoral System Choice* (2004).

Contributors: Ian Budge, Manfred G. Schmidt, Yves Mény, Gianfranco Pasquino, Josep M. Colomer, Hans Keman, Jan-Erik Lane and Svante Ersson.

COMPARATIVE EUROPEAN POLITICS

Third edition

Edited by Josep M. Colomer

Routledge
Taylor & Francis Group

LONDON AND NEW YORK

First edition published 1996
Second edition, 2002
Third edition, 2008
by Routledge
2 Park Square, Milton Park, Abingdon, Oxon, OX14 4RN

Simultaneously published in the USA and Canada
by Routledge
711 Third Avenue, New York, NY 10017

Routledge is an imprint of the Taylor & Francis Group, an informa business

Typeset in Adobe Garamond by
Keystroke, 28 High Street, Tettenhall, Wolverhampton

British Library Cataloguing in Publication Data
A catalogue record for this book is available from the British Library

Library of Congress Cataloging in Publication Data
   Comparative European politics / edited by Josep M. Colomer. – 3rd ed.
      p. cm.
   Rev. ed. of: Political institutions in Europe, 2nd ed.
   Includes bibliographical references and index.
   [etc.]
   1. Europe, Western–Politics and government. 2. Comparative government.
   I. Colomer, Josep Maria. II. Political institutions in Europe.
   JN94.A58C65 2008
   320.3094–dc22   2007048585

ISBN 10: 0–415–43755–5 (hbk)   ISBN 13: 978–0–415–43755–4 (hbk)
ISBN 10: 0–415–43756–3 (pbk)   ISBN 13: 978–0–415–43756–1 (pbk)
ISBN 10: 0–203–94609–X (ebk)   ISBN 13: 978–0–203–94609–1 (ebk)

CONTENTS

TABLES

NOTES ON CONTRIBUTORS

Ian Budge is Research Professor of Government at the University of Essex. His numerous authored or co-authored books include, most recently, *Mapping Policy Preferences: Estimates for parties, electors and governments, 1945–1998*, *The New British Politics*, *The New Challenge of Direct Democracy* and *Elections, Parties, Democracy: Conferring the median mandate*.

Josep M. Colomer is Professor of Political Science and Chair of Comparative European Politics at the University of Bristol. He is author of the books *Great Empires, Small Nations*, *Political Institutions*, *Strategic Transitions* and *Game Theory and the Transition to Democracy*, and editor of the *Handbook of Electoral System Choice*.

Svante Ersson is Lecturer in Political Science at Umeå University. He and Jan-Erik Lane are joint authors of *The New Institutional Politics* and *Politics and Society in Western Europe*.

Hans Keman is Professor and Chair of Comparative Political Science at the Free University in Amsterdam, as well as co-editor of *Acta Politica*. Among his publications are: *Doing Research in Political Science*, *Party Government in 48 Democracies* and the edited volume *Comparative Democratic Politics: A guide to theory and research*.

Jan-Erik Lane is Professor of Political Science at the University of Geneva and also teaches at the University of South Pacific. His most recent books are *Comparative Politics: The principal–agent perspective* and *Public Administration and Public Management*.

Yves Mény is Professor of Political Science and President of the European University Institute, in Florence. His most recent publications include *Democracies and the Populist Challenge*, *The Future of European Welfare: A new social contract* and *Challenges to Consensual Politics: Democracy, identity and populist protest in the Alpine region*.

Gianfranco Pasquino is Professor of Political Science at the University of Bologna and Adjunct Professor at the Bologna Centre of the Johns Hopkins University. Most recently, he has written *Sistemi politici comparati* and *Parlamenti democratici* (with Riccardo Pelizzo) and edited *Strumenti della democrazia*.

Manfred G. Schmidt is Professor of Political Science at the University of Heidelberg. His recent book publications include *Das politische System Deutschlands*, *Sozialpolitik in Deutschland: historische Entwicklung und internationaler Vergleich* (3rd edn) and *Political Institutions in the Federal Republic of Germany*.

CHAPTER 1

Introduction

Josep M. Colomer

Europe is the continent of old democracies, and democracy is the form of government which has triumphantly extended to the eastern part of that continent and many other parts of the world since late twentieth century. However, just when this typically European form of government is being accepted as never before, popular dissatisfaction with democratic outcomes, criticism of political decisions and unpopularity of politicians seem to be spreading. There is a far-reaching suspicion that this paradoxical growth of dissatisfaction with the real working of the most accepted form of government is related to the arrangements and structuring of political institutions in democratic regimes.

In this book political institutions and processes in fifteen European democratic countries, as well as in the European Union, are described, analysed and partly compared. We consider both institutions in the sense of rules of the political game and political organisations acting within that framework. Our main concerns are policy issues, political parties, electoral rules, elections, parliaments, state, regional and local governments, and the relationship between these institutions and the European Union, as well as the electoral, policy, coalition and strategic criteria used by political actors. Chapters are devoted to single-country analysis, in the cases of Germany, France and Italy, to sub-area studies in the cases of the islands of Britain and Ireland, the Iberian peninsula (Spain and Portugal), the Low Countries (Belgium, Luxembourg and the Netherlands) and the Nordic countries (Denmark, Finland, Iceland, Norway and Sweden), as well as to the European Union. (Some basic data are presented in Table 1.1.)

Table 1.1 Basic data

Country	Population, 2006 (millions)	Territory (000 km^2)	GNI per capita, 2006 (international 000 $)	Current constitution, year
Austria	8	84	33	1920 (1945)
Belgium	10	31	32	1993
Bulgaria	8	111	9	1991
Cyprus	0.8	9	21	1960
Czech Republic	10	79	20	1992
Denmark	5	43	34	1953
Estonia	1	45	15	1992
Finland	5	338	32	2000
France	63	552	31	1958
Germany	82	357	30	1949
Greece	11	132	23	1975
Hungary	10	93	17	1949 (1989)
Iceland	0.3	103	35	1944
Ireland	4	70	33	1937
Italy	59	301	28	1948
Latvia	2	65	13	1922
Lithuania	3	65	14	1992
Luxembourg	0.5	3	49	1868 (1948)
Malta	0.4	0.3	19	1964
Netherlands	16	37	33	1983
Norway	5	324	42	1814 (1945)
Poland	38	313	13	1997
Portugal	11	92	20	1976
Romania	22	238	9	1991
Slovakia	5	49	15	1992
Slovenia	2	20	22	1991
Spain	44	505	27	1978
Sweden	9	450	32	1975
Switzerland	7	41	39	1874
United Kingdom	60	245	34	1215/1707/1832

Note: GNI: gross national income in international dollars (purchasing power parity).
Parentheses denote the most recent year the constitution was enacted.

Source: World Bank.

The common historical and cultural features of the groups of countries mentioned allow us to isolate their specific institutions and compare their outcomes. In this introduction, relevant comparisons of some institutional features of all thirty countries in Europe are also presented. Common ground for further comparisons is offered by four general tables, several common tables for each chapter providing homogeneous and comparable data on parliamentary and presidential elections, left–right positions of political parties, governments and presidents, as well as a few country-specific tables on distinguishing features.

The new revised and updated edition of this book, now with the title *Comparative European Politics*, relies upon the first and second editions, which were published as *Political Institutions in Europe* (in 1996 and 2002). The success of the previous editions confirms the opinion of the authors when this project was initially conceived, that a clear, accessible and, at the same time, analytical and critical exposition of the institutional regimes of the European countries mentioned was a void to be filled in academic literature. This book may be used as an intermediate textbook for studies in Political Science, Comparative Politics, European Politics, Political Institutions or Constitutional Law, but as a whole or in some of its parts it can also be useful either for more introductory or more advanced courses in the same fields. In writing the text, it has not been assumed that the reader should be familiar with the abundant factual information provided here or that he or she should have prior knowledge of the analytical concepts sparingly used throughout.

For more than twelve years now, the editor has had the pleasure of working with an outstanding selection of European political scientists, well known for their insightful comprehension of the political systems of their countries and for their research and analytical skills. All the co-authors of this book have been in regular contact through the European Consortium of Political Research and other university networks.

THEORY AND EMPIRIA IN COMPARATIVE POLITICS

The applied analyses presented in this book attempt to fill a gap between political theory and empirical knowledge. For several decades, both a corpus of increasingly refined theoretical statements and great amounts of empirical data have grown up together in political science. Yet it is clear that formal deductive reasoning without reference to real facts, on the one hand, and merely inductive generalisations, on the other, have not exhausted the possibilities of intellectual progress in the discipline of politics.

Within the field of comparative politics – an admittedly large, plural and often evasive field – there is a tradition which pushes in a more appropriate direction. This is formed by all those pieces of research devoted not only to more or less accurate descriptions of political facts in several countries but also to advancing knowledge about similarities and differences among political structures and, at the same time, testing theoretical propositions about the real working of political institutions.

Nevertheless, one should be aware that discontinuities in the relationship between explanation and description in political science have also been partly provoked by the lack of a single, widely accepted methodological approach among the members of the discipline. Only progress in the consistency and rigour of theoretical assumptions and of analytical methods can create adequate conditions for articulating observations of the real world in a meaningful ensemble.

The development of political science has contributed in a discontinuous and fragmentary way to achieving this aim. As is well known, during the first part of the twentieth century the main influence in the study of politics came from constitutional law. Its characteristic subjects were at that time certain features of political institutions, such as relations between the legislature, the executive and the judiciary, the forms and types of government and, more incipiently, electoral laws. This tradition gave us important description and systematisation of political data and, with its universalistic claim, helped to enlarge the territorial scope of study to all parts of the planet. However, the typical approach of political law was normative rather than explanatory, and many of its works were pervaded by value judgements often supported merely by preconceptions in favour of or opposed to certain real existing political arrangements.

The 'behavioural' approach diffused by the mid-twentieth century had the salutary effect of contributing to reducing the former prescriptive focus while, at the same time, introducing new actors, such as real voters, political parties and interest groups, as the main subject of the study of politics. This in turn enlarged political studies and produced huge amounts of empirical knowledge and collections of data. However, its methods, focusing on inductive statistics and generalising reasoning, did not have the capacity to provide explanatory causality and falsifiable prediction. Furthermore, the 'sociological' emphasis on socio-economic structures, values inherited from education and family, party motives and ideology, public opinion and motives for voting, mostly considered as factors in the stability of political systems, led to neglect of the study of political institutions – a crucial intermediary between values and outcomes.

The rediscovery of institutions resulted both from a search for complementary explanations in this kind of empirical 'sociological' analysis and from some developments in formal political theory. The latter were in their turn the result of a new theoretical and methodological course, basically inspired by the deductive and formal, 'economic' style of reasoning (rather unfortunately labelled 'rational choice' by political scientists), sparked off since the 1970s. After a number of sophisticated models of 'market'-type interactions among political actors, the apparent lack of a theoretical explanation for real equilibriums or stable outcomes of those interactions led to the pursuit of new research in the institutional direction. Political institutions were, thus, rediscovered as a source of empirical regularities which were inconsistent with the findings of formal models previously built in an institutional vacuum. The theoretical scheme was then improved with concepts such as 'structure-induced equilibrium', that is, those collective decisions which are relatively stable, in spite of being made in social conditions prone to instability, because they are efficaciously produced by the institutional structure. In this approach, 'institutions' are considered in a rather abstract way simply as rules of the game, especially rules for making collective decisions. However, the analysis tends to be completed with 'organisations', that is, parties, pressure groups, economic and social bodies and other purposive actors trying to take advantage of the opportunities stemming from the existing institutions (Shepsle 1979, 1989; Riker 1980; Colomer 2001b, 2005).

Through all these developments, political science has made progress towards becoming a 'normal science'. Basically, scientific progress requires the following levels of knowledge: (1) definitions and classifications; (2) quantitative measurements; (3) causal hypotheses; and (4) explanatory theory. The state of the question at all these levels of knowledge is summarised in the following pages regarding the democratic institutions and processes in the European countries and the European Union (Colomer 2004b, 2007b).

SOCIAL STRUCTURES AND POLITICAL INSTITUTIONS

Two parallel debates in different fields of political science have been helpful in shaping a model of the political process which can be used for analytical purposes. The first line of progress took place in the traditional field of comparative politics. In the 1960s certain conventional statements formulated in a sociological perspective tended to underline the importance of homogeneous social structures and common values to the stability of democratic regimes (typically, Almond and Verba 1963). Given that at that time ethnic or cultural homogeneity – referring to religion, race and language differences – seemed greater in the United states than in plural Europe, the European turmoil of democracy and authoritarianism in the first half of the twentieth century appeared in this light to be deeply rooted in society and even hard to prevent or avoid again.

An alternative to these statements was forcefully presented by Arend Lijphart. According to his well-known contribution, a plural and heterogeneous society, such as many actually existing in Europe, may support a stable democratic regime if the institutional structure allows the expression of this pluralism, and if the prevailing conventions and norms of behaviour favour exchanges and co-operation among actors. On this basis Lijphart developed his categories of 'majoritarian' regimes – containing institutions such as plurality rule or majority rule electoral systems, bipartism, concentrated governments and unity of powers – and 'consensual' regimes – including proportional representation, multipartism, coalition governments, divided powers and federalism. Lijphart focused his attention on 'consociational' devices, that is, informal rules and customs conceived as tools to reduce the depth of ethnic and religious cleavages (particularly relevant in democracies such as those of Belgium, the Netherlands and Switzerland) (Lijphart 1984, 2007).

Indeed cultural or ethnic 'homogeneity' tends to be associated with small countries, which are the bulk of the current membership to the European Union, whilst most of the large and socially complex states should be considered 'heterogeneous'. If this simplification is accepted, we could restate the question in the following way. It is to be expected that monist institutions favouring high concentration of power can produce political efficacy, in the sense of good performance in decision-making, especially in small, homogeneous countries, while in large and heterogeneous states they tend to produce some unequally distributed political dissatisfaction among different groups in society (a 'majority tyranny'), which may favour manifestations of social unrest or inter-territorial tensions. On the other hand, institutional pluralism, separation of powers and federalism can produce negotiations and co-operation among parties, which may feed democratic consensus through a fair distribution of satisfaction with political outcomes among the different groups in society, but at the cost of some political inefficacy and governmental and policy instability.

This scheme seems consistent with that derived from other, more theoretical debate between some exponents of the 'sociological' and the 'rational choice' approaches in political science (for relevant references, see Dahl 1956; Riker 1982). According to the former, politics fought out on a single ideological dimension, such as the usual left–right axis, reinforces the lines of conflict. However, uni-dimensionality of the policy ideological space is considered to be a necessary condition for the existence of equilibrium, that is, a stable collective outcome, such as a policy or party membership of a government, in the latter approach. On the contrary, whilst cross-cutting divisions among the population are considered to favour consensus and egalitarian distribution of political satisfaction in standard political sociology, rational choice models found the existence of two or more ideological dimensions to be a source of policy and governmental instability through cycles of variable winning coalitions of minorities with intense preferences in the different dimensions. (For a comparison of statements and the findings of the two approaches, see Miller 1983.)

There is in fact a notable coincidence in the analyses of the two theoretical approaches, although they sometimes differ in their implicit value judgements. They coincide in stating that social and cultural homogeneity or uni-dimensionality of citizens' preferences – to use both vocabularies at the same time – favours equilibrium or policy and governmental stability, but also an unequal distribution of political satisfaction in society. Both also agree in seeing social and cultural heterogeneity or the multi-dimensionality of citizens' preferences as favouring disequilibrium or policy and governmental instability but also creating a potential platform for a more egalitarian distribution of average political satisfaction in the medium or long term.

If efficacy in decision-making was a priority value, a homogeneous society or, if that did not exist, as is mostly the case in Europe, a monist and unitary institutional framework favouring clear and robust decisions should be preferred. On the contrary, where social consensus is highly valued a pluralist institutional scheme reflecting the variety of society should be preferred, even though it would imply a certain abundance of vote-trading, strategic voting, coalition-building and splitting, inter-governmental bargains for further decentralisation and other practices of the sort.

Consistent with this analysis, a complete examination of all the attempts at democratisation in the world since the nineteenth century shows that higher rates of success, that is, longer duration of the corresponding democratic regimes, are achieved with parliamentary regimes using proportional representation and the corresponding multiparty systems and coalition governments – the typical continental European regime – to the extent that they can spread political satisfaction widely among different groups and feed subsequent support into the political regime. Likewise, the highest rates of failure, that is, replacement of democratic regimes with non-democratic ones, are produced by parliamentary regimes with majoritarian electoral formulas promoting high concentration of power in a single party, as in the typical British system, which can foster rejection of the regime among those excluded from government. Intermediate rates of success in establishing durable democracies are found for presidential and semi-presidential regimes, which imply some division of powers, but also inter-institutional conflict and instability. (For details, see Colomer 2001a.)

It is thus possible to establish a clear parallel between the two types of political regime distinguished by Lijphart in the applied analysis first mentioned, the two types of democracy considered relevant by Riker after revising Dahl in the second theoretical development, and the different rates of success in democratisation just mentioned. 'Monist' or 'majoritarian' institutions on the British model would correspond to 'populist' democracy, a model characterised by a high social concentration of political satisfaction and dissatisfaction. 'Plural' or 'consensual' institutions would correspond to 'liberal' democracy, a model characterised by high negotiation costs among parties, but also the opportunity for social consensus and broad democratic satisfaction.

Certainly, political institutions are useful. Expressed in standard terms, institutions form a necessary framework for human interaction and the peaceful solution of social conflicts, which at the same time attempts to promote social benefits. In a more theoretical manner, institutions may be conceived of as a means of overcoming co-ordination and co-operation problems in collective action for the provision of public goods and for achieving agreement among individuals with varied preferences and interests. However, institutions such as electoral systems, power relations between the legislature and the executive, and degrees of centralisation are not neutral but privilege certain policy alternatives, reduce the scope of the citizens' choice and give incentives to some particular behaviours. By introducing these biases, institutions promote the existence of collective decisions, and this is exactly the reason for their utility. But their degree of representativeness and, in consequence, the political satisfaction they create in society are varied (Brennan and Buchanan 1985; North 1990; Colomer 2001a, 2001b).

A COMMON ANALYTICAL FRAMEWORK

What we are trying to promote in this book can be called political analysis, a level of understanding of the real world which is neither mere factual description nor pure formal theory, although it relies upon empirical information and theoretical concepts. The book has been planned in the belief that theory should be able to explain real data, and that data are meaningless unless organised and interpreted by some theoretical framework.

Specifically, we have tried to draw from some recent political theory an agenda of questions for applied analysis, which in turn guides the search for a selection of empirical material. It is interesting to note that, even among American political scientists, a research agenda derived from certain recent theoretical developments has led to new interest in European politics. Europe is, obviously, the preferred setting for multipartism, parliamentarianism, coalition politics and corporatist negotiations. It is also the scene for the building of a new, very large, democratic and market-oriented 'empire' eroding the traditional bases of nation-states and promoting new types of intergovernmental relations.

Europe offers a relatively large number of country cases allowing strict comparative analysis of political institutions, since variables such as socio-economic structures and cultural traditions are not so varied and can be more easily isolated in explaining causal relationships. In particular, and as we shall see in the chapters that follow, different outcomes in rather similar cultural and institutional structures, such as those of Britain and Ireland, can be attributed to their different electoral systems; the different strategic behaviour of political actors in Belgium and in the Netherlands has led to different outcomes in terms of political performance and institutional change; in Scandinavian and Nordic countries similar outcomes are derived from significant consensual devices, such as patterns of negotiation among parties in parliament and corporatist policy concertation; and it is possible to attribute the great governmental instability in Portugal during its first years of democracy, in contrast with the governmental stability in Spain, respectively to their presidential and parliamentary institutional arrangements.

Systematic comparisons such as those just mentioned are limited to certain groups of countries in this book. However, we have tried to avoid at least some of the traditional criticisms of standard comparative politics: formal legalism and empiricism. With this purpose, all the authors of the following chapters have adopted a common, previously agreed upon analytical framework which is based on an implicit interpretation of the political process as a series of decision-making steps.

Each country or comparative chapter starts with elections. Usually a brief presentation of the main issue dimensions, where voters' political preferences can be placed, is followed by a thorough analysis of electoral rules.

Parties and party systems are then examined in the context of the two constraints just mentioned: the policy ideological space of citizens' preferences and the electoral institutions. Besides using standard categories to classify party systems, the authors devote attention to party strategies, trying in particular to characterize the predominance of either centrist or polarised trends.

Next, party competitive and coalition strategies are studied in parliament. The role of parliamentary rules ('institutions' in the strict sense) and the codes of behaviour of parties ('organisations' within the same approach) provide the setting for studying performance, legislative production and, according to country specifics, government formation.

Governments in their different formulae – which in the European context are basically reduced to parliamentary and semi-presidential – are subsequently approached. The analysis of executives is expanded to the bureaucracy and the institutions of corporatist intermediation or social concertation in order to explain outcomes in the shape of public policies. The relationship between the just-mentioned institutions and the judiciary is also addressed to some extent.

After this journey, from the citizens, through elections and parties, to parliament and government and their outputs, a 'transversal' analysis is sketched. It includes regional and local government, which shows an increasing trend towards decentralisation, as well as some challenges to the traditional model of the nation-state. Finally, the links between domestic and European institutions and the 'Europeanisation' of domestic party systems and other elements of the political process are explored.

In each chapter a final section attempts an assessment of the performance of the existing institutional framework. Real debates and alternative proposals for institutional reforms in several countries are used as a basis for forecasting their degree of institutional stability or change and their foreseeable effects.

Different emphases on any of these aspects depend on country specifics. In this way, particular attention is given to government and bureaucracy in the cabinet regime of Britain, federal relations in Germany, the relative powers of president and parliament in France, the electoral system and its reforms in Italy, party rule in the weakly institutionalised processes of decision-making in Spain and Portugal, coalition strategies in Belgium and the Netherlands, the strength and reforms of the welfare state in Nordic countries, party volatility in recent Eastern democracies, as well as the process of building European Union institutions able to be at the same time representative and effective in decision-making.

In spite of these varied emphases, which contribute to a better understanding of the similarities and differences among countries, the common general scheme has allowed the authors to organize country and comparative analyses into common topics and to use similar categories for selecting and dealing with the corresponding data. Comparisons centring on relevant variables are presented in all the chapters. More systematic and general comparisons between the complete political structures of different countries are attempted in apparently 'comparable' cases, which can be considered as 'sub-area studies' on account of their territorial proximity and common history and culture, although this comparability is also submitted to some critical revision. As a whole, the amount of information collected in all of them seems sufficient to yield an overall and quite detailed panorama of the design and working of political institutions in Europe in the early twenty-first century.

COMPARING INSTITUTIONAL MONISM AND PLURALISM

It seems possible to approach a relative estimate of the degrees of institutional and political 'monism' or 'pluralism' through the analysis of the actors involved in the decision process. We shall take into account the characteristics of the following: political parties, chambers in the parliament, a directly elected president, and regional governments in federal systems. The degree of monism/pluralism in an institutional structure will depend on how many of these actors must agree in order to make a policy decision, as well as on their power to make decisions by themselves in different ways from the other actors.

We can assume that a large number of actors and their election or formation in different ways will favour the likelihood of different political majorities in the institutions – in other words, pluralism. Nonetheless, some accuracy in measuring their number and relative decision-making powers must be introduced.

First, we can approach the party system. Multiparty and two-party systems correspond, respectively, to coalition and single-party governments. Highly pluralistic party systems, which can be characterised as those where fewer than half of the seats are in the hands of the two largest parties, can usually be found in Belgium, Denmark, Finland, Latvia, Lithuania, Poland, Slovakia and Switzerland, whilst moderately pluralistic systems and multiparty coalition governments can be found in Austria, Bulgaria, the Czech Republic, Cyprus, Estonia, France, Germany, Iceland, Italy, Luxembourg, Netherlands, Norway, Portugal, Romania, Slovenia and Sweden. In contrast, restrictive, close to two-party systems favouring single-party governments exist in Greece, Hungary, Ireland, Malta, Spain and the United Kingdom.

Second, we can deal with unicameral and bicameral parliaments. Bicameral parliaments exist in 13 of the 30 European countries considered, including the largest ones. We shall consider two features favourable to pluralism: the existence of different electoral procedures able to produce different political majorities in the chambers;

Table 1.2 Electoral rules for the lower or first chamber

Country	Seats	Formula	Magnitude	Ballot	Threshold (%)
Austria	251	proportional	42	open list	4
Belgium	212	proportional	15	open list	–
Bulgaria	240	proportional	240	closed list	4
Cyprus	59	proportional	9	closed list	1.8
Czech Republic	200	proportional	8	open list	5
Denmark	175	proportional	12	open list	2
Estonia	101	proportional	9	open list	5
Finland	200	proportional	14	open list	–
France	555	majority	1	two single ballots	12.5 runoff
Germany	656	proportional	656	two votes: list and single	5
Greece	300	proportional+bonus	5	open list	3
Hungary	386	mixed: proportional	10	closed list	–
		majority/plurality	1	single	5
Iceland	63	proportional	33	closed list	–
Ireland	166	proportional	4	transferable preferential	–
Italy	630	proportional+bonus	24	closed list	2
Latvia	100	proportional	20	open list	5
Lithuania	141	mixed: plurality	1	single	–
		proportional	70	open list	–
Luxembourg	60	proportional	15	open, cumulative	–
Malta	65	proportional+bonus	5	transferable preferential	–
Netherlands	150	proportional	150	open list	0.67
Norway	169	proportional	9	open list	4
Poland	460	proportional	11	closed list	5
Portugal	247	proportional	11	closed list	–
Romania	346	proportional	8	closed list	3
Slovakia	150	proportional	38	open list	5
Slovenia	90	proportional	6	open list	4
Spain	350	proportional	7	closed list	3
Sweden	349	proportional	12	open list	4
Switzerland	200	proportional	8	open, cumulative	–
United Kingdom	646	plurality	1	single	–

Note: Magnitude: average number of seats/district.

Source: Adapted and updated from Colomer (2004a).

and symmetrical powers requiring difficult bargains between them to agree on legislation. In only two of the cases considered, Germany and Switzerland, do we find the possibility of different political majorities and at the same time decision rules accepting an indefinite number of negotiation rounds between the two chambers. A recent reform of the electoral system in Italy has also increased the likelihood that the two chambers may have different political majorities. Indefinite negotiations between chambers are also open in Belgium. In all the other bicameral cases there is the possibility of different majorities, but with restrictive decision rules in favour of one of the chambers in limited negotiations (Austria, the Czech Republic, France, Ireland, Netherlands, Poland, Romania, Spain, the UK).

Third, the parliamentary or presidential scheme can also be evaluated. In 14 of the European countries considered there is a popular election of the president, but only in 5 of these countries does the president have significant executive powers – Bulgaria, Cyprus, France, Lithuania and Poland – a formula which has been called 'semi-presidentialism'. Among the rest of the countries, in 8 the ceremonial president is appointed by parliament and another 8 are parliamentary monarchies. Some government formation powers and the possibility of dissolving the assembly are allocated to some other directly elected presidents besides those mentioned, but also to certain parliamentary elected presidents and to a few monarchs; however, all of them usually exert these powers in accordance with parliamentary electoral results and majorities, which makes them less significant.

Table 1.3 Parliament and President

Country	Parliament	President
Austria	weak bicameral	elected
Belgium	weak bicameral	monarchy
Bulgaria	unicameral	elected, executive
Cyprus	unicameral	elected, executive
Czech Republic	weak bicameral	parliament
Denmark	unicameral	monarchy
Estonia	unicameral	elected
Finland	unicameral	elected
France	weak bicameral	elected, executive
Germany	strong bicameral	parliament
Greece	unicameral	parliament
Hungary	unicameral	parliament
Iceland	unicameral	elected
Ireland	weak bicameral	elected
Italy	strong bicameral	parliament
Latvia	unicameral	parliament
Lithuania	unicameral	elected, executive
Luxembourg	unicameral	monarchy
Malta	unicameral	parliament
Netherlands	weak bicameral	monarchy
Norway	unicameral	monarchy
Poland	weak bicameral	elected, executive
Portugal	unicameral	elected
Romania	weak bicameral	elected
Slovakia	unicameral	elected
Slovenia	unicameral	elected
Spain	weak bicameral	monarchy
Sweden	unicameral	monarchy
Switzerland	strong bicameral	parliament
United Kingdom	weak bicameral	monarchy

Finally, there are in Europe four formally federal countries – Austria, Belgium, Germany and Switzerland – but in all the larger states there is some degree of decentralisation, including in France, Italy, Poland and Spain, as well as in parts of the United Kingdom. Almost half of the population of the European Union live in

Table 1.4 Decentralisation

Country	Locals	Regions	% expenditure
Austria	2,359 local, most mayors	9 states	35
Belgium	589 municipalities	6 regions and communities	42
Bulgaria	264 municipalities, mayors		nd
Cyprus	86 communities and municipalities, mayors		5
Czech Republic	6,254 municipalities 14 regions		27
Denmark	98 municipalities 5 regions		62
Estonia	241 municipalities		25
Finland	416 municipalities 1 province		39
France	36,763 municipalities 100 departments	26 regions	20
Germany	12,431 local, mayors 323 districts, chairmen	16 states	43
Greece	1,035 municipalities and communes 57 prefectures and super-prefectures		7
Hungary	3,169 municipalities, few mayors 19 counties		26
Iceland	79 towns and municipalities		nd
Ireland	114 counties, cities and towns		20
Italy	8,100 communes, mayors 104 provinces, presidents	20 regions, most presidents	32
Latvia	530 local		26
Lithuania	60 municipalities		24
Luxembourg	117 municipalities		12
Malta	68 local		1
Netherlands	467 municipalities 12 provinces		35
Norway	431 communes 19 counties		41
Poland	2,489 communes, mayors 315 counties and districts	16 regions	30
Portugal	4,252 parishes 308 municipalities	2 regions	13
Romania	3,133 cities and municipalities, mayors 42 counties		nd

Table 1.4 (continued)

Country	Locals	Regions	% expenditure
Slovakia	2,887 municipalities, mayors 8 regions, presidents		18
Slovenia	193 municipalities, mayors		19
Spain	8,089 municipalities	17 autonomous communities	53
Sweden	290 municipalities 20 counties and regions		44
Switzerland	2,800 communes	26 cantons	58
United Kingdom	12,434 parishes, towns and communities 468 counties, boroughs and districts, few mayors	3 nations	29

Note: The second and third columns include only councils and offices elected directly by popular vote, not those appointed or indirectly elected. The last column indicates the percentage of decentralised public expenditure out of total public expenditure (including social security). Nd stands for no data.

Source: Author's elaboration with data from the Council of European Municipalities and Regions, Committee of the Regions of the European Union, Stegarescu (2005), as well as www.local.gov.uk and other local sources.

regional territories with parliaments and governments having legislative, executive and judicial responsibilities comparable to those of member states within their areas of competence, including transposing EU law directly into domestic law, especially in the 68 regions in Austria, Belgium, Germany, Italy and Spain. However, if the degree of decentralisation is measured by the usual index of proportion of public expenditure in the hands of the central government, the most decentralised countries are, in addition to those just mentioned, also some formally unitary states in which local governments enjoy high proportions of public resources, led by Denmark and Sweden, as shown in Table 1.4.

Other institutional features could be included in a more detailed analysis, such as the existence of constitutional courts and other independent institutions in particular policy areas, for example those of corporate bodies, central banks, etc. Yet the variables mentioned can be sufficient to approach the relative degree of institutional pluralism of several European countries and allow for some comparative comments.

A great variety of institutional combinations actually exist in the countries considered. At the top of our scale of pluralism we should place Switzerland, Germany and Belgium, all multiparty, bicameral and federal systems. In Switzerland, the paradise of local government, other institutions not included in our examination, such as the particular division between the legislature and the executive, and referenda by popular initiative would reinforce its score of institutional and political pluralism, in this case with extremely high consensus. In Germany, the permanent search for consensus in a context of divided power has led Manfred G. Schmidt, in Chapter 3, to present the German political system as resting upon 'a Grand Coalition of the federal government and the state governments, as well as a more or less hidden Grand Coalition between the incumbent parties in federal government and the major opposition party'. In Belgium, in contrast, traditional 'politics of accommodation and policy concertation' has been recently replaced with higher levels of 'confrontation and competition', to the point that 'co-operation across party-political elites which shared a common interest, namely a "unitary" Belgian state, [has] become increasingly difficult', as formulated by Hans Keman in Chapter 7.

Lower down the scale we should place France and Poland, with very similar institutional structures including multipartism and semi-presidentialism, which favour 'cohabitation' of differently oriented powers and coalition politics, as well as non-legislative regionalisation. In his chapter on France (Chapter 4), nevertheless, Yves Mény notes the shifts between periods of cohabitation and those of 'presidential executive' in which 'effectiveness, governmental solidarity, concentration of power and the authority of the leader take priority over pluralism, debate and checks and balances'.

Other countries experience different trade-offs between decision-making effectiveness, expected to be higher when the country is relatively small and homogeneous, and permanent negotiations otherwise. Regarding Italy, Gianfranco Pasquino remarks in Chapter 5 that the current institutional regime, although it is still in transition, responds to 'the need for an inclusive democracy in which, in contrast to the previous regime, which was blocked around the CD and permanently excluded both the extreme right and the Communist Party, all the relevant actors have found a role and the possibility of exercising some clout'. Spain has a distinctive profile with highly concentrated power and adversarial politics at the centre of the state, together with a high level of territorial pluralism, competition and decentralisation, as is also discussed in Chapter 6. In the chapter on the Nordic countries (Chapter 8), Jan-Erik Lane and Svante Ersson, focusing on Denmark, Finland and Sweden, note that the traditional combination of 'adversarial politics with consensus institutions' is waning in favour of lower political and social consensus, although the 'Scandinavian model' retains distinct features of compromise politics.

The twentieth-century model of a monist regime was, of course, the United Kingdom of Great Britain, but it has been experiencing significant reforms in recent times, especially territorial devolution of powers. Ian Budge remarks in Chapter 2 that a simple political regime favouring high concentration of power within a large, varied state gave governments a basis on which 'to exclude large societal interests from government decision-making, to re-establish the market as the major mechanism for economic and social decisions, despite the objections of disadvantaged groups, and to assert the overriding authority of the reduced central state over other political institutions'. At the extreme end of the scale, the best examples of monist and simple regimes are those with a unicameral parliamentary regime and a unitary state. These include the smallest countries, some with a certain degree of limited multi-party politics, such as Cyprus, Estonia, Iceland, Luxembourg, Portugal and Slovenia, and others more closely approaching a two-party system, such as Greece, Hungary and Malta.

A crucial development in European politics, which crosses all the chapters of this book, is relations between state and local politics and the European Union. These relations develop in two directions: states cede powers to the institutions of the Union and domestic politics are increasingly 'Europeanised'.

Through half a century, the political institutions of the European communities evolved from relations corresponding to an international organisation based on states' sovereignty to others approaching a federal union. During the first period most decisions were made by unanimity of the representatives of states' governments in the Council, while in the latter period states share more powers and the European Parliament, which is the only directly elected European body, plays a more significant role in inter-institutional decision-making. As is discussed in the final chapter of this book (Chapter 9), as a result of this process the current European Union can be considered to be neither an international organisation nor a state, but an 'empire' – especially by analogy with the process of building the United States of America about one hundred years earlier. But, as is the case with states, cities and other forms of polity, 'empires' can also be either democratic or dictatorial, and, if democratic, they can adopt different institutional formulas (Colomer 2007a).

The institutions and processes of the European Union can, thus, be analysed with the help of the same notions and measurable variables previously applied to the analysis of state and other political regimes. Nowadays the institutions of the European Union include parliamentary elections by proportional representation; a broadly aggregative, moderate multiparty system; parliamentary appointment and censure of the executive Commission; and a sketch of a two-chamber assembly formed by the Parliament and the Council. Both separation of powers and power-sharing characterise the relations between the European Union and the other levels of government across the territory, the variety of territorial formulas shaping a kind of large-scale, asymmetric federalism. All this clearly locates the Union on the side of the pluralistic and consensual mode of decision-making, in consistency with distinctive features of most democratic regimes across Europe.

BIBLIOGRAPHY

Almond, G. A. and S. Verba (1963) *The Civic Culture: Political attitudes and democracy in five nations*, Princeton, NJ: Princeton University Press.

Brennan, G. and J. M. Buchanan (1985) *The Reason of Norms: Constitutional political economy*, Cambridge: Cambridge University Press.

Colomer, J. M. (2000) *Strategic Transitions: Game theory and democratization*, Baltimore: The Johns Hopkins University Press.

—— (2001a) *Political Institutions: Democracy and social choice*, Oxford and New York: Oxford University Press.

—— (2001b) 'Disequilibrium Institutions and Pluralistic Democracy', introduction to J. M. Colomer (ed.) 'The Strategy of Institutional Change', special issue, *Journal of Theoretical Politics* 13 (3).

—— (ed.) (2004a) *Handbook of Electoral System Choice*, London and New York: Palgrave Macmillan.

—— (2004b) 'Political Science is Going Ahead (By Convoluted Ways). A commentary on Giovanni Sartori', PS: *Political Science & Politics*, 37 (4).

—— (2005) 'It's the Parties that Choose Electoral Systems (or Duverger's laws upside down)', *Political Studies* 53 (1): 1–21.

—— (2006) 'Comparative Constitutions', in R. A. W. Rhodes, Sarah Binder and Bert Rockman (eds) *Oxford Handbook of Political Institutions*, Oxford and New York: Oxford University Press.

—— (2007a) *Great Empires, Small Nations. The uncertain future of the sovereign state*, London and New York: Routledge.

—— (2007b) 'What Other Sciences Look Like', *European Political Science* 6 (2): 134–42.

Dahl, R. (1956) *A Preface to Democratic Theory*, Chicago: The University of Chicago Press.

Lijphart, A. (1984) *Democracies: Patterns of majoritarian and consensus government in twenty-one countries*, New Haven, CT: Yale University Press.

—— (2007) *Thinking about Democracy. Power sharing and majority rule in theory and practice*, London and New York: Routledge.

Miller, N. R. (1983) 'Pluralism and Social Choice', *American Political Science Review*, 77: 734–47.

North, D. C. (1990) *Institutions, Institutional Change and Economic Performance*, Cambridge: Cambridge University Press.

Riker, W. H. (1980) 'Implications from the Disequilibrium of Majority Rule for the Study of Institutions', *American Political Science Review* 74: 432–58.

—— (1982) *Liberalism against Populism. A Confrontation between the theory of democracy and the theory of social choice*, San Francisco: Freeman.

Shepsle, K. (1979) 'Institutional Arrangements and Equilibrium in Multidimensional Voting Models', *American Journal of Political Science* 23: 27–59.

—— (1989) 'Studying Institutions: Some lessons from the rational choice approach', *Journal of Theoretical Politics* 1 (2): 131–48.

Stegarescu, D. (2005) 'Public Sector Decentralization: Measurement, concepts and recent international trends', *Fiscal Studies* 26 (3): 301–33.

Sources for left–right party positions in all chapters

Benoit, K. and M. Laver (2007) *Party Policy in Modern Democracies*, London and New York: Routledge.

Budge, I., H.-D. Klingemann, A. Volkens, J. Bara and E. Tanenbaum (2001) *Mapping Policy Preferences: Estimates for parties, electors and governments 1945–1998*, Oxford: Oxford University Press.

Huber, J. and R. Inglehart (1995) 'Expert Interpretations of Party Space and Party Location in 42 Societies', *Party Politics* 1 (1).

Klingemann, H.-D., A. Volkens, J. Bara, I. Budge and M. D. McDonald (2006) *Mapping Policy Preferences II 1990–2003*, Oxford: Oxford University Press.

CHAPTER 2

Great Britain and Ireland

Variations in Party Government

Ian Budge

The United Kingdom included the territory of the present Republic of Ireland until 1922. The Republic inherited most of its political institutions and much of its political culture from the union. Though its secession was violent, relations between the successor states are probably the most intimate in Western Europe. English is spoken in both. England, with roughly five-sixths of the population of the British Isles, and above all London, with its overwhelming economic and cultural impact, remain the social centres of gravity whatever the formal political arrangements. Irish citizens can vote in all British elections, while inhabitants of the disputed territory of Northern Ireland are automatically entitled to both British and Irish citizenship.

Clearly territorial differences exist within the British Isles, otherwise there would not have been an Irish secession or devolution to regional parliaments in Northern Ireland, Scotland and Wales (1997–1999). But these are played out within a unifying cultural context. The central institutions of both the United Kingdom and Ireland are distinguished by extraordinary stability. Parliamentary government, with power centralised in a cabinet supported by a partisan majority in the lower house, goes back in both cases to the system which emerged in Britain in 1868, and which in its essentials (also at the bureaucratic level) has not been altered since. It has survived transferral (in the Irish case), two world wars, two social and political revolutions in the post-war period, and went on unchanged to the twenty-first century. Such stability is good in itself. But the limited ability of the traditional institutions to cope with an extended role may limit socio-economic intervention by government.

The strong cultural and political similarities between the United Kingdom of Great Britain and Northern Ireland and the Republic of Ireland render their political differences all the more interesting, as they can generally be traced to one or two key institutional contrasts which render party strategies, and hence political outcomes, very different between the two states. We thus have the ability to draw a highly controlled institutional comparison to see why, in spite of many resemblances, their contemporary politics differ so much. The basis of such differences is to be found in the electoral system and the way it reflects underlying cleavages.

ELECTIONS

Underlying cleavages and policy issues

The major British cleavage has usually been identified as class – based on accumulated social differences in type of occupation (factory-based manual work versus others), education, accent, lifestyle, place and type of housing, trade union membership, income and the life experiences which stem from these. Class cleavages were intensified in the inter-war period by the removal of cross-cutting territorial cleavages, with the secession of southern Ireland, and the general decline of religion as a serious political force. In voting terms class influences reached their apotheosis in the early post-war elections from 1945 to 1959.

Class as a political cleavage both produced and was sharpened by Labour and Conservative conflict over this period. The decline of the religious and Irish cleavages caused the weakening and near disappearance of the old cross-class Liberal Party. This transformed earlier three-party competition into effective two-party competition by 1935 – a situation which continued at the electoral level until 1964 and which, because of the electoral mechanisms described below, meant that Labour and Conservatives were the only serious competitors for governmental power until the 1980s.

The social bases of the class cleavage weakened after the 1950s. This was due in part to industrial and economic changes which reduced the numerical strength of the manual, factory-based, unionised working class, the core of Labour support. Services grew at the expense of manufacturing: manufacturing itself changed, reducing the role of both skilled and semi-skilled manual workers such as ship-builders and miners, and even of repetitive assembly-line operatives such as car workers. They were replaced by more skilled or more flexible workers, often part-time, with women increasing to half the work force and extensive immigration from South Asia and Eastern Europe. The life experiences of most workers became increasingly divergent from those of the traditional unionised manual worker, who stayed in one job, one establishment and often one house all his life. Economic change was intensified by the levelling effects of the comprehensive welfare state introduced by Labour from 1945 to 1948.

The traditional, static bases of the class cleavage thus began to erode quickly after 1959. This process was mirrored in the rise of Liberal voting and the increase of electoral volatility in the 1960s and 1970s. At first this led to rapid Conservative–Labour alternation in government. By the 1980s, however, as the Labour vote shrank

Table 2.1 Elections to the House of Commons, 1945–2005

Year	Turnout	Labour	Liberal	Conservative	Scots & Welsh	Others
1945	76	48	9	40	0	3
1950	84	46	9	44	0	1
1951	83	49	3	48	0	0
1955	77	46	3	50	0	1
1959	79	44	6	49	0	1
1964	77	44	11	43	1	1
1966	76	48	9	42	1	0
1970	72	43	8	46	1	1
1974	79	37	19	38	3	3
1974	73	39	18	36	4	3
1979	76	37	14	44	2	3
1983	73	28	25	42	2	3
1987	75	31	23	42	2	2
1992	80	34	18	42	2	4
1997	72	43	17	31	3	6
2001	59	42	19	33	3	6
2005	61	35	22	32	4	7

Note: 'Scots & Welsh' includes the Scottish National Party and the Welsh National Party (Plaid Cymru). Northern Irish and other minor party votes are included in 'Others'.

and the Conservatives gained a large enough plurality (42 per cent) to keep themselves permanently in government, it appeared that they were the main beneficiaries, and Labour the main losers, from the social changes that had been under way. Strengthened by a Social Democratic split from Labour in the early 1980s, the Liberal Democrats had also improved their electoral standing to a point where their results (especially in 1983) rivalled Labour's. These points are illustrated in Table 2.1, which shows voting support for the major parties as well as turnout for the post-war period.

The General Election of 1997 marked a turning point in party-political terms. Labour gained a large parliamentary majority over the Conservatives, though with only 43 per cent of the vote. The Liberals doubled their number of MPs to become a significant parliamentary force for the first time in the post-war period, while the Scottish and Welsh Nationalists held their ground. These results were more or less duplicated in the elections of 2001 and 2005: the major development was a collapse in turnout from just over 70 per cent to around 60 per cent The success of Labour and to a lesser extent the Liberals has been attributed to their ability to appeal to a new classless type of voter mainly in the South East of England while keeping their old bases in the peripheries. However, as Table 2.2 illustrates, the latter are now subject to erosion.

The territorial variation in British political loyalties is illustrated by Table 2.2, which reports the results of voting for the legislatures in Scotland, Wales and Northern Ireland. Recently, the Scottish Nationalist Party has emerged as the plurality party in Scotland. In mainland Britain, Scotland and Wales give strong support to Labour but also to Nationalist parties pressing for regional independence. In Northern Ireland the British unionists and Irish nationalists monopolise local representation.

Table 2.2 British regional elections, 1998–2007

	Labour	Liberal	Conservative	Nationalist	Others
Scotland – Parliament					
1999	39	14	16	29	2
2003	35	15	17	24	9
2007	32	16	17	33	2
Wales – National Assembly					
1999	38	14	16	28	4
2003	40	14	20	21	5
2007	32	15	22	22	9
Northern Ireland – Assembly					
1998	–	7	39	36	18
2003	–	4	49	41	6
2007	–	5	45	41	5

Note: In Northern Ireland, 'Conservative' includes Democratic Unionist and Ulster Unionist; 'Nationalist' includes We Ourselves (Sinn Féin) and the Social Democratic and Labour Party.

The English regions share Scottish and Welsh problems of industrial decline, unemployment and social deprivation and hence have mostly supported Labour. Generally speaking, the Conservative vote goes down and the Labour and Liberal votes go up the further one goes north and west from London.

The differentiated pattern of regional results illustrates a central point about the main British political cleavage – it is only partly based on class as such. It would in fact be more accurate to describe the central political division as an accumulation of regional and class conflicts rather than purely class ones – an accumulation in which the territorial and regional dimension is now more important than class, if they can be separated out at all.

The reason why territorial and class cleavages overlap, both socially and politically, is that the manufacturing and extraction industries associated with the nineteenth-century Industrial Revolution – mining, steel, shipbuilding and textiles – developed in the peripheries rather than the core of Britain – in Scotland, Wales, Cornwall and the North of England rather than in London and the South East. Thus the classical industrial proletariat also developed in these areas, in the new metropolises of Glasgow, Manchester, Leeds, Newcastle, Cardiff and their associated mining and mill towns. In many ways the culture and social experiences of these areas were shaped by the existence of the new class and its social and political struggles. Existing regional contrasts with the South East of England, the stronghold of established institutions and of the traditional elite, were reinforced by, and became entangled with, class ones.

Industrial change brought about the partial collapse of the older industries of the North and West in the last two decades of the twentieth century. The new service industries grouped themselves around London, the largest market and communications centre. At the same time the negative redistribution of wealth from poor to rich, fostered by Conservative governments from 1979 to 1997, hit most severely in the peripheries, where the poor were concentrated in larger numbers.

The 1980s thus saw a re-emergence of the territorial basis of British politics, where Conservative governments drew their parliamentary majorities from the South East of England and Labour MPs came almost exclusively from the North and West. At the extremes, the Conservatives had no representation in Scotland and Wales, while hardly a Labour MP came from South East England outside the deprived area of central London. However, the success of Labour in 1997 and 2001 in attracting voters from the South East now means that the Conservative political base there is threatened.

Sharp territorial contrasts underline the essential nature of political conflict in Britain, between a coalition of dispersed groups (both social and territorial) supporting Labour and a centrally located and privileged group supporting the Conservatives – who can thus enhance their electoral appeal as defenders of the national 'British' interest. The restored Liberals, who may yet bridge the gap between Labour and Conservatives, have been penalised by an electoral system which privileges regionally concentrated parties. They thus secured few parliamentary seats even when they received one-quarter of the national vote. Meanwhile nationalist parties, who have more concentrated local support, can extend their representation.

One can gain a further insight into the concentrated and cumulative nature of the central British political division by comparing it with the Republic of Ireland. Secession from the United Kingdom appealed to the most socially distinct stratum in Ireland, the rural Catholic peasantry and small-town bourgeoisie. It was violently opposed by Protestants, above all in the only industrialised area of the island around Belfast, in the North. Independence when it came was thus accompanied by partition – the rural south and west going to the republic while Northern Ireland stayed as a province of the United Kingdom.

Within the new republic there was no obvious social cleavage around which the new party system could organize. Incipient differences between the overwhelmingly largest city, Dublin, and the rest of the country were diverted by the immediate issue of whether to accept partition or to fight on. The nascent party system divided itself on these lines in the midst of an ongoing civil war. The pro-Treaty group which formed the first government became Party of the Gael (Fine Gael), while the constitutional opposition, and governing party for most of the time from 1932 onwards, became Heroes of Destiny (Fianna Fáil). Their names indicate the appeal of both to Irish nationalism. Both subscribed to the social doctrines enunciated by the Catholic Church. There was a tendency for Fine Gael to uphold the economic interests of Dublin and the east coast, as perceived by the upper bourgeoisie. In the 1930s Fianna Fáil constructed a western small-farmer and Dublin working-class alliance. These lines were very blurred, however, and easily overcome by tactical and election considerations. Fianna Fáil's creation of a near majority election coalition meant that Fine Gael's only chance of government office was to ally itself with smaller parties, often of a radical agrarian or proletarian nature. Increasingly, from the 1950s onwards, its ally was the Labour Party.

The Labour Party, an offshoot of the all-British Labour movement, had held aloof from the nationalist controversies of the 1920s in its pursuit of social reform. This gave it permanent minority status, averaging about 10 per cent of the vote in national elections. While giving support to Fianna Fáil in the 1930s, it went into coalition with

Table 2.3 Elections to the Irish parliament, 1948–2007

Year	Turnout	Labour	Fine Gael	Fianna Fáil	Others
1948	74	9	20	42	19
1951	75	11	26	46	7
1954	76	12	32	43	7
1957	71	9	27	48	16
1961	71	12	32	44	13
1965	75	15	34	48	3
1969	77	17	34	46	3
1973	77	14	35	46	5
1977	76	12	31	51	7
1981	76	10	37	45	8
1982	74	9	37	47	6
1982	73	9	39	45	6
1987	73	6	27	44	11
1989	69	10	29	44	17
1992	69	19	25	39	17
1997	68	10	28	39	21
2002	64	11	22	41	26
2007	66	10	27	42	20

Note: Votes are counted on first ballot.

Fine Gael in return for promises of reform in the 1950s, 1970s and 1980s. The increasing volatility both of voting and of the party system in the 1990s, associated with an economic boom and recession, produced an increase in Labour support (particularly in Dublin, to 26 per cent of the vote in 1992). This made Labour a desirable partner for Fianna Fáil in the new coalition government which emerged after the election of that year. Subsequently Labour governed with Fine Gael till 1997. A market liberal party, the Progressive Democrats, has been Fianna Fáil's preferred coalition partner from 1997.

One can say that the relatively loose and unideological nature of party politics in the Republic of Ireland reflects a widespread consensus on major issues, backed by its status as a small country on the European periphery. Its traditional neutrality exempts it from pressures to join in international alliances such as the 'War on Terror'. It can receive substantial benefits from the EU without attracting too much attention. Although the Church has been losing its social dominance, Catholic social doctrine on matters like abortion and divorce still holds sway, eased in practical and individual terms by the proximity of the UK (where both are available). The one threatening and immediate issue – what support to give violent Nationalism in Northern Ireland – has now been solved by the acceptance of a power-sharing Executive there and the establishment of an effective Irish–British condominium over the territory. The one long-term consequence is perhaps the political gains made by We Ourselves (Sinn Féin), the Irish Nationalists in both Northern and South Ireland. But these do not as yet pose much threat to the main parties of the South, especially since its Southern vote went down in 2007.

In contrast, British politics in the new century have been increasingly shaken by New Labour's support for intervention in Iraq and support for the United States in its War on Terror. While bipartisan, in the sense of being supported by the leadership of both main parties, the issue has split Labour internally, causing a haemorrhage of traditional activists and supporters – particularly on the peripheries of Britain. A first consequence is the steady decline of the party in both Scotland and Wales – signified by the 2007 success of the Scottish Nationalist Party (SNP) – and an erosion of its basis of support in Northern England. The British Conservative Party, in the meantime, has moved, under a new Leader, David Cameron, from a rightist to a centrist image, although his stand on policies remains vague.

Electoral system and party system

A comparison of the British and Irish electoral systems demonstrates, if proof were needed, that differences in the rules for aggregating votes into seats have a profound effect on the handling of these issues and on national politics in general. Ireland has a system (single transferable vote) more geared to obtaining proportionality between party shares of votes and of parliamentary seats than the British. It also offers voters more of a choice between parties and candidates. The British single-member constituencies with simple pluralities would have guaranteed Fianna Fáil, with a plurality of the popular vote in most elections from 1932, a near-permanent majority government in Ireland. Under the actual system of the single transferable vote in multi-member constituencies Fianna Fáil had instead often to form minority governments with outside support – and now coalitions. Conversely, the Irish system, applied to Britain, would have enforced minority or coalition government over the whole post-war period, with marked differences in party style and policies, not to mention the institutional workings of government.

Mainland Britain uses the 'first past the post' or single-member, simple plurality electoral system for UK elections. As the name implies, one MP is elected for each constituency on the basis of receiving more votes than any of his or her rivals. There is no requirement to gain a majority. In an extreme case an MP with 33 per cent or even 25 per cent of the vote would win the seat if (s)he got one vote more than any rival.

The consequence is that parties win seats if they have strong local support, and are in a position to win a majority of seats and form a government if such support extends over wide areas of the country. Local minorities do not get represented. A party with wide national support spread evenly, like the Liberal Democrats, gains relatively few seats. This is the reason for extreme discrepancies between the Liberal Democrats' national vote shares and seats. (In 1983 they and their partners took 26 per cent of the vote but just over 3 per cent of parliamentary seats.) Liberal Democrats are in a strong local minority almost everywhere and hence do not usually win seats. It is Labour and Conservatives who have enough support over wide areas to gain a large parliamentary representation.

However, as we have seen, this support is regionally concentrated – the Conservatives get pluralities in the South East of England, and Labour in the West and North, Scotland and Wales. Despite substantial minorities of the other major party's supporters existing in its rival's area of predominance, these minorities are not represented. The system thus exaggerates regional contrasts in support, so that Conservatives increasingly seem like a regional South East English party in terms of parliamentary representation.

Were a third party like the Liberal Democrats to get up to 37–38 per cent of the vote, its support would necessarily be enough in certain localities to pick up parliamentary seats very rapidly. This is a very high level to attain before gaining influence, however. In effect, 'first past the post' operates to consolidate and stabilise the existing party system and thus resists and deflects major movements for change. When these become very strong, it may register such change so rapidly as to destabilise the political situation even further.

The same considerations apply in regard to regionally strong parties like the Welsh and Scottish Nationalists. As these can generate concentrated regional support, they do not suffer from under-representation to the same extent as do the Liberal Democrats. The Scottish Nationalists are still underrepresented, however, to the benefit of Labour. Were they to expand their current one-third of the Scottish vote by another 10 per cent in UK elections they would suddenly gain a majority of Scottish seats. The political effect would be an immediate demand for independence.

The inflexibility of 'first past the post' thus enables national parties to ignore many political movements and the demands they voice. Where these become even more widely supported, perhaps because of the frustration generated by stalemate, the electoral system would create a critical situation by suddenly registering the strength of the movement. This may explain the fact that territorial or constitutional change in Britain is liable to come all at once, as in 1997–9, after a long period of inattention and non-response by policy-makers.

The electoral system has other effects on the style and conduct of British government. Members of Parliament do not have to contend with party colleagues for election. This directs their attention to national rather than local affairs, since what counts for getting elected is nomination by a national party, and that in turn depends heavily on leadership endorsement. The dependence of MPs on the national leadership also makes for strong party discipline in Parliament. Nominally party policy is agreed in parliamentary party meetings (subject to endorsement by the annual party conference). In practice the leadership dominates discussion in both, particularly when in government.

Both in its direct and in its indirect effects, therefore, the British electoral system operates to reduce the number of parties by restricting effective parliamentary representation to two. It also tends to give an unequivocal parliamentary majority to only one of the two, thus promoting the creation of strong single-party majority government in the teeth of what is effectively a three-party system at electoral level.

The Irish system works, in contrast, by allowing voters, within constituencies usually of three or four members, to rank candidates in order of their preference. Votes are aggregated by (1) establishing an 'electoral quota' which a candidate needs to be elected, which consists of total vote divided by number of seats plus one, (2) electing the most popular candidate and distributing his or her surplus of votes over the electoral quota to the other candidates in proportion to each one's share of second preferences in the elected candidate's total set of votes. (3) After this redistribution the second most popular candidate is declared elected and his or her surplus votes are redistributed among the remaining candidates in the same way. (4) The same procedure is followed until all seats are allocated.

The Irish system makes strong local support in the constituency very important for each candidate, since even if his or her party is preferred (s)he may be ranked well below party colleagues and thus not elected. There is no such danger under the British system (see below). This reinforces the strong localism of Irish deputies and their relative lack of interest in national affairs, which in turn contribute to the autonomy of the national leadership. More important, it creates considerable incentives to form electoral coalitions, as the parties within them can reward each other by urging supporters to give second preference to their partner. The electorally successful coalition of Labour and Fine Gael in the 1970s and 1980s used this tactic. The use of multi-member constituencies also ensures, in contrast to Britain, that strong local minorities can hope to gain a seat. Thus small parties do not need to be in a local majority to gain parliamentary representation. This feature of the system has kept Irish Labour going and, with the acceptance by Fianna Fáil of coalition government, gives Labour and progressive democracy a pivotal role in determining which of the larger parties will govern.

Two factors, however, have tempered the tendency to spread parliamentary seats between parties and create coalition governments. One has been the strong socio-political base of Fianna Fáil, which has made it into a near-majority government on many occasions. The other has been the bias of inherited British traditions and institutions (such as collective cabinet responsibility) towards single-party government. With the emergence of a four-party – or at least two-and-two-halves-party – system at electoral level, the single transferable vote has produced change towards a multi-party coalition system. So far in Britain the election system has prevented Parliament and governments from reflecting Liberal Democrat electoral successes. Not surprisingly a major Liberal Democrat objective is to change that.

PARTIES

As the above discussion indicates, British parties run the whole gamut of ideological tendencies found elsewhere in Europe, from minority nationalism through Green and left socialist parties to mainstream Labour, Liberal Democrats and Conservatives. Only Christian Democracy is lacking, although the Northern Irish Unionists and the Social Democratic and Labour Party are in effect based on religious cleavages – the first representing the Protestants and the other the Catholics of Northern Ireland. The Unionists are exceptional among the peripherally based parties in having socially conservative policies (though not economic ones – they could hardly be, as the province is so dependent on state subsidies). Their raison d'être is, however, to support partition and the incorporation of the province within the British state, just as We Ourselves (Sinn Féin), moderately left in terms of overall ideology, supports the union of Northern with Southern Ireland. Unionists have on occasion provided useful parliamentary support for the major parties at Westminster and been rewarded by a change of Northern Irish policy in their favour.

The Welsh and Scottish nationalists share a left-wing orientation – a natural position to take on the central–periphery cleavage which strongly characterises British politics. Indeed, their ideological tendencies are sometimes to the left of Labour's. Both gained votes in their respective regional elections in 2007. The Scottish National Party wants nothing less than Scottish secession from the British state. The Party of Wales (Plaid Cymru) stands more for devolution than for independence. Its core support is in Welsh-speaking North Wales, which creates internal divisions with English-speakers in South Wales, the most populous area of the country.

While the Green Party and various extreme groups on left and right have gained substantial votes in occasional European and local elections, none has mustered enough support to gain even one British parliamentary seat. The workings of the electoral system will continue to marginalise them for the foreseeable future. It is therefore with the mainstream parties – Labour and Conservative above all – that we ought to be concerned when we discuss the normal workings of politics in the United Kingdom as a whole.

The ideological positions of the major parties as summarised on a left–right scale (see Table 2.4) can be characterised from content analyses of the parties' own programmes at national elections. Left-wing support for greater government intervention in the economy and society, more welfare and social services, and peace and international solidarity abroad contrasts with a right-wing emphasis on individual freedom, incentives, traditional morality and military alliances. These are the 'core' left versus right positions which, on the evidence of their own manifestos, parties take. Labour is consistently to the left of the Conservatives on these points. Usually the parties maintain a fair degree of ideological distance from each other, though this may be modified by strategic and situational factors, when they move closer or take over some of their rival's policies. In the 1950s the Liberals switched between the Conservative and Labour positions, but from the 1960s onwards they became more resolutely centrist and ceased to 'leapfrog' the other parties.

While maintaining their own individuality the parties obviously modify their policies to gain voting support and win elections. In the early 1950s the Conservatives' pledge to accept most of Labour's post-war reforms moved them over

Table 2.4 Left–right placement of parties in Britain

	Welsh PCy	Scottish SNP	Labour LB	Liberal LD	Conservative Con	
Left	Centre-left			Centre	Centre-right	Right

Party names:
PCy: Party of Wales (Plaid Cymru)
SNP: Scottish National Party
LB: Labour Party
LD: Liberal Democrats
Con: Conservative Party

Source: Adapted from data in Huber and Inglehart (1995), Budge *et al.* (2001), Klingemann *et al.* (2006), Benoit and Laver (2007), and chapter authors' sources. See references in Chapter 1.

towards the left of the political spectrum. In 1964 and 1970 the two parties came quite close together. The rise of the 'New Left' in the Labour Party and of Margaret Thatcher's 'New Right' among the Conservatives produced a major ideological divergence in the 1980s. Labour's loss of four elections in a row caused far-reaching internal modification of its policies. It moved towards Conservative positions in 1987, returned to the left in 1992 but moved decisively rightward in 1997, 2001 and 2005 with full acceptance of the free-market economy. The Conservatives up to 2005 maintained their old policies of reducing state intervention in society by selling off public enterprises and imposing market-oriented reforms on the welfare state and the education system, but their third successive election defeat has caused them to modify these positions.

It is instructive that the way the major parties present their policies to the public emphasises the class elements in the basic political cleavage and de-emphasises the territorial element. This is partly due to Labour's desire to keep Scotland and Wales under control. Even after it proceeded with devolution in 1997–1999 its main concern was to co-ordinate regional and central action, rather than to leave regional legislatures and governments with any autonomous initiatives. The party has preferred to concentrate on social and economic policy for two reasons. One is straightforwardly electoral: to win power at British level, Labour needs to gain votes in the Midlands and the South East of England, where devolution has no positive connotations. It already has all the support in Scotland and Wales that it needs. The enhancement of social services and general redistribution are points on which all its present and potential supporters can agree, so it would be counterproductive to emphasise territorial questions too much in its electoral appeals.

The other factor shaping the Labour leadership's priorities lies in the party's origins as a class-based political movement and in the basic values built into the party as a result. The party's core beliefs centre on the question of social and economic equality. As we have seen, this is also a matter of central importance to the remoter peripheries where the underprivileged are more concentrated. Labour stands historically for the elimination of poverty, steady improvement in public services and in ordinary people's living standards, the narrowing of income and wealth differentials, wider and more evenly spread opportunities, and the abolition of social and legal distinctions based formally or informally on social status. Recently it has paid growing attention to racial and sexual equality as well as class equality. Its international outlook also originates in egalitarian values: traditionally it has supported transnational organisations, seeing them as a more effective road to international peace and world redistribution than military alliances. This is why the government's unquestioning support for America's proactive military policy has caused such divisions within Labour.

Unlike some other European socialist movements, Labour has downplayed political reform, seeing in the undefined reserve powers of the state and its formally unlimited parliamentary sovereignty a useful instrument for imposing social change. This accounts for its late support for devolution and unwillingness to consider radical constitutional change. In spite of its reforms after taking office in 1997 it is reluctant to support major political change, or to consider a formal electoral alliance with the Liberal Democrats, being still attracted by the untrammelled action as a single-party government which the present set-up gives it.

For the Conservatives, political power *per se* has been much more important and they have historically been willing to make more ideological concessions than Labour to get it. They have therefore been quite consistent in upholding the unitary British state and unlimited parliamentary sovereignty (which as we shall see gives effective autonomy to the leadership of the majority party), and in opposing attempts to codify the constitution, which would reduce governmental power *vis-à-vis* other groups in society. They have even been prepared to accept that at times Labour may have access to power, counting on their own electoral strengths to minimise such periods. In this they have not been mistaken. The Conservatives controlled the government for thirty-five years of the half-century from 1945. Although they lost the last three elections, they show no sign of abandoning their support for an 'elective dictatorship' of a single-party government based on a minority of the vote.

Conservative core values thus relate primarily to the idea of a strong state which will secure social order. Different elements in the party emphasise different aspects of this role – on the one hand as an instrument of law and order through police, courts, school discipline and traditional religious morality, on the other as a supporter of paternalism and hierarchy, with basic welfare for the less well-off. In the first part of the post-war period this latter point of view seemed electorally popular with the majority of the population, so the party pragmatically accepted it as a policy to gain power, which it held from 1951 to 1964. The subsequent Labour government's attempts to impose widely unpopular measures such as comprehensive (neighbourhood) schools and a further redistribution of wealth gave strength to a New Right element in the Conservative Party. This element mounted a radical attack on Labour policies, in favour of re-establishing an entirely free-market economy, cutting welfare and increasing wealth differentials. Traditional Conservatives who did not themselves feel the same attachment to a free market were reconciled to this stance by its reassertion of state authority in the face of the social opposition, particularly from trade unions, which the changes provoked (see the next section). This combination of 'free market, strong state' underlay Conservative policies from the mid-1970s onwards, reaching its full flowering in the period of Margaret Thatcher's premiership (1979–1990). The reassertion of state authority also applied to foreign policy, where it fitted happily with Conservative support for NATO and a strong military and diplomatic position. The electoral successes of Thatcherism, with its particular appeal to the upwardly mobile sectors in the South East and Midlands of England, reconciled even the non-free-marketers to the Conservative position during the 1980s.

The breakdown of the Thatcherite synthesis came with the question of closer British integration into the European Community, which pitted its 'free-market' elements against supporters of the 'strong state'. For them the concept of British sovereignty became increasingly important as it seemed to be threatened by the growing powers of the European Commission under the Single European Act of 1986–1987 and especially the Treaty of Maastricht of 1992–1993. For the free-marketers, led by Mrs Thatcher's successor, John Major, the liberalisation of trade within a larger European market was of greater importance, even though they diverged radically from other European governments on questions of social protection from free-market forces. The opposition between the two elements within the party overwhelmed the Conservatives after their electoral defeats in 1997 and 2001. After 2005 and the choice of a young more centrist leader, the Conservatives have emerged as more united in pursuit of power.

Labour is much more tied to its ideology. This is in large part due to the institutional structure of the party and the support base it gives to internally competing groups. The Labour Party was founded at the beginning of this century when various socialist groups came together with the trade unions. The latter provided support and an organisational base: the socialists provided activists and a constituency organisation. The two groups had somewhat different objectives and tactics, though of course both concurred in their ultimate aim of securing equality and advancement for the less privileged. The trade unions, however, had more immediate and pragmatic objectives: to secure their own power and position in industry, to extend immediate welfare benefits and in general to use pragmatic concessions and bargaining to secure immediate concrete gains for the working class. The socialist elements, strong in constituency associations, were keen to promote a radical reorganisation of society along egalitarian lines. Both sides could concur on the creation of the welfare state and nationalisation in the late 1940s but diverged in the 1960s over such matters as school conception and union privileges.

In recognition of the trade unions' financial support their leadership was given a predominant role in the party conference, the main policy-making body of the Labour Party, through the 'bloc vote'. Each union delegation cast the votes of all its members paying party subscriptions as a unified whole in favour of, or against, proposed policies. These votes overwhelmed those of constituency delegations. Generally, over the post-war period, the unions' votes helped to secure the election of a relatively pragmatic parliamentary leadership which could generally count on their support against the more radical left of the party.

By the end of the 1960s, however, several large unions had elected a more radical leadership which increasingly diverged from the party leader. The New Left of the party gained in power and proposed more distinctively left-wing policies. In turn this provoked an internal split and secession of centrist leaders to form the Social Democratic Party (1981), which was later absorbed by the Liberal Democrats. The split damaged Labour's electoral base and more than anything else was responsible for Labour's weakness in the 1980s and early 1990s. A centrist leadership regained control after the crushing electoral defeat of 1983. Under Tony Blair it promoted a much more pragmatic policy stance which took over many elements of Thatcherism and gained the party the sobriquet of 'New Labour'. This is unlikely to change under the new leader Gordon Brown.

The Liberal Democratic Party emerged from the fusion, in 1988, of the Social Democrats and the Liberals, one of the traditional parties which had been gradually squeezed out of power by Labour and Conservatives in the inter-war period. The Liberals predominated in the new party, and it is their core values which give it its distinctive ideological tinge – above all, concern with individual freedom. As we have seen, support for individual freedom could lead, as in the Conservative Party, to support for radical free-market measures and lack of concern for social security and welfare. This is what characterises many free-enterprise liberal parties on the Continent. In the case of the British Liberals, like their Scandinavian counterparts, concern for freedom led to support for welfare on the grounds that political freedom is impossible without some level of economic and social security for all. More direct preoccupations have been their opposition to censorship, advocacy of a written and limited constitution, and civil liberties – particularly in the context of repressive measures against Muslim terrorists. The Liberal Democrats have always been firm on regional devolution, on environmental protection and on extending the ownership of industry to the workforce, with workers having the same rights as management. They have also been the most consistently favourable of the parties to full integration with the European Union. And of course they have supported reform of the electoral system towards full proportional representation – both because it gives greater freedom of individual choice and because they are the party most penalised by the existing arrangements.

Liberal Democrat policies do not fit well into classic left–right divisions, which accounts for the Liberal Democrats' largely centrist position in regard to these. Of all the parties they are the most committed to the extension of political rights and to electoral reform – which would, given their central ideological position, make them the determining factor in choosing a Conservative or Labour partner in a coalition government. As it is, the existing electoral system shuts them out from effective policy-making and debate.

Whatever its idiosyncrasies, Britain fits quite well into the standard model of European party systems, with a well-organised left opposed to a well-organised right, and a significant centrist party competing at electoral if not at parliamentary level. Ireland is quite different. Its system of parties has long been regarded as the most distinctive in the world, even taking Canada and the United States into account.

The peculiarity of the Irish system has been to have two parties competing for power which are almost identical ideologically. As we noted above, Fianna Fáil and Fine Gael originated in the civil war between those not prepared to accept independence for the south and west of Ireland without the North (Fianna Fáil) and those who had signed the treaty accepting partition (Fine Gael) and who formed the first governments of the Irish Free State. The latter won the civil war but lost subsequent elections to Fianna Fáil, seeing their basic vote shrink to around 30 per cent of voters while that of Fianna Fáil oscillated near 50 per cent. The main difference between the parties stemmed from their history and the personal and clientelist networks it had caused them to build up. These networks were particularly important given the small size of the country (under 3 million population), its agrarian and rural basis, and the highly personal nature of political relations. There was an incipient socio-economic cleavage between the parties, Fianna Fáil being stronger among the small subsistence farmers of the west and among the small-town bourgeoisie, and Fine Gael representing the large farmers of the east and what big business there was in Dublin. With this support base Fianna Fáil has been more nationalistic, severing all remaining political links with Britain by 1949. Fine Gael has always been more cautious on the nationalist issue, favouring negotiations with Britain, the major customer of its core supporters on the east coast.

Neither party was anxious to get closely involved in the Northern imbroglio, however. The factions of the Irish Republican Army (IRA) want to overthrow established authority in the South as well as in the North, so governments of all parties

Table 2.5 Left–right placement of parties in Ireland

	Ourselves	Labour		Nationalists	Progressive
	SF	LB		FG FF	PD

Left	Centre-left	Centre	Centre-right	Right

Party names:
SF: We Ourselves (Sinn Féin)
LB: Labour
FG: Party of the Gael (Fine Gael)
FF: Heroes of Destiny (Fiannna Fáil)
PD: Progressive Democrats

Source: As for Table 2.4.

have interned their members and cautiously co-operated with British forces. With the Northern settlement nationalism has faded as an issue. Both parties are enthusiastically pro-European, partly to distance themselves from the British and partly in recognition of the economic benefits and direct subsidies membership of the European Union brings – notably the Irish economic boom from the 1970s.

In terms of left–right policies Fine Gael was originally at the right of the policy spectrum while Fianna Fáil, in keeping with its populist appeal, stretched over a wide range of the spectrum from centre-right to centre-left. In seeking to counter Fianna Fáil's near-majority position among electors, however, Fine Gael exploited its rival's refusal to go into coalition even when it lacked a Dáil (parliamentary) majority, and formed coalition governments with small agrarian-populist parties and Labour in the 1950s, and with Labour from the 1970s to 1990s. As a result – and perhaps even in anticipation – its policies moved leftward in these decades.

This rendered the major Irish parties less distinguishable than ever. The general thrust of their policies on the economy and society in a traditionally Catholic country is best described as Christian Democrat, and they certainly pay great attention to the Social Encyclicals of the late nineteenth century and to current papal announcements on these topics. Abortion is effectively banned and divorce was legalised only in 1995.

Socially, however, there has been great change in the Republic over the last twenty years. Church attendance has dropped off and the authoritative position of the Catholic hierarchy has been repeatedly challenged, not least through appeals to the European Court. This has fostered hostility towards the EU among traditionalist as well as left-wing sectors. Secular parties such as Labour, the Progressive Democrats and Sinn Féin have found growing electoral support, with increasing fragmentation of the party system and moves towards coalition governments. It may be, therefore, that we shall see a more normal European pattern emerging in Ireland, with the emergence of distinct left, centre and right blocs.

One other peculiarity of Irish politics is the role played by popular referendums, which occur quite frequently on important issues and are actively contested by the parties. The vote of 2001 rejecting the treaty expanding the EU was a recent example of this. Britain, like Ireland, has had a nationwide referendum on membership of the European Community (1975), and Scottish and Welsh electors voted on regional devolution in 1979 and 1997. Such popular consultations are only held, however, at the political convenience of governments and are not mandated by the constitution.

PARLIAMENT

The working British constitution (as opposed to its numerous ceremonial accretions, Bagehot 1867) is ruthlessly simple: a government supported by the majority party in the House of Commons can do anything. There is no written document to limit its scope. The government inherits all the powers of an undefined royal prerogative. The legal doctrine of parliamentary sovereignty ensures that government legislation cannot normally be challenged directly in the courts (for the one exception, see below).

There are of course practical limits to the powers a majority government can exercise: the trade unions are less powerful than they used to be, owing to Thatcherite legislation and high unemployment, but they and other interest groups can still thwart particular policies when they feel strongly enough. More important, central government has no direct field administration in most domains and is thus dependent on other bodies – often politically opposed to it – to implement its policies. This often renders them more symbolic than real.

Despite such practical limitations, the absence of legal and constitutional restraints does put British governments among the most powerful in Europe. Irish governments inherited the tradition of strong authoritative rule from Britain. Within their limits they have the same freedom of action when supported by a Dáil majority. However, their limits are more strictly drawn, both by a written constitution – which does therefore permit legal challenges – and by the entrenched position of one of the most traditional and strongest Catholic Churches in Europe. No government would consciously risk a confrontation with the Church, and when the two have blundered into conflict, usually on social issues, the government has generally lost. In recent times governments have also lost referendums on important moral and European issues.

The strength of government *vis-à-vis* parliament and other bodies favours in Britain, and to a lesser extent in Ireland, the idea of the party mandate. This is the constitutional doctrine that the electoral programme of the party given the majority of parliamentary seats has been endorsed by the electorate, and that the government is entitled – indeed, required – to put its programme into action while in power. This widely held point of view severely downgrades the importance of Parliament, as it gives the government direct popular authority. It is true that such authority is conferred by obtaining a majority of seats in the House of Commons. But thereafter the leadership of the majority party can go ahead on its own and feels entitled to the compliance of Parliament in enacting its programme. Similarly the rank and file of the majority party are charged only with providing loyal voting support. Withdrawing such support or persistently criticising government is flouting the popular will.

These attitudes – widely held among both populace and political elite – secure strict party discipline in support of the government. They even ensure a compliant opposition, as it too accepts that the government has secured popular endorsement. This despite the fact that, owing to the working of the electoral system, British governments never secure the support of a majority, only that of a plurality – New Labour governed in 1997 and 2001 on the basis of 42 per cent of the popular vote and 36 per cent after the election of 2005. The mandate doctrine also has considerable ambiguities. What exactly are the policies which have been endorsed? Explicit pledges made during the election campaign? The priorities sketched out in the party manifesto? Anything the government chooses to do during its term of office?

If one analysed mandate theory in detail the exact basis of government action might be unclear. One advantage to governments of having an unwritten constitution is that its leading doctrines escape precise analysis and definition. The mandate theory can thus be invoked whenever and in whatever context the government has need of it. By and large its claim, with all its consequences in terms of loyal party support and muted opposition, is accepted.

This vitiates other potential roles for Parliament – as a scrutinising and revising body, for example. All parliamentary proceedings are overshadowed by the results of the last general election or by the prospect of the next. They are a forum for largely ritual debates. Approval of government measures is automatic. The purpose of parliamentary debates is not to change minds on the floor of the house but to influence public opinion for or against the government. Control over parliamentary proceedings is thus in the hands of the leadership of the two main parties and primarily of the government. Expressing individual opinions against the party line is difficult, as is the evolution of a purely 'parliamentary' 'cross-party' view. It can be seen that parliamentary procedures, like those of the electoral system, favour the two main parties at the expense of the others, making it difficult for the latter to get any media exposure at all through Parliament. The main party leaderships, in contrast, appear in televised debates and newspaper reports very frequently.

The emphasis on authoritative government backed by popular mandate – the 'elective dictatorship' – explains what would otherwise seem anomalous in a parliamentary democracy – the obsessive secrecy of governments and bureaucracy about what they are doing. This denies to those outside, including MPs, much opportunity for informed comment or constructive criticism of government action. The maintenance of 'official secrecy' is enshrined in draconian legislation which makes not only disclosure but the receipt of classified information a criminal offence. Bureaucrats are required not to disclose information to, and even to mislead, parliamentary committees investigating government policy.

These bizarre outcomes become understandable in the context of doctrines which regard governments as uniquely empowered, by election, to carry through the popular will. The major function of official secrecy is thus to protect the government from challenge, or even embarrassment, internally. In doing so the retention and selective management of relevant information is a powerful tool. The classification of what is an official secret is in the government's and bureaucracy's own hands, and is buttressed by 'D notices' to the media requiring total silence on matters defined as important for defence, certificates to judges preventing classified evidence being disclosed in court, extremely severe libel laws and the 'lobby' system of briefing certain privileged journalists with 'unattributable' information favourable to the government's position.

These practices have been partially breached by the practice of investigative journalism in recent years, making full and embarrassing use of increasing numbers of leaks from dissident civil servants and government members. The House of Commons has also developed the institution of semi-permanent select committees – bodies of MPs from all parties, sometimes with an opposition chairman – which 'shadow' a particular ministry or department (e.g. Defence, Employment, the Environment, Home Affairs, etc.). These committees conduct investigations into important aspects of the ministry's work, or on particularly controversial decisions that have been made. Their reports are informative and authoritative, partly because they have the power to call civil servants and ministers to testify.

However, their scope is severely limited by the institutional constraints mentioned earlier. In the first place they have to operate within the ongoing, party-based, adversarial confrontation between government and opposition. This means that, in order to secure cross-party agreement within the committee between MPs from all sides, they cannot investigate matters at the forefront of the party debate. But these, of course, *are* the most important parts of current policy. Second, in order to secure cross-party agreement on the final report, the committee must not be too critical of the government, otherwise its supporters on the committee will dissent. And, third, the committees are as hampered by official secrecy as anyone else. Civil servants' loyalty is defined as lying with the current government, not Parliament, and they are encouraged to be 'economical with the truth' in a famous phrase of a former head of the civil service, even to Parliament.

Parliament has two houses. Besides the House of Commons, with its 646 directly elected MPs, there is the House of Lords, reformed in 1999. Members are now nominated for life on the recommendation of a committee (whose members are nominated by government). The object is to maintain a rough party balance. In recent years the active members, about 200 in number, have been drawn largely from these nominees. As they are people of individual weight and some news value, their speeches can have considerable impact. The Lords' debates are much less partisan than those of the Commons, as the government's survival does not depend on them. As a result their select committees have less difficulty in mustering cross-party support for their point of view, and can function better than in the Commons.

However, the influence of the House of Lords is indirect and diffuse. Its non-elective base clearly puts it in a disadvantageous position. It has merely delaying and not veto powers over legislation. While this may be strategically important in the case of governments with small House of Commons majorities or nearing the end of their term, the Lords can normally be overridden and are therefore a purely marginal factor in the power equation. (The Seanad is in a similar position in the Irish case.)

Parliament as a whole, and the House of Commons in particular, is thus to be interpreted more as a context in which government operates than as a constraint on its powers or as an independent scrutineer and critic of its activities. It provides the forum in which the partisan contenders for power meet, but in itself it is fairly neutral. The adversarial relationship between government and opposition puts a premium on party discipline and loyalty, which in turn undermines any possibility of concerted action independent of the party leaderships. The only body with a clearly recognised role independent of government is the official opposition – the other main party with aspirations to, though not possession of, governmental power.

However, the official opposition consists of only a minority in Parliament and so cannot claim to represent that institution as a whole against the government. It is much more readily identified with a (defeated) partisan viewpoint. Most of its pronouncements are aimed at winning the next election. So debate occurs only at a very general level, on set pieces of legislation and policy rather than on the bulk of government business, and in an adversarial rather than a constructive manner. It is not seriously intended to improve government policy but to present it in a good or bad light to the electors. In any case the government often acts under extra-parliamentary (Crown prerogative) powers, where parliamentary debate can only review something already done rather than attempt to modify it for the future, as with the decision to go to war in Iraq.

The weakness of Parliament as an institution, the dominance of the government and the role of the official opposition as government-in-waiting have been recognised in political and constitutional textbooks for a long time. Democracy was, however, thought to inhere in the challenge presented to the government by the opposition: government policy would thus always be constrained by the need to retain general

Table 2.6 Governments of Britain, 1945–2007

No.	Year	Prime Minister	Party composition
1	1945	C. R. Attlee	Labour
2	1950	C. R. Attlee	Labour
3	1951	W. S. Churchill	Conservative
	1955	A. Eden	Conservative
4	1955	A. Eden	Conservative
	1955	H. Macmillan	Conservative
5	1959	H. Macmillan	Conservative
	1963	A. Douglas-Home	Conservative
6	1964	H. Wilson	Labour
7	1966	H. Wilson	Labour
8	1970	E. Heath	Conservative
9	1974	H. Wilson	Labour
10	1974	H. Wilson	Labour
	1976	J. Callaghan	Labour
11	1979	M. Thatcher	Conservative
12	1983	M. Thatcher	Conservative
13	1987	M. Thatcher	Conservative
	1990	J. Major	Conservative
14	1992	J. Major	Conservative
15	1997	A. Blair	Labour
16	2001	A. Blair	Labour
17	2005	A. Blair	Labour
	2007	G. Brown	Labour

support for the next election. In the light of mandate theory, independent parliamentary criticism or debate was felt to be irrelevant or even to get in the way of the direct relationship which should exist between government and people.

Such views were, however, elaborated for a two-party system in which the main parties were evenly balanced, so that there was fairly frequent alternation in power or at least the prospect of it. Under constant electoral threat a party government may be expected to modify its policies to what is acceptable to the mass of centrist voters. The problem with the contemporary system is that it is a three-party system in which the third party, the Liberal Democrats, is seriously under-represented. The governing party thus regularly wins power on the basis of around 40 per cent of the votes – only 20–25 per cent of the electorate!

Adversarial debate between the two main parties is further weakened as an instrument of democracy by increasing government control over the means of mass communication. Manipulation of the media by 'spin doctors' has become an important element in maintaining New Labour's appeal. Various governments have also used their tenure in office to bully the BBC, penalise independent television companies critical of them and get sympathisers on to the control boards of both these organisations. Parliamentary debate will clearly be ineffective unless it can reach the public through the media in a relatively unbiased form. Increasing government influence over the media militates against that.

Under these circumstances the system of strong government and weak Parliament no longer seems designed to respond sensitively to changes in the popular will. Rather, it operates to muffle debate and to steamroller policies through without regard to opposition – a buttress of party hegemony rather than democracy. The most likely agent of change in current constitutional arrangements would be a coalition government, which under the existing electoral system is likely to emerge only from a Liberal Democrat breakthrough. This in itself is unlikely, though not totally impossible, so the probability is that the dominance of governments over Parliament, and indeed over most other political institutions, will continue.

The changes that frequent recourse to coalition government could make in Britain are illustrated in Ireland, where such a change did take place in the 1980s (Table 2.7). Fianna Fáil governments from the 1930s subordinated Parliament to the Executive, as in Britain. The trend was even exacerbated by the concern of most TDs (Deputies) with local events in their constituencies rather than national affairs. This meant that the government could often buy support, or buy off opposition, by distributing local favours. Changes in the party system reduced Fianna Fáil's ability to rule on its own during the 1980s. First Labour and Fine Gael formed a coalition (1982–1987), then Fianna Fáil found it needed a Progressive Democrat or a Labour alliance. Coalition government now seems to have arrived in the Republic, with a concomitant rise in the importance of Parliament as the site where coalitions are formed and negotiations over both personnel and policy take place. Coalitions are unlikely to be as monolithic as single-party governments, therefore the prospects in Ireland are of an increase in policy-relevant debate and parliamentary voting, which has now become decisive in respect of government policy.

Table 2.7 Governments of Ireland, 1948–2007

No.	Year	Prime Minister	Party composition
1	1948	J. A. Costello	Fine Gael, Labour, Clann na Talmhan
2	1951	E. de Valera	Fianna Fáil
3	1954	J. A. Costello	Fine Gael, Labour, Clann na Talmhan
4	1957	E. de Valera	Fianna Fáil
	1959	S. Lemass	Fianna Fáil
5	1961	S. Lemass	Fianna Fáil
6	1965	S. Lemass	Fianna Fáil
	1966	J. Lynch	Fianna Fáil
7	1969	J. Lynch	Fianna Fáil
8	1973	L. Cosgrave	Fine Gael, Labour
9	1977	J. Lynch	Fianna Fáil
	1979	C. J. Haughey	Fianna Fáil
10	1981	G. M. D. Fitzgerald	Fine Gael, Labour
11	1982	C. J. Haughey	Fianna Fáil
12	1982	G. M. D. Fitzgerald	Fine Gael, Labour
13	1987	C. J. Haughey	Fianna Fáil
14	1989	C. J. Haughey	Fianna Fáil, Progressive
	1991	A. Reynolds	Fianna Fáil, Progressive
15	1992	A. Reynolds	Fianna Fáil, Labour
16	1994	J. Brutton	Fine Gael, Labour
17	1997	B. Aherne	Fianna Fáil, Progressive
18	2007	B. Aherne	Fianna Fáil, Progressive
19	2007	B. Aherne	Fianna Fáil, Progressive, Green

Note: The first party indicates the Prime Minister's affiliation.

GOVERNMENT AND BUREAUCRACY

Cabinet and Prime Minister

We have talked about 'government' in the British context as if it were an undifferentiated institution, but in fact the exact form of the 'government' is as ambiguous as everything else in the unwritten constitution. The one definite thing we can say about it is that all members of the government have to be drawn from one of the two houses of Parliament, and that in practice the vast majority of them will be MPs. At one level the government is everyone occupying a position under the Crown, down to unpaid parliamentary private secretaries who act as dogsbodies in Parliament for the more important ministers. Calculating it in this way, the government has over 100 members. They are all MPs or peers of the majority party and will lose their position if they vote or speak against policy either in public or in private. They are thus important in controlling the majority party. At majority party meetings held to discuss policy, typically of around 350 MPs, the 100-odd government members only have to find another 80 or so supporters to dominate the meeting. Party members are then under intense pressure to support the agreed policy. In this way a government and 100 backbench supporters can dominate the proceedings of the 630-odd MPs in the House of Commons, if necessary.

Otherwise the lower-ranking members of a government do not have much weight and they will certainly not decide its policy. This is also true of middle-ranking ministers, who may have some say in specialist matters that concern their own department or ministry but who do not much influence government policy overall. The real core of a government is the cabinet, the central co-ordinating and policy-making body, which meets regularly once a week under the convenorship of the Prime minister to take major decisions and to resolve disputes and controversies which have found their way up to its level. The cabinet is both a partisan body, consisting of the main figures in the majority party leadership, and also the effective centre of the executive.

Most individual members of the cabinet will be in charge of one of the more important ministries or departments into which the executive is divided (Table 2.8). Thus they have a double workload deriving from departmental responsibilities on the one hand and cabinet responsibilities on the other. A few cabinet ministers will be relieved from departmental responsibilities, charged, confusingly, with 'ceremonial' functions such as Chancellor of the Duchy of Lancaster or Lord President

Table 2.8 Major departments and agencies of British central government

Department name	Department functions
Cabinet Office	Co-ordination and implementation of policies
Treasury	Economic planning and financial control
Privy Council Office	Legislative programme
Constitutional Affairs	Oversight of court system
Home Office	Police, prisons, immigration, citizenship
Northern Ireland Office	Government policy in Northern Ireland
Welsh Office	Government policy in Wales
Scottish Office	Government policy in Scotland
Department for Environment, Food and Rural Affairs	Countryside, agriculture, rural development
Department for Transport, Local Government and the Regions	Liaison with local government; supervision of rail and roads
Department for Work and Pensions	Social security, disability and employment
Department of Health	Government health policy and National Health Service
Department of Trade and Industry	Trade policy, energy and science
Department for Education and Skills	Schools and universities
Department for Media, Culture and Sport	Museums, broadcasting policy
Foreign and Commonwealth Office	Foreign relations including European Union
Ministry of Defence	National security

of the Council. Their real job, however, is to deal with non-departmental party and political business and to convene cabinet committees to deal with specialist matters.

Besides its political importance as the final source of authority and ultimate decision-making body, the cabinet derives its central position from the fact that it is the sole co-ordinating body in British government. This is not to say that there are not hundreds of interdepartmental committees. As we shall see, however, these can take final decisions only if all concerned agree. Where they do not, disputes even over trivial matters can go all the way up to cabinet for resolution. Conversely, centrally important but agreed matters may not go to cabinet at all because they are agreed and time is scarce.

Cabinet ministers are in a paradoxical position with regard to each other and to the Prime Minister. The latter appoints them to office: (s)he can also promote them or dismiss them. Collectively, on the other hand, they can in effect destroy the Prime Minister by withdrawing their support. However, it is difficult for the cabinet to act collectively independently of the Prime Minister. For in replacing him or her they are automatically putting one of themselves in the position – a move which will reward some and penalise others, especially the main contenders. A prime ministerial resignation is therefore liable to be precipitated by external events – a dramatic policy failure, an impending or actual general election defeat – rather than by a spontaneous revolt of cabinet members.

The relation of cabinet ministers among themselves is collegial and adversarial at the same time. They are colleagues in the sense that their political position depends on the success, particularly the electoral success, of the government and party to which they belong. Hence they must co-operate in ensuring that success, and in backing the Prime Minister's attempts to assert central authority over the governmental machine and over the majority party.

The constitutional form taken by collegiality is the doctrine of collective responsibility whereby each member of the government (not simply cabinet members) is supposed to support all governmental measures and to take public responsibility for them (even should they privately disagree). While the doctrine has been vitiated by the growth of investigative journalism, which probes into internal disputes, and by the growing use of leaks and anonymous disclosure of confidential information to reporters, it is still preserved through official secrecy and the management of information. Cabinet ministers are generally powerful enough to let their dissent be made known when they want it to be. It is the middle-ranking and junior members of the government who are most under pressure to signify total agreement and to defend government policy, on pain of dismissal.

The need for cabinet ministers to differentiate themselves from each other and to pursue their policy disputes into the public domain reflects the adversarial side of their relationships. This is structural and stems from two aspects of their interactions with each other, one political and one institutional.

On the political side the cabinet contains a number, usually two or three, of senior figures in the majority party who are the most likely people to succeed the Prime Minister if (s)he is forced to resign. Each of these heirs apparent has associates and supporters among other ministers. This clearly makes for rivalry and jostling for position. If the government seems in a good position, with the party united, the economy booming and election prospects good, the Prime Minister will be safe from challenge, and this source of rivalry will subside. Sudden crises or scandals, as well as a re-emergence of internal party divisions, occur increasingly frequently, however, in the rapidly changing modern world, and they are always liable to weaken the Prime Minister's position and to reawaken rivalries in the cabinet.

There is, however, a more everyday source of tension which arises between all ministers but particularly between those in the cabinet. This stems from their position as head of an agglomeration of bureaucrats and functions organised into a particular ministry or department of state. There are about 70 of these, of which 12–15 particularly important ones are represented in the cabinet – the Treasury (finance), Foreign Affairs, Home Affairs, Health, Education, the Environment, Defence, and so on. As we shall see when we discuss the bureaucracy, relations between ministries are expected to be adversarial. Very often direct clashes occur, as between Environment, which may want to designate an area for protection, and, for example, Defence, which wants to use it for intensive military practice. At the very least ministries will clash over sharing out money and will confront the Treasury, which has an interest in cutting spending.

The whole style and dynamics of policy-making in Britain are geared to advocacy and opposition of policies. Policies will not get far unless they are backed by a department prepared to argue for their merits. A general discussion is ensured by forming a committee with other departments which declare an interest, and arguing it out, with some defending and others attacking the policy. While admirable for ensuring critical discussion, such adversarial attitudes spill over into the cabinet when, as often happens, no agreement on the matter can be reached below that level. The lack of any significant co-ordinating mechanisms below cabinet level means that disputes very often do spill over, though always into a cabinet sub-committee with the interested parties represented before reaching the full cabinet.

Such disputes are muted and concealed by the doctrine of collective responsibility discussed above and by the common interest ministers share in re-election. Cabinet conventions have evolved in the context of single-party government, and the effects of adversarial decision-making are usually contained by it. A look at the Irish experience in the 1980s, however, shows that the strict application of cabinet conventions to a coalition arrangement can cause ruptures between the partners. In the 1982– 1987 Irish coalition of Fine Gael and Labour the latter took the more 'social' spending ministries while its more conservative partner took the 'central' finance ministries. As Fine Gael was the larger partner and British traditions of majority voting and collective responsibility applied in cabinet, Labour had to acquiesce in silence to cuts in social programmes which it had promised, electorally, to protect. The end result was a rupture with its election partner of twenty years, due not just to policy disputes but to the way cabinet conventions exacerbated them. Labour's wary attitudes to its coalition partners of the 1990s – which included both Fine Gael and Fianna Fáil – go back to this experience. Coalitions are now run on the basis of equality between the partners.

Recent criticisms of cabinet government in the British case relate above all to co-ordination and implementation of government policy by ministries and agencies. These problems have been exacerbated to some extent by 'hiving off' some government services to private contractors or nominated 'quangos' (quasi non-governmental bodies). To bring together and concentrate the efforts of the diverse departments and bodies dealing with a particular problem the Prime Minister's office has been strengthened, with the Deputy Prime Minister acting as 'enforcer'. The Prime Minister has increasingly taken personal control of major government policies or crises like the recent wars. Typically, however, attention is diverted to another crisis before the first one is resolved, as with the outbreak of foot-and-mouth disease in 2001. It remains to be seen whether these interventions in the government machine are any more effective for the actual implementation of policy than what went before.

Civil service and bureaucracy

The most notable feature of the central bureaucracy is its grouping into autonomous ministries and departments. There is no agreed list of these, but in a broad way one can say there are about fifteen centrally important ministries represented by their political heads in cabinet and about seventy fairly important ministries and offices of various kinds. A list of some of them is given in Table 2.8.

Only one or two people in each ministry are appointed by the current government: these are the MPs or peers who act as political heads and representatives of the department in the government. They may bring in a political adviser but there is no ministerial *cabinet* supervising all aspects of internal administration, as in France, for example. More likely a new minister will work with the permanent, non-politically appointed civil servants they find running the department, with a qualified right to choose among unknown candidates for posts in their private office. British politicians are exceptionally dependent on their bureaucrats not only for policy implementation but also for policy advice. This makes the nature of the civil service, as the central bureaucracy is called, their early socialisation, appointment and career expectations of particular importance in understanding British government.

Of course, like all bureaucracies, the civil service is hierarchical and employs large numbers of people at the lower levels (clerical and manual workers) who hardly count in policy-making. Above them are executive officers charged with implementing already agreed policies. The more successful of these may work their way up to the level of policy-making, undertaken by the 6,000–10,000 persons at the top of the civil service hierarchy. Most of these, however, are recruited directly by the civil service itself, through competitive examination and interviews geared to the university curriculum, and within that to the model set by the elite universities of Oxford and Cambridge. There have in fact been repeated complaints, from the Fulton Commission of the late 1960s onwards, about the extent to which the top levels of the civil service are dominated by Oxbridge graduates. Marginal changes have taken place but the style as well as the graduates of Oxford and Cambridge still dominate the upper levels.

What does this imply for policy-making? In the first place it means that higher civil servants share a particular ethos which is quite resistant to governmentally inspired change, and which to a considerable extent isolates them from the common experience of the mass of British society. This contributes to a preference for shutting off their discussions from ill-informed intervention (hence to a heavy stress on official secrecy and classified discussion) and for admitting only approved interlocutors to the policy club. It also favours a generalist approach to policy-making. Rather than having a technical education in the areas they administer, the assumption is that the non-specialist administrator will be better able to put together advice from a variety of sources, including the technical grades of the civil service itself, and come up with a better overall policy than could have been produced by any one specialist.

Higher civil servants thus transfer quite readily between jobs and even departments in the course of their career. However, they make their mark by advancing the perceived interests of their current team, whether it be a section or the department as a whole. Each ministry is likely to have a set of policy preferences built up over the years, and known as the 'departmental view', often based on supporting favoured interests or clients. The model civil servant regards his or her role as an advocacy one, just like a lawyer in the British courts. While in a particular department or section (s)he will promote its interests, even though the previous year, in another department, (s)he was engaged in attacking them.

Given the frequency of ministerial changes within governments, a politician can expect to spend less than two years, on average, at a particular ministry. On arrival, mostly without previous experience or knowledge of the ministry, (s)he depends on civil servants for information and guidance. The fact that both have an immediate interest in promoting the importance and influence of the department gives them some common ground, of course, as does the social background which Conservative ministers in particular will share with top policy-makers. There will also, however, be potential divergences, particularly where either the minister or the government has plans for change in important policies affecting the ministry. On the face of it, the bureaucratic policy-makers would seem to have all the advantages in a confrontation with their minister. They have control of the records and information about past decisions. To a large extent they control the minister's agenda and the (civil service) personnel who service him or her, down to the level of the private secretary. They also control the relevant policy network which is the source of technical advice and political consensus-building round proposals.

These resources are generally sufficient to push ministers or governments who have not thought about the policy area much, or who have only very general and vague ideas, into supporting the departmental view. This situation can be reversed, however, when ministers have more experience, and particularly when the government as a whole is firmly committed to a particular programme which has a popular mandate, as was true under Mrs Thatcher and Tony Blair. Recent examples have been 'New Labour' changes in education and the National Health Service.

Ireland inherited a traditional British type of civil service, already largely autonomous and centred on Dublin, when it gained independence in 1922. Thus much of what has been said about the general style of the British civil service, particularly its division into ministries with their own departmental view and adversarial relationships, applies also to the Irish case. The administration is highly centralised in Dublin and is largely staffed and run by graduates of the two universities there. It has perforce had to be highly conservative and restrictive during most of its existence, confining itself to the minimal functions of state, because of the general shortage of resources up to the 1970s and the financial crises of the 1980s. Social services have never developed to the British level – in part because of limited resources, in part because of the opposition of the Catholic Church to any interference in family relationships.

The exception, partly of necessity, has come in the field of industrial development. The need to develop the economy so as to stem emigration and depopulation has led to an innovative and relatively successful approach to attracting overseas firms to locate in Ireland, partly through financial inducements and partly through free-trade zones in the west. Of necessity the agencies and departments involved in industrial policy have had to be autonomous and innovative, able to take immediate decisions free from the need to negotiate overmuch with other departments.

Other differences from Britain stem from the small size of the country and the even greater centralisation on one city, Dublin. Bureaucrats are almost all personally known to each other. It is easy to get in touch. Thus in some ways in Ireland bureaucracy is a more unified force than in Britain: it is also easier to agree on policy because the limits of the possible are much narrower. The traditional caution and financial conservatism of Irish bureaucracy were well adapted to the conditions of the 1980s and 1990s, and attuned to similar instincts in Fine Gael and Fianna Fáil.

Interest groups

One of the reasons why British central ministries evolve different policy preferences and opinions lies in their relations with outside specialists and interest groups. All ministries have their own 'policy networks' extending down to local level, on which they rely for information and gaining compliance for their policies. In return ministries adopt many of the views which circulate inside the network and promulgate them in government.

The advantages of this arrangement for both sides are obvious. Interest groups can hope through their sponsoring department to have an influence on government policy and legislation before they are adopted, which is much more likely to shape them in the way they want than if they were to campaign publicly after they had been promulgated. On the other hand, the department wishes to be able to say that its policies have the support of all or some of the groups they are likely to affect. They also need to have technical information, for example on how much a proposed environmental protection measure will cost the industries affected. In spite of having specialist civil servants – economists, statisticians, engineers – on tap, the ministry lacks the resources to gather all the information required. The generalist nature of the civil service as a whole renders it particularly dependent on advice from outside specialists and makes it generally more likely to take a reactive than a proactive role in policy-making.

It must be said, however, that this process of interaction is not an open one accessible to all who have views on the policy area with which a ministry is concerned. There are quite strict requirements for obtaining 'insider' status with a ministry and 'club rules' which it is essential to obey. To a considerable extent the interest groups involved become 'captives' of the civil servants. Confrontational tactics and rhetoric must be eschewed: interest groups must avoid leaks to the media and accept what comes out of the policy process. What they get on the other hand are confidential regular meetings with civil servants and politicians in which they can argue the case for their view of the policy, and put forward the technical considerations which support it. A perfect example of the type of 'insider' relationship which can form policy is the motorists', road hauliers' and road contractors' relations with the Department of Transport, which have reinforced its support of new motorways and roads.

Past relations of the same kind have obtained between the National Farmers' Union and the former Ministry of Agriculture, Fisheries and Food; between the Department of Trade and Industry and the Confederation of British Industry (CBI); between the former Department of Employment and the trade unions. However, such relations are subject to change, both from overall government policy and from the entry of new groups (such as supermarket chains and food consumer associations) into the policy arena. The Department of Employment changed under Thatcherite policies from an advocate to a controller of trade unions. In general Conservative governments from 1974 to 1997 were suspicious of interest groups, believing that they themselves had the (free-market) answers to the problems confronting them, and that business and the unions would try to subvert these if they could, rather than accepting and enforcing them. They preferred, therefore, to break with the quasi-corporatist practices of the past and felt much less need to consult affected interests than their predecessors had done. This tradition has continued under 'New Labour'.

There may be some justification for government scepticism about the groups the civil service naturally tends to consult, particularly in the economic field. The groups tend to be 'peak' associations, federations of a widely disparate membership of other bodies. Such peak associations are well staffed, with good research departments, and are naturally well placed to get reliable information from their members. They are thus able to meet the information needs of their sponsoring department in the civil service.

What they are much less able to do is to trade consent for concessions on policy, as they have no binding sanctions over their own members. Thus wage or price limits agreed with government at the top level are always liable to be breached by individual businesses or unions, which were often successful under the weak governments of the 1960s and 1970s in extracting concessions over and above those made at the national level.

There is a certain logic therefore in the Conservative position that regulation needs to be imposed from above by a strong authoritative state, and unruly interests forced to comply by legal sanctions applied through the court system. Imposition from above worked well against the isolated and weakened trade unions of the early 1980s, which were also hit by the high unemployment produced by the government's monetarist financial policies. The limitations of intervention, on the other hand, were shown by the attempt to maintain high taxes on petrol which were met with wide popular protests in the autumn of 2000. Another area where policy-making by imposition has produced patchy results from the government's point of view is education. The total exclusion of the teaching unions from the Department of

Education has resulted in boycotts and strikes, and disaffection is now spreading to the medical professionals of the National Health Service.

There are still advantages, therefore – even for governments with a mission – of consultation with interest groups. However, this is a long way from saying that all such groups are allowed free entry even to the ministries that do consult.

An overview of policy processes

We have shown that central decision-making in Britain brings together elected politicians, career civil servants and interest-group representatives – who may themselves be a very mixed bag of people. The relative importance of the various actors changes according to circumstances. First, while civil servants are always present, in certain cases they are more autonomous than in others. Education reforms have involved politicians very heavily. Safety and health at work are handled predominantly by the interests concerned.

Second, governments may be more or less ideological. The Conservative governments of the 1980s were unusually so. But as governments spend longer in office they tend to run out of ideas and may be grateful to civil servants who have their own agenda of problems to be tidied up. This seems to have happened with major projects for computerisation under New Labour as its attention was distracted more and more overseas.

Third, the importance attached to negotiations with interest groups varies from government to government. The traditional interpretation of British politics has emphasised the centralisation and cohesion of the system. The cabinet, elected on a party programme, supported by a disciplined majority in the House of Commons, aided by a competent and obedient civil service, is capable of making far more coherent policy than that which emerges from the coalition governments of Continental Europe or the American division of powers between the legislative, executive and judicial branches.

This view needs to be modified, for a number of reasons. British political parties, and so cabinets, are coalitions of people of clearly differing views, who are also political rivals to a considerable extent. There are also divisions within the administrative sector itself. Departments differ in their attitudes and concerns. The Department for Environment, Food and Rural Affairs is much more supportive of farm subsidies, as is the Ministry of Defence of military spending, than is the Treasury. As a major part of the job of ministers is to represent the interests and attitudes of their departments, such differences create conflict not only between civil servants but also between their ministers in the cabinet.

The administrative style of British government, as we shall see in more detail below, has always been to entrust the implementation of policies to other people – notables serving on nominated bodies, courts, local authorities and, in some areas, interest groups. Such devolution limits the degree of control central government enjoys. It was traditionally said that a French Minister of Education could tell you at any hour of the day what every child in France was studying; British governments have not been able to break local control of education even though it has been reduced. Administrative devolution saves central government the expense and difficulty of running schools directly; it also limits the degree to which the Secretary of State for Education can make real decisions about what happens in schools.

The coherence of central decision-making has also been limited by the weakness of 'umbrella' interest groups speaking for broad social groups, particularly unions and employers. The CBI and Trades Union Congress (TUC) have very little control over their members: governments thus deal with interest groups which have not themselves achieved the same degree of unity as interest groups in, say, Austria or Sweden. In consequence they have to broker more conflicts than their counterparts in countries with more centralised interest-group systems. At times central decision-makers are themselves disoriented by contending and conflicting claims from groups.

Central decision-making still offers opportunities to politicians who know what they want and how to achieve it. The Thatcher and Blair governments show that elections can indeed make a major difference in British politics. Yet behind the apparent simplicity lies the complexity of interaction between different spheres – politics, administration and interests. Within each sphere there is less unity than might be expected. British government is formally and constitutionally highly unified. In reality it is quite fragmented.

Policy outputs: patterns of government expenditure

We have discussed the processes of decision-making in Britain: what do they add up to in terms of the substantive policies which are actually adopted? We can check this by seeing how the central government has divided its budget between different areas of expenditure in the post-war period. Expenditure is not all there is to policy – clearly the government can make important changes in the legal sphere, or in regulatory policy, or sign treaties such as those enrolling Britain in the European Community without the commitments affecting spending very much.

Admitting this, it is still the case that the share of the budget allocated to areas like social services is crucial to large numbers in the population. Most areas require some spending to make policy effective, so reductions or increases in the budget percentages devoted to them are crucial indicators of where governments put their priorities. The share of overall resources spent by British governments increased from around one-third of gross domestic product (GDP) in the 1950s to approaching half in the mid-1980s, so the question of its allocation is centrally important in terms of its sheer weight in the economy. Budgeted spending has been shown to relate to the priorities stated by the government party in its election programme, so it is also important in a programmatic sense, as showing how the ruling party carried its policies through into action. We have calculated how percentage allocations of the budget varied in different policy areas in each year of the post-war period. By and large, the long-term trends continue regardless of whether the government is Labour or Conservative. The shares for defence and agriculture drop steadily over the whole period, while expenditure on the social areas of health, social security, education and housing generally goes up – as does the share for the police, courts, prisons and general 'administration of justice'. Of course the budget percentages do not tell the whole story about government spending, since they do not tell us directly how much is spent in each area in absolute terms. As we know that the total government share of GDP was going up, however, the relative increase signifies that actual spending on public services increased sharply over the post-war period, relative to static or declining expenditures in areas like defence.

What this illustrates is how the Conservative governments of the 1950s accepted the welfare state as they said they would. Indeed, they went further than mere acceptance, spending more and more on welfare. So did the Labour and Conservative governments of the 1960s and 1970s. With Mrs Thatcher came a change, however. In most 'social' areas expenditure dropped or was contained (the exception being the general area of social security, where increasing outlays on unemployment benefit as a result of privatisation and industrial closures caused by other government policies kept payments up relative to other areas). The Thatcherite turnround is most dramatically illustrated in the area of subsidies to public housing, reduced to almost one-fifth of their former percentage by 1985. As the government had cut its expenditure as a share of GDP from 45.1 per cent in 1980 to 42.8 per cent in 1986, this represented a real reduction in most social entitlements. In the 1990s expenditure on public services gradually increased again, particularly after 'New Labour' came to power in 1997.

What these figures show is that Conservative ideological commitments to 'rolling back the frontiers of the state' in favour of private provision and the free market did carry through to public policy under Mrs Thatcher, just as the promise of New Labour to defend and consolidate the welfare state was also reflected in allocations. Whatever the inefficiencies of the central policy process, it is clear that governments do manage to translate programmes into action, at least in broad terms and in some areas.

The general spending allocations we have described follow something of the same pattern over all Western democracies, though perhaps less markedly than in Britain. This is also true of Ireland, where expenditure in general and allocations to the 'social' side of the budget surged in the 1970s, but then experienced cuts during the economic and financial crises of the 1980s. Even though Labour was in coalition with Fine Gael for much of this period, it failed to reverse or even to modify such cuts substantially. These continued under the Fianna Fáil coalition with the free-market Progressive Democrats. Renewed economic growth in the 1990s and Labour's influence in its coalitions with Fianna Fáil and Fine Gael supported a promised expansion of the welfare programmes, which survived its loss of power in 1997.

INTERGOVERNMENTAL RELATIONS

Regional and local governments

As has been noted at several points, British central government in London has no field administration in most policy areas. Instead it relies on other bodies, primarily regional and local governments, but also autonomous nominated boards ('quangos') and even interest groups and professional bodies, to implement its programmes in detail. Such arrangements are not unusual in European federal states such as Germany, where the *Länder* carry through the bulk of centrally inspired administration. It is anomalous, however, in a state which (at any rate in constitutional theory) is so centralised as the British. In Wales, Scotland and Northern Ireland, under the devolution arrangements, regional executives and administration have taken over most social and domestic affairs.

These new bodies represent an interesting innovation in British constitutional practice. They are not unprecedented since Northern Ireland previously had a regional administration (1922–1972) and various islands (the Channel Islands and the Isle of Man) have always had local autonomy. Formally the powers of the new regions differ among themselves, Wales having mostly administrative oversight over its affairs while Scotland and Northern Ireland have legislative control of most domestic matters (social services, education, justice and development). Tax powers are in all cases very limited, so the British government has ultimate 'control of the purse' in regard to regional expenditure. In many ways devolution has simply meant leaving bothersome peripheries to their own devices provided they do not make too much trouble. Central government retains direct control of England, with 52 million of the 60 million inhabitants of the United Kingdom.

The regional set-ups have allowed for limited constitutional experiments. In Wales and Scotland constituency MPs elected to the local legislature have been supplemented by list MPs elected on the basis of party strengths in larger districts. This has diluted the tendency of 'first past the post' to give the plurality electoral party a legislative majority. In practice this has meant that the dominant Labour Party has had to form coalition executives with the Liberal Democrats. In turn this has resulted in the Assembly and Parliament having more power, with some policies being adopted which run counter to British New Labour policy. There is obvious scope for conflict between regional and central governments, particularly with the new Nationalist-dominated Executive in Scotland.

The Republic of Ireland inherited its institutional structure from Britain, so that it has a broadly similar division of labour between the central administration and county and town councils elected locally. Popular resistance to the British administration in the late nineteenth century, however, meant that the central departments in Dublin took many more direct powers (over police and education, for example) than in Britain. As local politics are traditionally non-partisan in many areas, and Fianna Fáil and Fine Gael share much the same fiscal and social policies, the kind of local–central conflicts which developed in Britain in the 1980s are absent in Ireland, and the traditional balance between centre and peripheries has thus not shifted so much in the recent past.

The absence of a direct central presence in localities means in practice in Britain that if a policy is decided on, in education for example, the Department of Education does not routinely implement the policy through its local offices – it has none. Still less does it send instructions direct to the schools, over which it has no immediate authority. Instead it sends details of the new policy to the directors of Education and the education committees of borough and county councils, requesting or requiring compliance and asking for reports on progress.

Clearly this indirect mode of proceeding is subject to delay and sometimes non-compliance, particularly if the policy has not been passed as legislation and thus does not have the full force of law. Non-compliance can become full-scale obstruction, as in federal systems, if the local government is politically opposed to central government policy. Owing to the fact that local elections take place over a three-year period, and thus often when the government party is in the trough of its popularity cycle, there is an in-built mechanism in Britain for parties in control locally to differ from the one in power at the centre.

Where policy is generally agreed, of course, the situation does not necessarily lead to an impasse. Politicians are not the only people involved in local decision-making. Local bureaucrats are professionals and specialists in their own areas – finance, public health, sewage and so on: they have a national career pattern and will often have close links with their fellow specialists or civil servants in the relevant national ministry. They probably indeed have closer links with their national 'policy network' than with fellow officials in their own local authority.

However, even such networks, professionally predisposed to relay and implement national policies, need to be consulted and won over if the process is to go smoothly. This is even more true of the professionals' political masters, ideologically opposed to central government anyway. As we noted, the style of governments since 1979 has not been to consult, but to impose directives with a strong ideological content. The result has been constant conflict with local government, which in many ways has represented a more effective opposition to central policies than the parliamentary opposition.

The central government has two major weapons in trying to enforce its will at local level. In the first place it provides one-third of local government revenue (another one-third comes from local taxes and one-third from service charges). In the second place, through its control of Parliament it can pass legislation binding on lower bodies.

In forcing compliance upon local authorities governments have relied on a variety of measures, all of them still available but which have changed in emphasis from fiscal instruments to direct intervention and then to indirect legislation over the years. The first concern in the early 1980s was to reduce public expenditure in general, and social expenditure in particular. As local government was responsible for more expenditure in these areas than central government, a prime concern was to restrict its spending. This was done by 'capping' the revenue of recalcitrant councils. The central government published financial targets for each authority. Those which exceeded them found their central subsidies reduced. When they tried to raise local taxes to compensate, legislation was passed to prevent them doing so beyond levels set by the centre.

A less direct policy has had more success and was increasingly deployed in the 1990s by both Conservative and Labour governments. It consists in reducing the area of operation of local government by two means, both backed by legislation.

First, for functions which remain with local government, such as the environment and social work, 'internal markets' are to be created. The council is to be in the position of a purchaser of services and is obliged by law to put services out to tender and accept the cheapest contractor. However unwillingly, therefore, councils are to be forced to apply 'value for money' market-driven values, if necessary by the government taking them to court. This policy also reduces a council's labour force and its general importance in its locality, as well as its autonomy of action. The 'internal market' was also employed to reorganize central services such as the National Health Service, putting managers in charge instead of health professionals such as senior doctors.

A second policy, again backed by legislation, is to limit and transfer the functions of local governments. This has been done either by outright privatisation (bus services) or by transferring the service to the control of an authority nominated by central government (police, some health functions, redevelopment and planning powers in certain areas). In education, schools under the control of local authorities (as all state schools were prior to 1989) have been encouraged to 'opt out' and form independent trusts, negotiating directly with the Department for Education.

'Quangos' have always been a feature of administration in Britain. Lacking direct agents, British governments have relied on such bodies where local governments were unable to act. Often administrative powers have been granted to professional bodies so they can regulate their members' standards and conduct. The British Medical Association, not the Department of Health, tries and disciplines doctors, as do the corresponding associations of dentists, nurses, lawyers and a string of other professions. Marketing boards elected by farmers run purchasing policy for areas of agriculture. The National Society for the Prevention of Cruelty to Children polices child-care legislation.

Nominated boards have also run functions for government. The board of governors of the BBC has managed a major section of radio and television for seventy years and the health authorities have always been nominated. What has changed, however, is (1) that nominated boards have increased their numbers, responsibilities and budgets at the expense of local government, and (2) that their membership is no longer drawn from a broad, middle-class, all-party spectrum but is predominantly made up of government supporters, often businessmen.

A disquieting aspect of many of the new quangos is the absence of accountability to either taxpayer or customer. The various consumer 'charters' issued by government to guarantee standards of service cover only technical detail and in any case seem unenforceable and unenforced. On policy matters there is no knowing what goes on inside the new authorities, other than the scandals occasionally uncovered by investigative journalism. When these are revealed they are often covered up. A case in point was the £3 billion investment in unworkable computer systems by the National Health Service, where privileged contractors were exempted from public competition. Here, as in other cases, the government has every motive to protect its own nominees and use official secrecy to smother investigation. Corruption and clientelism do not seem to be widespread in the British *sottogoverno* yet, but there is some evidence to indicate that they are spreading.

The European Union

Apart from the House of Commons and local councils, the European Parliament is the only other body whose writ runs in Britain and which derives its authority from direct election. As with local government, the increase in the power and standing of the EU institutions in Britain has been resented by central governments which like to think of themselves as the only arbiters of the national interest. Conservative rhetoric of the last sixteen years has generally portrayed the European Union as a set of foreign institutions interfering unreasonably and arbitrarily with British freedom of action. At the same time, however, governments have acceded to the extension of Community powers, notably in the case of the European Single Act of 1986–1987 and the (truncated) Treaty of Maastricht forced through, despite internal splits in the Conservative Party, in 1993. The New Labour government also accepted the European Convention on Human Rights into English and Scottish law (1999).

Conservative ambivalence towards the European Union can be understood in terms of their attachment to the twin ideas of 'strong state, free market', which are not always in accord. There would be relatively little controversy about membership among Conservatives if the free-market element came without political strings. The extension of the free market internationally is seen as the corollary of its extension internally, and British governments have been consistent in this – Britain's is probably the least protected national market in the Union, and the governments of the early 1990s were among the foremost advocates of further GATT agreements on world free trade.

Her attachment to the extension of the free market explains the otherwise puzzling episode of Mrs Thatcher's support for the far-reaching Single European Act. The Act was seen purely in terms of expanding the free European market – somewhat oddly, in the light of the political institutions the Conservatives were building at home to consolidate and guarantee their own market reforms. The far-reaching political powers the European Commission acquired to enforce the single market took the government by surprise and to some extent accounted for the internal Conservative divisions over ratification of the later Treaty of Maastricht and their opposition to the Euro. Latterly both main parties have concurred on burying the European issue as Britain shifted its focus to the 'War on Terror' in support of the United States and in opposition to France and Germany.

One aspect of EU membership, however, whose influence is only now being realised is the European Court. Lacking a guaranteed written constitution, Britain lacks also a court with the formal power to strike down legislation as unconstitutional. Indeed, the doctrine of absolute parliamentary sovereignty explicitly denies British courts the right to do so. However, the European Court of Justice does operate with a constitution – the Treaty of Rome, the Single European Act, the Treaty of Maastricht – which binds member governments and in terms of which their legislation *can* be struck down.

British courts have recognised and applied rulings of the European Court which do this and hence can be said to have acquired powers of constitutional review by the back door. The European Court takes a broad view of the obligations implied by EU agreements, and defers to the European Convention on Human Rights, which Britain made part of its own law in 1998–1999. It may well thus end up imposing an effective charter of individual and social rights in Britain of a kind which has traditionally been resisted as a constraint on parliamentary and government action. Moreover, as the courts do not depend on government consent to impose these rulings, their acts represent an alternative channel of political action for groups wishing to challenge government policy, particularly under repressive anti-terrorist legislation which increasingly curtails individual liberties. British interest groups excluded from consultation in Britain have in fact often challenged government decisions at European level, and local governments may well join them in the future.

As is generally the case at the institutional level, Irish relations with the European Union follow the British. As internal political conflict is less acute, and there is a written constitution, there has been less need to appeal against government decisions, except in the social field. There the inability of government or courts to query Catholic social teaching has meant that pro-abortion groups in particular have had a welcome opportunity to bring in the European bodies. One example involved freedom of movement for women seeking an abortion outside the Republic. One political difficulty which prevented the government winning the referendum of 2001 on expansion of the Union was indeed its implications for such social questions.

On most other aspects of the EU Irish governments and parties happily accept the full implications of membership. A voice in the Commission and the Parliament gives this small peripheral country an importance it would not otherwise have. Economic subsidies, particularly for agriculture, are vital to the economy. The European connection gives Ireland a chance to break out from British dominance. Traditional neutrality is something of an issue, which came up in relation to the foreign aspects of EU expansion, but the inability of the EU to agree on foreign policy means that the likelihood of Ireland being called upon to act in military matters is remote.

The courts

The fact that English courts lack the power of constitutional review (the Scottish courts have sometimes asserted it) does not mean that they lack political power. Quite the contrary: they can wield substantial political power, mainly because politicians want them to. That is why legislation is so often written in a vague way, positively requiring judicial interpretation. Phrases like 'after due consideration . . .' (a minister may take a particular decision) or 'taking into account all reasonable circumstances . . .' invite the courts to interpret what is reasonable or relevant. English law, moreover, relies heavily on precedents from past judicial rulings and decisions, which are often weighty enough to modify interpretations of current legislation. One might well ask, 'Who needs formal judicial review in a situation like that?'

The political role of the courts has been enhanced by recent governments, which, rather than confront the trade unions (or, latterly, local government) directly, have preferred to pass restrictive legislation which the courts must then apply. Governments can be fairly confident that the judges, chosen from an elite group of lawyers and predominantly upper-class privileged males, will generally support their legislation in such cases. As with businessmen nominated to quangos, there may be individuals who are reformist or radical in outlook, but the majority can be relied upon to follow the preferred policy line.

During the 1980s this was in fact what the courts did. They were assiduous in punishing unions financially for overstepping the limits of government legislation and in imprisoning and fining those engaged in extended picketing. In disputes between central and local government they generally found in the former's favour. They upheld doctrines of official secrecy, whether in civil actions designed to prevent disclosure (the *Spycatcher* trials involving newspapers' right to report information already published abroad) or in criminal cases involving imprisonment of civil servants accused of 'leaking' information. (Juries sometimes refused to convict because of the draconian penalties involved.)

The increasing use of the courts to enforce disputed aspects of policy has thus proved very effective from the government's point of view. Passing structural legislation to enforce political and social change (such as competitive tendering in local government) is an effective strategy because it 'objectifies' such change, taking it out of day-to-day politics; makes direct opposition illegal; leaves the messy business of detailed enforcement to others; and reduces direct government responsibility for the area concerned once the legislation is in force. This is in line with other policies discussed above, such as 'hiving off' ministerial responsibilities to autonomous agencies.

In general, therefore, it can be said that the courts are effective agencies of government policy rather than autonomous actors in the political process. Given the privileged background of judges, they are likely to act as a brake on social or economic legislation passed by any non-Conservative government, as they have in the past with regard to trade union immunities. Their acceptance of the overriding authority of the European Court of Justice and integration into law of the Convention on Human Rights are, however, pushing them into a wider assertion of individual rights, and into social stances which sometimes run contrary to official policy (e.g. annulling the deportation orders for immigrants or suspected terrorists to their home countries).

INSTITUTIONAL CHANGES AND REFORMS

The electoral system in Britain, with its single member constituencies and plurality winners, is the principal obstacle to any major constitutional reform. It has facilitated the creation of artificial parliamentary majorities and single-party governments based on a (large) minority of the electorate. Interacting with this electoral situation, policies have become more ideological and less aggregative. Ideological certainty gave the Conservative governments of the 1980s a basis on which to exclude large societal interests from government decision-making, to re-establish the market as the major mechanism of economic and social decisions, despite the objections of disadvantaged groups, and to assert the overriding authority of the central state over other political institutions. These tendencies have been carried on by New Labour since 1997.

Major institutional changes were accompanied by measures which have had profound socio-economic effects: (1) massive selling off of public enterprises and property to private individuals and firms; and (2), connected with this, but also due to taxation changes and cuts in state benefit, a large increase in the wealth of the top

10–20 per cent of the population and a reduction in the standard of living of the lowest 25 per cent.

Such changes have been as fundamental as those which created the modern welfare state and the mixed economy under the Labour government of 1945–1951. Like them the Conservative governments of the 1980s and 1990s relied on the traditional institutions of government to put changes into effect: ministries, with a somewhat adversarial relationship among themselves, co-ordinated by a single-party cabinet using the doctrines of parliamentary sovereignty and the electoral mandate to enforce its own programme. Again this is a set-up which has been largely accepted by New Labour.

The absence of institutional innovation at the centre, particularly the lack of co-ordinating mechanisms other than the cabinet, may be seen as retrogressive in political terms. Reasserting traditional cabinet supremacy under the Prime Minister means that the cabinet will continue to be overloaded, and that his or her authoritative intervention will be focused now on one ministry, now on another, while the remainders take largely autonomous decisions in their own fields. This bodes ill for effectively tackling social exclusion and the improvement of public services, central planks of the Labour mandate conferred in the last three elections.

New Labour's accession to power in 1997 was expected to be a turning point in British political history, ushering in an era of political as well as social reforms. While some have been initiated, they went neither so far nor so fast as many wished. Moreover, the Blair government's style – autocratic, hierarchical and centralised – went against the spirit of many of the changes they themselves were making.

Thus devolution in Northern Ireland, Scotland and Wales broke with many of the centralised traditions of British government. However, the Prime Minister tried to keep control of the executives in his own hands by using local Labour predominance to put in his own nominees. Regional autonomy and powers were limited, while at the same time the government tried to subordinate local government in England even further.

So far as Scotland and Wales were concerned central manipulation has not succeeded. The introduction of an element of proportional representation into their electoral systems meant that no party had a legislative majority and coalitions with the Liberal Democrats became necessary. These pursued an independent policy line, showing how an all-British coalition might work if it ever came to power. Now the SNP Executive in Scotland seems bound to take an independent policy line.

The Labour government centrally, resting on massive parliamentary majorities, can afford to ignore its remote peripheries and concentrate on getting English local government to do what it wants. It is likely, however, that a failure to improve public services sufficiently, and alienation of health and education professionals by its attempts to do so, will reduce the government majority in the future. This might make it necessary to seek Liberal Democrat support for a coalition.

A Labour coalition government with the Liberal Democrats would inevitably lead to electoral reform as that is the key change that would consolidate the latter's political position. Any system of proportional representation would render the parties more equal and would favour a permanent coalition, with the Liberal Democrats in the decisive centrist position. This would represent such a definitive break with current political processes that the nature of all the central institutions would change. Parliament would open up, the cabinet would no longer attempt to be monolithic, official secrecy would break down, while the adversarial relationship between ministries would be subsumed into wider political bargaining between coalition partners.

How this might all develop can be shown from the case of Ireland. Apart from its electoral system and written constitution, Ireland has almost exactly the same institutions as Britain – unsurprisingly, as they were, after all, inherited from the United Kingdom. In the Irish case, parliamentary sovereignty and cabinet government have worked to sustain one-party rule, contrary to the influence exerted by the single transferable vote system at electoral level. The result was that Fianna Fáil was able to form single-party governments over most of the period from 1932 to 1982. However, the electoral system prevented it from consolidating its position as an absolute majority party. It was often dependent on outside support in parliament and so forced into policy compromises. This tendency has intensified in the last twenty years with coalition governments. Political compromise has also been promoted by other factors: (1) the very slight policy differences between the two leading parties; (2) the powerful position of the Catholic Church, which has always had a veto over any disputed aspects of social policy; (3) extreme resource constraints, due to the peripheral nature of the country in Europe; and (4) the need, supported by the mass of the population and almost all parties, to keep out of the conflict in Northern Ireland.

The economic boom of the 1970s facilitated the expansion of social services. With its collapse, controversy in the 1980s centred on the question of whether such expansion could be maintained, along with challenges to the hitherto dominant Catholic morality (e.g. on the general position of women and on birth control). Party disputes were muted, however, as the electoral system facilitated the emergence of several parties and consequent coalition governments. Decisions about social services thus involved the (moderate) Labour Party with one or other of the two traditional parties. Compromise and coalition bargaining rather than confrontation became the norm, aided by the economic recovery of the 1990s. The traditional institutions of government, centring on cabinet co-ordination of the ministries, were able to cope because of the small size of the country and the relatively modest expansion of services. Within the limits of the practicable, the institutions of British government appear to have served the republic well. The sole innovation, the electoral system, has helped to soften the more confrontational aspects of British government in a useful way.

In Britain coalition would substitute a more open and possibly more consensual form of government for the current 'elective dictatorship'. Our comparisons between the British and Irish situations suggest that electoral reform is the *sine qua non* for all political and possibly much social change. With Scottish and Welsh devolution it has come already to Britain, and may spread to the Westminster system sooner than we might think.

BIBLIOGRAPHY

A useful website on British politics is www.pearsonedt/budge.

Elections

Budge, I., D. McKay, K. Newton and J. Bartle (2007) *The New British Politics*, 4th edn, London: Pearson.

Chubb, B. (1963) 'Going About Persecuting Civil Servants: The role of the Irish parliamentary representative', *Political Studies* XI: 272–86.

Miller, W. (1981) *The End of British Politics?*, Oxford: Clarendon Press.

O'Leary, C. (1979) *Irish Elections, 1918–77. Parties, voters and proportional representation*, Dublin: Gill & Macmillan.

Sinnott, R. (1993) *Irish Voters Decide. Voting behaviour in elections and referendums in Ireland, 1918–92*, Manchester: Manchester University Press.

Parties

Budge, I., H.-D. Klingemann, A. Volkens, J. Bara and E. Tanenbaum (2001) *Mapping Policy Preferences: Estimates for parties, electors and governments, 1945–1998*, Oxford: Oxford University Press.

Gamble, A. (1988) *The Free Economy and the Strong State. The politics of Thatcherism*, London: Macmillan.

Klingemann, H.-D., A. Volkens, J. Bara and I. Budge (2006) *Mapping Policy Preferences II 1990–2003*, Oxford: Oxford University Press.

Mair, P. (1987) *The Changing Irish Party System. Organisation, ideology and electoral competition*, London: Pinter.

Parliament

Bagehot, W. (1867) *The English Constitution*, Oxford: Oxford University Press.

Kavanagh, D. (1981) 'The Politics of Manifestoes', *Parliamentary Affairs* 34 (1): 7–27.

Government

Artis, M. J. (ed.) (1989) *Prest and Coppock's UK Economy*, London: Weidenfeld & Nicolson.

Hofferbert, R. I. and I. Budge (1992) 'The Party Mandate and the Westminster Model: Election programmes and government spending in Britain 1948–1985', *British Journal of Political Science* 22: 151–82.

Intergovernmental relations

Griffith, J. A. G. (1981) *The Politics of the English Judiciary*, London: Fontana.

Rhodes, R. A. W. (1988) *Beyond Westminster and Whitehall*, London: Unwin Hyman.

Stoker, G. (1991) *The Politics of Local Government*, 2nd edn, London: Macmillan.

CHAPTER 3

Germany

The Grand Coalition State

Manfred G. Schmidt

Germany experienced more radical regime changes in the nineteenth and twentieth centuries than most other nations. In little more than 130 years the country has been governed by a constitutional monarchy (1871–1918), an unstable democracy during the period of the Weimar Republic (1919–33), National Socialist totalitarianism (1933–45), military occupation (1945–9), two separate German states in the period from 1949 to 1990, a liberal democratic one in western Germany and a communist one in the eastern part of the country, and since unification of West and East Germany in 1990 a unified democratic state.

Most observers in the early post-World War II period were pessimistic about the future of Germany's democracy. Too heavy seemed to be the political and economic load the country had to shoulder through the National Socialist past, military defeat, wartime destruction, occupation and the influx of 12 million refugees and people expelled from the eastern territories of the German Empire during the war and in the post-war period. Yet Germany's post-1949 transition to democracy, as studies of the political culture of the country have demonstrated, turned out to be a 'success story'. The reasons for this success were manifold. The explanatory factors that deserve first mention are the total discrediting of alternatives of a National Socialist or Communist nature. Of central importance was also the support for democracy on the part of the Western occupation powers and on the part of most West German political elites at the local and the state level. The factors that were conducive to democratic consolidation in West Germany also include the restoration of the economy and its high growth rate in the 1950s and 1960s. No less important were the reconstruction and expansion of a welfare state, which distributed and redistributed economic resources on a massive scale to the less wealthy and socially weak groups of West German society. The success of Germany's democratic transition manifested itself not only in high levels of political stability and governability, efficient alternation of government and insignificance of anti-system parties, but also in the preference for the rapid accession of the German Democratic Republic to the Federal Republic in 1990.

ELECTIONS

Political parties and voters

The role of the strongest party in the 2005 election to the lower house of the Federal Republic (the Bundestag) was taken by the Christian Democratic Union (CDU) and its Bavarian sister organisation, the Christian Social Union (CSU). This is consistent with a long series of elections: in most of the national elections the strongest party had been the CDU and the CSU, with an average share of the vote of 43.2 per cent in the 1949–2005 period. However, in the 2005 election to the lower house the CDU's share of the vote dropped to 35.2 per cent and thus to a level slightly above the SPD (34.2 per cent), the second largest party in 13 out of 16 national elections and the strongest party in three elections. Politically the CDU and CSU are centre-right people's parties of a religious, inter-confessional, inter-class and pragmatic conservative reformist complexion. Also of the people's party type but with a major stronghold among the unionised sections of blue-collar and white-collar workers and among weakly religiously affiliated voters is the SPD. In elections to the lower house the SPD gained an average share of 37.4 per cent of the vote in the period from 1949 to 2005. Less than 10 per cent of the vote was mobilised by the Liberals, the Free Democratic Party (8.8 per cent), while the Green Party, or Bündnis '90/Die Grünen (the official name since 1993), which made its entry on to the parliamentary scene in the late 1970s in state parliaments and in 1983 in the lower house, won between 1.5 and 8.6 per cent of the vote.

Smaller parties have also competed for votes. But their share has been low or insignificant with the exception of the early 1950s and the post-1990 period. In the early 1950s the German Communist Party, the Unified Germany Federation/Bloc of the Expelled and Dispossessed (GB-BHE) and regional parties, such as the Bavarian Party, mobilised 4–6 per cent of the vote. Furthermore, since the lower house election in 1990 the Party of Democratic Socialism (PDS), the successor organisation to the Socialist Unity Party (SED) of the former German Democratic Republic, and nowadays the Left, won between 2 and 8 per cent of the vote (see Table 3.1). In contrast to France or Italy, right-wing parties have been largely unsuccessful in the Federal Republic of Germany. And in contrast to the English-speaking family of nations, secular conservative parties have been absent from the post-1949 party system in Germany.

Judging by the distribution of voters by political-ideological families, the natural centre of gravity of politics in pre-1990 West Germany fell in the area between a

Table 3.1 Elections to the German lower house, 1949–2005

Year	Turnout	Communist KPD/PDS/Left	Green Gr/B90	Socialist SPD	Liberal FDP	Christian CDU-CSU	Right	Others
1949	79	6	–	29	12	31	2	20
1953	86	2	–	29	10	45	1	13
1957	88	–	–	32	8	50	1	9
1961	88	–	–	36	13	45	1	5
1965	87	–	–	39	10	48	2	2
1969	87	–	–	43	6	46	4	1
1972	91	0	–	46	8	45	1	0
1976	91	0	–	43	8	49	0	0
1980	89	0	2	43	11	45	0	0
1983	89	0	6	38	7	49	0	0
1987	84	0	8	37	9	44	1	1
1990	78	2	5	34	11	44	2	2
1994	79	4	7	36	7	41	2	2
1998	82	5	7	41	6	35	2	4
2002	79	4	9	39	7	39	–	2
2005	78	9	8	34	10	35	1	3

Note: Party vote is measured as a percentage of the total second vote.

Communist and post-communist: KPD: 1949 and 1953 (banned in 1956 by a ruling of the Federal Constitutional Court); DKP: German Communist Party, 1972–87; MLPD: Marxist-Leninist Party in Germany, 1987; PDS: Party of Democratic Socialism, 1990–2002; PDS/Left party 2005.

Greens: Greens (Die Grünen and since 1993 Bündnis 90/Die Grünen).

Socialists: SPD: German Social Democratic Party (Sozialdemokratische Partei Deutschlands).

Liberals: FDP: Liberal Democratic Party (Freie Demokratische Partei).

Christians: CDU–CSU: Christian Democratic Union/Christian Social Union (Christlich Demokratische Union/Christlich Soziale Union).

Right: DR: German Imperial Party (Deutsche Reichspartei), major party of the right, 1949–61; NPD: National Democratic Party (Nationaldemokratische Partei), 1965–87; The Republicans (Die Republikaner), 1990–2005.

Others: GB/BHE: Unified Germany Federation/Bloc of the Expelled and Dispossessed; DA: Democratic Coalition; FVP: Liberal Popular Party.

centrist position and centre-right. German unification has altered this distribution insofar as the East German party system has been marked by a weaker role of the CDU/CSU and the SPD than in West Germany, a strong position of the PDS, or the Left, and the weakness of the Liberals and the Green Party.

Compared with the Weimar Republic period, the ideological distance between the political tendencies in the western part of the country has been significantly less, and the willingness and capability of the established parties to co-operate with their opponents significantly greater. The accession of the former German Democratic Republic and the rise of the PDS, or the Left, however, changed the pattern insofar as this party adopts a leftist-socialist position in the party system. From this results an increase in political polarisation in post-unification Germany, albeit at a level well below that of the Weimar Republic and below that of the 'polarised pluralism' Italian style. The degree of party concentration also indicates a further contrast between the First and the Second German Republics. The party system of the Weimar Republic was notorious for its very high level of fragmentation. In contrast to this, the degree of party concentration in West Germany, and to a somewhat lesser extent in unified Germany, has been high, and higher than in most other member countries of the European Union (EU). Furthermore, the ideological spectrum of the parties represented in the national parliament in most of the period from 1949 to 2005 has been narrower than in the Weimar Republic and in most other democracies based on proportional representation. This is largely due to the absence of an agrarian party, a secular conservative party of the Anglo-American conservative type and a larger extreme right-wing party, such as Hitler's German National Socialist Workers' Party.

What accounts for the distribution of power between the political parties and tendencies in the Federal Republic? Why are the two major political camps divided between Christian Democrats and their coalition partners, mostly the Liberals, on the one hand, and Social Democrats and their allies on the other – such as the Greens in 1998–2005 or in 1969–82 the Liberals, and in post-1990 Germany the PDS in some of the East German states? To a significant extent, the answers to these questions must be based on the structure of cleavages and the impact of issues and candidates on the voters' choice.

The relative strength of centre and centre-right tendencies in Germany, above all in the pre-unification period, mirrored a distinct distribution of preferences. Measured by the distribution of voter preferences on the left–right scale, West German voters have been less inclined to adopt centre-left or leftist positions than voters in many other advanced democracies, such as France, Italy and Spain. But in contrast to nations with a strong centre-right or right-wing tendency, such as Ireland, the Federal Republic of the pre-1990 period was also representative of a position in the middle group.

The advantage of the centre and centre-right tendencies over the Social Democratic tendency in the pre-unification period mirrored to a considerable extent the impact of the cleavage structure on electoral behaviour. The major cleavages in the Federal Republic of Germany are religion and class. Particularly important to an understanding of politics in the pre-1990 Federal Republic is the relative strength of the religious cleavage, while the class-based division is somewhat weaker. Religion and class still play an important role in structuring voting behaviour in post-unification Germany, but less so in eastern Germany. Major social and economic trends, such as secularisation, the decline of the industrial sector and the rise of a service sector economy, have significantly reduced the overall importance of the religious cleavage and the class cleavage. German unification amplified this process, with the weakness of a traditional class cleavage in East Germany and a very large proportion of East German voters without affiliation to one of the churches as the major factors.

Other things being equal, the distribution of preferences on the left–right scale and the cleavage structure were conducive to a somewhat weaker long-term position of leftist parties in general, and of the SPD in particular. The position of the SPD has also suffered from the relative decline in the size of the Social Democratic core constituency in the industrial sector of the economy. Moreover, since the late 1970s the position of the SPD has been challenged by the rise of the Green Party, since the 1990s in East Germany by the post-Communist Party, and since 2005 by an alliance between the PDS and a West German-based leftist opposition party, nowadays the Left. Compensation for the loss of votes due to changes in cleavages and structural trends has been difficult for the SPD to achieve, but not impossible, as the national election in 1998 demonstrates. Three trends contribute to a compensation for these losses in this election: first, higher competence scores of the SPD in relevant issue areas, such as social justice; second, popular candidates, at that time above all Gerhard Schröder; and, third, the relative weakness of the major opponent, the CDU/CSU, prior to the national election of 1998.

Socio-structural trends have posed challenges not only to the SPD, but also to the Christian Democratic parties. The CDU/CSU has suffered losses in voter support due to secularisation in general and a relative decline in the proportion of voters with a strong religious affiliation in particular. These trends have been exacerbated by the post-1990 trends in East Germany. Weak religious affiliation of the East German electorate, the weakness of entrepreneurial culture and a small entrepreneurial strata, as well as the legacies of the former Socialist state, all pose unfavourable circumstances for Christian Democratic parties, and also for the Liberals, in the new German states. Until the mid-1990s, the Christian Democratic parties managed to compensate for many of their losses in other segments of the electoral market, mainly thanks to a comparative advantage in the types of issue salient in elections and issue competence and also due to the weakness of the Social Democratic opposition. But the compensation for the loss of votes itself proved to be too fragile. A wide variety of reasons were responsible for this. The Degeneration of a party in power for a lengthy period has played a role, and voters' frustration due to welfare state retrenchment and a protest against ambitious pro-European Union policy, such as the unpopular policy on introducing the Euro, the common European currency, were also important. Furthermore, regarding the popularity of the major candidates, Gerhard Schröder, the SPD candidate in the elections in 1998, 2002 and 2005, outperformed the chancellor candidates of the Christian Democratic Party, Helmut Kohl, Edmund Stoiber and Angela Merkel.

While socio-structural trends and the patterns of competition on the electoral market were more favourable to the non-socialist tendencies over a long period until the late 1980s, the overall balance of forces is different in the post-unification period. This is due to long-term trends such as secularisation and de-industrialisation, but it also mirrors unification effects and short- or medium-term change in issue competency and candidates. In contrast to the pre-1990 period, the balance between the major political tendencies in unified Germany as mirrored by shares of the vote is skewed in favour of left of centre parties. For example, the total share of the vote for major non-leftist parties, the CDU/CSU and the FDP, exceeded the 50 per cent mark until the national election in 1990. However, after 1990 that share declined, dropped to an all-time low of 41.4 per cent in 1998 and rose to 45.0 per cent in 2005. In a similar vein, the ratio between the vote for the major non-leftist parties and the vote for the major leftist parties (that is, the SPD and the Greens) dropped from scores larger than 1.0 before unification to 1.0 in 1994 and less than 1.0 since 1998. Whether this pattern will remain stable is difficult to forecast, because voters are more volatile than before. Hence, short- or medium-term determinants such as candidates, issues and issue competency play a more important role in shaping voting behaviour. From this results a higher level of uncertainty for the competing political parties as well as for the study of electoral behaviour.

Electoral system

The relatively high level of party concentration in the Federal Republic of Germany is at least partly attributable to cleavage structures and voters' preferences, but it also mirrors the impact of a distinctive electoral system. Germany's formula for elections to the national parliament is proportional representation on the basis of universal suffrage for citizens of German nationality aged eighteen or over. The special feature of the electoral system of a lower house is that voters have two votes, the first for a constituency candidate and the second for the party lists. One half of the 598 basic seats in the sixteenth legislative period of the lower house (since 2005) are allocated through relative majority votes in constituencies, and the other half through party lists in each of the sixteen states (*Länder*) of the Federal Republic. The decisive vote is the second vote, not the first. The reason is that the distribution of the second vote largely determines how many parliamentary seats a party will receive, while the first vote determines which candidates get those seats. The second vote prescribes proportional representation, whereas the first vote adds a personalised component to the electoral formula. The distribution of the second vote and the transformation of votes into seats according to the Hare–Niemeyer formula of quota and largest remainders generate a high level of vote–seats proportionality in the outcome, much higher than, for example, the degree of proportionality in most other democracies.

There are, however, two restrictions on proportionality. The first restriction concerns the 5 per cent clause. According to the 5 per cent clause of the lower house Elections Act, only parties with at least 5 per cent of the second votes or, alternatively, three constituency seats through relative majority in the first votes win rights to a proportional share of seats; that is, they can use their second vote. (But with one or two seats through relative majority in the first vote and less than 5 per cent in the second vote, as with the PDS in the national election in 2002, a party keeps these seats.) 'Excess seats' are the second restriction on pure proportionality. 'Excess seats' result from the possibility of a party winning more constituency seats than its proportional share of second votes would indicate. In that case the party retains its excess seats, and parliament is enlarged accordingly, as for example in the sixteenth legislative period of the lower house (since 2005), when the number of seats rose from 598 to 614.

Most of the political debates and most studies of electoral behaviour have focused on elections to the lower house (Bundestag). That perspective necessarily underestimates the importance of federalism and the impact of elections to state parliaments in each of the sixteen states on the composition of the state govern-ments and of the influential upper house (Bundesrat), which plays a major role in national policy-making. The electoral systems in the constituent states of the Federal Republic differ from the rules of the game in lower-house elections in nuance and detail, but all of them are members of the family of proportional representation. However, party preferences and election outcomes differ widely between national elections and elections to the state parliaments. The CDU–CSU vote, for example, varied in the elections to state parliaments in 1990–2006 from a minimum of 18.7 per cent in Brandenburg (1994) to a maximum of 60.7 per cent in Bavaria (2003), while the SPD vote varied from an all time low of 9.8 per cent in Saxony (2004) to 54.4 per cent in Saarland (1990). Hardly less dramatic have been the differences in the vote for the Liberals, which varied from 1.1 per cent (Saxony 1999) to 13.5 per cent (in Saxony-Anhalt in 1990).

Election outcomes in the German states have major effects on politics and policy at the national level because they affect the distribution of the votes in the upper house and hence are important for federal legislation. Consider, for example, the situation prior to the national election in 2005. At the national level the SPD–Green coalition held the reins of power. But none of a total of sixteen states were governed by a red–green coalition at that time and three others an SPD-dominated government, carrying altogether only 11 out of the 69 seats in the upper house. Nine state governments with a total of 43 upper house votes out of a total of 69 were controlled by the CDU or CSU, the opposition party in national parliament. And four states were at that time governed by grand coalitions between the CDU and SPD.

The party composition in the states has a major impact on the partisan composition of the upper house, the Federal Council, composed of deputies of the state government. Owing to the powerful role of the upper house in legislation – most major legislation in domestic affairs requires the explicit consent of the majority in the upper house – this constellation of political forces introduces powerful consociational elements to the architecture of government in Germany and often requires Grand Coalitions between the incumbent parties and the major opposition party. From this results the choice between blocking the decision-making process in the upper house or governing Germany by a Grand Coalition of the federal government and the state governments, as well as a more or less hidden Grand Coalition between the incumbent parties in federal government and the major opposition party.

PARTIES AND PARTY STRATEGIES

The German party system has undergone major changes both in respect of the total number of effective parties and the ideological distance between the various political tendencies. A large number of parties, a high level of fragmentation in the party system and a complex cleavage structure (class, religion, centre–periphery, anti-communism versus communism, and native population versus refugees and exiles) characterised the party system in the first and second legislative periods (1949–57). However, the total number and the relative importance of smaller parties declined rapidly, largely due to rapid social change, high economic growth rates, effective social and economic integration of weaker social groups through expanding job opportunities and welfare provision, and political mobilisation on the part of the CDU–CSU and the SPD. What had been a party system with a degree of fragmentation not too dissimilar from that of the Weimar Republic was transformed into a three-party system in the 1960s and 1970s. That party system was composed of a centre-right people's party of Christian Democratic complexion, a centre-left

SPD and a smaller liberal party. In this period, the Liberals were positioned as kingmaker.

Measured by indicators of political ideological heterogeneity, the German party system of the 1960s and 1970s embodied almost perfectly the case of moderate pluralism rather than one of polarised pluralism Italian style, to borrow from Giovanni Sartori's typology of party systems. Notwithstanding its relatively high level of concentration, Germany's party system proved more open to new parties than most observers were expecting, as was demonstrated by the rise of the Green Party in the 1980s and the rise of the PDS mainly in eastern Germany after 1990. Furthermore, in contrast to one-party dominant 'uncommon democracies', such as Japan under the rule of the Liberal Party, Germany's post-war democracy has been marked by major changes in the partisan complexion of national government. These include the replacement of the CDU–CSU-led government by a Grand Coalition of CDU–CSU and SPD in 1966, the change in 1969 from the Grand Coalition to a SPD–FDP coalition, the substitution of a new CDU–CSU–FDP coalition for the social–liberal coalition in 1982, the formation of a red–green coalition in 1998, and the most recent change in power in 1998, which resulted in the formation of the second Grand Coalition of the Christian Democratic parties and the Social Democratic Party in 2005.

Policy positions

Policy positions differ from one party to the other. On most left–right scales, for example on the Huber–Inglehart left–right scale of the mid-1990s, the PDS is located at the left extreme pole and the Republicans are the rightist party *par excellence*. In contrast to this, the CDU/CSU occupies a centre-right position, the SPD finds itself left of centre and to the right of the Greens, while the FDP is located in a centrist positions (see Table 3.2). This pattern is broadly consistent with the overall policy positions of the parties in Benoit and Laver (2007), although the positions vary from one policy area to the other. Policy positions of the parties vary for a wide variety of reasons. These include different social constituencies. The Christian Democratic parties, for example, are the main representatives of the property owners, farmers, the old middle class, business and religiously affiliated voters, but they also comprise a sizeable proportion of wage-earners, old-age pensioners, voters from lower-income classes and religiously non-affiliated citizens. Insofar as the Christian Democratic parties are organisations of an inter-confessional, inter-class and prag-matic conservative reformist, if not populist, character they may even be regarded as an approximation to the 'catch-all party'.

The policy positions of the CDU–CSU mirror the complex structure of its social constituency. The CDU has been described as 'a new attempt to unite practising Catholics and Protestants in a modern centrist party, mainly in reaction to their experience of Nazism'. Moreover the policy profile of the CDU–CSU is marked by 'adherence to Christian values, democratic constitutionalism, a liberal social order, the social market economy, European unity and the reunification of Germany' (Klingemann 1987: 296). Others have emphasised the combination of pro-market

Table 3.2 Left–right placement of parties in Germany

Left	Green	Socialist		Liberal	Christian
L	Grü	SPD		FDP	CDU/CSU
Left	Centre-left		Centre	Centre-right	Right

Party names:
L: Left Party (Linkspartei).
Grü: Greens (Bündnis 90/Die Grünen).
SPD: German Social Democratic Party (Sozialdemokratische Partei Deutschlands).
FDP: Liberal Democratic Party (Freie Demokratische Partei).
CDU/CSU: Christian Democratic Union/Christian Social Union (Christlich Demokratische Union/ Christlich Soziale Union).

Source: As for Table 2.4.

and pro-welfare state positions which the CDU has advocated, and have pointed out that a 'social market' approach, or 'social capitalism', is the trademark of Christian Democratic public policy. In organisational terms, the CDU of the 1950s and 1960s was in many respects mainly a *Kanzlerwahlverein*, a loose association geared to promoting the Chancellor. In the 1970s, it was transformed to a highly organised modern people's party.

A heterogeneous social constituency, pragmatism and religious affiliation have also marked the CSU, the Bavarian sister organisation of the Christian Democratic Party. But in contrast to the CDU the CSU has placed more emphasis on issues of regional concern, populism, a significantly higher level of state intervention and a conservative stance on civil rights issues.

The SPD is the oldest of the political parties in modern Germany and the one with the longest democratic tradition. Originally the SPD was mainly a party of organised labour, deeply rooted in the milieu of the German working class. In the post-1949 period the SPD has been gradually transformed from a class-based mass integration party into an ideologically moderate centre-left party. The SPD has mobilised voters mainly from workers and social-income earners, private-sector employees and public servants, blue-collar and white-collar workers and from materialists and post-materialists. The policy preferences of the SPD emphasise social justice, social equality, high levels of welfare state provision and an influential role of the state in regulating the society and the economy.

The Free Democratic Party, the liberal party, is asymmetrically located between the CDU–CSU and the SPD. The liberal party, it has been argued, is for 'people who found the CDU too close to the Churches and the SPD too close to the trade unions'. The liberals' economic and political ideology mirrors the interests of a social constituency pervaded by a middle-class entrepreneurial ideology and the predominance of secular views. The primary political goals of the liberal party, it has been argued, are to be found in the preservation of individual freedom, a market-oriented economic policy and the rejection of socialist planning and of clericalism. However, that picture needs to be complemented by differences between the FDP and the bigger parties. In contrast to both the CDU and the SPD, the Free Democratic Party is not linked with the interests of the social-income earners, such as old-age pensioners and recipients of social assistance, and not affiliated to the trade unions. As a strong advocate of private enterprise the FDP is closer to the CDU–CSU on economic issues. However, on most civil rights issues the SPD or the Green Party rather than the conservative CDU–CSU is the more natural coalition partner for the FDP.

The Green Party, or Bündnis '90/Die Grünen, is an offspring of the change in values from giving priority to materialist concerns to post-materialism. Ecological and gender issues as well as pacifism have been among the major concerns of the Green Party, although the Greens do not have a monopoly in these issue areas. A particularly large proportion of the voters and party members of the Green Party are to be found among the better-educated generations, above all among people working in personal social services. Regarding policy positions, the Greens advocate ecologically oriented left-wing post-materialist policies, with a major emphasis on environmental protection, the phasing out of nuclear energy, a liberal migration policy, citizen participation, as well as a high degree of decentralisation and autonomy in the structure of the polity. Organisationally, the Green Party is a loose coalition of decentralised groups and factional tendencies, inclusive of the proponents of an uncompromising ecologist stance in policy, the so-called fundamentalists, on the one hand, and the so-called realists, i.e. advocates of a more reformist and moderate approach to policy-making and coalition building with centre-left or liberal parties, on the other. The merger between the West German Greens and the East German Greens in 1993 strengthened the more moderate tendencies within the Green Party. And so, too, did the participation of the Greens in federal government in the period between 1998 and 2005.

In contrast to other political parties in Germany, the PDS – or the Left/PDS, the new label adopted in summer 2005, or the Left, the label taken up in 2007 – is a post-communist leftist party. Historically, the PDS is the successor organisation to the Socialist Unity Party, the communist state party of the German Democratic Republic. The new label the Left mirrors the formation of an alliance between the PDS and a West German-based leftist opposition party against market-oriented reforms. According to its party programme, the Left is a radical socialist party. However, more detailed analysis reveals heterogeneous profiles. First of all, the Left is much stronger in East Germany than in West Germany. Second, the Left is composed of different factions – from protest movements to radical democratic socialists and orthodox communists of the Stalinist and Leninist tradition. Its rank and file also includes supporters of the theory and practice of socialism in the style of the former German Democratic Republic, especially the East German intelligentsia and party faithful, but it also counts former members of the Social Democratic Party as followers. And, as a protest party, the Left benefits from economic problems and disappointed expectations in the process of unification. The vote for the Left can therefore at least partly be regarded as an indicator of disappointment with the impact of unification. The Left has been regarded also as a potential, if not real, anti-system party. However, the profile of the Left is more diverse. It oscillates between anti-system radicalism, socialist nostalgia, opposition against capitalism and 'pro-capitalist policy', on the one hand, and, on the other, relatively moderate policy-making in government, such as in the state of Berlin, where the leftist party presides together with the SPD over a policy of massive fiscal retrenchment.

Policy distances and coalition strategies of the parties

According to an influential view, the competitiveness in Germany's party system in the 1950s and 1960s had declined dramatically. This view has been most forcefully advanced in Otto Kirchheimer's theory of the 'waning of opposition' and the rise of 'catch-all parties' (Kirchheimer 1966a, 1966b). According to Kirchheimer, Germany was a prime example of both processes. Studies of party manifestoes have at least partly supported Kirchheimer's view by pointing to the change from conflict orientation to consensus: 'In a comparative perspective . . . post-war German parties seem the most consensual of all' (Klingemann 1987: 321). The range between the extreme poles in the party system of the Federal Republic in the 1960s and 1970s was indeed smaller than in most other constitutional democracies and much smaller than during the period of the Weimar Republic.

However, the 'waning of opposition' view overestimates the decline and underestimates the possibility of re-polarisation, as in the post-1969 period. Moreover the 'waning of opposition' view veils the continuity of significant policy differences between the German political parties. On economic issues the major policy difference has long been an inter-bloc conflict between the centre-left, the left and the Greens on the one hand and the centre-right parties and the Liberals on the other. Moreover, on most civil rights issues, such as abortion, and political rights issues, such as citizen participation and citizenship issues, and also on foreign policy issues, the major division has been that between the SPD and the Liberals, and to some extent also the Greens on the one hand and a more conservative stance by the Christian Democratic parties on the other.

The existing policy differences allow for widely divergent coalition governments in Germany. On economic policy and on other issues concerning the division of labour between the state and the private sector, the most natural coalition has long been a Christian Democratic–liberal alliance. On civil rights issues, on political rights and in many foreign policy areas the natural coalition partner for the Liberals has been the SPD rather than the CDU. The policy differences and commonalities prior to unification and in unified Germany also allow for the formation of a Grand Coalition between the CDU/CSU and the SPD in some of the states, such as in Bremen (from 1995 to 2007), Schleswig-Holstein (since 2005) and Saxony (since 2004), as well as in federal government (since 2005). Furthermore, the policy positions and the office-seeking strategies of the parties in the post-unification environment place the SPD in a particularly favourable position. The SPD's options include a Social Democratic–liberal coalition, such as in Rhineland-Palatinate (since 1991), a red–green coalition, such as in federal government between 1998 and 2005 as well as in several states, among them Northrhine-Westfalia (1995–2005), and coalitions between the SPD and the PDS or the Left, such as in Berlin since 2001.

In contrast to majoritarian models of democracies, coalitions have been the typical form of government in the Federal Republic of Germany. However, the coalition patterns in post-war Germany are also at variance with those of many other democratic states outside the world of majoritarian democracy. A wide range of variation has marked the coalition status of the federal governments in the Federal Republic. The dominant coalition type is a surplus majority government (if the CDU and the CSU are counted as separate parties, although they do not compete with each other). Minimum winning coalitions were in power over a somewhat shorter period (1969–72, 1976–82, 1987–91 and 1998–2002). Single-party governments (1960–1) and minority governments (November 1962, November–December 1965 and September 1982) were the exception rather than the rule. The coalition patterns in the states have been even more diverse. All-inclusive coalitions were prevalent in the immediate post-war period. When the Cold War began, all-party coalitions were replaced by coalitions, which excluded the Communist Party, and, later on, by surplus majority or minimum winning coalitions of different political composition. Although a clear trend towards centre-right–liberal coalitions or, alternatively, centre-left–liberal governments emerged in the 1950s, Grand Coalitions of the CDU and the SPD have been a familiar phenomenon at state level.

The rise of the Green Party in the late 1970s and 1980s also had a distinctive impact on coalition building. The outcome has been red–green coalitions, at first at the state level only, and between 1998 and 2005 also at the level of the federation. Since the early 1980s the environmentalists of the Green Party entered coalitions with the SPD in seven states: in Hesse (1984–7 and 1991–9), West Berlin (1989 to January 1991 and in 2001), Lower Saxony (1990–94), Bremen (1991–5 and since 2007), Brandenburg (1990–4), Schleswig-Holstein (1996–2005) and in Northrhine-Westfalia (1995–2005).

The formation of an SPD–FDP coalition in 1969 and the adoption of a conflict-oriented stance in opposition on the part of the CDU/CSU marked the end of the era of *rapprochement* between the Christian Democratic parties and the SPD. A higher level of political polarisation in the party system resulted also from controversies over issues of the new politics and new social movements in the 1970s and 1980s, such as the environmentalists, the anti-nuclear energy movement and the peace movement, and over issues regarding the East German transition to a market economy in the post-1990 period. In this period, political conflicts intensified to such a degree as to resemble the bitter disputes of the early 1950s between the Christian Democratic parties' emphasis on a pro-market economic policy, rearmament and the rapid integration of West Germany into the international and supranational organisations of the West and the SPD's emphasis on nationalist reunification, and a democratic socialist economic policy.

However, in most of this period the higher level of polarisation had to be reconciled with the requirements of co-operative politics inherent in the structure of the political institutions of Germany's Second Republic. This has been largely due to divided government, or divergent majorities in the lower and upper houses, such as from the early 1970s to 1982, when a social–liberal coalition in power at the level of the federal state faced an opposition party in control of the majority of the seats in the upper house. A similar pattern existed in the second half of the Kohl era from 1991 to 1998, when the CDU–CSU–FDP coalition lost the majority of the seats in the upper house, and from 1999, when the red–green coalition lost the majority in the upper house until 2005. The outcome consisted of a combination of confrontation and co-operation, and, hence, the coexistence of competition, partisan struggles and majority rule together with blocked decision-making or, conversely, consensus formation through compromises or unanimity in decision-making. From this results a unique pattern of confrontation and co-operation between government and opposition. Particularly in legislation subject to an affirmative vote of the upper house, the major opposition party gains a co-governing position in this game. A better understanding of that constellation and its Grand Coalition outcome requires a more detailed study of parliament, government and federalism. It is on these topics that attention will now be focused.

PARLIAMENT

Parties in parliament

In contrast to presidentialism American style and in contrast to French semi-presidentialism the Federal Republic has a parliamentary system of government. The lower house (Bundestag), upon the proposal of the Federal President, selects the head of the government, the Federal Chancellor. The Chancellor is dependent on the support of the majority of the Bundestag. He or she can be dismissed from office only by a vote of constructive no confidence, that is, by the election of a successor by the majority of the members of the lower house. This prevents negative majorities – that is, majorities for voting a Chancellor out of office but insufficient to vote in favour of a new head of the executive – and inhibits major changes in government within a legislative period. But that does not preclude the possibility of a major change in power, as the successful constructive vote of no confidence against Helmut Schmidt (SPD) and for Helmut Kohl (CDU) on 1 October 1982 showed.

In contrast to monarchical forms of parliamentary government, Germany's parliamentary democracy is republican in nature. Its executive is divided into the Chancellor, the head of government, and the Federal President, the head of state. The two are of unequal political weight: the distribution of power favours the Chancellor. The Chancellor holds a powerful position *vis-à-vis* both parliament and the President, while the President's role is mainly confined to the exercise of 'dignified' ceremonial functions. The exception is the President's role in periods of major political crisis, for example when a Chancellor does not obtain a stable majority of the votes in the upper house (Bundesrat) or when a motion of the Chancellor for a vote of confidence is not carried by the majority of the members of the lower house (Bundestag). In such a situation the President dissolves the parliament, as in 2005. The normal case, however, is marked by dominance of the Chancellor and a weak role for the President. It is largely for this reason that Germany's parliamentary government has been described as Chancellor-dominated parliamentary government or a 'Chancellor's democracy'.

As in most other parliamentary democracies, Germany's parliamentary system is based on a powerful role for the parties in the selection of the political leaders, in policy-making and in patronage. The parties are so powerful that Germany's Second Republic has been classified as a major example of a 'party state', that is, a state in which all major political decisions are shaped, if not determined, by political parties. Although the full applicability of the 'party state' view to Germany is debatable because an unusually large number of 'veto players' circumscribe the scope for action left to the parties, the selection of candidates for elections to the lower house, as well as the selection of the Chancellor, is almost exclusively controlled by the political parties. While half the total number of seats in the lower house is in theory available to non-partisan candidates, provided they gain a relative majority in the electoral districts, in practice only party candidates win parliamentary seats. With very few exceptions, deputies have been party members and have been subject to the respective parliamentary group's voting discipline.

Thanks to the high level of proportionality inherent in the electoral system, the distribution of parliamentary seats among the parties closely follows the distribution of votes. In all but three sessions of the lower house (1972–76, 1998–2002, and 2002–2005), the CDU–CSU, comprising the CDU deputies and the CSU representatives (who are separately organised in the CSU territorial group), has been the strongest parliamentary group. Social Democratic deputies have formed the second largest parliamentary group, followed by the Liberals, and, since the 1980s, the representatives of the Green Party and, in the sixteenth Bundestag, the deputies of the Left/PDS. The list of small parties which have held parliamentary seats includes the Communist Party, the right-wing Imperial German Party and the Bavarian Party in the first legislative period from 1949 to 1953, the Centre Party in the first and second sessions, the German Party until the third session, and after unification the PDS or the Left.

Standard indicators of governability mirror the high level of political stability that has been achieved in Germany's post-1949 democracy. An example is the length of time required to form a government, and the average life of the government can be taken as a further illustration. The mean score for the total number of days required to form a government after an election is 38, with a minimum of 24 in 1969 and 1983, and a maximum of 65 in 2005. Most of the selected cabinets have survived periods of considerable length. The mean survival period has been between three and four years and, thus, has been significantly higher than the survival period of cabinets in Italy, Belgium and the Netherlands, to mention just a few examples. In most cases the selected government remained in office throughout the period, but there have been exceptions to the rule, as in 1972, 1982 and 2005, when a vote of confidence and a vote of no confidence, respectively, made way for the dissolution of parliament before the full term.

The high survival periods of selected cabinets are at least partly attributable to the existence of internal pluralism in the political parties combined with tough discipline and party solidarity in voting in the lower house. While migration from one parliamentary group to another was a common phenomenon among the smaller parties in the 1950s, the migration rate in parliament declined rapidly, with two exceptions. Measured as the percentage of the total number of deputies migrating between parliamentary groups, the migration rate dropped from 22 per cent in 1949–53 to 16 per cent, 6 per cent and 0.4 per cent in the subsequent legislative periods, and increased, albeit moderately, after changes in party composition in 1969 and 1982, and in the first post-unification legislative period. The migration rate varies with the size of the political parties: the largest rate of defection from one parliamentary group to another occurred among the smaller parties, except for the Liberals, while the smallest overall migration rate marked the two major parties in the Federal Republic, the CDU/CSU and the SPD. The noteworthy exception is the 1969–92 period, when defection from the parliamentary group of the SPD resulted in the SPD losing its majority in the Bundestag.

Voting procedures in the lower chamber

Absolute-majority and two-thirds-majority rules dominate the voting procedures in the lower house (Bundestag). The selection of the Chancellor, the vote of confidence and the constructive vote of no confidence require the approval of the so-called 'Chancellor's majority', that is, the majority of the members of the lower house. Legislative changes in the constitution require two-thirds majorities in the lower and the upper houses. Furthermore, a two-thirds majority in each of the houses is also needed for selection of the judges of the Federal constitutional Court and for a parliamentary vote on the impeachment of the President for wilful violation of the Basic Law or any other federal law. Because each of the political parties in Germany regularly gains less than 50 per cent of the votes and seats, a two-thirds majority, in practice, requires the formation of an oversized coalition or an all-inclusive coalition as well as co-operation between the governing parties and the major opposition party. The two-thirds-majority rule thus strengthens the consensus democracy component and the Grand Coalition component in Germany's polity.

More detailed analysis of the legislative process demonstrates the applicability of this view also to legislative activity below the threshold of constitutional change. The upper house (Bundesrat) has a qualified veto in areas of non-mandatory legislation, although that veto can be overridden by majorities in the Bundestag of a size equivalent to the size of the veto majority. With respect to Bills, which are subject to an affirmative vote of the upper house, however, the upper house has full veto powers. This is particularly important because until the reform of federalism in 2006 up to 6 out of 10 Bills and, in practice, most legislation on major domestic issues, were subject to mandatory approval by the upper house. Thus the governance of the Federal Republic through legislation requires in most cases the formation of a Grand Coalition of the incumbent parties and the major opposition party, and a coalition of the federal government and the majority of the state governments. This is central to a fuller understanding of politics and policy in Germany.

Particularly important are these Grand Coalition requirements in a period with a divided government, i.e. a period in which the governing parties find themselves confronted with a numerical majority of states ruled by the opposition party in the upper house. As pointed out above, a divided government characterised most of the period of the SPD–FDP coalition in 1969–82, but it also shaped politics from May to October 1990, from early 1991 to 1998 in the period of the CDU–CSU–FDP coalition and from 1999 until 2005 in the period of the red–green coalition.

In a divided government the opposition party is *de facto* positioned as a co-governing party, as long as the state governments' deputies vote along partisan lines (which is often the practice on issues of major policy importance) and as long as the government and the opposition prefer a compromise to a blocked decision-making process.

Legislative performance

In a famous study Max Weber differentiated between two types of parliament. One is the 'working parliament' (Weber 1988: 350), which emphasizes mainly committee work, legislation and control of the executive; the other is a parliament in which attention is focused mainly on parliamentary debates. The German lower house comprises both types of parliament. But the dominant part is the working Parliament. For example, studies have revealed the *de facto* priority of committee work (which is mainly done behind closed doors in Germany) over public deliberation in parliament. In the first fifteen legislative periods of the lower house (1949–2005), for example, 31,648 committee sessions were counted, almost ten times the total number of plenary sessions. Other measures of legislative performance support the view that the Bundestag is a productive and efficient parliament. For example, the average annual number of tabled Bills in the Bundestag amounted to 661 in the first fifteen legislative periods, and the total number of Bills passed – an average of 428 in each legislative period – was not dramatically lower. Legislative activity is also mirrored in the duration of the legislative process, measured by the average duration across all legislative periods from the date on which a Bill is tabled until the promulgation of an Act. According to this measure, legislative Acts span a period of 187 to 266 days.

Most legislation concerns issues and areas below the level of constitutional change. Only a small minority of legislative Acts involve changes in the constitution. Most of the constitutional changes were legislated in the following four periods: first, from 1953 to 1957, i.e. in the period of a two-thirds-majority coalition of the Christian Democratic parties, the Liberals and the German Party/Federation of the Expelled and Dispossessed (GP/BHE); second, in the period 1966–9, the period of the Grand Coalition of the Christian Democratic parties and the SPD, in which the government presided over a two-thirds majority; third, in 1990–4, that is, in the period of the unification of West Germany and East Germany and legislation on the implementation of the Maastricht Treaty on European Union; fourth, in 2006, when the reform of federalism demanded a wide variety of changes in the constitution.

The extent to which party differences have an impact upon parliamentary legislative activity has been much discussed. That most Bills are passed unanimously, one group of observers argues, points to small party differences. Others argue that the relative policy importance of a Bill matters and that these differences reveal major party differences. Very important Bills or important legislative Acts, for example, often do not encounter opposition party approval. Examples include reform projects of the red–green coalition government in power from 1998 to 2005, such as the reform of citizenship in 1999, and the phasing out of nuclear energy. In contrast, unanimous approval or near unanimity is often achieved only with Bills of lesser policy relevance. However, the complete picture is more diverse. There have been major Bills which met with the approval, usually after extended bargaining, of the incumbent and the major opposition parties, such as legislation on German unification, on privatisation of telecommunication and railways, and on the introduction of the Euro, the common European currency.

Overall, however, the data on legislation in the 1980s and in the period after unification until 2005 indicate declining proportions of Bills that were passed unanimously in the lower house. This largely reflects an increased level of political polarisation between the governing coalition and the opposition parties, but it also mirrors the trend towards a confrontational style in opposition behaviour. However, a complete picture requires us to take into account the legislative vote in the Joint Mediation Committee of the two chambers. The Joint Mediation Committee has a permanent membership of 16 representatives of the lower house (before unification 11), in proportion to the parties' share of seats, and 16 delegates from the upper house (before unification 11). The committee considers on appeal all legislative disagreement between the two houses. This has been the case in 13 per cent of all legislative acts of the lower house. *De facto* the Joint Mediation Committee has become a powerful mechanism of compromise-seeking and decision-making on the basis of Grand Coalitions between the incumbent parties and the opposition as well as between the federal government and the state governments.

Particularly important has been the role of the Joint Mediation Committee in the first two sessions of the Bundestag (1949–57), in most of the era of the SPD–FDP coalition (1969–82), in the second half of the era Kohl (1990–98) and in the period in which the red–green coalition normally could not count on more than a minority of the votes in the upper house (1999–2005). In these periods, between 11 and 16 per cent of all Bills tabled in the Bundestag were submitted to the Joint Mediation Committee. Most of these Bills were settled in the Joint Mediation Committee through compromises between all or almost all participants after extended bargaining. This is a further indication of the major political actors' tendency to comply with the co-operation requirements inherent in Germany's political institutions. That compliance mirrors a consensus among the political elites on essential norms and values, but it can also be attributed to a cost–benefit calculation by the parties. According to that calculation, the benefits deriving from co-operation are higher, and the costs lower, than those that would accrue from non-co-operation and hence blocking political decision-making. However, it must be added that blockage of the political decision-making process cannot be excluded, as the fate of the tax reform of the Kohl government in the thirteenth legislative period (1994–8) demonstrates, to mention only one spectacular example.

GOVERNMENT AND BUREAUCRACY

Party composition of government

In most of the period under investigation (1949–2007), the Christian Democratic parties have long been a major player in the process of government formation.

However, the Christian Democratic parties' control of the reins of power has been contingent upon parliamentary support from smaller coalition partners, with the exception of the aftermath of the national election in 1957, in which the CDU and CSU gained more than 50 per cent of the seats in the national parliament. Among these smaller parties the Liberals have frequently been strategically positioned. In the period up till the mid-1990s the FDP was often the kingmaker, as its coalition policy determined whether the CDU–CSU or the SPD gained access to the centre of power. The important position of the Liberals in the party systems is also mirrored in the partisan composition of national governments. Although the FDP is the smallest of the three established parties, it has participated in government since 1949 for longer than any other party. At the federal government level the Liberals held office in 1949–56, in 1961–6 and from 1969 until 1998, with a short interval in 1962 and in September 1982 due to the breakdown of the SPD–FDP coalition. In the period from 1949 until 2007, the FDP thus participated in government for almost 31 years out of a total of 58 years, while the Christian Democratic parties, although of an electoral strength many times greater than the Liberals, did so for almost 39 years. The SPD has had to content itself with 25 years in office (1966–82, 1998–2005 and 2005–). However, in contrast to the single-party government of a social-democratic complexion in Austria, Britain, France, Spain or Sweden, the SPD has never been in a hegemonic position in national government. The SPD has had to share power with the CDU–CSU from 1966 to 1969 and since 2005, with the Liberals over a period of 13 years (1969–82) and with the Green Party from 1998 to 2005 (see Table 3.3).

Compared with other democracies in the post-World War II period, the extent to which left parties have participated in national government in Germany, measured by the share of cabinet seats (29.3 per cent in 1950–2005), is moderate. The extent to which Social Democratic parties have controlled the reins of power in federal government in Germany is lower than in Belgium (31.6 per cent), Finland (31.0 per cent), Greece (36.4 per cent) and Britain (38.1 per cent), and much lower than in Austria (50.7 per cent), Denmark (50.9 per cent), Norway (66.7 per cent), Sweden (78.9 per cent) or Spain (48.3 per cent) (the data are for 1950–2005 and in the case of Spain for 1977–2005). In contrast to the weak role of the left parties in government, the centrist or centre-right tendency has been a major incumbent party in Germany, similar to the centrist parties in the Benelux countries and in Italy until the decline of the Christian Democrats. In contrast to this, secular conservative parties, or 'rightist parties', have not participated in government in the Federal Republic of Germany. This marks a crucial difference between politics in Germany and in the family of English-speaking nations.

Parties have, of course, natural preferences for particular portfolios, depending upon the nature of their political programme and manifestos as well as on the preferences of the social constituencies. The overall pattern of the distribution of ministries among incumbent parties in the Federal Republic has been as follows: The largest party in a coalition normally takes the Ministry of Finance, the Ministry of Labour and Social Affairs, the Ministry of Defence, frequently also the Ministry of the Interior and the more state-interventionist ministries, such as Transport, Research and Technology, and Housing. But Grand Coalition may differ from these

Table 3.3 Governments of the Federal Republic of Germany, 1949–2005

No.	Year	Chancellor	Party composition
1	1949	K. Adenauer	Christians, Liberals, Nationalists
2	1953	K. Adenauer	Christians, Liberals, Nationalists, GB/BHE
	1955	K. Adenauer	Christians, Liberals, Nationalists
	1956	K. Adenauer	Christians, Nationalists
	1956	K. Adenauer	Christians, former Liberals, Nationalists
3	1957	K. Adenauer	Christians, Nationalists
4	1961	K. Adenauer	Christians, Liberals
	1963	L. Erhard	Christians, Liberals
5	1965	L. Erhard	Christians, Liberals
	1966	K. G. Kiesinger	Christians, Socialists
6	1969	W. Brandt	Socialists, Liberals
7	1972	W. Brandt	Socialists, Liberals
	1974	H. Schmidt	Socialists, Liberals
8	1976	H. Schmidt	Socialists, Liberals
9	1980	H. Schmidt	Socialists, Liberals
	1982	H. Kohl	Christians, Liberals
10	1983	H. Kohl	Christians, Liberals
11	1987	H. Kohl	Christians, Liberals
12	1991	H. Kohl	Christians, Liberals
13	1994	H. Kohl	Christians, Liberals
14	1998	G. Schröder	Socialists, Greens
15	2002	G. Schröder	Socialists, Greens
16	2005	A. Merkel	Christians, Socialists

Note: Former Liberals: DA, later renamed FVP, merged with DP in 1957, and with CDU in 1960. The first party indicates the Chancellor's affiliation.

patterns. In the second Grand Coalition, for example, the smaller coalition party, i.e. the SPD, took not only the classical welfare state ministries, but also the Ministry of Finance and the Foreign Office. In centre-right–liberal coalitions and in centre-left–liberal coalitions, the FDP frequently gained control of the cabinet seats of the Ministry of Justice, the Ministry of Economics and the Foreign Office. With the exception of the red–green coalition, the ministries in the law and order domain have mainly been within the jurisdiction of centre-right or liberal tendencies. In contrast, the ministries at the heart of the welfare state have been allocated to the CDU–CSU and the SPD, thereby restoring the centrist stance that characterised social policy in the Weimar Republic until 1930.

Political parties play a major role in the Federal Republic. In contrast to the pre-1949 regimes the constitution of the Federal Republic and legislation such as the Parties Act spell out the legitimate political rights of the parties. These include officially guaranteed participation 'in forming the political will of the people' (Article 21 of the Basic Law) and responsibilities, such as a democratic structure for the parties' internal organisation, and the duty to publicly account for their assets and for the sources and the use of their funds. Furthermore, the political parties have largely exploited the room for manoeuvre available to them. According to a widely shared view the outcome has been a 'party state' (*Parteienstaat*), in which the parties and their deputies in parliament take all or almost all major political decisions.

The 'party state' view rightly points to the importance of political parties, but it tends to neglect the institutional constraints on party behaviour. Among these, the following deserve mention: political-administrative constraints, the networks existing between the state and organised interests, the momentum and selectivity inherent in intergovernmental relations at the national level and within the European Union, the tradition of self-administration in social security and in local government, the autonomy of the judiciary, the delegation of public functions to experts such as an autonomous central bank, constraints stemming from Germany's high level of integration in international and supranational organisations, and from free collective bargaining between employers' and employees' associations on wages and working conditions. These constraints add up to an unusually large number of 'veto players' and de facto 'co-governing actors' in the Federal Republic of Germany. It is on some of these constraints on the 'party state' that attention will now be focused.

Political and administrative structure

A political party that gains access to the reins of power at the national level in Germany governs a central state of modest size, which is tied down by a highly fragmented state structure. More specifically, few federal ministries have the resources to implement and monitor the policies enacted by the federal government. With few exceptions, such as defence and foreign policy, public administration is not a responsibility of central government but of the state government (*Länder*), local government, experts in institutions such as the central bank, and para-public institutions of the welfare state, such as the Federal Employment Agency (Bundesagentur für Arbeit) and the health and social insurance funds, not to mention the right of trade unions and employers' associations for free collective bargaining on wages and working time. The national government in the Federal Republic of Germany thus govern without having direct control over the administration of most of its policies and without having direct control over major tools of economic policy.

The consequences are non-trivial. In economic policy, the federal government, although widely regarded as politically responsible for macro-economic outcomes, disposes only of limited resources to control macro-economic outcomes. For example, only 30 per cent or less of the total budget of general government is at the disposal of the federal government (while the states, local government and the social insurance funds are in charge of broadly 70 per cent of the budget). Furthermore, monetary policy, which has been transferred to the European Central Bank, is completely beyond the control of the federal government. Moreover, the consequences of delegating administrative responsibilities are numerous. The process of implementation of most legislation brings old and new players together, such as administration and governments at the state level and para-public institutions of social and labour market policy, which all retain considerable discretion in applying federal legislation. Furthermore, the federal government will attempt to make legislation as detailed as possible so that its intentions will be realised in the process of implementation. Last but not least, the delegation of administrative responsibilities hands leverage of considerable strength to state administrations, state governments and para-public institutions not only in the implementation of the law but early in the legislative process. This creates a strong pressure on the parliamentary majority and the government to harmonise legislation at an early stage with the expertise and the preferences of governments and administrations at the state level and the experts of the various para-public institutions.

Following Max Weber's theory of bureaucracy, some scholars have interpreted the administrative structure of the Federal Republic in terms of his hierarchical and monocratic model of public administration, derived largely from the experience of Prussian and French absolutism. However, this perspective has proved inappropriate to a better understanding of the politico-administrative structure of the Federal Republic of Germany. A more adequate perspective requires differentiation between three models of administrative intermediation of interests: (1) the French model of institutional isolation of a monocratic and centralised administration from societal interests; (2) a fragmented multi-centre administration characterised by a low degree of isolation from societal tendencies and a large number of access points for organised interests, typified by the US model; (3) the intermediate category of the Swedish model, defined by a strong tradition of professional bureaucratic administration, similar to that of France, and implementation based on autonomous authorities, as in Sweden's labour market policy, rather than on hierarchical monocratic administration.

The German case approximates the Swedish model of decentralised and delegated public administration, although administrative interest intermediation in some policy areas comes closer to the French model, such as fiscal administration, or the US model, such as the public administration of agricultural policy, which has largely been captured by interest associations representing German farmers.

Regardless of the degree of formal incorporation into the administrative process, consultation by the administration with the relevant interest groups is characteristic of legislation and pre-legislative activity in practically all policy areas in Germany. The rules of procedure of the federal ministries even require officials to consult representatives of interest groups when drafting legislation related to an interest association's area of concern. Organised interests are, thus, expected to speak for their constituency. Furthermore, the participation of these interest groups is regarded as necessary and legitimate. Due to the fragmented state structure, a wide variety of access points are available to interest groups at the national, state and local levels, as also in the para-public institutions. This is the institutional base of a widespread practice of bilateral consultation and co-operation between the state and private interest organisations in Germany.

Most of the interactions between administrations and interest groups in the German polity are of a sectionalist nature, while cross-sectoral co-ordination is almost completely absent from the state–interest group networks. A sectionalist bias also characterises the corporatist linkages in Germany's political economy. In contrast to fully developed neo-corporatism, as in Austria until the 1990s, Germany's liberal corporatism is of a sectionalist nature and is confined to a limited number of policy areas, such as unemployment insurance and labour market policy, health care and – from the mid-1960s until the late 1970s – incomes policy.

Sectional interest intermediation and bilateral consultation will normally generate a higher level of political integration of social groups and can improve the intelligence in state intervention, other things being equal. However, following the neo-corporatist view, according to which neo-corporatist interests' intermediation generates better macro-economic performance, it can be argued that the sectionalist nature of corporatism in the Federal Republic, and hence the absence of the cross-sector co-ordination of fiscal policy, wage policy and private investment, constrains economic policy to a large extent. But at the same time trade union power and the massive demand for social security among a large proportion of the electorate have been strong enough to block the route towards a potentially successful alternative regime, namely that of a more liberal political economy with lower levels of social policy and less ambitious job protection.

INTERGOVERNMENT RELATIONS

The Federal Republic, it has been argued, is a 'semi-sovereign state' or a state which embodies high 'dispersal of power', that is, a government Goliath tied down by powerful formal or informal checks and balances and co-governing institutions, such as coalition government, the Federal Constitutional Court and autonomous institutions, and federalism. Federalism also merits particular attention in the context of the study of intergovernmental relations. Public policy in the Federal Republic rests not only upon a high degree of intertwining of policy-making between the federal authorities and the states (*Länder*), comprising assured participation rights and the veto powers of the upper house in major legislation. Public policy in Germany also resides in joint planning and administration between the federal government and the state governments in a wide variety of matters that require co-operation and shared responsibility between the federal government and the states. The major examples are: since the reform of federalism in 2006, financial planning, economic development and science and research; and, included in the pre-2006 period, spending on tertiary education and environmental policy. Policy-making in these sectors has been intergovernmental in character, a feature which is exacerbated by inter-governmentalism within the political institutions of the European Union. At the same time, policy-making within the context of Germany's party state is also shaped by party competition. Policy-making is thus influenced by the coexistence of two modes of conflict resolution: one based on bargaining, techniques of compromise-seeking and consensus formation, similar to the practice of consociational democracy, whereas the other rests upon majority rule, as in a pure majoritarian democracy.

Germany's federalism is institutionalised in a federal government and sixteen states with a wide variety of relations between the various governments. In contrast to the pre-unification period, sharp economic disparities mark post-1990 federalism, above all disparities between the poorer states in the east and wealthier or rich states in the western part. Moreover the accession of the former German Democratic Republic to the Federal Republic on 3 October 1990 shifted the balance between the states of the federation in favour of the more northerly and Protestant areas. Furthermore, owing to the high level of secularisation in East Germany, the share of religiously non-affiliated voters has increased. Last but not least, the party composition of the state governments differs widely.

The heterogeneity of federalism in unified Germany poses a twofold challenge for the states and the federal government. Economic reconstruction of eastern Germany and the creation of a common standard of living in eastern and western Germany require, over a lengthy period, a massive west–east transfer of public resources equivalent to roughly 5 per cent of gross domestic product (GDP) per annum. The west–east transfer has intensified conflicts over the distribution of the costs involved between the political parties, between the federal government and the states, between capital and labour, and between government and the central bank, not to mention divisions within the *Länder*. The large differences between the states in unified Germany are a particularly heavy burden on federalism, because its institutional set-up and the repertoire of strategies available to its participants at the time of unification were all premised on the assumption of a relatively homogeneous federation.

One implication of the post-1990 situation is that the states have found it more difficult to form coalitions against the federal government, the other is potentially greater room to manoeuvre on the part of the federal government *vis-à-vis* the states, provided that the federal government has sufficient political will, skill and resources to form coalitions with a majority of the states, including states from the political camp of the opposition party.

Germany's federalism has often been misunderstood. In contrast to the American model, political authority in the German federalism is not allocated to any one level of government but is shared by the federal government and the state governments. More specifically the state governments are in charge of most areas of public administration and have a major say in federal legislation. But note that the administration of the major parts of the welfare state is largely within the jurisdiction of para-public institutions, above all the social insurance institutions and the corporatist Federal Labour Office, and thus is not within the direct reach of state administration. Furthermore, most major federal legislation requires a majority in the popularly elected lower house, and in the upper house made up of delegates of the state government executives who cast their votes *en bloc*. Moreover, the states have a considerable share of the responsibility for the planning and formation of public policy through a wide variety of institutions of co-operative federalism and through self-coordination, such as through the quasi-governmental conference of the state ministries of education.

Germany's federalism comprises a network-like system of interlocking politics, which bridges the high level of vertical and horizontal differentiation and fragmentation of the decision-making process. Within these policy networks, all participants find themselves in a series of interdependent decision-making structures. This interdependence, together with the willingness and ability of the major political actors to co-operate, has pervaded German federalism to a very large extent. From this results extended bargaining as the dominant mode of conflict resolution. In most cases, techniques of consensus formation have been successfully adopted and have secured unanimous votes or near unanimity, while pure majority rule or minimum winning coalitions are rare.

Table 3.4 Germany's states compared

State	Number of votes in the upper chamber	Cabinet offices share		
		SPD	CDU/CSU	
Baden-Württemberg	6	11	75	
Bavaria	6	5	–	90
Berlin	4	55	30	
Brandenburg	4	71	16	
Bremen	3	74	12	
Hamburg	3	73	9	
Hesse	5	67	19	
Mecklenburg-West Pomerania	3	42	33	
Lower Saxony	6	48	36	
Northrhine-Westfalia	6	62	23	
Rhineland-Palatinate	4	28	61	
Saarland	3	31	58	
Saxony	4	3	95	
Saxony-Anhalt	4	46	32	
Schleswig-Holstein	4	30	56	
Thuringia	4	12	80	

Note: The left column indicates the number of votes in 2007. The right column indicates the percentage of cabinet portfolios of the major parties; SPD: Social Democrats, CDU/CSU: Christian Democrats and Bavarians, during the period 1949–2006 (Baden-Württemberg and Berlin 1952–2006, Saarland 1957–2006, and Brandenburg, Mecklenburg-West Pomerania, Saxony, Saxony-Anhalt and Thuringia 1990–2006).

Each participant in the interlocking politics network has veto power of considerable strength. Dramatic effects on policy can result from the combination of this veto power and the impact of a divided government, such as in the period from 1991 to 1998 and from 1999 to 2005. Within this context, Bills subject to an affirmative vote of the upper house (which was standard for more than half of all legislative Acts prior to the reform of federalism in 2006 and for most important legislation) force the federal government to choose between compromises with the upper house majority and, thus, with the opposition party and, alternatively, acceptance of a blocked decision-making process. The choice for the major opposition party is co-operative co-government or confrontation. The latter, however, leads to decision-making processes being blocked. In practice the governing parties and the opposition party have in most cases chosen a co-operative strategy, usually after a longer period of confrontation and negotiation. But there are also exceptions to this rule, such as the confrontation between the CDU–CSU and SPD in the thirteenth legislative period (1994–8), which blocked a major tax reform project of the CDU–CSU–FDP coalition, as well as major conflicts between the red–green Schröder government and the opposition party in the 1998–2005 period.

The political risk involved in a co-operative solution of the conflict between the parties is considerable. The governing coalition and the opposition will have difficulty 'selling' the co-operative strategy to their respective social constituencies and particularly to those activists who demand confrontational rather than co-operative strategies. Thus the choice of a co-operative solution, and the underlying Grand

Coalition structure of these co-operative moves, may well generate political discontent, dissatisfaction and exit of disappointed voters. It is therefore a natural inclination of the parties involved in this process to adopt a dual-track strategy, both co-operation and confrontation in legislation and in the symbolic presentation of the choices or, alternatively, co-operation in legislation but with a confrontational style in the political rhetoric of partisan struggles. The latter, however, fuels adversarial politics and tends to undermine the co-operation potential required for legislation in the hidden 'Grand Coalition State' in the Federal Republic of Germany.

The constitutional state

The Federal Republic has been shaped by processes of 'learning from catastrophes', such as the breakdown of the Weimar Republic, National Socialist rule in 1933–45, and the collapse of the political, economic and social order in 1945. The National Socialist state in the period up to 1939 was notorious for its dual structure, i.e. the co-existence of relative predictability of the legal system in most economic affairs and unpredictability in almost all other aspects of political and social life. That dual structure was increasingly superseded by a totalitarian regime during World War II. The primacy of National Socialist politics over the law stands in great contrast to the legal structure of the Federal Republic. The 'founding fathers' of the Federal Republic's constitution placed major emphasis on the formation of a constitutional state, the independence of the judiciary, judicial review and the establishment of a powerful Federal constitutional Court. The effects could not have been more dramatic: the rule of law, the institutionalization of the constitutional Court as the guardian of the constitution and a 'law- and court-minded people' have replaced the unpredictability inherent in Germany in the 1933–45 period.

The omnipresence of the law in the Federal Republic is striking. 'There is hardly an area of human relations in Germany untouched by some rule, order or regulation', wrote a leading US expert in German constitutional politics (Kommers 1976: 50). Even more striking is the powerful role of the Federal Constitutional Court in politics and policy-making. The Court is the guardian of the constitution, empowered to review on appeal any alleged violation, including legislative acts, and to void laws that violate the provisions of the Basic Law. The Constitutional Court is autonomous and independent of any Justice Ministry. As in many other democracies, political parties participate in the selection of the judges of the court. However, owing to the federal structure of the Federal Republic, the states also play an important role in the process of recruiting constitutional judges. Half the sixteen members of the court are selected by a Bundestag committee composed of twelve deputies in proportion to the parties' share of seats, and half by the Bundesrat, in each case on a two-thirds-majority rule. The two-thirds-majority threshold is built into the Act establishing the Federal Constitutional Court, while the mandatory participation of the two houses has been made part of the constitution. The method of selecting the judges of the Court ensures influential roles for the federal government, the state governments, the governing parties and the opposition party. Furthermore, the two-thirds majority *de facto* requires the formation of a Grand Coalition, or an all-inclusive coalition of the political parties, and unanimity, or near-unanimity among the state governments and the representatives of the lower house.

Open access to the process of judicial review is a distinctive feature of the judicial system in the Federal Republic. Constitutional issues usually reach the agenda of the Court by one of three routes. Most common is the route via complaints on unconstitutionality entered by an individual who claims that one of his or her constitutionally protected rights has been violated by a public authority. A second route is through judicial review of actual court cases that raise constitutional issues, or review of the compatibility of specific legal norms and constitutional provisions. The third route by which causes come before the Constitutional Court is through the process of abstract judicial review, that is, the review of the constitutionality of legislation as a general legal principle without reference to a specific court case. Abstract judicial review can be requested by the federal government, or by state governments, or by one-third of the members of the lower house and thus, for example, by the opposition, provided it is strong enough. In practice opponents of a Bill have used abstract judicial review procedure as an instrument to continue a political dispute through legal means and this has been a potentially powerful weapon in the hands of the opposition party in particular.

The Court is also the final arbiter in constitutional disputes between different levels of government, such as constitutional conflicts between the states and federal government. Furthermore the Constitutional Court is responsible for protecting the constitutional and democratic order against groups and individuals seeking to overthrow it. Moreover, it is within the authority of the Constitutional Court to decide on presidential impeachment, the impeachment of federal or state judges, and to scrutinise petitions for review of the process and outcome of elections.

The Court is famous for an impressive record of constitutional interpretation in a wide variety of important matters. These include the treaties on the foreign policy of *détente vis-à-vis* the Eastern European states inaugurated by the SPD–FDP coalition in 1969 (*Ostpolitik*), abortion law, co-determination in industry and the constitutionality of the route to German unification, to mention only a few examples. From a civic rights perspective, the Court has been praised for its protection of human rights. From a democratic perspective, much can be said in favour of the Court's role as guardian of a constitutional democracy. From a technocratic systemic point of view, it can be argued that the Court has relieved parliament, government and opposition of responsibility in a wider variety of highly controversial issues, such as abortion or the reform of public radio and television. From a policy-oriented perspective, the Constitutional Court has been criticised for exhibiting a high level of judicial activism, adopting an overtly political role, usurping the legislative and policy-making prerogatives of parliament and government, and for not exercising sufficient judicial restraint. In the view of many observers, a conservative or liberal stance is characteristic of the Court's policy. Others have pointed to a more pluralist pattern in the decisions taken by the Court. It has also been argued that the Court's interference with parliamentary and government prerogatives varies with time, depending at least partly on the scope of the legislative activity of the various cabinets and parliaments.

Although considerable disagreement exists on the details of the Court's stance in policy-making, it is uncontroversial that the Federal Constitutional Court, through its decisions, but also thanks to anticipation of judicial review on the part of legislators, has been a major determinant of the courses of action open to the legislature and government. From the perspective of a top-down model of public policy, a powerful constitutional court, such as the German Constitutional Court, can be regarded as a major restraint to policy-makers. The restraint is amplified by the impact of powerful courts below the level of the Federal constitutional Court, such as the Federal Social Court, whose responsibilities are mainly in the area of adjudication on legal aspects of social policy; the Federal Labour Court, the major arbitrator in disputes on federal labour legislation and workers' rights; and the administrative courts, which have become controllers of public administration and political arenas for the continuation of political disputes over high-technology policy by legal means.

The overall outcome of the powerful position held by the judicial system in general and the Federal Constitutional Court in particular has been the unprecedented degree of juridification of Germany's polity, economy and society. It is for these reasons perfectly appropriate to regard the law as one of the major pillars upon which the distinctive 'semi-sovereignty' of the modern German state rests.

Trading state and European integration

The political construction of the German state and its foreign policy, it has been argued, has been characterised by 'semi-sovereignty' and priority for a 'civilian power'. The analysis presented so far supports this view although Germany's participation in multilateral peacekeeping and peace enforcement has added a new component to the foreign policy stance of the country since the mid-1990s. But this does not violate the view that semi-sovereignty is a major characteristic of Germany's foreign affairs. The degree of international or supranational integration, as exemplified in NATO and EU membership, is very high, compared with pre-1945 regimes and with other large countries or central powers. While conflict and co-operative partnership between the major parties, federal government and state government, as well as between labour and capital, can be regarded as the dominant principle of co-ordination in the domestic political arena, the *Leitmotiv* of Germany's foreign policy stance comprises integration into the West and multilateralism together with the transfer of sovereignty to international and supranational organisations, security partnership and the predominance of a 'trading state policy' (Staack 2000) rather than a 'great power' approach to foreign policy.

Trading state policy and security partnership were based upon military components, such as rearmament and NATO membership, on economic elements, such as the integration of the German economy into the world market, and upon genuinely political dimensions, such as the transfer of sovereignty rights to international and supranational organisations. Political and economic dimensions were also at the heart of the integration of the Federal Republic into the European Union: the taming of the power of the German state was a major motive for the foundation of the community of the European states in the 1950s. And so, too, was the intention to create an efficient and sound environment for economic growth, social progress and peace through economic and political European integration. Part of the deal was inevitably the transfer of a considerable proportion of national sovereignty to the supranational European level. Over a longer period, this transfer was largely confined to a few selected policy areas, particularly agricultural policy, and tariff and trade regulation. Owing to the acceleration of European integration in the 1980s and, subsequent to German unification, in the early 1990s transfers of sovereignty began to involve to an increasing extent selected areas of economic policy, environmental policy and transport, as is demonstrated in the Joint Internal Market and in the efforts to implement the Maastricht Treaty on European Union, effective since 1 November 1993, in which parameters were set for European monetary unification.

Despite the technocratic character of government in the European Union and notwithstanding the high level of compartmentalisation in EU policy-making, the political leadership and the established parties in Germany have been among the advocates and activists of European integration. This is at least partly attributable to the economic and political benefits that German diplomacy and German industry have derived from European integration, but it also mirrors a desire for undisputed political visions on the part of the political class.

Generally speaking, European integration has received considerable support from almost all major political actors in Germany, with the exception of half-hearted support from the German states. While the states supported the case for economic integration, they have attempted to draw the line at further expanding the level of political integration. This mirrors the apprehension of the state governments, and most politicians at the state level, that continued European political integration would undermine federalism and, thus, would destroy the *raison d'être* of the states, the *Länder* as they are called in German. In the parliamentary debate on the Maastricht Treaty, and in legislation on that treaty, the *Länder*, however, gained substantial concessions from the federal government. The major instrument for safeguarding the interests of the states is a fundamental change in the Basic Law. The new Article 23 of the Basic Law, implemented in December 1992, allocates a variety of access points and veto points to the states on practically all issues regarding the transfer of sovereignty to the European Union of concern to the states. Thus the Maastricht Treaty has not resulted in the downgrading of the states, but rather in the upgrading of their position in the policy machinery in Germany and within the network of EU institutions and national institutions.

The extent to which the European Community has altered the political institutional structures of politics and policy in Germany has been a matter of controversy. According to the 'internationalist' school of thought, politics and policy in the Federal Republic are nowadays to a large extent shaped by the requirements of the European integration process and by legislative and executive acts of the European Union. In contrast, the 'nation-state'-oriented school of thought argues that national politics and national policy-making do still significantly shape the parameters of the timing and substance of the EU policy-makers, and circumscribe the extent to which European legislation and EU policy are implemented in Germany. An intermediate view emphasises a wide range of sectoral variation in governance structures at the national and EU level and the interaction of EU-driven and nation-state-driven determinants. According to this view, some policy areas are, indeed, governed by coalitions composed of specialised Euro-bureaucracy and sectionalist national administrations, such as policy on trade and tariffs, and agricultural policy, while others are mainly controlled at the national level, such as the core institutions of the welfare state. There are also areas in which a Euro-bureaucracy is governing, with the European central bank as the major example.

A further point needs to be mentioned in this context. Most EU interventions are attempts to achieve a higher level of standardisation, or harmonisation, in some of the legal and institutional aspects of the member countries. However, to achieve effective and legitimate standardisation, or harmonisation, requires a high level of harmonisation of intermediary institutions, such as political parties, trade unions, professional groups and the mass media. This type of harmonisation, however, is largely lacking in the process of European integration. A practical implication is that a Europeanised public space does not yet exist in Europe. Policy-making of the EU and for the EU thus lacks a general European public – a clear manifestation of a major democratic deficit of the European Community.

Public policy and the 'semi-sovereign state'

The Federal Republic is notorious for its high level of institutional fragmentation and dispersal of political power. This is largely attributable to federalism and extended delegation of public functions to para-public institutions or societal interest associations as well as to deeper European integration. Moreover, the analysis of the constitutional structures of the country reveals a complex mix of 'majoritarian democracy' and 'consensus democracy', to borrow from Arend Lijphart's (1999) vocabulary. Furthermore, voters' alignments, the party system and proportional representation have generated a distribution of power which requires coalitions as the typical form of government. These factors also narrowly circumscribe the freedom of action of the federal government and generate an unusually large number of institutional and partisan veto players. It is largely due to the impact of these restrictions on the federal government that policy changes in domestic politics are often mainly gradual and incremental and that major policy changes are particularly difficult to achieve. Dramatic changes in policy are not excluded, as the case of the Kohl government's unification policy in 1990 or the decision to join the common European currency shows, but dramatic changes have been the exception rather than the rule. This can be a major obstacle to the preference for radical policy change of centre-left or left-wing governments, but it also inhibits efforts to achieve radical policy change on the part of rightist or centre-right governments. However, the potential for policy inertia inherent in a state in which many veto players exist can also be a major hindrance to elasticity in adjustment to major exogenous or endogenous shocks, such as unification, the ageing of society, reduced rates of economic growth, ambitious social policy efforts or low birth rates.

Additionally, the short-term elasticity of its political institutions, together with the consensus requirement inherent in the structure of Germany's democracy, can provoke 'voice' or 'exit' of members and voters of political parties. This is basically due to the gap that exists between the expectations of most voters on the one hand and the political process and political outcomes on the other. Most voters expect that the party they have chosen will adopt competitive strategies and outcomes of the winner-takes-all type. Most voters thus premise their expectations on a majoritarian democracy model. However, Germany's polity, in reality, is a unique combination of majoritarian and consensus democracy within a federal and 'semi-sovereign' setting, and therefore generates outcomes resembling those of a consociational democracy. Germany's democracy is thus precariously positioned midway between the effective taming of state power and problems in the effort to secure support for, and legitimation of, the political parties. This may be regarded as the institutional infrastructure of the popular criticism of the political parties and the 'party state'.

Although the 'semi-sovereign' structure of the German state gives priority to incremental policy change, it does not exclude the possibility of minor or major political innovation. Minor innovation is demonstrated by the co-existence of continuity in national institutions and widespread flexibility and experimentation in less visible arenas of politics, such as the para-public institutions, in the economy and in the networks of co-operative federalism. Major innovations occurred in the 1953–7 period, that is, during the period of a hegemonic CDU–CSU-led government, such as the decision to rearm Germany and to enter the European Community. Major innovations occurred also in the 1966–9 experiment of a Grand Coalition of the CDU–CSU and the SPD, and in the politics of German unification in 1989–90. Major reforms of the red–green coalition after 1998, such as the phasing out of nuclear energy and the privately funded, though also state-supported, pension scheme introduced in the 2001 pension reform are further examples. There has also been leeway for expanding the scope of government, measured by government revenue, or general government expenditure, as a percentage of GDP. Germany is a member of the club of 'big government' countries. Most of the increase in public expenditure as a percentage of GDP was allocated to the expansion and maintenance of a comprehensive welfare state, which is complemented by a hardly less ambitious network of labour protection schemes.

The institutional apparatus of the national polity has been conducive to a distinctive pattern of public policy. Co-operative federalism may hinder dramatic and radical policy changes, but it facilitates distributive incrementalism and secures a sufficient level of institutional elasticity. Similarly, the logic of policy-making in centre-left and centre-right quasi-catch-all coalitions is inherently favourable to welfare largesse, particularly in periods of rapid economic growth. Furthermore, while a decentralised state structure impedes fully fledged Keynesian management led by central government, it strengthens, along with the independent central bank, the aim of controlling inflationary pressure rather than combating unemployment. Focusing on the political economy, the aggregate outcome of these institutional factors and others discussed above has been a distinctive public policy in the Federal Republic: 'a policy of the middle way' between the extremes marked by social democratic welfare capitalism along Swedish lines and North American market-oriented capitalism.

Germany's 'policy of the middle way' is a unique combination of market-oriented liberal economic policy, policy measures of a social democratic nature and a policy of a Christian Democratic complexion. The policy of the middle way has four constituent parts: first, price stability; second, the aim of achieving efficiency *and* equality; third, big government of the transfer-intensive kind; and, fourth, a state which delegates major public functions to experts and to societal associations of para-public status.

The political and economic outcomes of the Federal Republic, particularly in the pre-unification period, have been widely regarded as a success story. However, three caveats must be added to the 'success story' view. One concerns the limits of the policy of the middle way, such as the failure of the effort to maintain or restore full employment. Moreover, the costs involved in the policy of the middle way have been considerable. Its price in the post-unification period has been particularly high. Friction between the major components of the middle way policy has been greater since unification, with the trade-off between ambitious social policy goals and employment as a major example. The third caveat concerns the winners and losers of the middle way. The core group of winners consists of social classes with capital income from the ownership of firms, shares, monetary assets and land; employed persons in the primary labour market segments; old-age pensioners with a working life of forty to forty-five years and few spells of unemployment, or with no experience of unemployment at all, and with wages or salaries above the average and, hence, a relatively high social income. It is important to emphasise – and this must be regarded as the key to understanding the political foundations of the middle way policy – that the core groups of winners are at the same time the core groups in the constituencies of each established political party.

The losers of the policy of the middle way are mainly to be found among the unemployed – in particular job-seekers with frequent spells of unemployment and the long-term unemployed – among groups with a short working life and a low income from work and, hence, a low income from social security schemes.

INSTITUTIONAL REFORM

Like many other advanced democratic states, Germany has been confronted with a variety of problems, such as reduced rates of economic growth, high levels of unemployment, high public debt, an ageing population, environmental pollution and political terrorism. Moreover, the Federal Republic has been exposed to unique challenges, such as the integration of roughly 12 million refugees and expelled after World War II, as well as the integration of eastern Germany's political, economic and social structure into a unified Germany. Despite the challenges, Germany's polity has proved to be relatively successful. For example, according to measures of political productivity, such as participation, freedom, stability, health of democracy and social policy effort, the Federal Republic, despite the institutional constraints of major reforms, might be regarded as a democratic 'success story'.

The relatively high level of performance of the country's political institutions and the requirement for co-operative strategies inherent in Germany's democracy have been among the major determinants of the debate on institutional reforms, and have narrowly circumscribed the options available to practically minded reformers. Of course, there are proposals for radical reform, such as radical overhaul of the constitution, the replacement of competitive federalism with unitarian co-operative federalism, the dismantling of the welfare state and, to mention it only in passing, the call for a revolutionary breakthrough on the part of the extreme left and the extreme right of the political spectrum. However, most such proposals are based on empirically dubious arguments about the high costs of maintaining the *status quo*, and equally dubious assumptions about the large-scale benefits and low cost of radical or revolutionary change.

More serious proposals for institutional reform have focused mainly on certain aspects of the institutional arrangements. One of these proposals concerns the 'party state' issue. Many critics of what they regard as a too powerful role for the political parties have raised their voices in favour of imposing more restrictions on party finances, party behaviour and party patronage, and have recommended more citizens' participation through adding plebiscitarian arrangements to the political structure. Others have opted for improving the knowledge base and the competence inherent in the national institutions. The nature of the recommendations varies from neo-liberal criticism of interest associations and the state–interest group nexus to the proposals for genuinely technocratic meritocratic reform concepts and to full support for creating and maintaining neo-corporatist relations between organised economic interests and the state. Furthermore, proponents of federalism emphasise the potential threat of European integration to the individual states of the Federal Republic, and demand low-speed integration or a halt to further integration. In contrast to this, the 'Europeanists' advocate accelerated economic and political European integration. There exists also considerable disagreement between the 'federalist' camp, mainly composed of the state-level executives and deputies to state parliaments, and the proponents of radical change in the delimitation of federal territory on the question whether the *Länder* have the size and capacity required to discharge the responsibilities laid upon them. Moreover, a potentially explosive debate is that conducted by defenders of the welfare state and proponents of further welfare state expansion on the one hand, mainly to be found among the unions, the welfare associations, the churches, the left wing of the SPD and the Left, and critics of comprehensive social policy, mainly composed of business interests, the Liberal Party and neo-classical economists, on the other.

Last but not least, German unification has triggered a debate on the constitutional structure of the country. The rapid accession of the former German Democratic Republic to the Federal Republic and the almost complete transfer of the West German legal, political and economic institutions to eastern Germany have avoided protracted parliamentary debate on matters of constitutional design. However, a minority has continued to demand radical amendment of the Basic Law. Politically more important has been the Joint Commission on Constitutional Reform. The Joint Commission was the product of Clause 5 of the Unification Treaty, which urged the legislature to consider issues of constitutional change raised by the unification of the two Germanies in 1990. The constituent assembly of the Joint Commission met in January 1992, and the report of the commission was published on 6 November 1993 (Gemeinsame Verfassungskommission 1993). Within the context of the main theme of this chapter, two major characteristics of the Joint Commission deserve mention: the composition and the lack of decisions by the commission. The composition of the Joint Commission was unique. Half its 64 members were deputies selected in the lower house in proportion to the parties' share of seats, and half were deputies of the upper house, among the latter 13 state minister presidents out of a total of 16 minister presidents. Thus the political parties and a substantial proportion of the core of Germany's political class deliberated on constitutional change in the Joint Commission on Constitutional Reform.

It is therefore not surprising that deliberation in the commission has served mainly to advance the case of the 'party state', and the case of institutional guarantees for the German states, such as that enshrined in the new Article 23 of the Basic Law. In contrast to this, most other proposals for constitutional reform have been disregarded as unlikely to attract the two-thirds majority required for constitutional change in the upper and lower houses, such as the proposal to add referendum democracy components to the political constitution of the Federal Republic, to mention just one example.

The decisions and lack of decisions made by the Joint Commission are amenable to explanation. The key to an understanding of the politics and policy of the commission lies in its personification as an institution, which is distinctive to the Federal Republic. The Joint Commission was composed of two Grand Coalitions. One of them was the Grand Coalition of the major established parties, above all the CDU–CSU and the SPD; the other consisted of a broad coalition of the federal government, with its parliamentary majority and a two-thirds majority in the upper house, and thus a two-thirds majority among the state governments.

This is part of a more general message to be derived from the political institutions in Germany. It is almost impossible in the Federal Republic of Germany not to be governed by a Grand Coalition of federal government and state governments and a Grand Coalition of the major established parties – hidden or formal. Diverging majorities in the lower house and the upper house exacerbate this requirement. Particularly in periods of formal coalitions between the CDU/CSU and SPD but also in periods of diverging majorities, the Federal Republic of Germany can therefore be regarded as the embodiment of the Grand Coalition state, a consociational democracy German style.

BIBLIOGRAPHY

Origins and political regime

Beyme, Klaus von (2004) *Das politische System der Bundesrepublik Deutschland. Eine Einführung*, 10th edn, Wiesbaden: VS Verlag für Sozialwissenschaften.
Conradt, David P. (2005) *The German Polity*, 8th edn, New York: Longman.
Dalton, Russell L. (1993) *Politics in West Germany*, 2nd edn, New York: HarperCollins.
Katzenstein, Peter J. (1987) *Policy and Politics in West Germany. The Growth of a Semi-sovereign State*, Philadelphia: Temple University Press.
Schmidt, Manfred (1987) 'West Germany: The Policy of the Middle Way', *Journal of Public Policy* 7 (2): 139–77.

—— (2003) *Political Institutions in the Federal Republic of Germany*, Oxford: Oxford University Press.

—— (2007) *Das politische System Deutschlands. Institutionen, Willensbildung und Politikfelder*, Munich: C. H. Beck.

Wolfrum, Edgar (2006) *Die geglückte Demokratie. Geschichte der Bundesrepublik Deutschland von ihren Anfängen bis zur Gegenwart*, Stuttgart: Klett-Cotta.

Elections

Falter, Jürgen, and Harald Schoen (eds) (2005) *Handbuch Wahlforschung*, Wiesbaden: VS Verlag für Sozialwissenschaften.

Jesse, Eckard (1990) *Elections. The Federal Republic of Germany in Comparison*, New York and London: Berg.

Parties

Benoit, Kenneth and Michael Laver (2007) *Party Policy in Modern Democracies*, London and New York: Routledge.

Kersbergen, Kees van (1995) *Social Capitalism. A Study of Christian Democracy and the Welfare State*, London: Routledge.

Kirchheimer, Otto (1966a) 'The Vanishing Opposition', in Robert A. Dahl (ed.) *Political Oppositions in Western Democracies*, New Haven: Yale University Press.

—— (1966b) 'The Transformation of the Western European Party Systems', in Joseph LaPalombara and Myron Weiner (eds) *Political Parties and Political Development*, Princeton: Princeton University Press.

Klingemann, Hans-Dieter (1987) 'Election Programmes in West Germany, 1949–1980: Explorations in the Nature of Political Controversy', in Ian Budge, David Robertson and Derek Hearl (eds) *Ideology, Strategy and Party Change. Spatial Analyses of Post-war Election Programmes in 19 Democracies*, Cambridge: Cambridge University Press.

Laver, Michael and Ben Hunt (1992) *Policy and Party Competition*, New York and London: Routledge.

Schmidt, Manfred G. (1980) *CDU und SPD an der Regierung. Ein Vergleich ihrer Politik in den Ländern*, Frankfurt and New York: Campus.

—— (2002) 'The Impact of Political Parties, Constitutional Structures and Veto Players on Public Policy', in Hans Keman (ed.) *Comparative Democratic Politics: A Guide to Present Theory and Research*, London: Sage.

Parliament

Beyme, Klaus von (1993) *Die politische Klasse im Parteienstaat*, Frankfurt: Suhrkamp.

Feldkamp, Michael F. (2005) *Datenhandbuch zur Geschichte des Deutschen Bundestages: 1994 bis 2003*, Baden-Baden: Nomos.

—— (2006) 'Deutscher Bundestag 1987 bis 2005: Parlaments- und Wahlstatistik', *Zeitschrift für Parlamentsfragen* 37 (1): 3–19.

Schindler, Peter (1996) 'When Parties Matter: A Review of the Possibilities and Limits of Partisan Influence on Public Policy', *European Journal of Political Research* 30 (2): 155–83.

—— (1999) *Datenhandbuch zur Geschichte des Deutschen Bundestages 1949 bis 1999*, 3 vols, Baden-Baden: Nomos.

Weber, Max (1988) 'Parlament und Regierung im neugeordneten Deutschland', in Max Weber, *Gesammelte Politische Schriften*, Tübingen: Mohr.

Government

Green, Simon and William E. Paterson (eds) (2005) *Governance in Contemporary Germany. The Semisovereign State Revisited*, Cambridge: Cambridge University Press.

Hartwich, Hans-Hermann (1970) *Sozialstaatspostulat und gesellschaftlicher Status quo*, Cologne-Opladen: Westdeutscher.

Helms, Ludger (2005) *Presidents, Prime Ministers, and Chancellors. Executive Leadership in Western Democracies*, Basingstoke and New York: Palgrave.

Lehmbruch, Gerhard (2000) *Parteienwettbewerb im Bundesstaat*, 3rd edn, Wiesbaden: VS Verlag für Sozialwissenschaften.

Lijphart, Arend (1999) *Patterns of Democracy. Government Forms and Performance in Thirty-six Countries*, New Haven and London: Yale University Press.

Maull, Hanns W. (1991) 'Germany and Japan: The New Civilian Powers', *Foreign Affairs* 69 (5): 91–106.

Niclauss, Karlheinz (2004) *Kanzlerdemokratie. Regierungsführung von Konrad Adenauer bis Gerhard Schröder*, 2nd edn, Paderborn: Schöningh.

Pempel, T. J. (ed.) (1990) *Uncommon Democracies. The One-party Dominant Regimes*, Ithaca, NY: Cornell University Press.

Schmidt, Manfred G. (2000) *Demokratietheorien: Eine Einführung*, 3rd edn, Opladen: Leske & Budrich.

—— (2005) *Sozialpolitik in Deutschland. Historische Entwicklung und internationaler Vergleich*, 3rd edn, Wiesbaden: VS Verlag für Sozialwissenschaften.

Schmidt, Manfred G. and Reimut Zohlnhöfer (eds) (2006) *Regieren in der Bundesrepublik Deutschland. Innen- und Außenpolitik seit 1949*, Wiesbaden: VS Verlag für Sozialwissenschaften.

Staack, Michael (2000) *Handelsstaat Deutschland. Deutsche Außenpolitik in einem neuen internationalen System*, Paderborn: Schöningh.

Zohlnhöfer, Reimut (2001) *Die Wirtschaftspolitik der Ära Kohl. Eine Analyse der Schlüsselentscheidungen in den Politikfeldern Finanzen, Arbeit und Entstaatlichung. 1982–1998*, Opladen: Leske & Budrich.

Intergovernmental relations

Kommers, Donald (1976) *Judicial Politics in West Germany. A Study of the Federal Constitutional Court*, Beverly Hills: Sage.

—— (1997) *Constitutional Jurisprudence of the Federal Republic of Germany*, 2nd edn, Durham: Duke University Press.

Landfried, Christine (1996) *Bundesverfassungsgericht und Gesetzgeber. Wirkungen der Verfassungsrechtsprechung auf parlamentarische Willensbildung und soziale Realität*, 2nd edn, Baden-Baden: Nomos.

Scharpf, Fritz W. (1984) *Optionen des Föderalismus in Deutschland*, Frankfurt and New York: Campus.

—— (1999) *Governing in Europe. Effective and Democratic?*, Oxford: Oxford University Press.

Institutional reform

Gemeinsame Verfassungskommission (1993 *Bericht der Gemeinsamen Verfassungskommission*, Deutscher Bundestag 12. Wahlperiode, Drucksache 12/6000, 5 November 1993.

CHAPTER 4

France

The Institutionalisation of Leadership

Yves Mény

The five decades of constitutional stability that France has experienced under the Fifth Republic are a record by French standards. Since the 1789 Revolution only the Third Republic (1875–1940) has lasted longer. Yet there have been numerous events that might have brought down the new political regime of 24 October 1958: take-over threats and attempts on the life of its founder, General de Gaulle; the 1962 rebellion of both right-wing and left-wing members of parliament against the presidentialisation of the regime; the student, and social, revolution of 1968; the uncertainties surrounding the left's accession to power in 1981 and the *cohabitation* of majority and opposition first in 1986 and 1993 and again in 1997. In short, many people expected the Fifth Republic constitution, like de Gaulle himself, to be no more than 'a bad moment to live through' (Paul Reynaud). It seemed to be a short-term solution to a short-term problem – the difficult decolonisation process that the Fourth Republic was unable to address from the beginning to the end of its short life.

But the apparently fragile Fifth Republic did more than survive the challenge of events. It is only with hindsight that analysts can assess the capacity of institutions to resist the hazards of circumstance. At the time, observers and participants in the political game found many reasons to be sceptical about the longevity of the new institutions. Several factors combined to increase their doubts.

First, the constitution seemed made for one man, de Gaulle, who inspired it and tailored it to his shape, almost entirely on the model sketched out in his famous Bayeux speech of 16 June 1946. Paraphrasing Sieyès, who asked himself what there was in the constitution of the year VIII and replied, 'Bonaparte,' it could be said that in 1958, for many French people, the constitution was de Gaulle, the strong man rising out of the chaos. A referendum – more of a plebiscite – was held under the slogan 'Yes to the constitution means yes to de Gaulle' (28 September 1958; 80 per cent said 'Yes'). Once the first moment of euphoria had passed and the difficulties that brought down the Fourth Republic had been resolved, people expected a return to normal, a return to the republican tradition of strong parliamentary regimes in force since 1875. So there was constant reference in the 1960s to an imaginary 'Sixth Republic' constructed according to various designs put forward by parties or individuals fond of constitutional re-engineering. This rhetoric has continued up to now, up to the 2007 presidential campaign.

Second, the new regime, in substance as well as in the words of its founders and their acolytes, portrayed itself as a break with the preceding system. It was against excessive parliamentarianism, against the rule of parties, against parliament's monopoly of legislation, against a weak executive and against politicians. The very radicalism of this denial of the past, in words at least, made some people fear that, once decolonisation had been achieved, an alliance of critics and opponents would be prepared to sweep the Fifth Republic away or at least take their turn to make sweeping changes to the form and content of the constitution. The right had not forgiven de Gaulle for his 'treason' in giving Algeria independence. Some of the left could not forget the troubled origins of the Fifth Republic (the Algerian revolt of 13 May 1958, the military pressure), the 'ultimate' in wickedness in the eyes of Communists and a few Fourth Republic stars (Pierre Mendès-France, François Mitterrand). The *notables* (people of local or regional prominence) did not want to prolong a regime that threatened to reduce their influence. Political scientists pointed to the regime's authoritarian features, and constitutional lawyers drew attention to the ambiguities of a system which did not fit the conventions or normal classifications of constitutional law. Was it direct democracy or representative democracy, a parliamentary or a presidential regime? French constitutional history shows that sudden changes are rarely productive. Once the enthusiasm for radical change has passed, and the pleasure of a fresh start has gone, new regimes make way for reformers and revolutionaries who, in their turn, promise better todays or brighter tomorrows. For many people the rupture of 1958 carried the seeds of failure of the new regime within itself.

Third, the idea of regime change was, it could be said, rooted in habits and minds. Within the space of twenty years the French people had experienced the demise of the Third Republic and the birth of the Vichy state on 10 July 1940; the confrontation between the Vichy regime and the French National Committee set up in London on 24 November 1941; the provisional government of the French Republic created under de Gaulle's authority on 24 April 1944, which ruled concurrently with the Laval government brought in by the Eleventh Constitutional Act of 18 April 1942; the referendum of 21 October 1945 confirming the French people's reluctance to bring back the Third Republic, and the simultaneous election of a Constituent Assembly; the drawing up of a draft constitution while France was governed according to the provisional regime set out in the Act of 2 November 1945; the rejection of that draft on 5 May 1946 and the drafting by a second Constituent Assembly (elected 2 June 1946) of a second version, approved on 27 October 1946 out of weariness more than enthusiasm (one-third said yes, one-third said no, one-third abstained);

the revision of the constitution on 7 December 1954; and the dissolution of 2 December 1955. As if these twenty years of constitutional incoherence were not enough to give rise to a feeling of uncertainty, political events added their contribution: five years of war in continental Europe; the incessant, murderous colonial struggles in Indochina, Madagascar and Algeria; the denial of values inscribed in the preamble to the constitution to cover up torture and cleaning-up operations in colonial wars that were settled with hundreds of thousands of deaths (mostly of local people); the breaking of political and electoral promises (left-wing manifestos, right-wing practices); and, finally, government instability: there were twenty-two cabinets during the Fourth Republic, including the last, that of de Gaulle, given power on 3 June 1958 in a final surprise development. As Leon Blum foretold, 'One would leave the provisional only to enter the precarious'. By voting massively for de Gaulle and the new constitution French people demonstrated their willingness to have done with the past. But that same past gave them the right to be dubious and sceptical, to retain that doubt and scepticism which made Lampedusa write in *Il Gattopardo* (*The Leopard*), 'Things have to change to stay the same', and Americans utter the cynical phrase 'The more things change the more stay the same'.

With hindsight, events disproved the doubts. The Fifth Republic did not just innovate in the field of constitutional design. It brought in strong leadership at national level that served as a model for other social and political institutions – to the extent that authority and efficiency were promoted everywhere at the expense of pluralism and collegiality (the principal exception doubtless being university institutions). It contributed to the restructuring of political parties and interest groups. In addition the new institutions revealed unexpected dimensions beyond those sought by their authors. For example, the evolving role of the Constitutional Council and the ideological and political use of the preamble to the constitution have unexpectedly enhanced the state of law. However, the most fascinating aspect of this unplanned institutional development remains the way individuals and groups have manipulated it in their own interests. The technocratic elite took over the executive machinery, whereas the parliamentary elite, denied a significant input into the legislative process, withdrew to their local bastions and turned the Senate into the periphery's power base. The left-wing parties, initially hostile to the institutions, used them to their advantage when they came to power. The voters themselves played the electoral and referendum rules like experts, giving power to the right (in 1968, for example) or to the left (in 1981, 1988 or 1997, for example), then refocusing their aim at the next election (the departure of de Gaulle in 1969, the Socialist defeat in 1986, no overall majority in 1988 and the defeat of the President's party after a misguided dissolution of the National Assembly by Chirac in 1997). The rational voter, increasingly independent of the party organisations and freer of sectoral loyalties (class and religion), has contributed greatly to the institutionalisation of the regime and to its evolution. (S)he gave unconditional support to the presidential leadership, tempered by some punishment when it went beyond the acceptable (1967, 1969, 1986, 1988, 1993, 1997); inflicted a change of government (1981, 1995), and then *cohabitation* (1986, 1993, 1997), on the very parties which had argued against it in the name of the institutions; and made sophisticated use of the different types of elections and voting systems to 'send a message' to the political class, especially in elections where little was at stake (e.g. local and European elections). In short, the institutions, as the rules giving access to power and about the exercise of power, giving a structure to political life, are at the heart of the political game.

In consequence the French political system cannot be reduced to the rules it sets itself or to the principles it proclaims. It is the product of past and current events. It swings between the goals which inspired it and the constraints and burdens which are imposed upon it. Numerous paradoxes and contradictions affect its structure, existence and evolution. Permanent tensions between values and needs modify its internal equilibria and transform its fundamental characteristics, either imperceptibly or abruptly. The government's strength has varied widely according to circumstances and personalities. The Constitutional Council evolved within a few years from being insignificant to having a central role. The parties have in turn been taken apart, reconstructed and weakened again, to the extent that the party system of 1958 was unlike that of 1965, and in 1990 had little in common with that of 1970. Over the last forty years governments have been supported either by a single-party majority, or by a party with no overall majority, or by coalition majorities. The 2007 elections mark a further change. The very fragmented party system has been substituted in the National Assembly by a *de facto* two-party system (UMP and Socialist Party) due to the collapse of minor parties and the 'guillotine effect' of the electoral system.

The constitutional rules are constraints imposed on the political players but are also resources manipulated by political entrepreneurs. It is this tension that gives the political system its specific shape.

ELECTIONS AND MOBILISATIONS

Although it is popularly believed that France is an ancient democracy, the assumption needs to be qualified. The franchise was restricted until 1848; secrecy at the ballot box was not guaranteed until 1913–14; women did not acquire the vote until 1945 and the voting age was not lowered to eighteen until 1974. There was no judicial supervision of changes in constituency boundaries until 1986 (and they have not been adjusted since) and, in the current state of the Constitutional Council's jurisdiction, there is no control of referendum Bills. In short, although it would be absurd to deny democratic credentials to France, and to the Fifth Republic especially, it would be just as absurd to think of it as a quasi-ideal democracy.

Popular participation: referendums and elections

The Fifth Republic constitution and the Gaullists' use of the institutions demonstrate clearly that authoritarian practices can be accompanied by constant appeals to the electorate. The period 1958–62, in particular, illustrates the mixture of charismatic and legal–rational legitimacy that made the infant Fifth Republic such a special regime. French people had to vote twice in 1958 (referendum and parliamentary elections), once in 1961 (referendum) and three times in 1962 (two referendums and a parliamentary election), in addition to local elections. These six national polls, characterised by a high electoral turnout, always supporting General de Gaulle and the Gaullists without fail, punctuated a period of marked restrictions on civil liberties because of the Algerian war. This exceptional regime became the rule. A state of emergency, a regime hardly compatible with real guarantees of fundamental rights, was imposed from 1955 to 1962 in Algeria, and from April 1961 to May 1963 in mainland France, with the emergency regime introduced under Article 16 super-imposed on it from April to September 1961. Thus, while elections and popular participation were necessary ingredients of democracy, they did not capture all its essence.

Referendums

The use of referendums was one of the innovatory hallmarks of the Gaullist regime. In France plebiscites are associated strongly with the First and Second Empires, and one can understand why republicans had a particular aversion to them during the Third Republic. The Fourth Republic used a referendum for approving the constitution, but without enthusiasm and under pressure from de Gaulle (even then). It was only after 1958 that the referendum acquired respectability. Between 1958 and 1962 it became a real governmental tool, thanks to the 'direct dialogue' it introduced between the head of state and voters, above the heads of parliament and parties. The constitution envisaged the use of the referendum in *three* situations: to approve a Bill dealing with the organisation of public authorities or institutions; to authorise the ratification of a treaty which, 'without being contrary to the con-stitution', would affect the running of governmental institutions; and to approve a Bill to revise the constitution, if so requested by the President, after the text, in identical terms, has been voted by both houses. However, only the first of these three possibilities has been much used in practice, each time controversially. Since 1995, following a constitutional reform suggested by Chirac during his electoral campaign, the President of the Republic is able to call a referendum on a wider range of issues, including economic and social policy and public services reforms. But this option has not been exercised.

The use of the referendum under the Fifth Republic has several characteristics which differentiate its use from that in some other Western democracies. First, the process resembles direct democracy only superficially and spuriously. Although the people as a whole are asked to pronounce on a Bill, they have no power to take the initiative, either in making a proposal or in formulating the question. They have three choices only: to approve, reject or abstain. The practice of the Fifth Republic turned the referendum into a procedure at the disposal of the executive, especially of the head of state. During de Gaulle's time the referendum was exclusively the affair of the head of state, the government's 'proposal' (or that of parliament, which was careful to avoid such initiatives!) generally ratifying a presidential decision already taken. Thanks to this instrument, General de Gaulle could obtain not only the people's full consent but full power, usually solicited by a game of double questions to which only one answer could be given. Although de Gaulle's successors tried to use the referendum (Pompidou in 1972, Mitterrand in 1988 and 1992, Chirac in

2005) they took care not to put their own authority on the line, thus contributing to the modification of the referendum as forged by Gaullist practice. In fact, the referendum is always a risky operation, as is shown by recent experiences. More often than not, the electorate is not so much interested in the question officially at stake than in the possibility of sending a – usually negative – message to the men in power. At best, the President has to be happy with a polite indifference and a low turnout.

In the second place the referendums of 1962 especially, and of 1969, which would have modified the constitution without going through the revision procedure offered by Article 89, aroused intense argument between the majority and opposition parties. Recourse to Article 11 in 1962, introducing the election of the head of state by direct universal suffrage, precipitated a major crisis, defined by the president of the Senate, Gaston Monnerville, as a 'deliberate, self-willed, premeditated and outrageous violation of the constitution of the Fifth Republic'. The reform was nevertheless adopted by a majority of the French people, but only after Pompidou's government, accused of 'dereliction of duty', had been brought down, the house dismissed and a new election held in which the well-organised Gaullist majority triumphed. The debate and arguments have gradually subsided, François Mitterrand himself admitting that a sort of 'constitutional convention' would allow Article 11 to be used to revise the constitution.

Elections

The Fifth Republic has been generous in its use of elections, which, as well as designating local and national representatives, are also a powerful device for legitimation. Periods when there is no consultation of the electorate (e.g. 1989–92) are rare.

Two contrasting periods in the use of voting mechanisms during the Fifth Republic can be distinguished. The first, extending from 1958 to 1979, was characterised by the standardisation of electoral systems and their common alignment on a preferred mode, the two-round majority system, either for a single candidate or for a list of candidates. After 1958 the majority voting system was used for parliamentary elections. The 1962 reform extended its use to presidential elections, and it is also used for local and county elections.

In addition, the method of selection imposed by this voting system ('voters choose in the first round, eliminate in the second') is reinforced by provisions that encourage alliances among the left and among the right, and thus towards bipolarisation. For example, in the presidential election only the two best-placed candidates in the first round can stand in the second round; and in towns of more than 30,000 inhabitants, under the 1964 Act governing municipal elections, the list of candidates obtaining an absolute majority in the first round or a relative majority in the second round could take all the seats! What is more, candidates or lists in municipal, county or parliamentary elections had to obtain at least 10 per cent of the votes cast in the first round to be eligible to stand in the second round, a barrier raised during Valéry Giscard d'Estaing's presidency to 12.5 per cent of registered voters (which in the case of high abstention rates can have such a devastating effect that sometimes only one candidate is left on the battlefield).

This system, which contributed to the formation of what Maurice Duverger called 'the bipolar quadrille', reached the peak of its perfection in the late 1960s. But its constraints quickly appeared once it no longer fitted in with the new ideological, political and social tensions created by the 1968 crisis, de Gaulle's departure and changes in French society. With hindsight, the first indications could be seen in the presidential election of 1969, which became a contest between one candidate from the right and one from the centre, the left candidate having been eliminated. In addition, with no revision of the 1958 constituency boundaries, criticism of the distorted results of parliamentary elections became ever more heated. The left made a change to proportional representation its hobbyhorse.

In 1979, with the first direct elections to the European Parliament, the worm was introduced into the fruit by a curious coalition. Centrists, Socialists and Communists, tired of the smoothing-out effect of the two-round majority system being at their expense, were fairly favourable to proportional representation. The European Community institutions preferred proportional representation, used in all member states except Great Britain and France. The Gaullists, though in principle hostile to proportional representation, came round to supporting it because they wanted France to be a single constituency, so as to demonstrate the indivisibility and sovereignty of France. The introduction of proportional representation at the national level was the first breach in the majority-rule system. When the Socialists and Communists came

Table 4.1 Elections to the French National Assembly, 1958–2007

Year	Left	Communist PCF	Green V	Socialist SFIO/PS, MRG	Centrist MRP, PR/UDF		Gaullist RPR/UMP	Right FN	Other
1958	2	19	–	20	35		18	3	4
1962	2	22	–	20	23		32	1	–
1967	2	23	–	19	18		38	1	–
1968	4	20	–	17	15		44	0	–
1973	3	21	–	22	25		24	–	4
1978	3	21	–	28	20		26	–	3
1981	1	16	–	38	22		21	0	2
1986	2	10	–	32	–	42	–	10	5
1988	0	11	–	38	–	38	–	10	3
1993	1	9	10	19	–	38	–	13	10
1997	2	10	6	29	15		17	15	6
2002	3	5	6	27	5		43	12	6
2007	3	4	4	28	8		46	4	3

Note: Party vote is measured as a percentage of votes cast on first ballot.

Communist: PCF: French Communist Party (Parti Communiste Français).

Socialist: SFIO: French Section of Workers' International (Section Française de l'International Ouvrière). PS: Socialist Party (Parti Socialiste). MRG: Movement of Left Radicals (Mouvement des Radicaux de Gauche).

Centrist: MRP: Movement Republican Popular (Mouvement Républicain Populaire). PR: Republican Party (Parti Républicain). Since 1978 UDF: Union of French Democracy (Union de la Démocratie Française).

Gaullist and Conservative: RPR: Rally for the Republic (Rassemblement pour la République). From 1986 to 1993: Joint candidacies with the Centrists. UMP: Union of People's Movement (Union du Mouvement Populaire).

Right: FN: National Front (Front Nationale).

to power the dismantling continued. A (not very) proportional representation system was introduced for municipal elections, with prizes awarded to a list winning on the first or second round. The d'Hondt formula of proportional representation was introduced for parliamentary elections in 1985, but replaced again since 1986 with the single-member, two-round majority system. Proportional representation was introduced too for regional elections (with *départements* as constituencies). In sum, the Fifth Republic now possesses a full palette of extremely varied electoral rules that have not been without influence on the 'destructuring' of parties (the formation of wings and factions) and alliances. Elections thought to be 'with nothing at stake' (*sans enjeu*, that is, not deciding a country's general political orientation) increasingly resemble the United States' 'mid-term elections'. Voters, freed from some electoral constraints and more aware that one election does not change much, have adapted their voting behaviour. They vote more according to the political moment and the 'message' they want to convey than to an increasingly weak partisan allegiance. This new fluidity, the product of a more volatile electorate, less determined by social and cultural factors (class, religion), consisting of what have been called 'rational voters', has harmed the main parties and allowed new political forces to emerge. The Greens and the National Front were able to burst on to the electoral scene thanks to a combination of elections 'with nothing at stake' and electoral rules that have a less drastic effect on minor parties than the majority rule. The municipal elections of 1983 and 1989, the European elections of 1984 and 1989, and the regional and parliamentary elections of 1986 were occasions for these 'outsiders' to advance at the expense of the famous 'gang of four' (Communists, Socialists, Centrists and Gaullists). The apex of this versatility was reached during the last ten years. After having elected Chirac and a sweeping rightist majority in 1995 the French electorate voted *en masse* for the left in 1997 but sanctioned the Socialist Prime Minister Jospin in 2002 when he was placed third in the presidential race. However, the failure of the small parties of the extreme left, as well as of the National Front of Le Pen in 2007, and the overwhelming success of Sarkozy both in the presidential and parliamentary elections have a taste of déjà-vu about them. It is reminiscent of the 1962 situation, accentuating even further its features in terms of both presidentialisation of the regime and simplification of the party system.

Thus the electoral evolution of the Fifth Republic took a path of progressive bipolar restructuring of the Fourth Republic's fragmented parties and electorate. This was followed by a weakening towards crisis point of a system which had stabilised only on the surface. In 1988, for the first time under the Fifth Republic, the coalition in power did not obtain an absolute majority in parliament. It was unable to legislate or govern without recourse to the ingenious devices introduced by the authors of the Fifth Republic constitution in pursuit of 'rationalised parliamentarianism', a euphemism for 'limited parliamentarianism'.

Indifference and protest

Elections, as noted above, are undoubtedly necessary to the proper functioning of a democratic system, but not sufficient. Acknowledging that, in the absence of more appropriate methods, elections are one of the better means of expressing views, their validity depends both on the conditions and rules which govern them (e.g. voting methods, fairness) and on voter commitment.

The abstention rate is one way of measuring the acceptability of this process of expressing opinions. The abstention rate in France is always calculated in relation to registered voters. (In the United States, for example, it is measured in relation to potential voters.) Electoral registration is not mandatory (even though it is almost automatic in small towns), and it is estimated that almost 10 per cent of potential electors are not registered. Apart from this fringe of deliberate absentees from electoral participation, the number of abstainers is regarded as medium range. About a quarter of voters desert the ballot box in national elections, though the variation between elections is not negligible. The abstention rate can exceed 30 per cent when two elections are held close together and the second election is judged less important than the first (e.g. the parliamentary elections of 1962 and 1988 and 2007 when abstention reached 40 per cent). But it may fall to below 15 per cent (e.g. 13 per cent in the second round of the presidential election of 1974, and 14 per cent in 1981 and in 2007). On the other hand, participation is lower in department and municipal elections in large towns. Participation of registered voters in French elections is about average for Western democracies; it is much higher than in US national and local elections or in UK local elections, and comparable to the ones in Germany or Italy, where there is a tendency towards a general decline. Nevertheless, the most noteworthy phenomenon of recent years has been the tumbling of participation rates in by-elections, or in polls not perceived as important by the electorate. Only one-third of voters (encouraged to abstain by the right, it is true) participated in the referendum ratifying the Matignon agreements and the associated legislation on New Caledonia.

Further polls (regional elections and a referendum in 1992, parliamentary elections in March 1993, European elections in 1999 and local elections in 2001) show persistent abstention (about one-third of the electorate abstained), though without enabling us to talk about a real 'exit' phenomenon. Indifference or dissatisfaction with regard to government parties is also expressed in other ways: spoilt or blank ballot papers (nearly 1.5 million in 1993) and the dispersal of votes in favour of 'protest' parties (e.g. hunters, ecologists, the extreme right, regionalists). For instance, in March 1993 the 'government parties' received only two-thirds of the vote, whereas they attracted more than 80 per cent of voters in 1981, when the Communist Party still had a monopoly of 'protest', with 16 per cent of the votes.

But yet another characteristic typifies French political life: the periodic eruption of violence and protest that contradict or counterbalance choices expressed through the ballot box. Unlike societies which have succeeded in channelling violent social relations into institutions that translate them into peaceful, formal and symbolic forms (e.g. British adversarial politics), and unlike countries where violence is expressed less in the political arena than within society itself (American crime, Italian mafia), the French system has always experienced street demonstrations that bring pressure to bear on power. The peasant and urban revolts under the *ancien régime*, the *sans-culottes* of 1789, the Parisian uprisings of 1793, 1830, 1848 and 1871, the populist demonstrations of 1934, the workers' strikes of 1936, the 'political' strikes of 1947 and the Poujadists of the 1950s were similar expressions of what an American sociologist (J. Pitts) would describe as a 'delinquent community'.

The Fifth Republic does not escape the general rule. Governments from 1958 to 1991 were repeatedly confronted with explosions of temper as brutal as they were unpredictable, despite frequent elections and a generally supportive electorate. Some violent episodes had fundamental origins in the process of state reconstruction and decolonisation; for instance, France experienced endemic violence from 1955 to 1962 during the Algerian war. But bombs and assassination attempts have also peppered the rebellions of small nationalist groups in Corsica, Brittany and the Basque country. New Caledonia was on the verge of civil war from 1984 to 1988. In Réunion and the Antilles radical violence flared up suddenly, even though voters there continued to legitimise the mainland authorities over the years with electoral support which increased rather than declined.

As well as these national, nationalist or regionalist 'revolutions', sectional protest groups used violence in a more or less spontaneous way during strikes and demonstrations without it being organised or systematic. Farmers destroyed public buildings, and tradepeople and shopkeepers sacked local tax offices as a favourite way of expressing their demands. The erection of barricades in 1968 was part of this strategy, in which symbols and emotions are put to political use. There is now hardly any demonstration which does not end in ritual destruction and clashes with the police. How can these 'French passions' (Theodore Zeldin) be explained? Some observers locate the roots of the phenomenon in the way French people are socialised and educated. They argue that the French, subdued from childhood (within the family, at school) by a strong authority which does not allow discussion, can choose only between submission (passive obedience) and periodic revolt. This explanation has some salience. But other factors must undoubtedly be considered – for example incapacity or at least a poor capacity to organise group activity. Parties, unions and sectional interests have not been able to group their potential clientele into stable federations. The current fragmenting and weakening of the main ideological organisations has made the situation even more volatile. Nothing has replaced the framework once provided, for example, by the Church or by the Communist Party. The trade unions are incapable of mobilising their troops and, when discontent explodes, must adapt to the more or less confused and unrealistic demands of spontaneous 'co-ordination committees'.

Finally, the state shares responsibility for the brutal assaults it sometimes suffers. From the time of the monarchy until today interest groups have been unwelcome in 'the seraglio of power'. Groups are regarded as scarcely legitimate (since in principle only the elected are worthy) and held at a distance. In order to be heard they must often demonstrate their representativeness through noise and anger. Then we see the paradox of a state, initially haughty and disdainful, which does not negotiate with the mob, suddenly ready to concede anything and forgive anybody because there is no other way out of the *impasse*. The all-powerful state is replaced by the state ready to go to any lengths to re-establish social peace. Governments should learn from experience. But the phenomenon is repeated so often that it seems they do not. Social groups, on the other hand, have understood the lesson; they know violence pays and that it is more effective to smash shop windows than to participate in an official planning inquiry. One of the chief defects of the French political system is thus revealed: it is still able to offer its citizens only a choice between two equally unsatisfactory options: individual action (e.g. ignoring or circumventing regulations and conventions) or violent revolt, since adequate channels of communication at citizens' disposal are lacking.

POLITICAL PARTIES

The French party system is unusual among Western democracies. It is characterised by the fragility, instability and weakness of parties. This feature is not new or special to the Fifth Republic. But the 1958 institutions and the political events of the last forty years have given it a particular stamp.

The party system: decomposition and recomposition

Until the 1988 and 1990 Acts on the financing of political parties and electoral campaigns, parties had no special legal status. They were organised as ordinary associations under the 1901 Act, or even as *de facto* associations. They could easily fall within the category of organisations forbidden under this law or under the decree of 1936 outlawing groups that threatened the 'republican form of government'. Legal guarantees and financial resources were not conceded to some parties that might have deserved them on account of their influence. But parties have never been so weak, so incapable of hammering out programmes, mobilising activists or attracting the voters as they have been since the 1990s. Is this decline inexorable? Or are we coming to the end of a period of disintegration that heralds a restructuring of the French political landscape? No answer to the question is possible at the moment because the parties have been affected in the last forty years by such varying fortunes, including periods of decline followed by periods of popularity. Only one thing is certain: no party has been able to consolidate the gains or progress it has made at some points in its history.

Table 4.2 Left–right placement of parties in France

Communist PCF	Green V	Socialist PS	Democrat MD	People UMP	National FN
Left	Centre-left		Centre	Centre-right	Right

Party names:
PCF: French Communist Party (Parti Communiste Français).
V: Greens (Verts).
PS: Socialist Party (Parti Socialiste).
MD: Democratic Movement (Mouvement Démocratique) (ex-UDF).
UMP: Union of People's Movement (Union du Mouvement Populaire).
FN: National Front (Front National).

Source: As for Table 2.4.

The right: from Gaullist imperialism to fragmentation

In 1958 the Fourth Republic parties 'collaborated' in the construction of the new regime more or less enthusiastically – with the notable exception of the Communist Party, which showed almost complete hostility to General de Gaulle and his institutions. It was the right which rallied most vigorously to the colours of the new regime, but on the basis of a misunderstanding. It was persuaded, like the military and the French settler population of Algeria, that de Gaulle would retain Algeria within the bosom of mainland France. Besides, the reinforcement of the institutions in favour of the executive was bound to please an electorate attached to the values of order and authority. Nonetheless, Gaullism presented itself under its own flag and hit the bull's-eye in the parliamentary elections of 23 and 30 November 1958. The Gaullists (Union for the New Republic, UNR) obtained 20 per cent of the vote, while the National Centre of Independents and Peasants (CNIP) increased its share of the vote to 22 per cent, compared with 15 per cent in the 1956 elections. Thus the traditional right not only did not suffer from the emergence of Gaullism but made substantial gains from the electorate's shift to the right (the right obtained 56 per cent of the vote as against 46 per cent in 1956). However, the triumph of the traditional right did not last much beyond the period of domination over Algeria.

Electoral Gaullism was climbing irresistibly to power. The UNR and its allies obtained 36 per cent of the vote in 1962, whereas the CNIP vote collapsed (less than 10 per cent). In 1967, despite the majority parties' mediocre score, Gaullist candidates bearing the 'Fifth Republic' label maintained their share of the vote at 38 per cent. In the June 1968 'elections of fear' their score was unprecedented: 44 per cent of the vote. For the first time since World War II, one party, the Gaullists (by now called the Union of Democrats for the Republic, UDR), had obtained an absolute majority of seats. The right seemed, therefore, to have been comprehensively reconstituted, since extreme-right voters joined the Gaullists in favour of an amnesty for the last rebels of the Algerian war. Extreme-right candidates received a fraction of the vote: 0.13 per cent in 1968. The election of Georges Pompidou to the presidency in 1969 nibbled away part of the centre vote. This temporary triumph was short-lived, because the 1969 conservative advance tended to marginalise and then drive away part of the popular vote that de Gaulle had been able to attract and retain. The right risked becoming a minority, since to the defection of part of the electorate were added the internal conflicts of the 1974 presidential elections. Jacques Chirac headed a conspiracy in favour of Giscard d'Estaing and against Chaban-Delmas, the Gaullist candidate, dividing the electorate and the Gaullist movement. Having resigned his post as Prime Minister, Chirac succeeded in August 1976 in a take-over bid for the UDR, which became a powerful machine focused entirely on promoting him and his objective: winning the 1981 presidential election. From then on he was seen as the divider of the right, against Chaban-Delmas in 1974 and against Giscard d'Estaing in 1981. The bitterness aroused by this treasonable behaviour made it difficult for him to appear as the potential organiser of a federation of the right. What was more, the leaders of the parliamentary and presidential right were the accomplices and victims of the campaigns of a right-wing press that from 1981 to 1986 gave vent to the New Right's ideas and prepared the ideological ground for nationalists and an extreme right wing promoted by an outstanding orator, Jean-Marie Le Pen. However, by defeating or marginalising all potential challengers from the right (starting with competitors in his own party, such as Balladur), Chirac has remained the only winning card. In spite – or because – of his inability to govern after the parliamentary defeat of 1997 (following a misconceived dissolution on the initiative of Chirac himself), Chirac appeared as the only serious candidate capable of defeating his leftist opponent Lionel Jospin. But the 2002 presidential election took an unexpected and dramatic direction. Jospin lay behind Le Pen in the first round, leaving the French electorate with the worst possible scenario: a second round opposing Le Pen to Chirac, who won by 82 per cent of the votes but with weak political support in the country.

Helped too by the coincidental timing of elections 'with nothing at stake' (by-elections, local elections, European elections) and by the introduction of proportional representation, the extreme right, enlarged by populist protest, became solidly implanted, and represented 12–15 per cent of the electorate. During the 1990s, it constituted the third right-wing political force, and in large measure determined the political debate and the strategies of the Gaullist party (now the Realignment for the Republic, RPR) and the UDF. Although the National Front, like the French Communist Party (PCF) of the 1950s, was a party outside the system, it became, as the PCF did then, though in a different context, the ideological reference point in relation to which the other political parties positioned and defined themselves. The rapid growth of the National Front and its entry into the party system were striking illustrations of the fluidity and fragility of that system. In five years a small group was able to climb into the first rank of parties, almost on a level with the two large structures of the right and centre (the Gaullists and the UDF), and over-taking the PCF. The problem of the right-wing parties in power was to contain this growth and to try to win back lost voters. For many years they were unable to set up a clear strategy, hesitating between rejection and complacency. The National Front played this ambiguity to its advantage, surfing on the protest mood of the French electorate during the 1980s and 1990s. It even managed to come second in the first round of the 2002 presidential election by eliminating a very fragmented left from the second ballot.

It was only with Nicolas Sarkozy that the right was able to impose itself as a credible alternative. Without making any real concessions to the National Front's ideas, Sarkozy was able to convince the popular electorate (which for a large part were also former Communist or Socialist voters) that he could better deliver on issues such as law and order, immigration and unemployment. At both the presidential and parliamentary elections in 2007, the National Front was brought back to its level of twenty-five years ago. Combined with a leadership close to retirement (Le Pen is over 80 years old), this strategy might bring to an end the extreme right/populist interlude which has been so detrimental to the political system over the past twenty-five years.

The centre: in search of an indefinable identity

A centrist electorate exists. The centre has for thirty years provided political change by making the balance shift sometimes to the right and sometimes to the left. It forced de Gaulle into the second round of the presidential ballot in 1965, and in 1988 refused Mitterrand the benefit of an overall parliamentary majority. But this electorate is fickle and unstable, split between right-wing impulses and left-wing ideals. Its leaders (in parliament or in local government), unable to control it, try to steer (or follow) as best they can. Under the Fourth Republic the centre had managed to construct a relatively powerful party structure with the creation of the Republican Popular Movement (MRP), one of the three large forces produced by the Liberation period. But the MRP, despite the social concerns of its leaders, remained the prisoner of its more conservative electorate and dependent on the clerical–secular cleavage still so salient during the Fourth Republic. Even though the MRP was part of almost all government coalitions under the Fourth Republic, it only represented 11 per cent of the electorate at the dawn of the new republic in 1958, compared with 29 per cent and 26 per cent, respectively, in June and November 1946. It did not really gain from its support for General de Gaulle during the Algerian war, since its remaining electors were also attracted to the hero of 18 June 1940. When the MRP broke with de Gaulle over the European issue (May 1962) it was abandoned by part of its electorate, and its share of the vote fell to 9 per cent in the 1962 parliamentary elections.

In spite of the surprisingly high polling of the centrist candidate in the presidential election of 1965 (he obtained 4 million votes), and the centrist unexpected success in the presidential election of 1969, when the president of the Senate, Alain Poher, gained more votes than the left-wing candidates and went into the second round in competition with Georges Pompidou, the centre was never able to find a programme which would attract voters or to build an organisation worthy of a real party. Following the departure of General de Gaulle, centre politicians aligned themselves with the decision already expressed by a large part of the electorate and joined the right-wing camp. This process started with Pompidou, was completed during Giscard d'Estaing's presidency and confirmed with the Socialist victory. After the 1988 presidential election and Mitterrand's promise of an 'opening to the centre', centre politicians made some signals of reconciliation towards Michel Rocard. But faced with Mitterrand's unwillingness to engage in a formal alliance, operation 'Opening' was limited to the seduction of a few *notables* and the entry on to the scene of a few personalities (non-political), called 'representatives of civil society' especially for the occasion. In 2002, the leader of the centre, Bayrou, ran for the presidency, trying to challenge Chirac, but failed. His second try in 2007 was apparently more success-ful, attracting more than 18 per cent of the electorate during the first round of the presidential elections. However, this major breakthrough lasted no more than two weeks. His new party launched in the wave of this success won a mere 7.5 per cent of the vote in the first round of the parliamentary elections and only four MPs in the second round.

The left: from disunity to collapse

Although out of power from 1947 until the end of the Fourth Republic, the PCF remained the largest French party, a party with a relative majority that obtained more than one-quarter of the vote in 1956. Affected, like other parties, by the Gaullist tide, it obtained only 19 per cent of the vote in 1958, and, because of the change in the electoral system, its parliamentary representation fell to just ten deputies. But its declared hostility to Gaullism (despite some acknowledgement of the positive aspects of Gaullist foreign policy, notably the retreat from NATO's military command structure, the recognition of China and criticism of American policy in Vietnam) allowed it to maintain its position and 'capitalise' on discontent. Thus it obtained an average of 21 per cent of the vote during the period 1962–78. Until the parliamentary elections of 1973 the contrast with the Socialists (SFIO) or the Federation of the Democratic and Socialist Left (FGDS) was striking. The decline of the non-Communist left seemed unavoidable despite attempts at renewal and restructuring. The SFIO just managed to survive in 1958, thanks to its support of the constitution and its participation in de Gaulle's government, obtaining 15.5 per cent of the vote on 23 November 1958. But its subsequent opposition led it to fall back to 12.5 per cent on 18 November 1962. Efforts to reconstruct the radical and Socialist left, with the aid of political societies ('the clubs'), allowed it to climb back, encouraged especially by Mitterrand's unexpected score in the presidential election of 1965. The FGDS, founded by Mitterrand, obtained nearly 19 per cent of the vote in 1967 and so did creditably in comparison with the Communists. This federation was the result of the failure of the 'Grand Federation' initiated by Gaston Defferre in preparation for forthcoming presidential elections. In the minds of its promoters, its goals were to fight Gaullism and to set up a force comparable to, if not larger than, that of the PCF, by constructing a Democratic and Socialist Federation. The federation was supposed to bring together the SFIO Socialists, the radicals, Mitterrand's Convention of Republican Institutions (CIR) and the Christian Democrats (the MRP). But the opposition of Joseph Fontanet (MRP), who banned the term 'Socialist', and of Guy Mollet, who waved the banner of anticlericalism, wrecked the plan. Ambitions were lower when Mitterrand took up the torch again with his FGDS. Despite a programme published on 14 July 1966, the 'Little Federation', which excluded the Christian Democrats, was hardly more than an electoral alliance whose main advantage was to reduce the number of left-wing candidates. The 1967 elections were not a success in terms of votes but, thanks to the new discipline, allowed the left to gain fifteen more seats than in 1962. However, the SFIO did not want to go further with federation. The final blow was dealt to the FGDS by the 'events' of May (from which it was absent, except for Mitterrand's unfortunate declaration of 28 May 1968, announcing his candidature for a presidential post which was not available). The radicals left the federation, and Mitterrand resigned in November 1968. The old left was once more divided and weakened, while the Communist Party maintained its position. But the Communist and non-Communist left were both being harried by organisations calling themselves radical, even revolutionary, that took off during the May 'events': the Unified Socialist Party (PSU), created in 1960 by 'the new left', which fought

Gaullism but was not willing to join the PCF or by the SFIO of Guy Mollet; and Trotskyites and Maoists.

Discussions about re-approaching the 'clubs' and the SFIO started again at the end of 1968. Personal and institutional disagreements remained so strong that the Socialist Party (PS) created at Alfortville represented the betrothal of a lame duck (the SFIO) and a scraggy lark (the Union of Socialist Groups and Clubs (UGCS) of Alain Savary). Gaston Defferre was designated as presidential candidate. It was a descent into hell for the non-Communist left, whose candidate obtained 5 per cent of the vote, against 21 per cent for the Communist candidate. From these ruins it was at least possible for Mitterrand to come back with some force to propose his idea of what the party should be and what political strategy it should follow.

The Epinay congress of 11–13 June 1971 set Socialists faithful to the 'old party', grouped round Savary, against the mixed bunch who wanted a new party (without being agreed on its content or arrangements). Mitterrand defended the idea of an alliance with the PCF that would permit a rebalancing of the two families of the left. The task seemed difficult because, in contrast to the Socialists, who had foundered in 1969, the PCF had maintained its position. It had reaped the benefit of the socio-economic strife of 1969 and improved its image by distancing itself from the USSR (condemning the Soviet invasion of Czechoslovakia in August 1968) and by accepting the principle of pluralism and alternating governments should it be elected. Despite their differences, the Socialist Party and the Communist Party reached an agreement on 16 June 1972, signing a 'Common Programme of Government'. At the same moment, left-wing radicals separated from the Radical Party of Jean-Jacques Servan-Schreiber, formed in January 1973 the Movement of Left Radicals (MRG), which, in its turn, signed the Common Programme.

Fifteen years after the inauguration of the Fifth Republic, twenty-six years after the post-World War II split, fifty-three years after the foundation of the Communist Party at the Congress of Tours, the left seemed to be on the way to turning the old myth of 'the reunification of the working-class movement' into reality. The 1973 elections did not completely fulfil the hopes invested in this venture, but the pump was primed. The Socialists obtained 19 per cent of the vote, against 21 per cent for the PCF. This early progress received a strong boost at the time of the presidential election, when Mitterrand, sole candidate of the left, was only just over 400,000 votes behind Giscard d'Estaing (less than 1 per cent of voters). At the Assembly of Socialism of October 1974 this success led to the further incorporation into the PS of parts of its outlying fringes (the PSU and the French Democratic Confederation of Labour, CFDT). Michel Rocard, Robert Chapuis and a few thousand activists joined the PS despite the reservations of a final stubborn group which kept the PSU going, come what may. But the PCF found the Union of the Left no help, whereas the PS and Mitterrand reaped the reward of their strategy. In particular, in the local elections of spring 1977 the PS and the MRG advanced and profited more than did the PCF from the gains of the united left (58 towns of over 30,000 inhabitants were won by the left, 35 of which were run by Socialists). The Communist Party used the updating of the Common Programme, which it especially wanted and which was justified by the change in economic conditions (the 1973 oil crisis), to raise its price, demanding that the nationalisation programme should be considerably expanded.

The break-up of the Union occurred on 23 September 1977. The 1978 elections did not seem to punish this new divide, since the PCF still obtained 21 per cent of the vote and the PS–MRG alliance gathered 25 per cent. Nevertheless the division and quarrels within the left contributed to the achievement of the governmental majority.

With hindsight it was clear the small decrease in the PCF vote was in fact the beginning of its descent into hell, punishment for a party incapable of adapting to the new realities, a party which remained Stalinist in numerous aspects of its internal functioning and its policy decisions. From now on, all the PCF's efforts to get out of its downward spiral only accelerated its fall, whereas the PS swept from victory to victory. The PCF share of the vote fell to 15 per cent in June 1981, to 11 per cent in the European elections in 1984, to 10 per cent in the parliamentary elections of 1986 and to 7 per cent in the first round of the presidential elections in 1988. At the beginning of the 1990s the PCF share of the vote was stable at about 10 per cent, very much behind the PS and overtaken by the National Front, but fell again in spite of the efforts of its new leader, Robert Hue. Not only has the PCF by now been superseded by the Greens, it is also challenged by the extreme-left parties, which together obtain a larger share of the vote than the PCF. Over the same period the PS–MRG, bolstered by its leader's triumph, achieved 37.5 per cent of the vote and won an absolute majority of seats in 1981. Even when defeated in 1986 it still attracted 32 per cent of the vote. It climbed to 35 per cent in 1988, missing an absolute majority by a few seats. Although the PCF agreed in 1981 to associate itself with the Mauroy government (it obtained only four ministerial posts), the exercise of power was no more helpful to it than opposition had been. Obliged to swallow the indignities of the austerity programme, it finally withdrew from the Fabius government in July 1984, which enabled it to criticise the Socialists' management more strongly. But the repercussions were not only electoral. The PCF lost its activists (its intellectuals, for the most part, had left much earlier), its local bastions and thus its logistical and financial support. Georges Marchais, famous for his television performances, became no more than a sad clown whose comments were scarcely of interest, they seemed so out of touch. In the past, the PCF either seduced or frightened. It no longer attracts voters, and excites at best indifference among its opponents. Instead, the Socialist Party, after the 1993 *débâcle*, managed to recover strongly in part because of the policies and mistakes of Chirac and of his Prime Minister Alain Juppé. Even more than in 1981, the 1997 victory of the Left coalition was a 'divine surprise'.

During the five years of cohabitation, the leftist government achieved many good economic and social results but failed to renew its programme and to convince its allies to rally behind Jospin as the candidate of a united left in the 2002 presidential elections. The extreme dispersion of left votes put Jospin in third position behind Le Pen. In spite of this defeat, neither the PS nor the PCF drew lessons from this bitter experience. The PS, under the chairmanship of François Hollande, tried to hide its ideological crisis and its internal divisions. They were exacerbated further by the deep division created by the referendum on the constitutional Treaty in May 2005. The left of the party, led by Laurent Fabius, chose to vote 'no' while the rest opted for 'yes'. While managing to reconcile these contradictions on the surface, the

PS found itself without a natural leader for the presidential elections. Primaries were, for the first time, organised, leading to the unexpected victory of Ségolène Royal; for the first time a woman was chosen as a presidential candidate but this major innovation was not enough to compensate for the political, organisational and ideological crisis of the party. Once more the Socialist Party had to start from scratch in order to adjust to the changes of the time. Its good fortune and at the same time its weakness is that it remains the only party of government on the left. The extreme left has no hope of gaining power and the PCF is unable to change and to learn from events (such as gaining a miserable 2 per cent of the vote at the presidential elections in 2007). This is all the more challenging for parties of the left, which permanently represent less than 50 per cent of the electorate and which can expect to win under only two conditions: a divided right and/or the capacity to attract part of the centre-left electorate.

Institutional constraints

It was thought for a long time that voting and institutional constraints (the two-round ballot system and the corresponding bipolar choice in the presidential election) had brought about a simplification of political life and imposed discipline and reorganisation on the parties. In other words, these constraints were supposed to have had a beneficial effect in encouraging the parties to reform themselves. There was some evidence in support of this analysis until the 1970s. However, the argument neglected the impact of two leaders, very different but both of exceptional stature, de Gaulle and Mitterrand. With one of them dead and the other placed in an institutional position which did not allow him to play the role of party leader, the centrifugal forces increased, under the very same influence of the rules of the constitutional game. What in practice is the fundamental goal that is at stake? It is the presidential election, which encourages, as it ought, the competition of those who think, rightly or wrongly, that a 'national destiny' awaits them. This competition first arises inside the parties, if several leaders seem to have the makings of a future President (e.g. as suggested by opinion polls). It results in the exacerbation of personal conflict, factional strife, strategies and alliances whose contribution to party division is increased the more outside factors (e.g. popularity ratings, media comment) intervene. For a presidential election to reinforce the parties, two conditions – not present in France – should be fulfilled: there should be two main parties only, and candidates should be subject to selection, whether in public (as in the United States) or inside the parties. In the absence of these conditions the parties themselves become the goal at stake and the site of great, and sometimes absurd, battles. French parties, born in a parliamentary context, class-related, ideologically based, do not fit well into such a scheme. General de Gaulle was right: the head of state of the Fifth Republic needed a gathering or realignment of the people, not a party. The posthumous revenge of the founder of the Fifth Republic is that the institutions born in 1958 have not, contrary to what was first thought, restructured or founded a modern party system.

That is why the party 'crisis' of the 1980s was not a short-term incident. Although it was masked for a long time by presidential charisma and by the constraints of the electoral system, the crisis is now obvious. The progressive modification of institutional constraints from the 1980s (the changes in electoral systems) did not cause these transformations. But it revealed and promoted them. Until 1979 the homogeneity of the electoral system was total. The two-round ballot majority system was used for all types of elections, from municipal ones to the presidential election. After 1979 a combination of elections 'with nothing fundamental at stake' and a diversity of electoral rules offered new opportunities to voters and groups that had hitherto been marginalised. With the fall of the Berlin Wall, the collapse of ideologies, the growth of new challenges (the environment, immigration and the demands of ethnic minorities), the French parties became like their European equivalents, i.e. in crisis. But the crisis is more deadly in France because French parties have never constituted the backbone of the political system.

The 2002 and 2007 presidential elections confirm this point. In 2002, the left lost because of an excessive fragmentation and Chirac won mainly because the electorate was put in the impossible position of having to choose between him and Le Pen. In 2007, Sarkozy's victory was not only the result of his programme and charisma. For the first time since the beginning of the Fifth Republic, the dominant party of the right was able to vote and choose the candidate. The same happened within the Socialist Party, where a 'beauty contest' was set up in order to choose the candidate from amongst the 'elephants' (the faction leaders). For the first time, here too, the candidate was chosen by the party on the basis of a real competition. It is still too soon to say if these changes are provisional or if they are an indirect consequence of the limiting of the presidential mandate to five years, a change which accentuates, furthermore, the presidentialisation of the system and might have an impact on the leader/party relationship.

PARLIAMENT

Rules and discipline

Parliament under the Fourth Republic, despite a few constitutional provisions soon ignored, was a parliament, it could be said, 'having neither faith nor law' (*sans foi, ni loi*). It violated even the clearest constitutional provisions with impunity, played ducks and drakes with others, manipulated electoral laws, annulled the election of candidates who displeased it (in 1956 the Poujadists), passed special laws (the state of emergency) and brought discredit on itself with its budgetary procedures, capricious motions of censure and its impotence even in the election of the President of the Republic. Since it controlled the agenda and was in charge of its own sittings and committee organisation, the Fourth Republic parliament had in fact considerable freedom of action – or, rather, licence. It is scarcely surprising that the founding fathers of the Fifth Republic wanted to react against this state of affairs. Yet it is surprising that later commentators should have measured the decline of parliament under the Fifth Republic by the standards of this model.

The Fifth Republic parliament is undeniably subject to severe restrictions that were applied (with excessive zeal) from the beginning. Constitution designer Michel Debré's basic premise – which proved to be erroneous – was that the numerous deep cleavages across France made it impossible to aggregate opinions and votes around a majority pole on one side and around an opposition pole on the other (as in Great Britain). What 'nature' could not offer had therefore to be brought about through 'artifice', i.e. rigid rules defining the function of parliament. In this respect the constitution effected a true revolution by comparison with the two previous republics, because it constrained parliament within strict limits:

1 Parliamentary sittings were reduced to two ordinary sessions of about three months each, which were not modified to a nine-month single session until 1995.
2 The assemblies' standing orders had to be approved by the Constitutional Council, making encroachments contrary to the letter and spirit of the constitution difficult.
3 The government controlled the agenda and the organisation of debates.
4 The number of standing committees was reduced to six, each really a 'mini-parliament' ill suited to effective consideration and amendment.
5 The range of parliamentary intervention is limited by Articles 34 and 37, which fix 'the domain of law' (areas in which parliament is free to legislate) and 'the domain of regulations' (issued by the executive), where parliament cannot intervene.
6 The financial powers of parliament are limited by Article 40, which declares out of order any Bill or amendment entailing a decrease in public revenue or an increase in expenditure.
7 Controls over the government (motions of confidence or censure) can be applied only according to strict provisions laid down in Articles 49 and 50.
8 Finally, multiple procedural provisions further reinforce the government's position by giving the executive a panoply of means to bypass or reduce parliamentary obstacles, for example the 'package' vote, and the government's power to declare that a vote on a particular text will be treated as a motion of confidence.

The 'rationalisation' of parliament, the expression most commonly used to describe and justify these reforms, has been much written about and has attracted innumerable criticisms. Yet the reforms are hardly original, since they are merely an importation of British parliamentary procedures. The scandal is in the contrast with the preceding 'golden age of parliament' and in the way the procedures were applied by the first rulers of the Fifth Republic. The constitutional provisions were severe but their application was even more so (Suleiman 1986).

In fact the executive was helped in its task, particularly by public opinion and by the judgements of the Constitutional Council. The government's task was facilitated politically by the disrepute parliament earned under the Fourth Republic, a reputation carefully nurtured by the political leaders of the Fifth.

Furthermore, the humiliation of parliament was the result of parliamentary 'self-flagellation'. In effect, the reduction in the parliament's power would not have been so steep and sustained had members of parliament not lent a hand. Two factors within parliament contributed to reinforcing the ascendancy of the executive at the expense of the National Assembly in particular. First, training in majority-party discipline – a phenomenon unknown in France before the Fifth Republic – was accomplished in almost military style, MPs accepting without a murmur the governmental edicts passed down by party managers. Second, parliament marginalised itself, reducing itself almost to the role of rubber stamp through members' poor professionalism and high absenteeism.

What is parliament for? Representation, decision-making and control

The representative function

Parliament is composed of two chambers: the National Assembly and the Senate, which in a unitary system seems constitutionally bizarre. Why seek representation through two chambers? It either risks pointless conflict or leads to a large consensus. The explanation owes nothing to the rules of democracy but much to the liberal political tradition. If the power to check constitutes one of the essential components of a liberal regime, then the second chamber's main justification is in moderating the excesses of the lower chamber.

Though this counterbalancing principle is so ingrained that it is now hardly ever discussed, the Senate's unrepresentative character is a sword of Damocles suspended over this venerable institution. Senators are indirectly elected by an electoral college made up of some 80,000 'grand electors' (mostly directly elected local government councillors); thus the democratic element is extremely attenuated. Its principal merit in a system of concentrated power like the Fifth Republic remains that of 'checking'. No doubt it is this characteristic that makes the Senate 'untouchable' despite its weak representativeness. Its strength derives mainly from the fact that it has become the voice of the most influential lobby in France: the local communities (in particular communes and departments). However, it is rather shocking that due to its mode of selection the Senate has been a bastion of the right consistently since 1958.

The representativeness of the National Assembly is incontestably superior, even though it is imperfect, whether from a political or a sociological point of view. Politically it is undeniable that the single-member, two-round majority system does not answer perfectly the requirements of representation. It is a 'French speciality', other democracies preferring proportional systems (with the exception in Europe of the United Kingdom, which uses a one-round plurality system). Since 1958 no parliamentary majority has been based on a majority of votes (this was also the case in 1986 after the Socialists had introduced a very disproportional proportional system). In addition, the minor parties are barred from the second round by a high 'exclusion threshold' (currently 12.5 per cent of the electorate), and the middle-ranking parties are under-represented if they have not concluded electoral pacts. Two examples suffice to illustrate the extent of this under-representation, in particular for the parties positioned in the extreme corners of the political chessboard. In 1958 the PCF, which received 19 per cent of the vote, won only ten seats, while the Gaullist National Union for the Republic (UNR), which received 18 per cent of the vote in the first round, won 207 seats thanks to votes transferred in the second round. In 1993 the National Front, with 12.5 per cent of the vote, obtained no seats, while the UDF, whose score was only 50 per cent higher (19 per cent of the vote), acquired 206 deputies. These inequalities in representation have been aggravated by the constituency map, both because constituency boundaries have been gerrymandered and because demographic disparities have increased over the years. Even though the new constituency boundaries drawn in 1987 removed the most blatant discrepancies the situation remains imperfect, as the results of the 1988 elections illustrate. The PS and the Movement of Left Radicals (MRG) almost won an absolute majority (they lacked a mere thirteen seats), though they obtained altogether only 36 per cent of the vote in the first round. In 1993 the right, with 37 per cent of the vote in the first round, made a clean sweep with 448 seats. The phenomenon was repeated in 1997, 2002 and 2007.

The decision-making function

Governments have always been active in the drawing up of legislation, but the weakness of the French parliament appeared in all its depth when it proved incapable not only of drawing up legislative proposals but even of simply approving them. This incapacity led to governments under the Third Republic turning to 'decree laws', and under the Fourth Republic to 'framework laws': a symbolic case of theoretical omnipotence emerging as practical impotence.

Nevertheless, honour was saved, because infringements of the theoretical and legal use of orders were presented as exceptions or violations. The Fifth Republic was considered scandalous when it claimed to put the clock right, i.e. to reconcile law with practice: in other words, to recognise the important role of the administration and government in drawing up legislation, to constitutionalise and thus to legitimise what had been seen until then as errors or stop-gap procedures. But this endeavour (Articles 34 and 37 of the constitution) proved fruitless, since it too was founded upon a utopian premise: the belief that it was possible to draw a line between the important and the secondary, the principle and the application, the fundamental and the subsidiary.

The best illustration of the ambiguity of parliamentary decision-making powers is without doubt the procedure for issuing regulations in Article 38, which is the constitutional codification of the practice of 'decree laws'. As with 'decree laws', the use of regulations (*ordonnances*) removes almost all power from parliament, since the ratification process is reduced to the tabling of a Bill that is never discussed, and the content of regulations is only vaguely defined in the relevant enabling law. However, this dismal observation should be balanced by a reminder that enabling laws have never been numerous, they have not always been used effectively, the Constitutional Council's control over their use is increasingly vigilant and, finally, parliament still has a right to amend regulations. More important, the use of *ordonnances* often demonstrates a sort of 'tribute of vice to virtue', since it could be said that governments of the Fifth Republic have used regulations even when they had majority support in parliament, because parliamentary debate is not as ineffective or as second rate as it is sometimes portrayed to be. If parliamentary power – and the mobilisation of opinion that debates can produce – was as futile as is claimed, the use of regulations would be unnecessary.

It is doubtless in budgetary and financial matters, and in foreign policy, that parliament's powers have been weakened most dramatically. Not only does the constitution forbid parliament to increase costs or decrease public revenue, but the government is reluctant to accept proposals affecting its own plans, even when they imply no extra cost, or would bring in extra revenue in ways unacceptable to the Minister of Finance. This curtailment of parliamentary powers is considerable by comparison with both a parliamentary regime like Italy and a presidential one like the United States, where the assemblies have sizeable prerogatives over revenue and expenditure.

Although the government has more room for manoeuvre than parliament (e.g. decrees for bringing forward or annulling expenditure, a 'freeze' on budgets, or staged implementation), it too has limited freedom, because it exercises real choice over an estimated 5 per cent of the budget at most. Moreover, when members of parliament resist, they can make themselves heard: the explanation of generous central government grants to local authorities is not simply central government generosity. The inextricable jungle of local taxation is partly due to multiple amendments of budgetary and other laws by elected national representatives acutely conscious of their local interests. Recently, a Bill was passed which, while modernising the budgetary process to make it more efficient, allows parliament more freedom for intervention and control. In addition, for the first time under the Fifth Republic, Nicolas Sarkozy has announced that the Budget and Finance Committee Chair will be offered to the opposition.

The role of parliament in foreign policy is even more marginal. At best parliament is called upon to ratify *faits accomplis*, though certain members (notably the chairs of the Foreign Affairs and Defence Committees) are rather better informed about decisions. Under the Fifth Republic this 'presidential reserved domain' was shared only slightly with the Prime Minister during the periods of *cohabitation* (1986–8, 1993–5 and 1997–2002), though the competition between Mitterrand and Chirac or Chirac and Jospin did not profit parliament. On the contrary, majority and opposition both seemed paralysed by the fear of causing their respective leaders problems. Neither the policy of *détente* nor the withdrawal from NATO's command structure, neither the Franco-German reconciliation nor the Franco-American skirmishes were inspired by or decided in parliamentary debate. Parliament was at best a forum for criticism or approval of a decision that had been taken or a line that had already been decided. On this point as on others the Mitterrand republic hardly differed from the Gaullist republic, as the 'management' of public opinion during the Gulf War of January–February 1991 showed. Parliamentary debate was reduced to its simplest form, representatives of the parliamentary groups being kept regularly informed by the Prime Minister. On the other hand, there were at least eleven televised interventions by the head of state between August 1990 and February

1991. Parliament is without doubt the first victim of the 'rule by the media' that has taken over in Western democracies.

The control function

Unquestionably it is in its controlling function that parliament has adapted least well to the needs of the time, in particular under the Fifth Republic. Parliamentary control over the government can take several forms. It can be purely partisan, that is, voiced by the opposition. Its function is to criticise government activity, to condemn abuses or violations of the law and to counter with its own policy proposals. This type of 'control' may attract attention, but it is effective only under some conditions: when the government is supported by a heterogeneous group of members, with a bare minimum or no absolute majority; or when the opposition mobilises public opinion sufficiently to force the government to withdraw under the combined pressure of internal forces (within parliament) and external forces (in the streets). These conditions have not been rare under the Fifth Republic. But in strictly constitutional terms this 'control' is considered an empty threat since, 'by definition', the majority supports the government.

A second type of control, considered in the classic typology as 'control with a penalty', involves the transformation of the parliamentary landscape: a significant section of the majority party (or parties) decides to cross the Rubicon and vote for a motion of censure put down by the opposition. If the motion secures the majority required under the constitution the government is forced to resign, and the President must decide whether to proceed to a dissolution of parliament and put the question to the electorate. This type of control is drastic. In the constitutional field it is like nuclear arms against conventional weapons: in theory it has a dissuasive effect, but it could not be used often without destabilising the system. The Fifth Republic illustrates this situation very well: one government only, that of Georges Pompidou, was brought down, when a section of the parliamentary majority broke ranks with General de Gaulle in 1962. The consequences (dissolution of the National Assembly and elections won by de Gaulle's supporters) show without question that the executive's power of dissuasion (dissolution) is more powerful than parliament's power of dissuasion (a vote of censure). While these techniques are still used in certain fragmented parliamentary regimes (Belgium, the Netherlands, Israel), elsewhere they tend increasingly to be stored away with other constitutional antiques. One cannot conceive of a parliamentary regime without them, but at the same time there is little illusion about their impact.

There remains a third method of control, quieter and more subtle, which does not belong wholly to the majority or to the opposition. It requires much energy, perseverance and know-how on the part of parliamentarians. It consists of detailed, thorough and precise checking of the activities of government and its administration. The ways and means are infinite: oral and written questions, oral questions with debate, committees of inquiry or of control, special inquiries, reports, hearings and so on. But in all these cases partisanship has to be put aside, or at least reduced, in favour of an honest, critical and comprehensive investigation. Needless to say, that is not easy in a parliamentary regime, where the system is based on the institu-tionalisation of difference: the government, with its majority, governs; the opposition criticises. It is unsurprising, therefore, that the country where this method of control functions most intensively is the United States, where there is no clear, stable bound-ary between majority and opposition (majority and opposition determine themselves by varying continuously from vote to vote).

It is this absence of checks, more than anything else, that makes governments so powerful, particularly under the Fifth Republic. Too often the premium is on the *fait accompli* in the knowledge that control will be non-existent or ineffectual.

PRESIDENT AND GOVERNMENT: THE 'REPUBLICAN MONARCHY'

Two elements contributed to making the head of state of the Fifth Republic the 'republican monarch' that Michel Debré outlined at the time of the Liberation, under the pseudonym of Jacquier-Bruère: the constitution itself and the use subsequently made of it. At that time the length of the mandate (seven years) was considered as an element of this quasi-monarchical presidency. However, under pressure from the media and from an heterogeneous coalition (including Giscard d'Estaing and the Socialists) Chirac, who had declared himself hostile to the '*quinquennat*' the year before, had to swallow it rather than be defeated. After the reform adopted by a rather indifferent people on 2 October 2000 the presidential mandate was reduced to five years.

The principle: the constitution, the whole constitution, and nothing but the constitution

The President of the Fifth Republic benefits from a twofold advantage by comparison with the canons of classical constitutional law: the President has in some respects the advantages and privileges of the head of state in a *presidential* system; in other respects he enjoys the prerogative powers of a head of state in a *parliamentary* system. This ambiguous combination of roles ensures for French Presidents their unique powers, simultaneously giving them complete political irresponsibility and the strength to make decisions and pressure other constitutional bodies. Placed at the summit of a parliamentary regime, the head of state, as tradition expects, appoints the Prime Minister and, jointly with the Prime Minister, appoints ministers. The head of state can address messages to both houses but, in conformity with 'republican tradition', cannot speak direct to parliamentarians from within the chamber. He may dissolve the National Assembly, and appoints three members of the Constitutional Council, including its president. To these powers belonging specifically to the President are added those shared with the Prime Minister and government, in particular the signing of regulations and decrees, appointments to various civilian and military posts, as well as all measures decided in the Council of Ministers. There are no surprises hidden in this brief list of the principal powers accorded by the constitution: they descend in a direct line from the parliamentary tradition of the nineteenth century.

Table 4.3 Presidents of France, 1958–2007

Election	Year	President	Party support
1	1958	C. de Gaulle	Gaullists, Centrists
2	1965	C. de Gaulle	Gaullists, Centrists
3	1969	G. Pompidou	Gaullists, Centrists
4	1974	V. Giscard d'Estaing	Centrist republicans, Gaullists
5	1981	F. Mitterrand	Socialists, Communists
6	1988	F. Mitterrand	Socialists
7	1995	J. Chirac	Gaullists, Centrists
8	2002	J. Chirac	Gaullists, Centrists
9	2007	N. Sarkozy	Conservatives, Independents

Note: The first party indicates the President's affiliation.

But added to this first list are several prerogative powers not often awarded to a head of state under a classic parliamentary regime. Under Article 11 the President can call a referendum on the proposal of the government or the two assemblies. On the other hand, only the President can avoid a referendum on reform of the constitution by deciding to submit it to the two assemblies meeting in congress. If there arises a serious and immediate threat to 'the institutions of the Republic, the independence of the nation, the integrity of its territory or the fulfilment of its international obligations', and if there is an interruption in the regular functioning of the constitutional public authorities, Article 16 gives the President full powers and makes him a temporary 'legal dictator'. In the light of this extraordinary provision, without parallel in other Western constitutions, the powers in Article 15 (the President of the Republic is the head of the armed forces) and in Article 52 (the President of the Republic negotiates and ratifies treaties) are almost a relief. Like the President of the United States, the President of the French Republic is all-powerful in the ordering of peace and war, of weapons and diplomacy.

The 1958 constitution is thus ambiguous or, rather, ambivalent in its terms. It leaves ample margin for manoeuvre to politicians (who are not deprived of something to bicker over) and interpreters (who are not deprived of something to expound upon). In addition this baroque structure is crowned by Article 5, which solemnly opens Section II, devoted to the powers of the President of the Republic. This provision, which ought in principle to clarify and underpin the group of technical provisions that follow, has with experience provided an 'obscure clarity'. It has unleashed political passions and given rise to a thousand and one interpretations. The President of the Republic, proclaims the article, endeavours to ensure respect for the constitution. He provides, by his arbitration, for the regular functioning of the public authorities as well as the continuity of the state. He is the guarantor of the independence of the nation, of the integrity of its territory, of respect for Community agreements and treaties. There have been endless quarrels over the semantics among politicians, legal experts and political scientists about the word 'arbiter'. Some people, referring to legal tradition or sport, insist on the *neutrality* inherent in the function of arbitration. Others, especially de Gaulle's supporters, appeal to etymology and invoke the Latin word *arbitrium*, which implies the power to decide in an

Table 4.4 Governments of France, 1958–2007

Legislature No.	Year	Prime Minister	Party composition
1	1958	C. de Gaulle	Gaullists, Centrists
	1959	M. Debré	Gaullists, Centrists
2	1962	G. Pompidou	Gaullists, Centrists
3	1967	G. Pompidou	Gaullists, Centrists
4	1968	M. Couve de Murville	Gaullists, Centrists
	1969	J. Chaban-Delmas	Gaullists, Centrists
	1972	P. Messmer	Gaullists, Centrists
5	1973	P. Messmer	Gaullists, Centrists
	1974	J. Chirac	Gaullists, Centrists
	1976	R. Barre	Centrists, Gaullists
6	1978	R. Barre	Centrists, Gaullists
7	1981	P. Mauroy	Socialists, Communists
	1984	L. Fabius	Socialists
8	1986	J. Chirac	Gaullists, Centrists
9	1988	M. Rocard	Socialists
	1991	E. Cresson	Socialists
	1992	P. Bérégovoy	Socialists
10	1993	E. Balladur	Gaullists, Centrists
	1995	A. Juppé	Gaullists, Centrists
11	1997	L. Jospin	Socialists, Communists, Greens, Radicals, Citizens
12	2002	J. Raffarin	Gaullists, Centrists
13	2005	D. de Villepin	Gaullists, Centrists
14	2007	F. Fillon	Conservatives, Centrists

Note: The first party indicates the Prime Minister's affiliation.

autonomous manner (as in the expression *libre arbitre*, free will). But, in the end (in the absence of a *real* constitutional referee), the meaning of Article 5 was decided and imposed by the holder of the post, in particular by the first of them, General de Gaulle. The definition of presidential power results as much from the way it is exercised as from the constitutional text itself. It has been said that the constitution was tailored to fit de Gaulle. In certain respects this assertion cannot be denied. But, essentially, the clothes have taken shape with use, as the experience of *cohabitation* from 1986 to 1988, from 1993 to 1995 and from 1997 to 2002, in a contrary way, demonstrated.

The practice: the use of the constitution

In contrast to the United Kingdom, whose constitution consists not of a single, solemn document but of a multitude of texts, laws, traditions and 'conventions', France is very attached to the idea of a written, solemn, rigid constitution – so rigid that if the constitution is unable to deal with some problem or other there is a change in the regime and a new constitution is adopted that supposedly deals with the questions not resolved by the preceding version. However, this childhood illness of French constitutionalism has had a few periods of remission, of which the most important and most famous was the Third Republic. Recently, a more pragmatic approach has prevailed and many constitutional changes have been introduced through amendments approved either by popular referendum or parliamentary vote.

The Gaullist interpretation and use of institutions are thus not novel. They demonstrate evidence of the capacity for institutions to be transformed by convention. From 1958 on, the impetus for change was in the hands of the head of state, as interpreter and actor, with the more or less tacit support of the conservative majority, and a left-wing opposition that was critical but ambushed by the hornets' nest of Algeria. Thus the Gaullist transformation of the constitution was made possible by a combination of favourable elements: exceptional circumstances, the complicity of government and majority, and the lack of any constitutional body to condemn violations or one-sided interpretations of the constitution. The rebellion of the majority in 1962, when the Algerian War was over, could have closed one period and one type of application of the constitution. The more or less implicit consensus was broken. But in submitting the constitutional and political issues to the judgement of people (the referendum on changing the constitution to introduce the election of the head of state by universal suffrage; the dissolution of the National Assembly and the elections of 11 and 18 November 1962) de Gaulle made the electors the judges of the legal case. By giving twice, and massively, the approval de Gaulle requested, the electors ratified past constitutional practices and the conventions which until that time had benefited from majority, but not unanimous, support. In July 1981 the number-one opponent of Gaullism, François Mitterrand, had just been elected President when he ratified Gaullist presidentialism, adopting it for himself: 'The institutions were not made for me, but they suit me very well'. After Pompidou (which was hardly surprising), after Giscard d'Estaing (despite denouncing in 1967 'the sole exercise of power'), François Mitterrand in his turn put on the seven-league boots.

Who could resist such temptation? The head of state's powers are *indefinable* because literally *indefinite*, without finite limits. This thesis was demonstrated by its antithesis when the right, led by Jacques Chirac, won the 1986 and the 1993 parliamentary elections, as well as in 1997, when the left, led by Lionel Jospin, won, always against the incumbent President. In all cases, the President suffered a serious loss of power. With the end of parliamentary support the powers of the head of state underwent a severe redesign process. As Mitterrand conceded in a televised interview on 2 March 1986, 'No one imposes conditions on the President of the Republic. He appoints whom he wants to. But he must do it in conformity with popular will.' He could theoretically submit an issue to a referendum, but the government or parliament would have had first to propose it to him. He could summon parliament to an extraordinary session, but only at the request of either the Prime Minister or the majority of National Assembly members. He could continue to nominate people to civil or military posts, but only with the Prime Minister's counter-signature. In short, the all-powerful monarch's unbounded domain was reduced in this new political context to the defined space which the constitution assigns explicitly to the President without imposing special conditions, i.e. the right of dissolution, the right to nominate three members of the Constitutional Council, and especially Article 16, the formidable prerogative which stops a responsible government reducing the President's military and diplomatic prerogatives to purely formal powers. This last area was the only issue on which the Chirac government did not systematically keep the President at a distance (in other areas he increased the number of cabinet meetings chaired by the Prime Minister which the President did not attend, and restricted the minutes of meetings, which have to be sent to the President, to their essential points). The experiment of *cohabitation* has been particularly fascinating in this issue, with its inextricable mixture of politics and constitutional rules, and in the shrewd manipulation of symbolic powers and law.

The wide range of powers accorded by the constitution and, more important, those acquired by convention at the expense of other constitutional authorities require the President to possess some means of exercising his or her choice and imposing his decisions. The outcome is the result of compromise. On one hand, the government instituted by the constitution has no boundaries, but the President can stamp his mark on it by selecting ministers and the Prime Minister. On the other hand, the Prime Minister is surrounded by a team of faithful advisers, responsible for following up activities in the principal policy sectors, particularly issues in the presidential domain, whose day-to-day management is, moreover, the responsibility of ministries. This system is potentially conflictual, even explosive, because it multiplies the centres of decision-making and influence: the President, his or her advisers, the Prime Minister and his or her *cabinet*, and the ministers. Indeed, conflicts have not been lacking, but they have mostly been confined to the limited circle of decision-makers and have only occasionally boiled over into the media. It must be said that de Gaulle imposed from the outset a discipline and rigour the Fourth Republic had forgotten: conflicts are now regulated in the quiet of antechambers, or resolved by the departure of the dissatisfied or 'dissident' elements.

The presidential staff

The President exerts his influence and prepares himself for decision-making through standing and *ad hoc* councils, and with the help of their advisers within the President's general secretariat and the President's *cabinet*. The councils held at the Elysée (the President's headquarters), chaired by the head of state or a close collaborator, do not have equal importance. Some councils draft policy, decide general directions or take decisions, such as the Defence Council, which establishes defence policy and the overall budgets for the armed forces and examines the impact of international events on strategic and military decisions. In contrast, other councils are set up as specific, provisional responses to some problem stirring public opinion. Finally, Presidents can at will set up close councils on subjects of their choice to discuss a question they think crucial, settle a dispute between members of the government or examine some topical problem requiring close co-ordination between the Elysée, the Matignon (the Prime Minister's headquarters) and the most important ministries. For example, in August 1990 François Mitterrand held several close councils to examine the Gulf conflict. But for most of the time councils have less dramatic, more prosaic objectives. In policy areas where the President wishes to intervene directly they are the ultimate restricted meetings before the Council of ministers meets. This council, chaired by the President, is a place for neither debate nor confrontation but simply a body for the political legitimisation of measures settled beforehand or elsewhere. Thus there is, *de facto*, a hierarchy which lets Presidents impose their point of view, or that of their advisers. But this hierarchy of decision centres depends on the voluntary 'compliance' of the Prime Minister. When this political agreement ceases, as was the case during the periods of cohabitation, the close councils evaporate and the Council of Ministers becomes a formalistic exercise. The only ones then remaining are those explicitly specified in Article 15 of the constitution (Higher Councils and Committees of National Defence).

The President's general secretariat at the Elysée is the presidential decision-making centre. It comprises a small group of senior civil servants (between twenty and thirty), who are mostly members of the elite groups educated in the prestigious administrative schools. Secretariat members specialise in the activities of one policy sector so that they can keep the President informed, follow up issues in that sector and draw the head of state's attention to potential problems or desirable initiatives. The secretariat as a whole is placed under the direction of the secretary-general, whose function goes well beyond that of administrative co-ordination. The secretary-general is the closest collaborator of the President (the only one to meet the President daily), may represent the President in councils, and constitutes simultaneously a protective screen and an essential intermediary. This official is given delicate, discreet tasks and often plays a pivotal role in negotiations during the setting up of a new government. In delicate periods like those of *cohabitation* this role becomes crucial. In recognition of the influence and importance of the function, holders of the post have always been people of outstanding ability, entirely devoted to the head of state and of sphinx-like discretion. They have generally gone on to hold top posts, e.g. Bernard Tricot and Burin des Roziers under de Gaulle, Michel Jobert under Pompidou, Pierre Brossolette and Jean-François Poncet under Giscard d'Estaing, Pierre Bérégovoy under Mitterrand, Dominique de Villepin under Chirac. Many of them later become ministers or even Prime Ministers.

The President's general secretariat works closely with the government's general secretariat. More loosely attached to the Elysée general secretariat is the President's *cabinet*. This *cabinet* consists of a few advisers charged with 'following' the political aspects of a particular policy sector, whether in the 'presidential domain' in the sense defined earlier, i.e. the constitutional domain narrowly defined (diplomacy, defence), the 'reserved' domain (African questions), or on issues judged to be fundamental (finance, industry, environment) or of special concern to the President of the day.

Is this Elysian office the real government of France? Or is it rather a sort of parallel structure which 'shadows' the official government structure? In fact, it is neither: the Elysée machinery seems more an instrument for drafting and following up the head of state's orders, which, essentially, settle the broad lines of policy. It serves too, when necessary, as a supreme body for regulating conflicts that are particularly deep or important. With the reduction of the presidential mandate to five years and the election of Nicolas Sarkozy it seems that a further 'presidentialisation' of the system is taking place. The President himself and his team of faithful collaborators are fully involved in the detailed applications of the presidential platform.

The government: the men of the majority

The Fifth Republic has experienced coalition government, dominant-party government and even several years of *cohabitation*. It could be said, therefore, that all facets of the complex relationship between President, government and parliament have been explored. But one fact is constant and bears no exception: the government is always the expression of the majority in the National Assembly (a relative majority only from 1988 to 1991). The governmental structure, from this point of view, is much nearer the parliamentary than the presidential model, where the President always chooses the ministers, whatever the majority within the legislative chambers. This formative principle of government under the Fifth Republic was hidden by the head of state's broad margin for manoeuvre in the choice of ministers and, especially, of the Prime Minister, when supported by a faithful majority. People tended to assume the head of state had total freedom. In practice, during *cohabitation*, the President can hardly do other than ratify the Prime Minister's choice, though he can exercise a veto – but only with discretion – over inappropriate nominations. In 'normal' times the President can propose, even impose, ministers to whom the Prime Minister is hostile.

What is the Prime Minister, therefore? Second-in-command? Chief of staff? The king's valet? On this issue, too, judgement must be qualified. Certainly the Prime Minister is the President's man or woman. Certainly the Prime Minister is subordinate to the head of state. But this relative dependence does not exclude, within the secrecy of committee meetings and offices, harsh discussion, different evaluations and even quarrels. Moreover, even when there is no dispute over principles the means of applying them remain an area of often considerable latitude in the hands of the Prime Minister and government. The Prime Minister's leeway is reinforced by the administration's ability to issue procedural decisions and interpretative circulars and to commit more funding or less. In short, the vision of a Prime Minister reduced to implementing more or less passively orders from the Elysée does not stand up to analysis. It gives too much weight to formal hierarchies and legal provisions, and completely neglects the strategy of the actors, their capacity to create autonomous space and to influence, bluff, evade. It neglects the complex meanderings of decision-making and, especially, the implementation process. It forgets the networks and alliances which can form between members of the President's and Prime Minister's cabinets and, even more likely, the frequent compromises that emerge from positions which at the outset were antagonistic. Without denying the President's uncontested superiority – to state the contrary would be to go against well-established facts – the role of the Prime Minister and the members of the government should not be underestimated.

The Prime Minister is aided in his or her task by two institutions – one administrative, one political – that make powerful engines driving the governmental machine. The first is the General Secretariat of the Government (SGG), created in 1935 to co-ordinate government activity under the Prime Minister's authority. The Secretary-General of the Government is traditionally a member of the Council of state, benefiting from a continuity that enables him or her to play the role of 'memory' or 'pivot' of governmental action. It is a prestigious post of the first importance even though it does not attract great media attention. On its holder depend good co-ordination of the government's legislative activity (Bills and decrees) and the smooth running of procedures (following up decisions taken in the Council of Ministers which the Secretary-General attends), collecting ministerial counter-signatures, adopting measures of enforcement, drafting the government's submissions should the Constitutional Council request the annulment of legislative proposals. This structure, of quite modest size (about 100 people), is crucial, for it is through it and thanks to it that government projects take a legal form. It guarantees their coherence, continuity and good order.

The Prime Minister's cabinet is the political counterpart of this administrative machine. Here the preoccupation with continuity, legal correctness and smooth administration gives way to politics, speed and innovation. The cabinet officially comprises only about twenty members, under the authority of a cabinet director, assisted by deputy directors, specialist advisers and officials assigned to specified issues. The cabinet chief concentrates especially on the day's political issues and 'manages' the Prime Minister's political engagements. This official structure is swollen by the addition of 'unofficial' and 'clandestine' advisers, considerably increasing the number of staff. The entourage of Jacques Chaban-Delmas in 1970–2, for instance, was estimated at 200 people. The members of the Prime Minister's cabinet come generally from the top civil service and especially from the 'great bodies' of public servants (*grands corps*). Other people slip in from time to time: a few academics, some members of the Prime Minister's political team or local entourage. (Pierre Mauroy's *cabinet* contained many people from northern regions.) The recruitment principle is simple: competence and trust (or at least a strong recommendation). Generally fairly young (thirty to forty-five years old), *cabinet* members are assigned a policy sector which they 'cover' on behalf of the Prime Minister, whom they inform, advise and perhaps represent in inter-ministerial meetings. Specialist advisers and officials are the Prime Minister's 'functional equivalents', in permanent contact with their opposite numbers in the Elysée and the ministries in 'their' sector. Nothing is decided at a ministry unless they have been informed and have given the green light. The functions of the members of the Prime Minister's *cabinet* are extremely important and tend to be a staging post for those destined for high office in the public service, banking, industry and, of course, politics.

These structures of political and legislative co-ordination and organisation are required for a collegiate government that is simultaneously a political body and the top of the administrative structure. Though ministers are responsible for the policy sectors assigned to them, they have only limited autonomy under the Fifth Republic, unlike their counterparts in, for example, Germany or Italy. The Prime Minister of the Fifth Republic is not simply *primus inter pares*. He or she can impose decisions, take strong measures and force a recalcitrant minister to submit or to resign. Good coordination is necessary because a government is never, despite appearances, a united and homogeneous whole. Everything, on the contrary, encourages dispute, rivalry and competition – party or intra-party divisions, personality clashes, demarcation disputes, quite apart from the fierce struggle to obtain the maximum personnel and financial resources. The conflict is more than personal; it is structural. By the discipline they impose, the decisions they make and the method they practise, Prime Ministers must ensure a cohesion made even more problematical by one of the methods frequently used to keep allies/adversaries quiet: giving them a ministerial portfolio. External peace is then paid for in conflicts that are no less fierce just because they are internal.

Each minister is both a political leader and the head of an administration. Under the Fifth Republic a double depolitisation of the ministerial task was attempted: first by making the ministerial function incompatible with a parliamentary mandate and then by recruiting 'experts' from the senior civil service to numerous ministerial portfolios. Though not a total failure, these attempts have not yielded the hoped-for results. Although ministers resign from parliament and are replaced by their successors, they have become, *de facto*, 'super-parliamentarians', possessing more abundant resources for their local electoral clientele than other parliamentarians. As for the experts, so numerous that, on average, they represent up to 30 per cent of the ministerial team, they rapidly converted themselves into politicians. It was thus demonstrated, *a posteriori*, that running a ministry cannot be reduced to simple technical-administrative management.

On European issues, co-ordination of French decisions in Brussels is assured, under the Prime Minister's authority, by a lightweight body attached to the Ministry of Foreign Affairs, the General Secretariat for European Affairs (SGAE). Created initially to adapt central structures to the needs of economic co-operation within the Organisation for Economic Co-operation and Development (OECD), the SGAE plays a vital role in negotiations with the European Union and, according to general opinion (in France, but also abroad), has proved itself an effective instrument, allowing French negotiators to speak with a single voice on briefs previously settled in Paris.

At the summit of this strongly hierarchical structure is the Council of Ministers. Chaired by the head of state, it meets every Wednesday and takes the final decisions on Bills, decrees and individual appointments. Under the Fifth Republic it has superseded the Cabinet Council, except during the periods of *cohabitation*, when Jacques Chirac first and Lionel Jospin ten years later increased the number of cabinet meetings in order to oust the head of state. Important politically and symbolically, the Council of ministers is nevertheless a formality. Debate or discussion is rare and takes place only with the agreement or at the request of the President. It is more a 'recording studio' than a place for collective work and exchanges. Only time will tell if the new options chosen by Nicolas Sarkozy will last long: by reducing the number of ministers to fifteen, he declared his willingness to restore debates within the Council.

MYTHS AND PARADOXES OF DECENTRALISATION

The constitution of the Fifth Republic leaves us in no doubt: France is a 'single and indivisible republic'. However, political reality is more complex than political comment or legal provision would lead people to believe. Behind the façade of unity, fragmentation can be glimpsed. Behind centralisation a multiplicity of centres of decision-making and influence appear. Behind the centre–periphery confrontation collaboration can be discerned.

The republic: single and fragmented

Although the statutes of all local authorities are identical and regulations are supposed to apply everywhere, analysis of practical outcomes reveals extraordinary diversity, a jungle of special institutions and *ad hoc* rules that challenge Cartesian rationality. This situation stems first of all from the attitude of local authorities to the powers that all in principle enjoy, which in a way are their 'capital'. Some local authorities let their 'inheritance' lie fallow, i.e. they do not use them; others use their powers strictly and carefully; yet others adopt an 'entrepreneurial' strategy, exploiting to the maximum the legal, technical and financial advantages they enjoy; finally, some authorities promote 'risky' policies on the edge of legality, opening the way to new legal interpretations or taking the chance of being penalised by the central authorities.

To this first – inescapable – differentiation caused by variations in the use of identical legal resources must be added the potential for local governments to multiply *à la carte* the bodies through which they intervene or collaborate in providing local services. Thus there exist 12,000 joint bodies providing a single service, 2,000 joint bodies providing more than one service, and around 200 'metropolitan' bodies making possible the co-operation between the central commune and its periphery, no two of which match each other exactly in powers, resources, organisation or mode of operation. In addition there are thousands of mixed public–private companies (which are often 'mixed' in name only), offices (for cultural activities, low-rent housing, etc.) and public bodies whose number and scope are not known with any certainty.

In fact the local authorities – towns, counties and regions – form only the visible tip of the iceberg or, to use a financial metaphor, are 'holding companies' controlling all manner of subsidiaries. But there is no consolidated 'balance sheet' which might give a realistic, detailed view of this local galaxy. Looked at in another way, central government, in order to satisfy myths and symbols, has continued the absurd practice of issuing the same regulations for the counties of Lozère and the Hauts-de-Seine, the towns of Toulouse and Colombey-les-deux-Eglises, and the regions of Rhône-Alpes and Limousin. But the reality and the constraints of facts upset these neat arrangements, whose origins can be found in the Jacobin conviction that centralisation and uniformity go together.

Centre–periphery: mutual counterbalance and control

To use a well-known metaphor, there is interdependence and even, at the limit, osmosis between centre and periphery. The first evidence of this interpenetration of 'central' and 'local' is the composition of political personnel. Almost all national politicians, members of parliament and ministers hold a local political mandate (sometimes two) and, in addition, exercise numerous associated functions (chairing joint boards, districts and many local organisations, such as mixed companies and local public bodies). In France, as in many other countries, political careers often start at the local level. But only in France is there an almost systematic practice of accumulating elected offices. More than 90 per cent of members of parliament have at least one local mandate. In 1990 all mayors of towns with at least 80,000 inhabitants had a national mandate. The Act of December 1985 which limited the accumulation of mandates put a brake on the pathological situation in which a politician could be simultaneously a member of parliament, mayor, councillor of a county or region and sometimes also a member of the European Parliament. Premier Jospin proposed to adopt an even stricter line by limiting the accumulation to two mandates and prohibiting parliamentarians from being at the same time the executive of a local body. But it failed on this second account, given the fierce and winning resistance of the Senate, an assembly which exemplifies in its most acute form this type of practice. Nicolas Sarkozy, who himself held local and national mandates before his election, has given his support to this ongoing convention and tradition of French political life.

This 'personal union' has multiple consequences, both negative and positive. The high rate of parliamentary absenteeism noted above can be explained in part by the constraints of accumulation. The real power of veto, or at least the strong potential for lobbying parliament on local problems, should also be noted, witness the inability of successive governments – including those of de Gaulle in all his power – to rationalise the patchwork quilt of towns; the defeat of the referendum on a regionalisation proposal in 1969; the burying of several innovative reports; and the capacity of local authorities to extract central government resources and to make money from their contribution to policies decided by central government. The positive contribution from this confusion of roles is the benefit local experience brings to the legislator, and the awareness of local needs introduced into central government decision-making. In other words, the accumulation of offices and the local loyalties of national politicians may provide an antidote to centralisation, well described by Pierre Grémion as 'tamed Jacobinism'.

A second factor of interdependence stems from the institutionalisation of local factors in national political and constitutional life. This element often goes unremarked in France, whereas no one ever fails to mention the guaranteed representation of states by the upper house in a federal system. The institutional mechanisms put in place or preserved by the Fifth Republic give local authorities much more influence than they have in some other systems characterised as regionalised or decentralised.

The essential device for effecting the penetration of central power by local forces is the Senate, which can still be described, as under the Third Republic, as the 'Grand Council of the Towns of France'. In a system centralised in principle, the Senate constitutes in practice the equivalent of a federal senate. It derives its legitimacy not from the people but from the local authorities, through the local politicians and 'grand electors' who elect it. It has no constitutional power of veto over edicts it considers contrary to the local interest but, *de facto*, has a real conventional power of veto. It would be a very daring government that tried to impose substantial reforms on local government against the advice of the Senate. This would be to risk a war of attrition and, if parliament finally won, becoming bogged down. Since the failure of the 1969 referendum no one has been prepared to appeal directly to the people over senators' heads. The formula often used about the American constitution applies here too: the 'advice and consent' of the Senate is necessary if any reform affecting local authorities is to pass. The approximately 500,000 local government councillors are more than just one of the most powerful lobbies in the country; in contrast to many pressure groups, the local tax lobby is 'within the walls'. It was fashionable in the 1960s to denounce the 'colonisation of the provinces', a view of events that had some truth. But, in doing so, people omitted to analyse a parallel phenomenon, less visible, more hidden by political rhetoric: the conquest of the centre by the periphery, a healthy and necessary rebalancing of the Jacobin (and inappropriate) legal and financial structures.

Today, more than ever, local authorities constitute a fundamental element of the political system: not only are their existence and autonomy guaranteed by the constitution (the principle of being 'freely administered', Article 72) and by several legal interpretations of the constitutional Council since 1982, but they have a decisive influence at the heart of the republic. National elites are also local elites. The hierarchy of their values is not always that proclaimed by grand state principles, as is shown by the benevolent attention paid to local authorities, and the absenteeism of parliamentarians who are more interested in their county or town hall. The financial and economic weight of local government is growing; local governments' budget now represents 45 per cent of government expenditure (with the enormous advantage of supporting only one-third of the salary burden) and their capital investment represents three-quarters of all public civil investment. In sum, everything combines to make them a key part of the system – the Basic Law, the constitutional 'conventions', the influence of their elites, their financial weight and their crucial importance to the implementation of public policies.

CONTINUITY AND CHANGE

As emphasised at the beginning of the chapter, the Fifth Republic has shown evidence of exceptional longevity and a sizeable capacity for adaptation and flexibility. This condition is explained by the continuing support for the Gaullist institutions by the general public, and by the gradual adherence to them of those political and intellectual elites that were initially hostile. Although in the 1960s plans for a Sixth Republic burgeoned in parliament and the media, the initiatives gradually dried up in the 1970s and no longer appear except as a sort of 'ritual obligation' on the part of the left-wing opposition. The Common Programme of the left still suggested manifold changes, putting forward numerous measures to reduce 'presidentialism' in favour of returning to the more classical canons of parliamentarianism. The arrival of the left in power had two consequences: it legitimised a constitution that had at last allowed an alternation of governments, and explicitly ratified the unconditional rallying of the left to the Gaullist institutions. The candidates from both the centre (Bayrou) and the Socialist Party (Segolène Royal) brought the issue up again during the 2007 presidential campaign. It is an easy argument against the incumbents, and the economic or political costs of raising it are close to zero. But it sounds more and more rhetorical and its impact on public opinion is very limited.

The constitution has nevertheless undergone profound evolution during the forty-five years of its existence: first, *conventions* with the Gaullist interpretations and practice and the experiences of *cohabitation* in 1986–8, 1993–5, 1997–2002; second, formal amendments (5 constitutional amendments between 1958 and 1992, and 13 after that). The 1962 reform was radical and controversial, substituting presidential election by universal suffrage for the oligarchic method conceived in 1958 that gave power to the *notables* (the electoral college of 80,000 'Grand Electors'). The 1974 reform of the rules of appeal to the Constitutional Council was described with contempt as a 'mini-reform' but was very important for institutional development, transforming the Constitutional Council into a quasi-constitutional court. This 'incremental' change is worth pausing over, for it has been and remains fundamental, as much for the intellectual, ideological 'revolution' it has brought about as for the running of the system. French legal–political thought had been dominated by a phobia about 'government by judges', and by the assertion of the principle of the sovereignty of parliament and the law.

There was supposed to be no threat or check to the sovereignty of law. The law, the expression of the general will in revolutionary and then republican dogma, was by definition perfect and indisputable. This idealised vision started to be questioned during the inter-war period, when anyone could see that 'the sovereign was captive'. The sovereignty of the people meant, in practice, the capricious, disorderly sovereignty of members of parliament. The law itself fell from its pedestal because it was mostly supplanted by 'decree laws', in the absence of a parliamentary majority able to forge 'the expression of the general will'.

Certainly the object in 1958 was not to introduce control by constitution in the way that was being tried in the new Italian and West German democracies. Even less was it to import constitutional checks into a judicial system that would not lend itself well to the American tradition of control by constitution. The intention of the constitution-makers in 1958 was more specialised and precise: to safeguard the integrity of the institutional machinery of the Fifth Republic by hindering drastic revision. So a specialist body was set up to verify, first, that framework laws and regulations did not betray either the letter or the spirit of the fundamental law and, second, that parliament did not cross over into the regulatory domain, escaping from its own orbit as defined by Article 34. The Constitutional Council was set up as the guardian of the temple or, to put it bluntly, the executive's 'watch dog', the opposition's term. Only the President of the Assembly, on one side, and the Prime Minister and the head of state, on the other, had the power to refer to the council a law they thought might not conform to the constitution. The Constitutional Council, not very active, and dependent on the executive, was considered a 'rump' judge, arousing indifference at best; otherwise, contempt.

The internal evolution of the Constitutional Council was accomplished in small steps, but the last stage had the effect of a thunderclap on the political class. Let us recall the facts briefly. Until the end of the 1960s constitutional judges confined themselves to dealing with norms (organic laws, ordinary laws, Assembly regulations, amendments) adopted or discussed by parliament and their effect on the constitution as narrowly interpreted, that is, as ninety-two Articles of a technical character which, essentially, organised the 'code of conduct' of the public authorities. In contrast, the preamble which precedes the articles, referring to the 1789 Declaration of the Rights of Man and of the Citizen as well as to the preamble to the 1946 constitution ('the economic and social rights particularly relevant to our times'), appeared to be a noble gesture, a declaration whose beauty and grandeur were rivalled only by their uselessness.

The Constitutional Council did not change the order of things at one stroke. To begin with, as if only in passing, it noted the existence of the preamble. Hardly any-one paid much attention. But some months later, in 1971, the government realised with horror that the preamble was now a crucial element of the constitution. The Constitutional Council from then on considered the preamble to constitute an integral part of the constitution and regarded it as part of its role to verify that laws conformed to that collection of references whose character is more politico-philosophical than strictly juridical.

This unexpected blow might have remained merely 'sword-play' if the procedures for referring cases to the council had stayed unchanged. Given the competent authorities, referral would probably have occurred only in exceptional cases, where one of the chambers disagreed with the government and its majority pressured its president to appeal to the council. The contribution of Valéry Giscard d'Estaing was to give the internal evolution of the council the scope it merited. Among numerous measures envisaged as creating a sort of 'opposition's charter' he proposed granting the right of referral to the council to sixty parliamentarians. By definition those parliamentarians would belong solely to the opposition, since it is difficult to imagine the majority who had voted for a law inviting the censure of a judge. The opposition of the day jeered at the proposal and refused to vote for this mini-reform of the constitution, not realising that the modification would have consequences comparable to those set in train by the election of the President by universal suffrage. The Constitutional Council had become in its own way the arbiter, the guarantor of the institutions and, even more, of common values.

The combination of these internal and external transformations has set up a dynamic greeted with enthusiasm by some and with alarm by others. Whatever one's opinion of the development, several decisive factors have emerged over the last period.

First, the Constitutional Council has continued to extend its scope, not only by invoking the 'fundamental principles recognised by the laws of the republic' and referring to principles laid down in the 1789 declaration or in the 1946 pre-amble but also by revealing general principles which had not been explicitly stated. The Constitutional Council is indisputably a creative judge.

Second, the council has widened its scope by bringing under its control the exam-ination of old constitutional norms when they are modified by new laws. However, some regret its refusal to examine 'exceptional legislation' (the state of emergency arising from a 1955 Act) at the time of the extension of the state of emergency in New Caledonia (1985).

Third, in dealing with legislative norms which are so imprecise that the executive could use them in an abusive or overzealous way, the council has adapted the tech-nique of 'declaration of conformity, with conditions'. It lays down the conditions of application or interpretation that would enable the law to be accepted as conforming to the constitution.

Finally, 'fear of the police being the beginning of good behaviour', the council's influence is not only negative, applied after the law has been adopted. Its body of jurisprudence, and the principles it has enunciated and applied, now constitute a 'bible' that the executive and parliament must respect if they are not to risk judicial censure.

Further reforms are under discussion. The numerous criticisms levelled at the Socialist government in the early 1990s encouraged Mitterrand to distract attention by suggesting reform of the constitution, a 'tidying-up'. The sharpest criticism concerned the Council of Magistracy (the magistrates' governing body) in particular, at a time of corruption scandals, because of its dependence on executive power, and the High Court of Justice, ill suited to examine ministerial responsibility in a manner which reassured people (over the issue of contaminated blood). Mitterrand therefore decided to ask an *ad hoc* committee of experts (legal experts and political scientists with a variety of political allegiances) to draw up proposals for revising the constitution. The committee's report of February 1993 did not suggest radical reform but made a host of proposals for improving the way the institutions functioned. Two Bills deposited by Pierre Bérégovoy were hastily presented to parliament before the March 1993 elections, but the incoming right-wing government preserved only two elements, reform of the Council of the Magistracy and of the High Court of Justice. These reforms would modify nothing fundamental, just as those connected with the ratification of the Maastricht Treaty did not upset the institutional balance. Likewise the 1995 reforms enlarged both the President's power to call referendums and the parliament's powers by extending its session. However, some important changes have been introduced during – and in spite of – the cohabitation between Chirac and Jospin.

After the introduction of the parity principle (Constitutional Law of 8 July 1999), the institutions must guarantee equal opportunity to men and women and make any institutional effort to promote its realisation. According to this rule, for instance, it is mandatory to present a list of candidates – when such is the case – made up of an equal number of men and women listed alternately. Such an obligation in local elections has allowed women to accede *en masse* to the local councils. However, this 'affirmative action' has its own limits: the rule does not apply to elections based on individual candidatures in a single constituency; nor does it provide guarantees that women will get access to posts of influence, as is shown by their poor performance when it comes, for instance, to the election of mayors. Male supremacy has remained nearly unchallenged. However, this measure is a first important step in improving women's representation in a country where they constitute less than 10 per cent of the MPs. A further political move took place in 2007 when Sarkozy decided that the ministries would be equally allocated to women and men.

The abovementioned limitation of the president's term from seven to five years adopted in 2000 – the so-called *quinquennat* – is the latest important formal change of the constitution. It presents a big advantage: reducing a political mandate far too long given the prerogatives given to the President. But the snowball effects of such a reform have barely been evaluated or have been overestimated. For instance, it has been argued that by aligning the duration of the presidential and of the parliamentary mandates the 'risks' of *cohabitation* would be reduced. Nothing is less certain than such an assertion. First of all, it is only by chance that these elections take place more or less at the same time (as happened in 2002 because of the dissolution of the

National Assembly in 1997), but even in such a case the electors can split their vote. The mechanics of two different types of constituency play an important role: only two candidates in the second round for the presidential race; nearly 600 constituencies where triangular battles are possible and local considerations important. The reduction of the presidential mandate is undoubtedly a positive change, but taken in isolation from the rest of the constitution it constitutes in a way a leap in the dark. No real lesson can be drawn from a president (Chirac) who knew that his first *quinquennat* would also be his last mandate. The tone might be set by the new elected president (Sarkozy), whose style, age and ambitions are quite different.

The fundamental mainspring of the Fifth Republic, despite the modifications, the party-political contingencies and the potential for *cohabitation*, remains the central position occupied by the executive – a presidential executive in 'normal' times, a mixed executive in a period of *cohabitation*. Assisted by a powerful and prestigious bureaucratic elite, the executive of the Fifth Republic is at the heart of the political system, an arrangement that brings with it a certain level of 'democratic deficit'. Effectiveness, governmental solidarity, concentration of power and the authority of the leader take priority over pluralism, debate and a system of checks and balances. But few voices are raised to question seriously the fundamentals of a system that has the support and approval of the elites as well as of popular opinion as a whole, as is shown again by the contrast in political participation and turnout: nearly 85 per cent for the presidential election, 60 per cent for the parliamentary elections three weeks later.

BIBLIOGRAPHY

Elections and mobilisations

Cole, A. and P. Campbell (1989) *French Electoral Systems and Elections since 1789*, Brookfield, VT: Gower.
Pierce, R. (1995) *Choosing the Chief. Presidential Elections in France and the United States*, Ann Arbor: University of Michigan Press.
Wilson, F. (1987) *Interest Group Politics in France*, Cambridge: Cambridge University Press.

Political parties

Ambler, J. (ed.) (1985) *The French Socialist Experiment*, Philadelphia: ISHI.
Bartolini, S. (1984) 'The French Party System', *West European Politics* 7 (4): 103–27.
Charlot, J. (1971) *The Gaullist Phenomenon*, London: Allen & Unwin.
Duhamel, O. (1980) *La Gauche et la Ve. République*, Paris: PUF.
Ross, G., S. Hoffmann and S. Malzacher (1988) *The Mitterrand Experiment*, Oxford: Polity Press.

Parliament

Huber, J. (1996) *Rationalizing Parliament: Legislative Institutions and Party Politics in France*, Cambridge and New York: Cambridge University Press.

Suleiman, E. (ed.) (1986) *Parliaments and Parliamentarians in Democratic Politics*, New York: Holmes & Meier.

President and government

Jones, G. W. (ed.) (1991) *West European Prime Ministers*, London: Frank Cass.

Knapp, A. and V. Wright (2006) *The Government and Politics of France*, London: Routledge.

Mény, Y. (1992) *La Corruption de la République*, Paris: Fayard.

—— with A. Knapp (1998) *Government and Politics in Western Europe. Britain, France, Italy, Germany*, third edn, Oxford: Oxford University Press.

—— with Y. Surel (2000) *Par le Peuple, pour le peuple. Populismes et démocratie*, Paris: Fayard.

Suleiman, E. (1994) 'Presidentialism and Political Stability in France', in J. Linz and A. Valenzuela (eds) *The Failure of Presidential Democracy*, vol. 1, Baltimore: The Johns Hopkins University Press.

Continuity and change

Andrews, W. G. and S. Hoffmann (1981) *The Impact of the Fifth Republic on France*, New York: State University of New York Press.

Guyomarch, A., H. Machin, J. S. Hayward and P. Hall (eds) (2001) *Developments in French Politics 2*, Basingstoke: Palgrave Macmillan.

CHAPTER 5

Italy

The Never-ending Transition of a Democratic Regime

Gianfranco Pasquino

Since 1992–3 the Italian political system has been undergoing a political and institutional transition. More precisely, the Italian transition, which has so far not affected the democratic framework but the performance and the quality of its democracy, is characterised by two fundamental phenomena. The first phenomenon concerns the rules of the game, that is, the mechanisms through which political power is won, allocated and distributed and the overall institutional structure of the political system. The second phenomenon is represented by incessant and significant changes in the party system concerning the type of parties and their coalitional arrangements. In the meantime, there have been a couple of significant rotations in office between the two major coalitions, though curiously without any change in their leaders, and several governments have followed each other. Attempts have been made to reform the institutions and even the constitution. To no avail. As of 2007, there appears to be no solution in sight.

The fragile, but lasting, equilibrium that characterised the long first phase of the democratic Republic has disappeared and has not yet been replaced by a new equilibrium. To paraphrase Josep Colomer (1996: 16), the Italian institutional equilibrium that prevailed in the First Republic proved to be stable without being accompanied by 'a high degree of political efficacy or satisfactory representation'. A new equilibrium has not appeared. This is both because, 'given the bargaining strength of the actors, none of them would find it worthwhile to enter into a process of bargaining and political change' and because the main features of a potentially new equilibrium remain exposed to criticisms and subject to repeated attempts at negotiation and at subversion. Understandably, the electoral system is at the same time the most controversial of the new features and the most important one that needs to be revised if one wishes to pursue both partisan and systemic goals. However, the real problem is that the Italian model of government remains that of a traditional parliamentary system dominated by political parties that are by far less capable of providing stable guidance.

POLITICAL PARTIES AND THE PARTY SYSTEM

On the whole quite stable throughout the First Republic, the major actors remaining largely the same without any significant change in their electoral strength and governing power, the Italian party system has undergone a profound transformation since 1993. The electoral reform impinged upon a situation that was already characterised by some currents of change. More precisely, there had already emerged a new and peculiar political movement, first Lombard, then Northern League. Its political appeal was fundamentally based on two elements. The first one was a growing dissatisfaction with the existing parties, especially with governing parties, for their corruption, as revealed by the 'Clean Hands' investigation, as well as for their performance, as revealed by the state of the economy. The second element was the explicit revival of a territorial identity. In several areas of the North, this kind of identity had always existed. It was often translated and channelled into local lists, but it was almost as often courted and captured by, at the same time, the factional appeal of the Christian Democrats (DC) and the national appeal of the Communists (PCI).

Neither the DC nor the PCI cultivated local sentiments, feelings or grievances. For several reasons, prominent among them the international alignment of the cold war, Italian party competition was truly national. Elections were fought neither on local/regional peculiarities and demands nor on European perspectives and aspirations, but exclusively on national issues. However, local grievances, on the part of the North, which felt exploited by 'Roman politics' and suffocated by the 'Roman bureaucracy', and regional peculiarities always existed. The Northern League decided to unearth and to highlight them. Thanks to the gradual decline of the Christian Democrats and to the dramatic transformation of the Communist Party, the Northern League was very successful in making an issue of territorial identity. That said, one must not exaggerate the political and electoral success of the Northern League. At its highest electoral level, only about one out of four Northerners voted for the League. It was a considerable, but not extraordinary result. As to the amount of political success measured in terms of the writing of the national agenda, the appearance of one paramount issue can be attributed to the strength of the League: federalism. Variously declined, as decentralisation, devolution, federalism, even secession and independence, in the 1990s the issue of how many and which powers should be devolved by the centralised Italian state to regional authorities became, in fact, overriding. In terms of actual policies, it only produced some inevitable devolution of functions and the (almost) direct popular election of the presidents of the regional governments. But, then, it remains very doubtful whether the League and its shrinking electorate considered these results satisfactory. However, the presence of three ministers in the second government led by Berlusconi (2001–6), including, before his illness, their leader Umberto Bossi, as Minister of Institutional Reforms and Devolution, has helped to defuse most of the grievances. Today, though electorally influential in the North, the Northern League is essentially just a regionally based political party.

As to the other parties, three phenomena took place. The first one is the disappearance for all purposes of most of the historical parties. The second one is the more or less complete transformation of some of the historical parties. The third, most important and, in all likelihood, decisive phenomenon has been the creation and success of a brand new party: Let's Go Italy (*Forza Italia*). All these changes amount to the construction of a party system that is very different from the one that existed in the first phase of the democratic Republic and that shaped its functioning. However, for several reasons, as many other political structures were caught in the transition, not even the present party system can be considered fully consolidated. This lack of consolidation can be seen and evaluated with reference to the parties' names, their electoral strength and their coalition partners. New attempts at creating additional parties have been made and not all of them have failed. But the process of party proliferation and aggregation appears to be by no means over in 2007.

As to the disappearance of most of the historical parties, especially the Liberals, the Social Democrats and the Republicans, there are good reasons to believe that their time had already been exhausted and that they were being kept alive only thanks to two factors. The first one was the proportional electoral law, with very low thresholds for parliamentary representation. Had Italy utilised the German 5 per cent clause only four or five parties would have obtained parliamentary representation. The Italian proportional representation system granted parliamentary seats even to parties with less than 2 per cent of the national vote. Once in Parliament, small parties were also granted offices in the various, usually oversised, governmental coalitions led by the DC. Small parties were used by the Christian Democrats as a buffer in order to avoid a head-on confrontation with the Communists, but also because, to some extent, they were providing political representation for social sectors which would otherwise not support the DC. Together with governmental offices came a lot of patronage power and opportunities. This second factor was not only welcome, but also practically decisive for their survival. When, following the implementation of the new electoral law, the small parties disappeared from Parliament, they lost all any chance of surviving politically. However, it is also important to stress that their organisations had already fallen into disrepute because of the indictment on charges of corruption of all their general secretaries. Still, it remains appropriate to remark that the proportional electoral law really was the small parties' safety net and that patronage was the water in which they could stay afloat. The Christian Democrats had to rely on them to buttress their governments, but, few exceptions aside, in terms of policies the small parties' contribution to the way Italy was governed has to be judged minor and limited.

It was a different story for the Italian Socialist Party (PSI), both with reference to its political role and in terms of fully understanding its sudden disappearance. Always by far stronger than any of the small centrist parties, the PSI was always caught between two kinds of opposite pressures. On the one hand, there was the pressure to guarantee some governability by joining an alliance with the Christian Democrats; on the other, there was the pressure to function as a channel for the transmission of leftist ideas, preferences and expectations, especially those formulated by the PCI. Because of these pressures, the PSI suffered two serious opposite splits, in 1947 because it had moved too close to the PCI, and in 1964 because it had joined a governmental coalition with the DC. When in 1976 Bettino Craxi gained power within the party and then translated his newly acquired political power into govern-mental power, becoming Prime Minister in 1983, he drastically revised the overall strategy of the PSI. In government with the Christian Democrats, Craxi delib-erately decided to challenge the Communists in order both to reduce their electoral following and to demonstrate their irrelevance, that is, that they had no influence whatsoever on governmental decisions and policies. In addition, Craxi exploited his indispensable governmental role and his coalition power in order to acquire, often in a less than proper way, all types of resources necessary to run lavish electoral campaigns. When his strategy failed, that is, when it became clear that the Christian Democrats were not going to be displaced and replaced and that the (former) Communists had not been overtaken in terms of electoral support, Craxi appeared so weakened that several charges of corruption and embezzlement could be levelled against him. Under the weight of the accusations and while its leader went into exile in Tunisia, the PSI practically dissolved itself. By the end of 1993, the five parties – Christian Democrats, Socialists, Social Democrats, Republicans, Liberals – that had governed Italy for more than ten years in a five-party coalition known as *pentapartito* had either disappeared or were in shambles. Only the Italian Democratic Socialists (SDI) play an albeit minor role within the centre-left coalition.

The Christian Democrats themselves were, indeed, a shambles, but their vicissi-tudes are better analysed in terms of a difficult and largely failed transformation characterised by two developments. The first is that, following the fall of the Berlin Wall and of Communism in 1989, the Italian Communist Party changed its name, its logo, its organisation. It also suffered a serious split, giving birth to the hard-line Communist Refoundation (*Rifondazione Comunista*), and had become a largely different and much less influential political actor. Deprived of their traditional 'enemy', whose threatening existence could repeatedly justify a vote in their favour from many social sectors, the Christian Democrats first lost votes, then exploded into several fragments. Today there are three groups claiming the unavailable heritage of the Christian Democrats. Within the centre-left coalition, one finds former members of the Italian Popular Party (Partito Popolare Italiano, PPI), now in the Daisy (*Margherita*) and the Union of European Democrats (Unione Democratici Europei, UDEUR). The Union of Democratic Centre (Unione Democratica de Centro, UDC) has long positioned itself within the House of Liberties (*Casa delle Libertà*), but recently it has challenged Berlusconi's leadership and, while remain-ing within the centre-right, it has decided to play its own cards (in the hope of a proportional electoral law).

At the beginning of the political and institutional transition, there is no doubt that by far the two most important transformations concerned the extreme parties of the political spectrum: the Italian Communist Party and the Italian Social

Movement (MSI). Indeed, only the transformation of these two parties made it possible, as we will see later, for party competition to change its nature, its dynamics, its quality.

The long overdue transformation of the Italian Communist Party began in earnest immediately after the fall of the Berlin Wall when the Secretary-General Achille Occhetto announced the decision to change the name and the logo of the party. However, too much time elapsed between the announcement and the actual change, which took place only on 1 February 1991. Hence, not only were the positive effects postponed, but the opponents of the transformation could also organise a successful split, giving birth to Communist Refoundation. This split has deprived the new Democratic Party of the Left (Partito Democratico della Sinistra, PDS) of at least one-quarter of its electoral strength and, above all, of many committed party workers and militants. Moreover, Occhetto's own project, to launch a 'new political formation' open to additional contributions, a 'caravan' that many could join during its journey, meant that the party remained in a continuous state of flux. In the wake of the defeat in the 1994 national and European elections, Occhetto suddenly resigned and was replaced by Massimo D'Alema. Though a staunch defender of the traditional role of mass parties, D'Alema himself thought it was necessary to create a new organisation. In February 1998, the so-called Thing 2 (Cosa 2, because Thing 1 was the original attempt to create what had become the PDS) was meant to bring together former supporters and leaders of the Republicans, the Social Democrats, the Liberals, some Socialists (the so-called Labourites), the Social Christians and several other minor left-wing groups. The outcome was baptised Left Democrats (Democratici di Sinistra, DS). The operation was led from the top and was accompanied neither by mobilisation nor by enthusiasm. It was a purely bureaucratic merger, mostly of full-time politicians. Later on, the DS leadership played for a short period of time with the idea of joining the exploration of the Third Way as indicated by New Labour. Following serious electoral defeat in 2001, the party went through a long phase of restructuring under the new secretary Piero Fassino. However, even though the Left Democrats were a decisive component of the victorious centre-left coalition in 2006, electorally they remained stuck at 17.5 per cent of the national vote.

Stressing the imperative to construct a new and large political organisation providing the necessary support to Romano Prodi's government inaugurated in May 2006, the Left Democrats and the Daisy decided to join in a new Democratic Party. This party had to combine the strength of both the Left Democrats and the Daisy to become the largest Italian party, possibly polling more than 30 per cent of the vote. The process leading to the new party should be completed before the 2009 European elections. While the Daisy, itself not having made any electoral growth in 2006, appeared not to suffer from the decision to merge with the Left Democrats, heated controversies and yet another split have accompanied the dissolution of the Left Democrats. Not only have those who left the party indicated their preoccupation with the disappearance of a left-wing political organisation. The overall fear concerns a potential drift of the political alignment towards the centre and the lack of a truly reformist party, which Italy has, in practice, never had.

Obviously, the full governmental legitimisation of the former neo-Fascists of the Italian Social Movement (Movimento Sociale Italiano, MSI), now National Alliance

(Alleanza Nazionale, AN), must also be considered a democratic success, even more so if one looks at AN's share of the vote: more than double what the MSI used to poll. During its transformation, National Alliance too suffered a split, giving birth to the MSI–Tricolour Flame (Fiamma Tricolore), but the split has been less consequential than that of Communist Refoundation for the Left Democrats. Even when undergoing its transformation, National Alliance remained a rather well-organised party, entrenched in most areas of the country, and not only in the South, with two strongholds in Lazio and in Puglia. On the whole, National Alliance's President Gianfranco Fini has been capable of controlling and leading his party towards the image of a decent, conservative, nationalist, almost Gaullist, party. By so doing, he contributed significantly to the victory of Berlusconi's Pole of Good Government (Polo del Buongoverno) in 1994 and House of Liberties (Casa delle Libertà) in 2001. In fact, the role of National Alliance appears to be crucial for the party competition becoming and remaining bipolar and to Italy to retaining the chance of alternation in government of different coalitions.

Looking at the transformation of the Communists as well as of the neo-Fascists, one can appreciate how successful Italian democracy has been. Though at a high price, that is, the lack of alternation and the curtailing of political options, for more than forty years the democratic constitutional framework proved to be capable of preventing both anti-system parties from jeopardising and destroying its essential features. It has obliged them to transform their ideologies and their organisations and to play a different role, acquiring, enjoying and losing governmental responsibilities. The post-1993 structure of political opportunities has rewarded both the former Communists and the former neo-Fascists, but only after and because they have accepted the rules of 'the game in town'. If there are still problems and challenges for Italian democracy, it is unlikely that they will come from its erstwhile opponents.

It is one thing to transform and improve old parties, and a very different thing to create new parties, especially *ex novo*, that is, neither out of splits nor out of parliamentary realignments and/or regroupings. One can locate in the category of 'splits' practically all the parties born out of the Christian Democratic *diaspora* and the three parties born out of the transformation of the Italian Communist Party (Left Democrats, Communist Refoundation, Italian Communists). In the second category of 'realignments and regroupings', one would find as the only lasting and successful case the Daisy (Margherita), originally constructed around former Christian Democrats and Prodi's faithful supporters, but led by prime ministerial candidate Francesco Rutelli, coming from the very different political traditions of the Radical Party and the Greens. Finally, the merger of the Left Democrats and the Daisy and the implementation of a new electoral law may encourage the much needed and overdue general realignment of the Italian left.

All this said, in the 1990s only one party appeared that, in the confusing Italian political arena, truly deserves the definition of new: Let's Go Italy (Forza Italia, FI). Created in less than six months between the end of 1993 and March 1994, from scratch, with very little support from some minor and declining centrist splinter groups, Let's Go Italy has quickly emerged as the most important, indeed, the dominant party not only in the centre-right alignment, but in Italian politics. In the 2001 national elections, FI became the first Italian party, polling almost 11 million votes, 29.5 per cent of the total. In 2006, though on the losing side, it obtained 9,048,976 votes (23.7 per cent), remaining by far the largest party in Italy. The second largest party, the Left Democrats, had about 3 million fewer votes. Moreover, its electoral consensus is distributed in a balanced way in all Italian regions, with strongholds of over 30 per cent in both Lombardy and Sicily.

FI's success and persistence have baffled political scientists and commentators alike. No doubt Forza Italia draws a significant part of its success from being the party of a leader who happens to be a media tycoon and who has, understandably, put his media power in the service of his political vehicle. No doubt the party, though by no means totally absent from local areas, remains sporadically organised when it comes to local elections. No doubt its overall appeal is largely populist and anti-political, but it also has a neo-conservative programme. That said, if a 'party' is defined, as it should be, as an organisation of women (not too many) and men (most of them) looking for votes in order to get seats and offices, Let's Go Italy fits this definition beautifully. It is not exactly a professional electoral party, because it is excessively dependent on its founder and leader and not enough on a network of at least part-time professional politicians. Indeed, its major asset, Berlusconi's leadership, also seems to be its major potential weakness. As was clearly shown by the 2006 electoral campaign, run forcefully and almost exclusively by Berlusconi in person, there is no deputy leader, no designated successor, no heir apparent. While Let's Go Italy's success has also been nourished by its ability to attract and to 'recycle' former Christian Democrats and former Socialists, the profile of the party and, perhaps, its future are closely tied to and defined by its founder and leader.

By emerging at the time it did, in 1994, Let's Go Italy has performed a substantially partisan role, providing for the political representation of all those voters who felt themselves to be orphans of their previous discredited parties, but it has also fulfilled an important systemic role. In 1994 Let's Go Italy prevented the left from acquiring governmental power by default, that is, because of the disarray of all centre-right parties. Serving as a linchpin, both for the Northern League and for National Alliance, otherwise incompatible bedfellows, Let's Go Italy succeeded in winning national power. Because the two bedfellows were indeed incompatible, the centre-right government was quickly overturned and could not quickly reconstruct a viable coalition agreement to prevent the Olive Tree from winning the 1996 elections. Hence, throughout the remaining years of the 1990s, FI and its partners served as an opposition, not always well prepared and capable, but still a check on the centre-left government. In the 2001 elections FI led the centre-right to the conquest of a conspicuous number of seats and governmental power. However, its subsequent governing experience was not especially successful because of the many legal problems faced by Berlusconi the entrepreneur, and his exaggerated promises, which were not followed by a satisfactory performance. The 2006 electoral defeat left Let's Go Italy, like the Left Democrats, who are the smallest left-wing party in the European Union, too weak to be compared with governing European conservative parties, for instance the Popular Party of Spain or the Gaullists of France, not to say the German Christian Democrats. At the European level, much to its satisfaction, Let's Go Italy has finally joined the European Popular Party, acquiring, in spite of its Euroscepticism, an important claim to legitimacy. On the whole, its ruling class,

Silvio Berlusconi included, mainly consisting of professionals who are close collaborators of the leader, still appears inexperienced, often not competent, largely motivated by anti-political feelings.

The preceding analysis is meant clearly to suggest that Italian parties and the party system are not sufficiently consolidated. Most parties are weak, fragile groupings, almost personal vehicles. Most of them are bound to change and, possibly, to disappear. Therefore, the Italian party system, both in its format, number and type of parties, and in its dynamics – that is, the pattern of competition among parties – is still undergoing a process of unguided transformation. The prevailing pattern of party competition in the First Italian Republic was the one identified and formulated by Giovanni Sartori (1976): 'polarised pluralism', centred on the strength and the coalitional propensity of centrist parties, the exclusion of the PCI and the MSI from any participation in the government, and the impossibility of alternation. In the 1946–92 context, polarisation referred both to the existence of three poles – right, centre, left – and to the ideological distance separating them, which made impossible any coalition between the centre and, respectively, either the right or the left and, as a consequence, deprived the political system of any healthy rotation in government. The new pattern of party competition is considerably different, perhaps just the opposite. The new party system may be defined as 'moderate pluralism'. In this model, centrist parties, without disappearing completely, count far less and cannot dictate the type of coalition to be constructed. Electoral competition has become bipolar between two heterogeneous coalitions, and alternation is not only possible, but has actually taken place, allowing all significant parties a taste of governmental power. More precisely, alternation has become possible and feasible both because the centre can no longer constitute itself as an autonomous pole and because the ideological distance between the two major coalitions has on the whole

Table 5.1 Left–right placement of parties in Italy

Left	Democrat		Centre	Freedom	Northern
LSA	PD	IV	UDC	PDL	LN

Left	Centre-left	Centre	Centre-right	Right

Party names:
LSA: Rainbow Left (La Sinistra Arcobaleno).
PD: Democratic Party (Partito Democratico).
IV: Italy of Values (Italia dei Valori).
UDC: Union of Centre (Unione di Centro).
PDL: Party of Freedom (Partito della Libertà).
LN: Northern League (Lega Nord).

Sources: Updated from sources for Table 2.4 and Giannetti and De Giorgi (2006).

been significantly reduced. In the absence of better indicators, Table 5.1 focuses on the policy distance among all parties.

For a complete stabilisation of the parties and the party system and of the nature of party competition, much will depend on the electoral system and the way it is reformed. At this point a return to polarised pluralism appears very unlikely. However, there is little doubt that a reintroduction of proportional representation may indeed favour the exclusion of the extreme left, that is, at least of Communist Refoundation, but possibly also of the right, National Alliance. Of course, proportional representation will also offer the opportunity for diversified centrist alliances, in all likelihood still dominated by Let's Go Italy, to 'occupy' in a rather stable way the centre of the political alignment. This situation, returning the entire political system to the pre-1993 configuration, would make any future alternation in government quite difficult.

Summing up, in the present Italian political system neither single individual parties nor the party system can be considered stable and consolidated. As Table 5.2 shows, there have been considerable variations in the number, type and electoral strength of different parties. There is no reason to believe that the overall process of alignment, de-alignment, and realignment has come to an end. On the contrary, both another reform of the electoral law and the creation of the Democratic Party will bring about additional and significant transformations concerning both major coalitions, and even their continued existence, their respective ageing leadership, and their relationship and competition. Finally, while the voters seem to appreciate the type of bipolar competition that, facilitated by the post-1993 electoral system, has characterised the elections of 1994, 1996, 2001 and even of 2006, too many politicians still seem intent on searching for a different system exclusively in order to improve their partisan performances. At this point, there are good reasons to believe that they will not be successful, but their obsessive search prevents the

Table 5.2 Elections to the Italian Chamber of Deputies, 1994–2006

Year	Communists		Democrats		Rose		Centre	Conservative		Northern	Others
	RC	PdCI	DS	Marg	V	SDI	UDC	FI	AN	LN	
1994	6	–	20	16	3	2	–	21	14	8	10
1996	9	–	21	11	3	1	6	20	16	10	3
2001	5	2	16	15	– 2 –		3	29	12	4	12
2006	6	2	18	11	2	3	7	24	12	5	10
	SLA		PD	IV			UDC	PdL		LN	
2008	3		34	4			6	38		9	6

Note:

Communist: RC: Communist Refoundation (Rifondazione Comunista); PdCI: Party of Italian Communists (Partito dei Comunisti Italiani); SLA: Rainbow Left (La Sinistra Arcobaleno).

Democrat: DS: Left Democrats (Democratici di Sinistra); Marg: Daisy (Margherita); PD: Democratic Party (Partito Democratico); IV: Italy of Values (Italia dei Valori).

Rose: Rose in Fist (Rosa nel Pugno); V: Greens (Verdi); SDI: Italian Democratic Socialists (Socialisti Democratici Italiani).

Centre: UDC: Democratic Union of Centre (Unione Democratica di Centro).

Conservative: FI: Let's Go Italy (Forza Italia); AN: National Alliance (Alleanza Nazionale); PdL: Party of Freedom (Partito della Libertà).

Northern: LN: Northern League (Lega Nord).

stabilisation of the party system, even more so because all of them are trying to retain or to improve their political power through the shaping of a partisan electoral system.

THE ELECTORAL SYSTEM

The Italian crisis being institutional, that is, fundamentally the product of the unsatisfactory performance of the overall institutional system, one can neither discount the size of the change to be made nor hope to solve the crisis exclusively through the reform of the electoral system. It is worth recalling that the peculiar type of proportional representation utilised in Italy had, indeed, been a component and a cause of the unsatisfactory performance of the political system, especially after 1975, and of its crisis at the end of the 1980s. Still, had it been up to the politicians alone, no reform of the proportional electoral law would ever have been approved. It took two popular referendums, initiated by some dissenting politicians with the support of several social and cultural associations, to put the issue on the political and institutional agenda. The first referendum, held in June 1991, signalled to the politicians, the majority of whom had vehemently opposed it, that they were out of touch with the citizens' preferences. The second referendum, held in April 1993, was widely interpreted as a complete rejection of PR in favour of a plurality system. Obliged to draft a new electoral law by the referendum, approved by almost 90 per cent of the voters, the politicians attempted to make their partisan goals prevail over the citizens' systemic goals. The outcome of the electoral referendum fundamentally dictated that the law for the Senate had to combine three major principles. First, it had to be based on a plurality mechanism; second, it had to be applied in single-member constituencies; third, it had to be corrected with some proportional reallocation of seats. Indeed, the referendum had made it almost imperative that three-quarters of the senators (238) be elected by plurality in single-member constituencies while the remaining seats (77) had to be allocated proportionally on a regional basis, without utilising any of the votes that had served to elect the 'plurality' senators.

Technically, the law for the Chamber of Deputies had not been affected by the referendum, because the 'repealing' mechanism could not be made to work against any of its features. Therefore, at least in theory, the Chamber PR might have remained unchanged or could have been drafted according to different principles. Politically, however, under pressure from public opinion, the deputies felt it necessary, first, to reform their own law, second, not to stray too far from the electoral law for the Senate. The dominant criterion remained the same: three-quarters of the seats (475) had to be won in single-member constituencies by using the plurality formula. The difference from the Senate law is that the voters for the Chamber of Deputies are given two different ballots: one showing the names of the candidates in each specific single-member constituency; the other containing the symbols of the parties and up to four names of candidates (155) to be elected through a proportional mechanism in regional or semi-regional areas. In order to have access to the proportional seats, a party must win at least 4 per cent of the national vote calculated with reference to the second 'proportional' ballot. The electoral reformers intended the new laws to achieve a number of goals. The most important of these was a reduction in the distance between the voters and the candidates, to be achieved by the creation of single-member constituencies instead of the previous large PR districts. The second goal was the simplification of the party system by making it impossible for small parties to obtain parliamentary representation. The third was the creation of stable governmental coalitions capable of lasting for an entire parliamentary term.

Obviously, all these goals could not be attained in one single election, but public expectations ran very high. On the whole, there appeared to be widespread agreement that the new electoral law had fallen rather short of the purported goals. There had been no reduction in the political distance between voters and candidates. In the absence of any residency requirement, the most powerful politicians had repeatedly chosen to be parachuted into the safest constituencies. Some of them decided in any case also to occupy the head of one or more (at the most three) proportional lists in order to increase their chances of being elected (another reassuring clause of the law). Needless to say, to give one curious example, in 1994 the general rapporteur of the law, the former Christian Democrat Sergio Mattarella, won a seat in the Chamber of Deputies thanks to his candidacy at the top of a proportional list. Even Mario Segni, the Chairman of the committee that had promoted the elected referendum, was re-elected only because of the proportional component of the law. As to the second goal, the simplification of the party system, a few figures will suffice. Though it is difficult to count them, there were 12 parties represented in the 1992 parliament. In 1994 14 parties obtained parliamentary representation and in 1996 the number of parties had risen to 19. The 2001 figures indicate that only 5 parties or aggregations of parties have overcome the 4 per cent threshold. In order of magnitude, they are Let's Go Italy, the Left Democrats, the Daisy (consisting of four different centre-left groups), National Alliance and Communist Refoundation.

In the three elections held under this electoral law (1994, 1996, 2001), the fact that quite a number of single-member constituencies could be won or lost by very few votes allowed minor parties to survive. Their contribution in some marginal seats was considered invaluable, both because it might have been very important and because it cannot be truly and precisely evaluated. In exchange for their support in single-member constituencies, minor parties have been rewarded by being allocated several safe constituencies. The end result appeared to be not only that many small parties could survive, but also that many new parties could be explicitly created by exploiting the opportunities offered by the law (as will be seen in the section on the political parties on pp. 136–44). However, this trend was abruptly interrupted in 2001 when some overly ambitious political movements, such as Italy of Values (Italia dei Valori), created by the former Clean Hands magistrate and senator Antonio Di Pietro, and European Democracy (Democrazia Europea), launched by the former CISL trade union leader Sergio D'Antoni, missed, respectively by a small and by a large number of votes, the 4 per cent threshold.

Finally, as to what concerns the creation of stable governmental coalitions, the evidence is mixed. On the one hand, it is true that the major party and political actors, with the exception of many Christian Democrats who founded the Italian Popular Party, immediately understood that the new electoral law made it imperative to create electoral coalitions. It may also be that, at the time of the 1994 elections, the former Christian Democrats entertained the idea of becoming the key/pivotal player (*ago della bilancia*) between the two major coalitions, on the one hand the Pole of Liberties/Pole of Good Government and on the other the left-wing Progressives. They failed and the centre-left coalition known as Olive Tree (*Ulivo*) was created in 1995–6 by their merger. In any case, the Italian electoral coalitions were and remain significantly heterogeneous, diversified and composite, though several actors have tried to challenge them by staying outside. The lesson taught by the 2001 general elections is that the space for third forces has been drastically curtailed, perhaps even definitely so. Nevertheless, the heterogeneity of coalitions constructed more out of political necessity than because of programmatic convergence has produced unstable governmental coalitions (as we will see in the section devoted to the government on pp. 152–60) that have negatively affected both the centre-right and the centre-left. In sum, the electoral law drafted in 1993–4 has not served the Italian political system in a completely satisfactory manner. On the contrary, it has contributed only slightly to a better functioning of the political system, but it has made a significant contribution to the completion of the Italian transition.

In view of the 2006 national elections, the governing House of Liberties coalition reached agreement on a new electoral law. The decision to reform the *Mattarellum* (as it was ironically and critically dubbed by the political scientist Giovanni Sartori, '*matto*' being in Italian crazy, a kind of village idiot) was not grounded in a sober and technical assessment of its inadequacies or aimed at drafting a better law that could improve the overall functioning of the political system. The motivations of the reformers were highly partisan. All the polls suggested a crushing victory for the centre-left made even more impressive by the majoritarian components of the Mattarellum. Aware that a proportional electoral law might, at the same time, reduce the size of the likely victory of the centre-left and contain the losses of the likely defeat of the House of Liberties, and pressed both by the Northern League and by the former Christian Democrats of the UDC, who had remained adamantly 'proportionalists', Silvio Berlusconi threw his support behind a new electoral law. Technically, it was not a return to the proportional electoral law Italy had utilised from 1946 to 1992. Perhaps, its most important component was the allocation of a majority bonus. For the Chamber of Deputies, the bonus had to be given to the coalition receiving the highest number of votes that would have allowed it to obtain at least 340 seats (out of 630). For the Senate, due to a probably wrong interpretation of the constitution according to which the Senate is elected 'on a regional basis', it was decided to attribute the bonus region by region. The distribution of seats was, otherwise, proportional to all lists having received at least 2 per cent of the votes, but also to the list that, in its respective coalition, had come the closest to the 2 per cent threshold. The existence of a majority bonus has had two political consequences. On the one hand, it has encouraged the formation of pre-electoral coalitions and it has preserved the quality of bipolar competition that allows the voters to express their preference for a coalition and its leader. On the other hand, it has obliged the two coalitions to become as encompassing as possible, thus producing highly heterogeneous alignments (the centre-left considerably more so).

Most of the constituencies were very large indeed, being allocated more than 20 and often as many as 30 seats or more, because the House of Liberties feared that the process of redistricting and reapportioning would have prevented the approval of its law in time. Multiple candidacies were allowed, which meant that many party leaders put themselves on the top of their party lists in several constituencies (Berlusconi was the head of the Let's Go Italy lists in all Chamber constituencies). Finally, all party lists were blocked. The voters could only mark with an 'X' the symbol of their favourite party. This rule gave a tremendous amount of power to party leaders, who could not just choose the candidates but, knowing with some accuracy the distribution of the votes for their party, constituency after constituency, decide in practice who was going to be elected. The outcry coming from the centre-left did not, of course, focus on the technicalities of the new law. Many, perhaps the majority, in the centre-left had remained proportionalists in their hearts and minds. Many of the centre-left party leaders certainly appreciated the gift that was made to them, offering the power to send to Parliament their most faithful supporters. The protest of the centre-left was purely partisan. They reacted against the attempt to deprive them of a massive electoral victory and of a large parliamentary majority. Also, because of the many mistakes they made and the impressive electoral campaign run by Berlusconi, their fears almost became a self-fulfilling prophecy.

When all the votes were counted, the centre-left enjoyed a comfortable majority in the Chamber of Deputies and a razor-thin two-seat majority in the Senate: 158 vs 156 (the Speaker of the Italian Senate, himself elected by the senators of the centre-left, traditionally does not cast his vote). No wonder the electoral system remains an object of continuous discord and renewed confrontation. In fact, after defeat in a Senate vote, Romano Prodi's government was obliged to resign. Following a quick round of consultation with party leaders, the newly elected President of the Republic sent Prodi back to Parliament for a renewed vote of confidence. He clearly added that no dissolution would be possible before the approval of a better electoral law. Therefore, he solemnly and warmly invited all party leaders to devote themselves to a successful search for a new electoral law. All the well-known and traditional cleavages suddenly resurfaced between a minority of parliamentarians and party leaders who favoured a majority electoral system of the run-off French variant and a majority of parliamentarians and party leaders some of whom had never ceased proclaiming their devotion to a proportional solution.

However, the 'proportionalists' are themselves divided among several alternatives: the German system, the Spanish system, some Italian variants and some technicalities; the percentage level of the threshold clause and whether or not to provide for a majority bonus and its seat size. From an often confused and manipulated debate marred by the continuing search for short-term partisan advantages, two conclusions can be safely drawn. The first one is that the next Italian electoral law will contain a high degree of proportionality. The second conclusion is that it will not work satisfactorily and it will remain an object of political conflict and struggle. In the meantime, another popular referendum on repealing some sections of the existing law is in the making. Though it will only be capable of revising in a majoritarian direction the very bad existing electoral law, not producing an overall satisfying outcome, it is still considered a lethal threat by all minor parties. Hence it may serve to pave the way for a pre-emptive reform whose quality remains to be seen.

THE PARLIAMENTARY SYSTEM

The Italian parliament has always been a parliament of parties, that is, a parliament staffed, controlled and made to work by parties and party leaders; even more so after the 2005 electoral reform, which, as argued before, has given to party leaders the power to 'appoint' their parliamentarians. Depending on one's perspective, one may want to suggest that this outcome was either inevitable and beneficial or, on the contrary, the consequence of choices made by the constitution-makers and negative. The Italian parliament has been described both as 'central' in the institutional and constitutional framework, and therefore very influential on its own, and as just an 'arena' for dialogue, exchange, confrontation between parties, as well as between the government and the oppositions (in the plural). In order to explain and understand the different definitions and descriptions and, as a consequence, the implications for the working of parliament, one must take into account several factors.

It is likely that the most important of these factors is represented by the peculiar form of parliamentary government Italy has had since 1948. In principle, parliament was constructed by the constitution-makers to become a central player in the Italian political system. In fact, no government can come into being without an explicit parliamentary vote of confidence. One might also expect that no government would lose office without a parliamentary vote of no confidence. The reality has been quite different. All Italian governments have been created outside parliament by a previous agreement among party leaders that was ratified by the President of the Republic, who according to the constitution officially appoints the Prime Minister (and countersigns the selection by the Prime Minister of the ministers). Only one government has ever been defeated in parliament on an expressly requested vote of confidence: Romano Prodi's government, in October 1998, following his attempt to test the solidity of his parliamentary majority, a showdown he lost by one vote. Otherwise, all governmental crises have been extra-parliamentary, that is, the product of party disagreements and clashes leading to the resignation of the Prime Minister. This was also the case in the much debated alternation (*ribaltone*), when in November 1994 the decision taken by Umberto Bossi, the Northern League leader, to withdraw his support from Berlusconi's government delivered a parliamentary, and subsequently a governmental, majority different from the one that had obtained an electoral majority a few months before. Constitutionally, for an Italian government to exist only a parliamentary vote of confidence expressed by both the house and the Senate is necessary. Politically, several commentators and analysts, joined, of course, by Berlusconi himself, claimed that this kind of overthrow of his government violated 'the will of the people'. Note, however, that the will of the people had not directly empowered the 1994 Berlusconi government.

Party disagreements and clashes have never even been debated in parliament for at least two good reasons. First, the outgoing Prime Minister never wanted to exacerbate the political tensions thus forfeiting his possibility of returning to office. Second, knowing that, in the absence of any credible governmental alternative throughout the 1946–92 period, they were 'obliged' to collaborate with the same partners, the parties in government never wanted to expose in public, that is, in parliament, their differences of opinion and their disagreements. On the whole, therefore, Italy provides us with a case of a parliamentary form of government in which parliament is not at all central to the creation and dismissal of governments. Is the Italian parliament then central to the policy-making process?

According to the constitution, the legislative initiative belongs to each individual member of parliament, as well as to the government and its ministers (and to 50,000 voters capable of writing, signing and submitting to Parliament an appropriate Bill). In practice, members of parliament exercise their right of legislative initiative frequently and massively (the voters almost never). However, MPs' success rate is very limited. No more than approximately 10 per cent of the Bills approved by parliament are initiated by individual members of parliament or even by groups of them. In any case, those unsuccessful Bills serve an important purpose. They are messages sent to interest groups, associations of all kinds, electoral constituencies and the mass media. Therefore, it is the government and its ministers who are mainly responsible for legislation. Perhaps that is how it should be since the government and its parliamentary majority may then be considered accountable for what they have accomplished or failed to do. At least in the 1980s and 1990s it appeared that the issue of governmental accountability had become relevant to Italian voting behaviour.

As a consequence, the Italian parliament's role has been confined to carrying out certain specific tasks. Of course, one important and specific task consists in evaluating, amending and, in the end, approving the Bills introduced by the government. However, for several reasons, the Italian parliament is not very effective at performing these tasks. The first reason is that it is not well equipped to do so because of three major structural characteristics that merit some consideration. The first is that the Italian parliament is, all things considered, the last of the existing (non-federal) bicameral parliaments in which both houses enjoy exactly the same powers and perform exactly the same functions. This means that all legislation must pass through both houses and even small changes have to be ratified by a vote. There are two politically significant consequences of this arrangement. One is that the law-making process is very slow. On average a Bill of any importance will take at least nine months before being approved. Therefore no government can rely on normal parliamentary procedures to get its legislation passed. So most governments resort to decree legislation. Because even decrees have eventually to be ratified by parliament within sixty days of their promulgation, many of them will expire simply because of the passing of time. Quite a number of them will therefore be reintroduced, following the same path and encountering the same obstacles. However, since decrees are immediately effective and produce concrete consequences, even the most controversial among them will serve to regulate activity in some sector without ever having been approved by a parliamentary majority. This was so not least because the governing majorities had been unable to agree on exactly how to regulate those very activities. Finally, in 1996 the Constitutional Court declared these parliamentary and governmental procedures unconstitutional. Italian governments can still enact decrees, but no longer reiterate them (unless, of course, some of the clauses and some of the wordings appear satisfactorily changed).

Another consequence of the Italian symmetric bicameralism is that the law-making process is very unreliable. It is not simply that the government cannot control the timing of its desired legislation. It does not control the content, the output, either.

This lack of control over the content derives from another structural feature of the Italian parliament and is reinforced by a political feature as well. The structural feature is a consequence of the fact that all legislation must, as a first step, be referred to rather powerful parliamentary committees. It is within those committees that consociational practices, that is, opaque agreements and transactions among the parties in government and the oppositions, found and may still find an easy outlet. This is even more the case when those standing committees are given the power to pass legislation without going through a vote on the floor of the house. One-tenth of the members of a specific chamber and one-fifth of the members of a specific committee retain the power to send legislation to the floor. Therefore, when nothing of the sort happens it is clear that opposition parties have squared their disagreements and that most of the provisions of the Bill do meet opposition demands.

The political factor is, obviously, that throughout the entire first phase of the Republic all governmental majorities were divided on most issues. This condition has not improved in the post-1993 phase because the winning coalitions have been made up of heterogeneous partners and their prime ministers were never strong enough to dictate policies. Though much better placed because it enjoyed a conspicuous parliamentary majority, even Berlusconi's second government (2001–5) did not always have its way because of the conflicts within his own House of Liberties coalition that produced several important ministerial reshuffles and in the end a governmental crisis. On the whole, it remains appropriate to stress that, under most circumstances, three lines of division run through the Italian parliament. One is the classic clear-cut division between the parliamentary majority and the opposition. Always rather rare though not totally absent in the Italian parliament in the period 1946–92, it has almost become the rule after 1993. The second line of division is that between the government and its parliamentary majority, due to the frequent repositioning of the various parties. The third, the most frequent one, cuts through the parliamentary majority itself, giving the opposition a welcome opportunity to exercise the clout eventually deriving from its discipline and active participation in floor and committee votes.

It must be added that the Italian bicameral parliament seems to be a system congenial to a divided, undisciplined, absentee majority. In practice, what the governmental majority loses in one committee it may recover on the floor. What it loses in one chamber it may recover in the other. The price to be paid is always time, often some additional compromises. The Bill intended to regulate the conflict between private interests and public duties, fundamentally, though not exclusively, affecting the media tycoon Silvio Berlusconi, provides a case in point. Obviously, from the beginning, in the summer of 1996, it entailed a clash between the governing centre-left majority and Berlusconi's centre-right coalition. A first draft could be approved in the Chamber of Deputies exclusively because it was bland enough not to pose any serious challenge to Berlusconi's interests and properties. For a couple of years not much more could be done because the centre-left partners were divided on many clauses of the Bill. Finally, a very different and drastically revised text was approved though only by the Senate and just a few months before the May 2001 elections. Lacking the approval of the chamber, it could not become law. Though adamantly denying the existence of a conflict of interests, in 2004 Berlusconi was obliged to pass a law that, in fact, recognises and freezes the situation as it was with no additional consequence.

Finally, the Italian law-making process has always been somewhat erratic. There are several explanations for this. In the first place, too much legislation comes before parliament for approval. This is due largely to the nature of the Italian legal and bureaucratic system. Even minor decisions and regulations have to be translated into laws, or small specific laws (*leggine*). Second, relations of mistrust between the governing majorities and the oppositions have always prevailed. In the past, this was due to the fact that an opposition aware of its practical inability to replace the governing majority was unwilling to relinquish its power of control over the activities of ministers, even more so since the governing majority never accepted the idea and the practice of making individual ministers accountable to Parliament for their decisions. It could not do otherwise because each individual party felt obliged strenuously to defend 'its' ministers, threatening a governmental crisis. Therefore, the quantity and the quality of acceptable regulations by individual ministers are extremely limited. In any case, all governmental majorities have been totally reluctant to penalise their ministers for political incompetence or any other sort of mis-demeanour. Only one minister was ever obliged to resign following a parliamentary no-confidence vote against him. This occurred in 1995. The Minister of Justice who suffered this fate was not a member of any party and occupied his role in the non-political government, not relying on a predetermined parliamentary majority, led by Lamberto Dini, himself at the time without any party base.

The Italian legislative process has been further complicated by membership of the European Community/European Union. Until recent times, all European directives had to be approved and translated one by one by the Italian parliament into Italian law, taking up a lot of time and energy. Politically, the situation was never catastrophic because the left of the PCI/PDS was a pro-European unification party and actively co-operated to speed up this part of the legislative process. Finally, in the early 1990s the decision was made that tens of European Union directives could be approved and implemented through an annual Community Law, drafted by the competent minister, and meant to adequately revise existing Italian laws affected by those directives.

The second explanation for the unreliability of the Italian legislative process has to do with the composition of the Italian parliament. Especially, but not only, in recent times, the most visible aspect of the Italian parliament has been its party fragmentation. There have always existed many, rarely less than ten, parliamentary groups and too many party factions (there were at least five factions within the Christian Democrats, as well as within the Socialist Party until 1976 when Craxi became the party secretary). The result was that several exchanges of all kinds, among many political and non-political actors, were possible, attempted, performed. Not only did these exchanges require time, but their final product also appeared to be quite far from the original text and the preferences of the government. Hence, the various governments either rejected it or tried to reformulate it. In the latter case, the legislative process had to start all over again. In the Parliament elected in 2006 there are thirteen parliamentary groups, which, of course, goes a long way towards explaining the slowness and the difficulty of the legislative process. While agreements and compromises between the government and the opposition are made well-nigh impossible because of the tough bipolar competition, this type of confrontation contributes negatively, in terms of timing and outcome, to the legislative process.

Finally, parliamentary voting procedures have always been of great help to all sorts of more or less organised groups but not to the governing majority itself. Up to 1988 on practically all issues it was possible for a small number of parliamentarians to request and obtain a secret vote. After a protracted and acrimonious battle against secret voting waged by Bettino Craxi, then Secretary-General of the Socialist Party, mainly in order to curb Christian Democratic parliamentarians' lack of discipline and abundance of ties with interest groups, resort to it was severely curtailed. Today, secret voting in parliament is very infrequent, almost exceptional. However, only in a few cases are the results of the voting tallied in such a way as to allow interested public opinion to obtain precise information on how the various individual members of parliament have actually voted. Most votes are, in fact, simply not recorded. Only the final numerical result is recorded, though, of course, the position of each party can be easily deduced from the voting declarations of their representatives. The remaining weapon used by those who want to obstruct the working of parliament is the request that there at least half of the parliamentarians, the so-called *quorum*, are present at any vote taken on the floor, be it an article of a Bill or a single amendment. When no certified quorum exists, the session is first adjourned for one or more hours, then suspended for one day, finally postponed for one week or more. Even a small group of disciplined parliamentarians, at least twelve – that is, the number necessary to request a count on the existence of a quorum – can thus easily disrupt the working of the entire Italian parliament.

The almost total elimination of secret voting has not destroyed the power of the lobbies. The most powerful of them have only transferred their intervention and their pressure from the floor of both houses to their committee rooms and, whenever possible, to the ministerial offices and staff rooms. This relocation of power and pressure, which was already in the making, has only been accelerated by voting and procedural changes. It indicates that, on the whole, the Italian parliament is not a significant independent political player on its own. The move elsewhere of the lobbies sets the seal on the declining power of a body that is badly in need of some streamlining and restructuring, for instance as to the division of functions and powers between the House and the Senate. It also suggests that what badly needs an incisive reform may be the Italian model of parliamentary government and, therefore, not only the relationships between parliament and government, but the very nature, the structure and the power of the government.

GOVERNMENT AND BUREAUCRACY

In many ways the best starting point for the analysis of Italian governments in their policy-making capacity and in their relationship with the bureaucracy and with organised groups is their appointment procedure. Under the Italian constitution, the President of the Republic appoints the Prime Minister and, on the latter's nomination, appoints all individual ministers. In practice, that is, in what Italian jurists have called the 'material' constitution, the procedure has worked in the past and works in the post-1993 phase in a very different manner. In the past, only in exceptional and almost unique circumstances has the President of the Republic himself enjoyed enough political power and enough personal discretion really to appoint the Prime Minister. In most cases the President's role was confined to choosing from among the several names submitted to him by the Christian Democrats. Otherwise, he was practically obliged to accept the ready-made choices submitted by the secretaries of the parties which had agreed to join a coalition government. As to individual ministers, they were not proposed by the Prime Minister, but imposed on him by faction leaders of the various coalition parties. Because Italian governments have all been coalition governments, with the exception of some 'emergency' crisis-softening all-Christian Democratic governments, all the rules pertaining to portfolio allocation were consistently, almost scientifically, applied. Indeed, a precious hand-book existed for the allocation not only of portfolios, but also of all types of political patronage, that has come, most recently, to include even the offices of Speaker of the chamber and the Senate. It was named after its author, a top bureaucrat with Christian Democratic leanings, *Manuale Cencelli*, and detailed these rules in a very effective manner. As things were, it was no surprise that the President of the Republic, himself usually the product of this game, was essentially obliged, except on a couple of occasions, to ratify those complex agreements.

Among the implications of the 1993 electoral law one finds that putting forward a candidate for the office of Prime Minister has, for the two major coalitions, clearly become not only a requirement but also an asset. There is no doubt that in 1994 Berlusconi enjoyed a distinct advantage over the Progressives, who, because of mutual vetos, were unable explicitly to indicate the name of their candidate to Palace Chigi, the official residence of the Prime Minister. Romano Prodi, the 1996 leader of the Olive Tree coalition, certainly acquired for himself and for his coalition partners the advantage of being the Prime Minister designate. The same was true for Berlusconi in the 2001 elections. Finally, in a sense the 2006 elections represented the epitome of this extra-constitutional development that significantly ties the hands of the President of the Republic. In fact, in all these instances, the task of the President of the Republic was confined to accepting the *fait accompli* of the electoral results. However, the President of the Republic can still exert an influence on the choice of the ministers, as Oscar L. Scalfaro (1992–9) did in 1994 when he prevented Berlusconi from appointing as Minister of Justice one of his discredited lawyers. Similarly, President Carlo A. Ciampi (1999–2006) successfully argued the case both for a pro-European Union and competent Minister of Foreign Affairs in Berlusconi's 2001 Cabinet and against the appointment of an indicted parliamen-tarian of the Northern League to the Ministry of Justice. In any case, the overall procedure for the appointment of the Prime Minister and the ministers remains long and relatively complex, because Italian governments remain coalition governments and must accommodate the requests of several partners. Hence, all the traditional criteria reflecting the strength of the partners and the importance of the portfolios still operate.

Because the Italian institutional system is somewhat Byzantine, the appointment procedure can by no means be swift. It is a ritual requiring several days. Moreover, when there is a governmental crisis, and there were many between 1994 and 2007, almost all the old, time-honoured but criticised practices re-emerge. It was so when, in the wake of the demise of Berlusconi's first government, President Scalfaro appointed a non-political government. Following Berlusconi's suggestion and the centre-left positive advice, he selected Berlusconi's Minister of the Treasury Lamberto Dini to become Prime Minister and actively participated in the choice of his non-political ministers. Scalfaro was offered another chance to mastermind a solution to the governmental crisis that followed Prodi's defeat in Parliament. Without the president's support no D'Alema government would have followed. Notice that it was in Scalfaro's discretion, had he so desired, to proceed instead to an early dissolution of Parliament and to call new elections. As we've already seen, President Giorgio Napolitano adroitly managed the first governmental crisis of his term by explaining how and why he had decided to behave then and for the foreseeable future.

All things considered, then, one can say that since 1993 the powers of the President of the Republic have been somewhat circumscribed when it comes to the appointment of the Prime Minister whenever a general election produces a clear winner. Those powers can still be exercised whenever a governmental crisis intervenes during the life of a Parliament. Then, the President may explore two options: immediate dissolution of Parliament or appointment of another Prime Minister, but only if he has a reasonable chance of mustering a parliamentary majority and keeping it together and working. In sum, while the inauguration of Italian governments may have shifted towards a more 'immediate' and closer relationship with the outcome of the elections and the preferences of the voters, there still remain many opportunities for politico-institutional manoeuvres.

Since the selection and appointment procedures of the past seem to have, on the whole, survived, one can understand why Italian coalition governments continue not to be characterised by enough political cohesion or collective responsibility; and why the Prime Minister has never been in a position to acquire and retain enough power to lead his coalition government and to dismiss incompetent or disloyal ministers. Since no Italian Prime Minister enjoys the power to dissolve Parliament and all Italian prime ministers know that they can be replaced by their parliamentary majority or, more likely, when and because a strategically located party shifts its support, their ability to steer a clear uncompromising course have generally speaking been quite limited. In a sense, Berlusconi's 2001 government, which was based on a sizeable majority supporting an allegedly strong leader, can be taken to represent a test of how much the Italian politico-institutional system has changed (or not). Politico-governmental stability is a precondition of governmental effectiveness, and this may be the second test for Berlusconi's government and the ministers he claims to have personally recruited with reference to their competence. I am afraid that neither test has been passed satisfactorily. Not only has Berlusconi delivered far less than he solemnly and spectacularly promised when he signed on TV his personal 'Contract with the Italians', but he had to suffer a governmental crisis in April 2005. Moreover, he was repeatedly obliged to replace quite a number of his ministers even in top offices: three ministers of Foreign Affairs, one Minister of the Interior, two ministers of the Treasury, two deputy prime ministers and a host of minor ministers and under-secretaries.

In the pre-1993 period, faction leaders successfully proposed or imposed the names of individual ministers for two major reasons: first, because they were powerful within their respective parties and factions; second, because they were capable of representing the preferences of some interest groups supporting specific parties and factions and, as a consequence, could promise politico-electoral advantages to come. Ministries were a reward for past groups' behaviour or a commitment to future action.

To a large extent, powerful faction leaders and sub-leaders were put in charge of those ministries considered significant by their socio-economic reference groups. As a consequence, the powerful Small Farmers' Confederation, closely associated with the Christian Democrats, was the successful sponsor of almost all the ministers of Agriculture. It was impossible to become Minister of Education without the active support and the open acceptance of the very many Catholic associations operating in that field. The Minister of Industry had to entertain an almost symbiotic relationship with powerful industrial groups and for a long time with the National Association of Manufacturers (*Confindustria*). Almost as a corollary, the Minister of State Participation was to be the representative of the major public enterprises and was closely controlled by a specific DC faction.

A long time ago, two ideal types were formulated to describe and explain the relations between ministries and their socio-economic constituencies: *clientela* and *parentela*. *Clientela* is the relationship between a ministry's bureaucracy and the interests it is supposed to deal with. Due to lack of competence and resources,

Table 5.3 Governments of Italy, 1991–2006

No.	Year	Prime Minister	Party composition
10	1991	G. Andreotti	Christian Democrat, Socialist, Social Democrat, Liberal
11	1992	G. Amato	Socialist, Christian Democrat, Social Democrat, Liberal
	1993	C. A. Ciampi	Independent, Christian Democrat, Socialist, Social Democrat, Liberal
12	1994	S. Berlusconi	Let's Go Italy, National A, Northern League, Christian (CCD)
	1995	U. Dini	Independent, Left Democrat, Popular, Northern League
13	1996	R. Prodi	Popular, Left Democrat, Greens, Renewal
	1998	M. D'Alema	Left, Popular, Green, Social Democrats, Renewal, Christians (UDEur), Communist (PdCI)
	1999	M. D'Alema	Left, Popular, Democrat, Green, Social Democrat, Renewal, Christian (UDEur), Communist (PdCI)
	2000	G. Amato	Social Democrat, Left, Popular, Democrat, Green, Christian (UDEur), Communist (PdCI)
14	2001	S. Berlusconi	Let's Go Italy, National A, Northern League, Centre (UDC)
15	2006	R. Prodi	Left Democrats, Daisy, Communists (RC, PdCI), Values, Christian (UDEur), Rose (SDI, Radicals)
16	2008	S. Berlusconi	Freedom, Northern League

Note: The first party indicates the Primer Minister's affiliation.

the ministry's bureaucracy becomes almost a client of those interests. It comes to depend on them even for technical advice. Therefore the most important decisions are really drafted, shaped or at least implemented according to the wishes of powerful interests. To a large extent, according to Joseph LaPalombara, this was the case with the Ministry of Industry *vis-à-vis* Fiat.

Parentela is the relationship between a ministry's bureaucracy, and often the minister him/herself, and outside interests when they share the same perspective, the same goals, the same values. This was, and in all likelihood remained for a long period, the relation between the Ministry of Education and the many Catholic organisations and associations active in the education field. Especially so because the Minister of Education had always been, with one short-lived exception, a Christian Democrat. With the passing of time, *clientela* and *parentela* may have changed in intensity, but not in quality. For instance, until its abolition by popular referendum in 1993, the Ministry of State Participation remained the client of all public companies and was not meant to orient their activities or to evaluate their performance, but only to transmit their requests to the Council of Ministers and vent their grievances. For some time the Ministry of Labour, usually allocated to a minister with a union background or endowed with some union ties, worked in harmony with the unions. In a typical relationship of *parentela*, it transmitted their demands and supported them in the usually complex and long-drawn-out process of bargaining with the employers and their confederation.

Much, though certainly not all this, has changed. Not only has the disintegration of the old party system made it imperative for interest groups to look for a more flexible relationship with the bureaucracy, but it has also offered some of them more independence. However, especially in the 2001 electoral campaign it became clear that thanks to the bipolar confrontation the National Association of the Entrepreneurs (Confindustria) could choose sides and throw its full weight behind Berlusconi. For his part, the leader of the House of Liberties could claim that the Confindustria programme was 'his programme'. One would expect the trade union movement to make a similar choice, though in the opposite direction, that is, in favour of the centre-left. Instead, because of their longstanding political division into three different national organisations, the trade unions have been lukewarm towards the centre-left government. Even the left-wing union the Italian General Confederation of Labour (CGIL) did not consider the centre-left government 'its own government', but just a friendly government who could be, and in fact often was, criticised.

Though not uniquely present in the Italian case, *clientela* and *parentela* were far more pervasive than other patterns of interest interactions with political and bureaucratic decision-makers. In Italy, for a long period of time the politics of interest groups continued to be dominated by political parties, their factions, their experts, whose power derived from their position as party spokesmen or women and not from their technocratic expertise. In light of the weakness of the Italian bureaucratic apparatus, it has always seemed out of place even to speak of the possibility of 'iron triangles': parties, interests, bureaucrats. Often recruited according to political criteria, mostly promoted according to partisan criteria, rarely endowed with specific technical knowledge or abilities, utterly lacking any *esprit de corps* or professional pride, Italian bureaucrats, with the exception of a few relatively happy islands of integrity such as the Bank of Italy, some branches of the Ministry of the Interior and the Ministry of Foreign Affairs, were the happy prey of political sponsors, and of defensive and rent-seeking union activities.

The bureaucrats' inefficiency and short working hours are paid for by job tenure and limited demands on their energies. Obviously, this trade-off is not profitable for the state when it comes to a need for active intervention in some socio-economic areas. It has been and remains highly profitable for governing parties when it comes to the acquisition of electoral consensus. Often those relatively few ministers who want(ed) to govern – that is, to deal with interest groups on an equal footing – decide(d) to bypass the state bureaucracy. They proceed to create their own more or less restricted staff, their own political cabinet made up of loyal and competent collaborators. However, this way, on the one hand, the bureaucracy is not encouraged to improve its performance; on the other hand, the difficulties deriving from the implementation and the policy evaluation phases do not disappear. Indeed, by playing according to the rules, the disgruntled bureaucrats may seriously damage any governmental activity.

Overall, the Italian policy-making process can be characterised as of the *reactive* type and accomplished in *conditions of emergency*. More precisely, policy-making of some importance is rarely proactive, that is, initiated in the political sphere following the intuition of some clever politicians. On the contrary, it is usually reactive because it is the product of demands coming from some socio-economic sectors, from outside actors such as collective movements or interest groups, from international pressures and obligations. Policy-making of some importance is rarely the product of normal procedures in normal times. It is usually the product of emergency situations because suddenly an issue has become of burning importance. Perhaps the issue had been forgotten because of the lack of instruments to keep it on the political agenda. Perhaps it had been postponed for lack of consensus among the decision-makers. Perhaps it had been removed because of cultural inability to envisage a viable and acceptable solution, or because the groups pressing for a solution were not powerful enough, or because those opposing a solution were very powerful indeed. When the issue becomes salient, the solution becomes urgent.

There are several examples of reactive policies being adopted under emergency conditions. The entire story of the reform of the university system is a case in point. It had been debated for seventeen years and became an issue only following the violent student eruption of 1977. Still, the law was passed only some years afterwards. Probably the most significant case of a reactive policy taken into serious consideration only when it developed into an inescapable emergency is represented by reform of the electoral law. Since more information has already been provided above, suffice it to recall here that it took two popular referendums to put the reform of the electoral system on the political and parliamentary agenda. Though it was more than just a policy, the decision to embark on meeting all the criteria necessary to join the Euro was taken by the Italian government only at the last moment in autumn 1996 when it became clear that almost all the member states were ready and that the costs of staying outside were going to be extremely high. Finally, another good example of the next likely reactive policy will be the one concerning the pension system, which has already been postponed, because of the hostility of the unions, for several years.

Because the two patterns of relations between politics and organised interests that dominated in Italy were those of *clientela* and *parentela*, there was not even a meaningful political debate about neo-corporatism and its potential contributions to policy-making. Imported from the international literature, the expression was first precisely utilised in the late 1970s. In that period, characterised by high inflation and growing unemployment, the socialist–communist trade union (CGIL) showed signs of developing some neo-corporatist availability, quickly rejected by the Christian Democratic trade union (the CISL). Later, in 1981, a quasi-neo-corporatist agreement between the employers and all the unions was signed thanks to the then Minister of Labour. Not much progress was made in the early 1980s. Most developments were blocked and became a lost cause when in 1984 the Socialist Prime Minister Bettino Craxi decided to curtail the indexation system by decree after having played with the idea, now strongly sponsored by CISL leaders, of tying the unions to the government in a true neo-corporatist pact.

The problem with the creation of a neo-corporatist system was, however, not so much political as mainly structural. The two most important conditions for the construction and functioning of a neo-corporatist system were missing in the Italian case. First, the union movement remained divided along political and cultural lines. Second, the party of the industrial working class, the Communist PCI, was never even close to governmental power. The three main trade unions, the CGIL, the CISL and the UIL, were closely affiliated to their respective parties, namely the PCI (later, the PDS), the Christian Democratic DC and the Socialist PSI. From a cultural point of view, that is, in their bargaining strategies, Italian unions have always exhibited profound theoretical and practical differences. They are preoccupied with representing all the workers, mainly at the national level, and pursuing both economic and political goals (CGIL) or with representing only unionised workers, essentially at the local and plant level, with exclusively economic goals (CISL). They tend to be either soft (UIL) or tough (CISL and CGIL) on the employers, and either soft (UIL, CISL and the socialists within the CGIL) or tough (the rest of the CGIL) on the government.

Understandably, the sheer fact that the PCI, correctly regarded as the party of the industrial working class, never had nor could legitimately aspire to a governing role prevented the establishment and consolidation of that initial condition of trust indispensable for the emergence and functioning of a neo-corporatist system. The working class was understandably suspicious of deferring its day-to-day requests in exchange for future gains, since no political player was in a position to offer them a credible guarantee. The neo-corporatist attempts that were made between the 70s and the 80s remained half-hearted and appeared ill founded.

The nature of the relationship between unions, parties and coalition governments is still a matter of discussion, conflict and disagreement. In the meantime, however, for several reasons common to West European union movements, and for some reasons peculiar to the Italian case, Italian unions have lost membership, representativeness, power. They are now a declining player in search of a role. However, it remains difficult and costly to govern against the unions or without taking into account at least some of their preferences and obtaining some collaboration. Understandably, this is what the various centre-left governments have tried to do, offering both the unions and the industrialists the possibility of collaborating in the formulation of policies in the overall economic area as well as in the field of labour and industrial relations. These complex pacts, some of them requiring more flexibility on the part of the labour force in order to create more jobs, seem to have worked reasonably well. However, both the unions and the industrialists have expressed some dissatisfaction, but a new pattern of relationship is not in sight.

The Italian decision-making process is complex and cumbersome. All minor and major decisions are bound to pass through a series of stages and to seek the agreement of several players, incessantly engaged in reversible and opaque negotiations. In the last instance, all significant and insignificant decisions are subject to formal approval by a divided and not very disciplined parliament. It is no surprise, then, that the overall decision-making process is inevitably exposed to interference by many illegal activities. Where a multiplicity of actors takes part in allocating a conspicuous quantity of public resources, often to be disbursed according to party criteria, the likelihood of corruption is very high. Indeed, political corruption has been widespread in the Italian case and it remains a feature of the political system.

There have been basically two types of corruption. The first type, money paid out to policy-makers at all levels in order to influence their decisions, predominated in the long first phase of the democratic regime up to the mid-1970s. It must be added that, on the part of public companies, whose managers were appointed by governing politicians, this money was also intended to subsidise governing parties, their electoral campaigns and political structures. In the absence at the time of any system of public funding of political parties, this kind of financing was not only indispensable, but almost taken for granted, as quasi-legal.

Then, in 1974, in the wake of a major scandal involving oil importers who had bribed parties in government in order to secure higher prices for oil products following the Arab embargo, a law was passed financing political parties with state money. Among its provisions, the 1974 law forbade public companies from making donations to political parties. Therefore, to some extent, it liberated, so to speak, public managers from that kind of peculiar, sub-institutional obligation towards parties. However, the flow of 'black' money was not completely interrupted.

The second type of corruption became even more widespread and acquired a systemic character. In this instance, party secretaries and their collaborators, ministers, under-secretaries, members of parliament, and local politicians were active in exacting kickbacks on all public contracts and public works, licences and allocations of resources and activities. This scandal of massive proportions was uncovered first in February 1992 in Milan, then, few regional exceptions aside, throughout the entire country. It became known as 'Kickbacksville' (*Tangentopoli*) and the corresponding large-scale investigation was called 'Clean Hands' (*Mani Pulite*).

The extent and depth of corruption derived from two factors. In the first place, all governing parties justified their requests for money, often sheer extortion, to industrialists, builders and contractors by pointing to the existence of the Communist threat. Their leaders claimed to represent the dam against that threat. Money was needed for increasingly costly electoral campaigns to counterbalance the superior

Communist Party organisation. Of course, this motivation lost all credibility with the collapse of international communism and the transformation and decline of the former Italian Communist Party.

In the second place, industrialists, builders and contractors were well aware that the same parties and, often, the same politicians who had already been in positions of power for a long time retained a credible chance of staying there just as long again. A change of governmental coalitions was not in prospect and, as long as there was a powerful Communist Party, from their point of view it was not even desirable. Kickbacks to governing parties and politicians could be justified, at least partially, as the 'price of democracy' and, to a lesser extent, as a sort of tax on their activities. Paradoxically, but understandably, some streaks of consociationalism survived for a while, so that, especially in Milan, where the PCI had long been part of the governing majority together with the PSI, some money was more or less indirectly poured into Communist coffers as well.

Though conspicuous, kickbacks have not prevented all Italian political parties from running high deficits. These were largely due to skyrocketing electoral expenditures, but in some cases also to the search for personal enrichment and a luxurious standard of living. Finally, because of the advent of commercial TV, electoral campaigns had become unbearably expensive and, trying to catch up with both the Christian Democrats and the Communists, the Socialists needed more and more money. They could get it only by pointing to their permanent role in the government and by exchanging favourable decisions for 'donations'.

In Italy, the relationship between money and politics has always been controversial and from the very beginning the law on the state financing of political parties has been challenged. A referendum to repeal the law in 1978 showed simultaneously great dissatisfaction and the extent to which the PCI and the DC were entrenched. The two parties barely succeeded in defeating the request: 44 per cent of the voters were in favour of repeal, 56 per cent against. In the ensuing years, the political climate changed drastically. In April 1993 more than 90 per cent of voters decided by referendum to do away with the law; more precisely, to stop the funds going directly to party parliamentary groups though not the electoral reimbursement. Indeed, the 1994 electoral law explicitly provides for substantial electoral reimbursements. However, all parties need more money and spend more money for their organisations. Hence, they have surreptitiously step by step reintroduced a form of state financing not only of their activities, but also of their structures. In any case, political corruption has not disappeared from Italian politics. Indeed, the ranking of Transparency International puts Italy year in, year out around thirty-second in terms of public morality, just above Nigeria and well below all European democracies.

INTERGOVERNMENTAL RELATIONS

In order to understand Italian intergovernmental relations precisely, it is necessary to always keep one premise in mind: Italian governments have constantly been weak both in terms of their likely and predictable stability and in terms of their decision-making powers. Therefore, those institutions and groups that were interested in opposing a decision could just try to buy time and wait for the inevitable change in the government and/or the ministers and/or the policies. There has so far been no significant improvement either in the stability or in the decision-making powers of Italian governments. Indeed, two major changes indicate that many decisions will be taken elsewhere. Paradoxically, if this phenomenon is confirmed it may allow those Italian governments that are successful in gaining enough political stability to concentrate on a few, major decisions. The first very important change has been increasing Italian integration with the European Union. This is not a development that concerns Italy alone. However, some of its consequences have been more important for Italy than for other member states of the European Union. The case of the Euro is especially revealing. Italian public opinion and fundamentally all Italian governments, with the possible exception of the one led by Silvio Berlusconi from April to December 1994, have been, at least verbally, unabashedly pro-Europe in all its various expressions. This pro-European attitude has constituted a sort of threshold for the governmental acceptance of some parties. Gradually, though increasingly, the Communists shifted their position and their policies towards, at least in the late 1970s, full acceptance of and full participation in the European institutions and unification process. Hence, to some extent, one can say that the simple existence of a European democratic framework produced positive results for the Italian political system.

Leaving aside a longer story, in any case not made of active participation by subsequent Italian governments and of innovations suggested by them, the most important turning point has been represented by the criteria set at Maastricht in 1992 for joining the European Common Currency system. Though initially perplexed regarding the ability of his government successfully to meet those criteria together with the 'virtuous' European states, in 1998 Prime Minister Romano Prodi exploited the opportunity to put in order the Italian economic system, which had been disrupted by several years of 'merry financial dealings'. Long considered a sort of safety net, the process of European integration opened a not too large but very important window of opportunity for Italy through which it became possible to restructure the Italian economic system. Once the Italian economic system was put on its not too solid feet, it became necessary to continue to run the economy without deviating from the guidelines and the indicators of the Growth and Stability Pact. Then, 'Europe' has been utilised by several Italian governments in different ways. It provides an alibi: 'We, the politicians, are not responsible for these painful decisions; they are imposed upon us by Europe'. It is taken as a constraint: 'We, the politicians, cannot do more or differently; these are the demands of Europe'. It offers an opportunity: 'We, the politicians, can assure you that by behaving as Europe asks Italy to do great benefits will follow'. Above all it has worked as a safety net: 'Because we are part of a democratic Europe, no doubt the European Union will support democracy and the democrats in Italy as well as the Italian socio-economic system'. A few nuances of interpretation notwithstanding, only the extreme right, the Northern League and Communist Refoundation dare in different ways criticise the European Union and oppose some of its policies.

The overall consensus that the European Union is on the whole largely beneficial for the Italian economic and political system is not broken by any contrary view. Even the critics are not asking for Italy to abandon the European Union, but just to redefine some of its positions and some of its policies. However, several criticisms have been made of all Italian governments for their limited ability to influence the decision-making process at the European level. The responsibility for this falls on the traditional handicaps of Italian institutions: the ministers, Parliament, the bureaucrats, Italian regional governments. Frequently changing ministers can neither grasp the importance of some issues nor exercise enough influence on their European counterparts/colleagues. A slow-working and cumbersome Parliament can neither intervene before the European decision-making starts, by suggesting counter-proposals and giving guidelines and support to the ministers, nor respond in the implementation process by effectively and in a timely manner translating European regulations and directives into the Italian legislative system. Bureaucrats, often selected according to patronage criteria, can rarely carry the day with their European counterparts, also because they cannot rely on a steady guide from their respective ministers.

Paradoxically, the most important development in the relationships between Italy and the European Union has taken place in one area where prestige counts enormously but cannot be translated into political power, that is, in the appointment of European Commissioners. Because of successful though different combinations of *fortuna* and *virtù*, Emma Bonino (1994–9) and Mario Monti (1994–2004) were given the opportunity to demonstrate their knowledge of the problems and their solid commitment to the European unification process. Moreover, because of his success in leading Italy into the Euro, Romano Prodi has been rewarded with the much more demanding task of leading the European Commission in difficult times and in uncharted waters (1999–2004), presiding over a major process of enlargement. However, not much of this personal prestige and accomplishment has reverberated on the Italian political system.

Political and institutional problems similar to those existing at the national level can be easily found at the regional level. Frequently changing governments, technically incompetent and overstaffed bureaucracies, a larger than acceptable dose of political amateurism have meant that most Italian regions have been less capable of obtaining and of spending European regional development funds. As a consequence, while several regions in the Republic of Ireland, in Spain and in Portugal have improved their lot and have increased their standard of living, most Italian Southern regions, with the exception of Basilicata, have made no leap forward. Whether this is due to the quality of the politicians and the bureaucrats or to the institutional mechanisms and their limited decision-making autonomy remains to be seen. In fact, it will soon be possible to discern which, thanks to one of the few significant institutional innovations introduced in the 1990s: the (quasi-)direct popular election of the president of the regional governments. It is not so much the mechanisms utilised to elect the presidents of the regions that are of special importance. What count more are two other elements: the first is that the winner, which is the elected President, gets a bonus of seats that consolidates and stabilises his majority; the second element is that the President cannot be replaced before new elections. In fact, it appears that regional instability has been significantly reduced, making it possible to proceed to the implementation of the President's legislative programme. In addition to the perspective concerning powers of decision-making that are not new, but can finally be exercised to the full, depending on the personal and political capabilities of the presidents, there is another perspective from which one may want to evaluate the changes taking place at the regional level.

This perspective suggests that powerful regional presidents will attempt to acquire a new balance of powers between regional governments and the national government. A greater number of social, economic and political preferences will be taken into consideration, to the satisfaction of a greater percentage of voters in their respective regions. Of course, it is still too early to draw convincing lessons and definitive conclusions from the short Italian experience. Nevertheless, for the time being no full positive evaluation appears to be justified. Centre-left regional presidents have largely supported the actions and the proposals of the centre-left national government and centre-right regional presidents have challenged, in some cases with tremendous partisan determination, whatever the centre-left national government was proposing or doing. Both sets of regional presidents have been asking for more powers and more functions. For their part centre-left regional presidents have given a positive evaluation to the devolution law approved by the government. The law rejected by the centre-right opposition in Parliament has been predictably opposed by centre-right regional presidents, most vehemently so by the regional president of Lombardy and Veneto. When in 2005 the centre-right House of Liberties approved a constitutional reform shifting more powers to the regions, the centre-left opposed it and succeeded in having it, together (as we will see in the next paragraph) with all the other constitutional reforms, rejected by a popular referendum. Only future events will reveal whether a new more effective and more satisfactory equilibrium is reached. It will also be interesting to see whether the presidents of the Italian regions will acquire the national stature of US governors or, to resort to a more appropriate comparison, of the Minister-Präsidenten of the German *Länder*. At this point, in the case of the relationship between the Italian state and the regions, between the national government and the regional presidents, the situation must be defined as in transition. Their respective powers as well as their functions will probably be changing, but there are too many factors to be taken into account before making any appreciable prediction.

Always a sore point in the functioning of the Italian political and administrative system, the relationships between the politicians and the judicial system became tense and burning with the explosion of the investigation called 'Clean Hands' (*Mani Pulite*). In order to understand its developments, one must state very clearly at the outset that 'rule of law' is not exactly the most appropriate expression to define the Italian situation. Organised crime has always been powerful in Italy, so much so that, according to many analysts and commentators, in at least four Italian regions, Campania, Calabria, Sicily and Apulia, the state, that is, the police and the judges, cannot guarantee a decent amount of control of the territory and personal security. In those regions, the relationship between organised crime and politics is, indeed, very close. Protracted Mafia and *camorra* activities would be impossible without the connivance of some politicians; some astonishing political careers would be unimaginable without the support of organised crime. In some cases, it may not be necessary for the politicians to look for support from organised crime. It is the Mafiosi themselves who decide whom to support, when and why. The Mafiosi choose who is going to be the winning horse and throw their weight behind him or her. Afterwards, they will ask for something in exchange, brandishing as a minimum the threat of shifting their votes and funds to other candidates or, even, of revealing their ties. Many economic activities are controlled by organised crime, so much so that all Southern Italian regions are deliberately avoided by foreign investors. For too long, some sectors of the judiciary, of local administrators, even of the police, did not clearly and consistently oppose organised crime. Then, at the beginning of the 1980s, several courageous judges, such as Giovanni Falcone and Paolo Borsellino, and some loyal civil servants, such as the then prefect of Palermo, General Carlo Alberto Dalla Chiesa, decided to confront the Sicilian Mafia. In due time, they were all murdered. The major change with respect to the past is that Mafia killers and Mafia bosses have all been apprehended and condemned, but their supporters and protectors within the political world have so far escaped being pursued by the law. Apparently, for some politicians Mafia votes do not stink. And new Mafia leaders have already appeared.

That said, the area where the confrontation between some judges and the political class has been most frequent, most tense, most bitter has been in those many illegal activities related to the financing of political activities: unlawful contributions, fraudulent budgets, kickbacks, embezzlement. Although since 1974 in Italy there has existed a system of public financing of political parties, state money has never been enough to cover all the costs of some lavish electoral campaigns and some over-staffed party organisations (plus the personal enrichment of some politicians). Ostensibly, most party leaders and parliamentarians justified their illegal activities by stating that some corruption in the financing party activities and electoral campaigns is 'the price of democracy'. For a long time, parliamentarians were also capable of protecting themselves against judicial action by rejecting the parliamentary authorisation the judges had to request in order to investigate the behaviour of a parliamentarian and to bring him (almost never her) to trial. Then, the parliamentary rules were changed. Instead of it being necessary to muster an absolute majority to approve the judges' request, it became indispensable to muster an absolute majority to reject it. In this entirely new ball game and under pressure from the mass media and public opinion, it became almost impossible for most parliamentarians to block the requests of the judges. At the end of the 1992–4 Parliament, more than one-third of the total number of Italian parliamentarians – that is, more than 300 of them – had received a judicial notice. However, because the Italian legal system offers many loopholes and because, of course, most politicians can employ very powerful teams of lawyers, several trials were never pursued to the end and several offences enjoyed the shield of the statute of limitations.

It is probably not true that there is less public support today for the anti-corruption judges. On the one hand, there is less mobilisation in favour of the judges; on the other, the issue of political corruption is even more politicised because Berlusconi, some of his close collaborators and some of the judges he allegedly bribed have all been indicted. For many Italians, however, the evaluation of the judicial system is made not on the basis of the struggle between the politicians and the judges or by the magistrates against political corruption and organised crime. It is made on the basis of the day-to-day performance of the magistrates dealing with civil cases.

With the exception of a few hardworking judges, the Italian judiciary is made up of many civil servants who lead a bureaucratic life, who are promoted through a seniority system without any quality control of their activities, who enjoy short working days, long vacations and high salaries. Public opinion being mixed, it is difficult to predict what kind of reception any attempt to reform and/or to 'normalise' the judges (in Berlusconi's words, 'to bleach the red robes') will receive. The criticisms made by Berlusconi of the Constitutional Court have been more disturbing because the Italian Constitutional Court has in fact played its role of 'guardian of the constitution' commendably. It is one of the few Italian institutions not really in need of any reform, except, perhaps, the introduction of 'dissenting opinions'. To sum up, like most other Italian institutions, the judiciary appears to be in transition: from an imperfect situation of considerable professional and organisational autonomy with respect to executive power, often, however, bordering on the corporatist protection of privileges, towards an unknown future.

STRATEGIES FOR INSTITUTIONAL REFORM

Notwithstanding their personal and partisan evaluations, all Italian politicians, scholars and commentators are well aware that the present institutional system cannot remain as it is. Generally speaking, there are two major points of view deriving from the fact that the electoral system remains an object of major contention and continues to be exposed to partisan reforms, and from challenges coming from popular referendums. The premise is that the 'old' political system was constructed on a proportional electoral law and that it was made to work, deliberately and/or out of necessity, by a proportional distribution not only of seats and offices, but also of several types of resources. Indeed, according to many analysts, the proportional principle was carried to the point of sustaining a sort of consociational democracy and its arrangements. Hence, those who are still favourable to 'proportionality' would say that, if it proves impossible to draft a decent PR law, any more or less majoritarian electoral system must be accompanied by some appropriate checks and balances. Those who criticised the old proportional electoral law – among other reasons also because it had fostered consociational devices and states of minds – and succeeded in reforming it, take the opposite view. They argue that the 2005 electoral proportional law has produced negative unbearable consequences. Therefore, a reform of the reform is absolutely indispensable before new elections take place (elected in 2006, the existing Parliament's term ends in 2011).

While there appears to be some agreement on the need for reform or at least for cosmetic embellishments, there is no agreement on the fundamentals. Nobody is any longer advocating the British model, while officially, though not in practice, the Left Democrats maintain that they would be in favour of the introduction of the French run-off electoral formula. It is clear that no party will be able positively to impose its favourite electoral formula. Since it is also clear that too many parties within their respective coalitions enjoy the role of veto players, it seems easy to predict two plausible outcomes: (1) no reform at all; (2) a reform introducing some proportional formula for the translation of votes into seats, accompanied by a very low threshold for access to parliamentary representation. In the light of my overall interpretation of Italian politics in the past decade and my forecast for the next decade, I can draw two general conclusions: first, no reform of the electoral system will completely satisfy all party actors or the voters; second, the electoral system will continue to be an object of major political contention and controversy.

In the meantime, another discussion will remain heated both with reference to the method to be implemented in order to draft and approve any constitutional reform and to the substance; that is, precisely which reforms will bring to a successful completion the political and institutional transition, at the same time improving the functioning of the Italian political system and the quality of its democracy. As is perfectly understandable, a combination of personal and partisan preferences with systemic views has shaped the various proposals. The majority of politicians have evaluated the proposals put forward by their colleagues, by their parties and by the scholars engaged in this debate with an eye to their personal/political advantage or, more frequently, to their potential disadvantage. The debate has oscillated between those who are arguing that the reforms ought to be made with the agreement of all those involved (*quod omnes tangit ab omnibus probari debet*) and those who are advocating not only the right, but even the duty of a parliamentary majority to take responsibility and to make the necessary reforms. The centre-left, as is clearly indicated by the experience in 1997–8 of a special parliamentary Bicameral Committee entrusted with the power to draft proposals in four areas (the form of the state; the model of government; the judiciary system; parliament and the relationships with Europe), has taken the first position.

Under the chairmanship of Massimo D'Alema, then the Secretary of the DS, perceived to be the most capable Italian politician and the most committed to the success of the reformist efforts in order to prove his statesman-like qualities, the Bicameral Committee worked for one and a half years. However, no overall agreement was reached and, in June 1998, the leader of the opposition Silvio Berlusconi all but sank the proposals formulated by the Bicamerale. While Berlusconi's quasi official explanation was that the Committee had formulated low-profile proposals, his critics point to the fact that he had been unable to get what he wanted in terms of the reform of the judiciary, that is, tighter political control of all judicial activities. Be that as it may, in all other fields the Bicameral Committee had demonstrated that there are no widely shared solutions to the Italian institutional problems.

When the turn of the centre-right came, Berlusconi and his allies decided to go it alone. As I have indicated above, the House of Liberties redrafted almost half of the Constitutional Charter pursuing two fundamental goals. On the one hand, more activities and more power were, satisfying the requests of the Northern League, devolved to the regional governments. On the other hand, more political and institutional power was given, as both Berlusconi and Gianfranco Fini, the leader of National Alliance, had long advocated, to the Prime Minister. The new arrangement, to be accompanied by reform of the symmetric bicameralism providing for territorial representation of the regional governments, largely inspired by proposals coming from the centre-left, was dubbed 'strong premiership'. It was also meant to put aside forever the only alternative model that was circulating in the Italian constitutional debate, French-style semi-presidentialism. To a large extent, though never precisely enough and without appreciating all the historical and political features that could not be created by any institutional mechanisms, the strong-premiership model was supposed to be or to be equated with the so-called 'Westminster model': a powerful Prime Minister leading his parliamentary majority. This was something Italy never enjoyed, but it is doubtful whether it could be shaped under the prevailing Italian political conditions, in which the two major coalitions hide the reality of a still fragmented party system.

In order to give more power and a better legitimacy to its candidate for the office of Prime Minister, prodded, after several vacillations, by Prodi himself, the centre-left decided to hold primary elections. Open to all voters, who only had to sign a pledge in favour of the Olive Tree coalition and to contribute €1 to the organisational expenses and to finance the subsequent national electoral campaign (the majority giving much more), an unusual and unprecedented primary was held on 16 October 2005. Unexpectedly, more than 4,300,000 voters turned out to choose among six candidates. Supported both by the Left Democrats and by the Daisy, Prodi received more than 3 million votes. However, the momentum of this intense mobilisation was quickly wasted when all party leaders of the centre-left coalition rejected all requests to hold primaries for the selection of parliamentary candidates.

The electoral law had been an informal part of the package of more ambitious constitutional reforms formulated by the House of Liberties and approved by its sizable parliamentary majority before the dissolution of Parliament in February 2006. Vehemently opposed by the centre-left, those reforms amounted almost to an overhaul of the Italian constitution, not only because they affected 56 articles out of 138, but because they were meant to reshape the major Italian institutions: the Presidency, the government, Parliament, and their mutual distribution of powers, as well as the relationship between the state and the regions, in the form of adminis-trative and political devolution. In fact, in the House of Liberties' constitutional preferences there were two distinct logics. The first one was fundamentally to strengthen the powers of the Prime Minister with respect to both the President of the Republic and Parliament, or, more precisely, his/her own parliamentary majority. Hence, the President of the Republic was to be deprived of his power to appoint the Prime Minister and to dissolve Parliament, while in practice no parlia-mentary majority could replace the Prime Minister. The second logic was apparently to increase the powers of the regions at the expense of the 'central' state, though without giving fiscal autonomy to the regional governments.

In principle, both logics had been widely shared by several leaders and con-stitutional advisors of the centre-left. Indeed, the strengthening of the powers of the Prime Minister figured prominently in some of the centre-left constitutional projects. Therefore, their highly vocal opposition appeared a mix of partisan and expedient motivations. What could be said of the constitutional package is not so much that it was going to be a threat to Italian democracy, but that it was often confused and that it promised no improvement of the functioning of the political system. On the contrary, it might have backfired and led to frequent inter-institutional con-flicts. When not approved by a two-thirds parliamentary majority, all constitutional reforms may (not 'must') be submitted to a popular referendum if this is requested by 500,000 voters, or five regional councils, or one-fifth of the parliamentarians. In a show of strength, centre-left leaders successfully pursued all three paths to the popular referendum. A not so secondary purpose was to increase the involvement of the voters, to 'educate' and to mobilise them (against Berlusconi's government). The referendum was held on 26 June 2006 in the wake of the centre-left's electoral victory. There was a good turnout (52.3 per cent): 15,971,293 (61.3 per cent) voted yes to the cancellation of all the reforms, while 9,962,348 (38.7 per cent) voted no, that is, expressed their support for the reform. In only two Northern regions, Lombardy and Veneto, where the centre-right, especially Let's Go Italy and the Northern League, is electorally very powerful, did there appear to be a majority in favour of those reforms.

The reforms of the House of Liberties were defeated, but the overall issue of how to construct a better circuit connecting the voters to Parliament and parliamentary majorities with their prime ministers, and how to improve political representation by redefining the role and the powers of symmetric Italian bicameralism, are still very much alive. In fact, they are also somewhat tied to reform of the electoral law. But again there does not seem to be a satisfactory shared solution in sight. Since no transformation of the Italian model of government followed, all constitutional issues remain very much alive and are the object of serious controversies.

More precisely, the Prime Minister remains, at best, a *primus inter pares*. With the exception of the 2005 primary election, he (so far, no 'she') is chosen by party leaders, does not lead his parliamentary majority, may be replaced at any time because it is not up to him to make the decision to dissolve parliament and to call early/new elections. The traditional Italian problem of the instability of prime ministers has not yet found a solution. However, it is fair to stress that, because of the immense effort by Berlusconi to personalise his politics as well as all his electoral campaigns, and because of the bipolar competition, Italian voters have had the impression of being consulted and being allowed to vote directly for their Prime Minister. Constitutionally, of course, it is not so. However, there is no doubt that Berlusconi's role in the House of Liberties coalition is such that, politically, he has certainly achieved a sort of direct popular election of the Prime Minister. In any case, once in office, the Prime Minister will find that his powers are limited, that his majority is not compelled to be disciplined, that the bicameral system is resistant to any attempt to rationalise and speed up the decision-making process.

For those who believe that the Italian problem and, generally speaking, the most important problem of many political systems is not the speed of the decision-making process, but its quality, it is fair to add at least one remark. Not only has the Italian decision-making process always been slow and cumbersome; it has also not been transparent. In the First Republic this lack of transparency led to the politics of buck-passing. Since it was almost impossible to identify who was responsible for what was done and what was not done, it became politically fruitful/advantageous to pass the buck to allies, to the government, to the opposition and *vice versa*. The practice has only minimally improved in the present political transition. Political account-ability appears still to be an elusive goal, and/or an eluded request, so much so that the proposals for a semi-presidential model of government were criticised on two counts: on the one side, because in case of a coincidence between the presidential

Table 5.4 Level of satisfaction with Italian democracy

	1987	1991	1997	2000	2004	2006
Very satisfied/fairly satisfied	26	20	30	36	46	53
Not very/not at all satisfied	72	78	67	62	52	44
Don't know; no reply	2	2	3	3	2	3

Source: Eurobarometer, selected years.
Note: Numbers are percentages of people in survey polls.

majority and the parliamentary majority too much power would be concentrated in the hands of the Chief Executive; on the other side, because in the case of cohabitation there would be the likelihood of conflict between the President of the Republic and the Prime Minister. Seen from the Italian perspective of the ills of the political system, any coincidence of the two majorities could speed up the decision-making process but also impose a lot of political accountability on the President. Cohabitation may make the decision-making process more difficult and perhaps slower, but it would shift a lot of accountability onto the Prime Minister. So far Italian political actors, especially minor parties, which are accustomed to exploiting their black-mailing power over the larger parties of their respective coalitions, have responded that they do not want any of either. Vested interests, not only those represented by the parties in Parliament, have succeeded in blocking any serious and significant reform. As a consequence, the Italian political institutional system remains in a unhealthy state of transition.

GLOBAL ASSESSMENT

Any assessment of a political system is bound to be influenced by two types of elements. The first is the evaluation of the previous political system; the second is the criteria/measures that are utilised. In the case of Italy, there is a third complicating element: the state of transition affecting the entire political system.

The First Italian Republic collapsed under the weight of excessive corruption, because of its inability to reform itself and to produce alternation in government. It has unjustly been buried by criticism of its later vices and not evaluated in a fair manner for some of its long-term contributions to the establishment, consolidation and even the growth of Italian democracy. In one sentence, one should not refrain from remarking that between 1948 and 1993 the Italian Republic had become, in spite of its traditional institutions, an economic giant, but because of the inadequacy of its institutions had not progressed much beyond the stage of a political dwarf. The next phase of the Republic, definitely not yet a Second Republic, was inaugurated in 1993 amid many exaggerated expectations, but also in the wake of great dis-satisfaction and bitterness on the part of most citizens and some political actors. So far, for a variety of reasons, the new phase has not lived up to those expectations. The third phase is not yet in the making. However, major changes, positive and negative, have taken place. Some of them have already been hinted at in the previous paragraphs. Here, a few additional and more systematic comments will be made, specifically focused on the authorities and the regime.

As to the authorities, on the positive side it appeared for a time that renewal of the political class, also because of generational reasons, might finally introduce new energies and produce new ideas. Not so. The 2006 elections witnessed a repeat of the competition between the same two leaders (69-year-old Berlusconi and 67-year-old Prodi) who had confronted each other ten years before in 1996, both surrounded and advised by the same old collaborators. On the negative side, it must be stressed that many members of the old political class have survived and continue to play a significant political role even in the new system. The second aspect is that the renewal of the political and parliamentary class has largely been the product of the appearance and the success of Let's Go Italy and, secondarily, of the presence in parliament of the Northern League. However, the appearance and consolidation of Let's Go Italy have not set into motion a process of collective renewal of the political class. Let's Go Italy has brought into the political system a number of representatives of a specific sector of society: businessmen and professionals with limited political competence and scanty interest in learning about politics. Political incompetence and professional arrogance have not renewed, and could not renew, Italian political life. On the contrary, contempt for politics and amateurism have certainly increased the distance between the average voter and politics. The traditional Italian cynicism has been strengthened and the rate of abstention has slowly, though irresistibly, gone up. Finally, the encumbering presence in the political sphere of the wealthiest Italian businessman, media tycoon Silvio Berlusconi (and his professional collaborators), created a very tense situation characterised by actual and potential clashes and was worsened by his ascent to power, by his conquest of Palace Chigi. This was so not only because of the overall conflict between his private interests and public duties, but also because of his conflict with the judiciary and his pervasive control of the television system.

Following Pippa Norris's (1999) useful three-fold differentiation, the evaluation of the Italian regime can effectively be broken down into its three components: regime principles, regime performance and regime institutions. It may be difficult to disentangle the performance of the regime from the democratic principles. Nevertheless, there is little doubt that the Italians have always been dissatisfied with the workings of their democratic regime. The percentages tell the story. I have chosen six different points in time: 1987, at the height of the five-party government, just at the end of Craxi's term as Prime Minister; 1991, when the cracks in the old Republic were already appearing; 1997, one year after the beginning of the Olive Tree governmental experiment; 2000, when that governmental experiment was coming to a somewhat disappointing end; 2004, in the midst of the long governmental experience of Berlusconi's House of Liberties; and 2006, during the electoral campaign.

As the percentages convincingly indicate, there have always been deep-seated reservations about the way Italian democracy works. For more than a decade these reservations appeared not to be exposed to contingent factors. They were not exposed to easy fluctuations influenced by changes in the government. Nevertheless, and ironically, the first not major increase in the percentage of satisfied citizens, though admittedly it still did not amount to an absolute majority, appeared just one year before the centre-right defeated the incumbent centre-left government and in spite of an overall improvement in the quality of Italian democracy. Somewhat surprisingly, in recent years there has been a surge in the percentage of Italian citizens satisfied with the working of their democracy. In 2004, for the first time ever, more than half of Italians were expressing their satisfaction. Independent and reliable sources confirm that the findings of the Eurobarometer appear not to have been influenced by exogenous factors. My interpretation is that by the autumn of 2004, Berlusconi's coalition had offered, though with some internal tensions, a long period of governmental stability. Obviously, this rare achievement received a favourable rating and very significantly increased the percentage of Italians satisfied with the working of their democracy. Let me stress that in all likelihood Italians were giving a good mark not to the performance of the government, but to the working of their democracy, finally capable of assuring, if not the best of governments, at least a stable government. As to the small decline in the spring 2006 percentage, a plausible hypothesis would suggest that Italians may have reacted against the poor quality of the electoral campaign.

There is no doubt that democracy is the only game played in the Italian political system, but neither the players nor the way the game is played satisfy more than a slim majority of Italian citizens. As a consequence, a significant number of them, though comparatively not an excessive percentage (only about 20 per cent), tend to stay outside the political arena, that is, they do not even bother to vote. While, comparatively, the Italian abstention rate compares well with that of most European democracies, it has grown in the last three or four elections. On the whole, a limited degree of improvement in the workings of the institutions has been achieved. The reform of the electoral law, although imperfect and unfinished, has significantly and positively changed the type of the political-electoral competition. As discussed in the section on parties and the party system (on pp. 136–44), bipolar competition has created the need for an inclusive democracy in which, in contrast to the previous regime, which was blocked around the DC and permanently excluded both the extreme right and the Communist Party, all the relevant actors have found a role and the possibility of exercising some clout. Above all, alternation has not only become possible, but has already been practised a couple of times. Of course, some scholars have stressed that any alternation will create some, at least temporary, dissatisfaction among the losers (perhaps one might also measure the amount of 'happiness' of the winners). Analysts should, therefore, not make too much of the dissatisfaction of some sections, never the same, of the Italian voters. It is the cost of alternation. One can surmise that the majority of Italian voters are probably willing to pay that price. What makes that price excessive in some cases is the anxiety fuelled by the fact that the rules of the game, the procedures, the institutions are not fully established. They are not stable because both the debate concerning which institutions and the attempts to reform them seem to be heading in a partisan rather than a systemic direction. Unless, and until such time as, a single player or coalition of players succeeds in formulating new rules and constructing new institutions, the Italian political system and its democracy will continue to be the object of pervasive criticism, and understandably so. In sum, the proof of the vitality of Italian democracy is that it is still changing. The level of citizens' dissatisfaction with its functioning, but not with its principles, is evidence that enough Italians care about improving it.

ACKNOWLEDGEMENT

Much of the rewriting of this chapter was accomplished in the Hilary and Trinity Terms of 2007 when I was Monte dei Paschi Visiting Fellow at the Centre for European Studies at St Antony's, Oxford, whose hospitality I gratefully acknowledge.

BIBLIOGRAPHY

General works

Bufacchi, V. and A. Burgess (2001) *Italy since 1989. Events and Interpretations*, revised edition, Basingstoke and New York: Palgrave.
Colomer, J. M. (1996) 'Introduction', in J. M. Colomer (ed.) *Political Institutions in Europe*, London and New York: Routledge.
—— (2001) *Political Institutions: Democracy and Social Choice*, Oxford: Oxford University Press.
Hine, D. (1993) *Governing Italy: The Politics of Bargained Pluralism*, Oxford: Clarendon Press.
Pasquino, G. (ed.) (1995) *La politica italiana. Dizionario critico 1945–1995*, Roma-Bari: Laterza.

Electoral system

Katz, R. S. (2001) 'Reforming the Italian Electoral Law', in M. S. Shugart and M. P. Wattenberg (eds) *Mixed-Member Electoral Systems. The Best of Both Worlds?*, Oxford: Oxford University Press.
Pappalardo, A. (1996) 'Dal pluralismo polarizzato al pluralismo moderato. Il modello di Sartori e la transizione italiana', *Rivista Italiana di Scienza Politica* 26 (1): 103–45.
—— (2002) 'Italian Bipolarism and the Elections of 2006. End of the Line or Just a Connecting Stop?', *Journal of Modern Italian Studies* 11 (4): 472–93.
Pasquino, G. (2007) 'Tricks and Treats: The 2005 Italian Electoral Law and Its Consequences', *South European Society & Politics* 12 (1): 79–94.
Wertman, D. (1977) 'The Italian Electoral Process', in Howard R. Penniman (ed.) *Italy at the Polls. The Parliamentary Elections of 1976*, Washington, DC: American Enterprise Institute.

Political parties

Giannetti, D. and E. De Giorgi (2006) 'The 2006 Italian General Elections: Issues, Dimensions and Policy Positions of Political Parties', *Journal of Modern Italian Studies* 11 (4), December: 494–515.

Newell, J. L. (2000) *Parties and Democracy in Italy*, Aldershot: Ashgate.

Pasquino, G. (2003) 'A Tale of Two Parties: Forza Italia and the Left Democrats', *Journal of Modern Italian Studies* 8 (2): 197–215.

Sartori, G. (1976) *Parties and Party Systems. A Framework for Analysis*, New York: Cambridge University Press.

Parliament

Capano, G. and M. Giuliani (2003) 'The Italian Parliament twixt the Logic of Government and the Logic of Institutions', in J. Blondel and P. Segatti (eds) *Italian Politics. The Second Berlusconi Government*, New York and Oxford: Berghahn Books.

De Micheli, C. and L. Verzichelli (2004) *Il Parlamento*, Bologna: Il Mulino.

Della Sala, V. (1998) 'The Italian Parliament: Chambers in a Crumbling House?', in Philip Norton (ed.) *Parliaments and Governments in Western Europe*, London: Frank Cass.

Government

Della Porta, D. and M. Vannucci (1994) *Corruzione politica e amministrazione pubblica: risorse, meccanismi e attori*, Bologna: Il Mulino.

Dente, B. (ed.) (1990) *Le politiche pubbliche in Italia*, Bologna: Il Mulino.

Golden, M. (1988) *Labor Divided. Austerity and Working-class Politics in Contemporary Italy*, Ithaca: Cornell University Press.

LaPalombara, J. (1964, 1987) *Interests Groups in Italian Politics*, Princeton, NJ: Princeton University Press.

Verzichelli, L. and M. Cotta (2000) 'Italy: From "Constrained" Coalitions to Alternating Governments?', in W. C. Müller and K. Strøm (eds) *Coalition Governments in Western Europe*, Oxford: Oxford University Press.

Global assessment

Bull, M. J. and G. Pasquino (2007) 'A Long Quest in Vain: Institutional Reforms in Italy', *West European Politics* 30 (4).

Norris, P. (1999) 'Introduction: The Growth of Critical Citizens', in P. Norris (ed.) *Critical Citizens: Global Support for Democratic Governance*, Oxford: Oxford University Press.

CHAPTER 6

Spain and Portugal

Rule by Party Leadership

Josep M. Colomer

Except for the brief and distant period of union of Portugal with the Spanish Crown in 1581–1640, the peoples and rulers of the two countries of the Iberian peninsula have followed a long tradition of ignoring each other. After the loss of the greater part of their colonial empires, and during a large part of contemporary history, Spain and Portugal endured authoritarian regimes and remained cut off from the outside world. Even in their comparatively few commercial, cultural and media external relations, Spain was more in touch with other countries of continental Europe, and Portugal with Great Britain, than the two countries with each other.

Despite this mutual ignorance, the two neighbouring states followed rather parallel courses in the struggle between authoritarianism and democracy in the nineteenth and twentieth centuries. If we take a simple working definition of democracy as a political system with civil liberties and competitive elections by broad suffrage, in Spain we have to record a republic which lasted eleven months in 1873, a moderate monarchy between 1890 and 1923 and another five years of republic from 1931 to 1936. The rest of the time has been taken up by an oligarchic monarchy and two military dictatorships, that of General Miguel Primo de Rivera (1923–9) and that of General Francisco Franco (1939–75), the latter preceded by a bloody civil war. For its part, the Portuguese monarchy of the nineteenth century also swung between legitimist, moderate and liberal constitutionalist phases, but a democratic republic existed only between 1910 and 1926, and that, as in the Spain of the following decade, was highly unstable, ending in military insurrection. After a series of military governments, António de Oliveira Salazar installed a long-lived authoritarian and corporativist regime, which lasted from 1933 to 1974.

For many Spaniards in the second half of the twentieth century the first news from Portugal to catch their attention was precisely the overthrow of the dictatorship by the armed forces' insurrection of April 1974, which was styled a 'liberation by coup'. A year and a half later, in November 1975, the death of General Franco opened the road to democracy in Spain, albeit via the monarchy which legally succeeded him. The two countries thus followed different routes in the transition from their respective authoritarian regimes. In Portugal the sudden collapse of authoritarianism, in large measure provoked by the final colonial crisis, gave way to the formation of a provisional government made up of opposition parties which up to that time had barely been organised, then to a period of instability during which a new and extensive constitution was approved with a strong social reform content, and finally to a moderate stabilisation. In Spain, by contrast, reform of the dictatorship was begun by the monarchist government itself in negotiation with the authoritarian rulers, and only after the first competitive election was a constituent process initiated with alternative negotiations taking place between new reform rulers and the anti-dictatorship opposition.

The historic isolation of the two countries had left them on the margins of the Second World War, which allowed the two authoritarian regimes to survive and which also explains their later almost simultaneous entry into the United Nations Organisation in 1955. Nevertheless, Spain and Portugal managed to establish normal foreign relations only after they had consolidated their democratic systems, and although the anglophile Portuguese had been persuaded to join a free-trade agreement between various countries of the European periphery (the European Free Trade Association, EFTA), they did not jointly become members of the European Community until 1986.

There are some basic similarities and some striking differences between the institutional choices of the Portuguese and Spanish democracies. In both countries, uncertainty about the future during the first phase of the transition, together with the wish to establish a democratic system that would include minorities, as a reaction against the former exclusive authoritarianism, led to the adoption of electoral rules based on proportional representation. In both cases moderate multi-party systems exist, although, especially in Spain, with a strong tendency towards polarisation.

On the other hand, while in Portugal the influence of the Armed Forces Movement, which had overthrown the dictatorship, introduced the institution of a directly elected President, in Spain the monarchy inherited from Franco's rule could make itself compatible with democracy only through the establishment of a parliamentary system. Thus the first democratic generation in Portugal saw a high degree of conflict between the President, the Prime Minister and the Assembly, as well as a great deal of government instability, while in Spain there has been the greatest government stability in Europe.

Finally, while the relatively small size and homogeneity of Portugal permit a unitary state structure, centralised in Lisbon, the greater extent and diversity of Spain are the bases of substantial territorial decentralisation. Given the high degree of concentration of power into a single party in the Spanish central government, territorial governments with different political party orientations have become the main element of political pluralism in the system, although not always in favour of consensual, stable agreements.

These institutional differences, however, did not prevent the governments of the two countries adjusting to moderate public policies dominated by the attractiveness of centrist political positions. An important common feature of the two systems, which offers a useful perspective for comparative analysis, is the lack of institutionalisation of the paths of negotiation and conflict resolution; for the most part these are undertaken in direct relations between the leadership of the major political parties.

ELECTIONS

Before going on to analyse political institutions, it is useful to provide a brief introduction to the context of voter preferences in which these institutions are set; this context in turn is partly an expression of the economic and cultural structures of society.

Political ideology

Many Spanish citizens are quite capable of locating their political preferences on a two-dimensional policy and ideology space formed by the symbolic left–right and the nationalist axes. The first axis, the left–right symbolic representation, basically reflects two sets of policy issues. One is socio-economic, ranging from a preference for governmental intervention (public spending and redistribution), on the one hand, to the market (tax reductions and free enterprise), on the other. However, a relatively high level of material well-being has accorded less ideological relevance to social class than in other historical periods, while inducing a consensus favourable to economic growth and the general prosperity of society. The second issue is moral and religious, with the two opposites favouring either pluralist tolerance or traditional family values. Some surveys show this issue assuming greater importance in the way the electorate identifies itself ideologically, especially among the young.

Citizens' preferences on these two sets of policy issues may not always coincide, but the limited choice offered by the political parties tends to reduce the available alternatives and confine them to one single dimension. Thus the main alternatives offered by the parties are located on a left–right axis whose poles represent, on the one hand, positions more favourable to government intervention and moral pluralism (close to the social-democratic tradition) and, on the other, positions more favourable to the market (albeit with notable elements of protectionism and government assistance) and to traditional Catholic values (near to the social-Christian tradition). Typically liberal combinations of economic market and moral pluralism are, by contrast, weaker. The distribution of Spanish citizens' preferences on the ideological and synthetic left–right dimension tends to be unimodal. The mean of individual preferences is situated slightly to the left of centre, as has been traditional in neighbouring countries such as France and Italy, and in contrast to the majority of other European countries, where it is located rather more to the right.

Alongside the left–right ideological dimension, there is another relevant dimension, namely the national identification within which political issues such as decentralisation and multilingualism are reflected. Together with Belgium and Switzerland, Spain is one of the European countries in which this dimension explains a large part of citizens' preferences. In some communities, such as the Basque Country and to a lesser extent Catalonia, one can even observe greater ability on the part of citizens to place themselves on the national dimension than on the left–right dimension (by responding to whether they consider themselves to be more or less Spanish or rather Basque or Catalan or from another community). This two-dimensional aspect is reinforced by the existence of their own political parties within these communities.

More specifically, among the main issues in election campaigns in Spain have been social assistance, family aid, public pensions for the retired, reduction of taxes, as well as some moral-cum-religious questions, such as the teaching of religion in state-subsidised schools, divorce and abortion. Emphasis has also been given to inter-territorial rivalries, especially in the distribution of public resources, as well as to the relations of the central government with nationalist parties. In some elections other issues have taken saliency, such as law and order, terrorism, the record in government of the party in power, especially as regards economic growth, and the probity of the parties and candidates.

In the Portuguese case socio-economic and moral-religious issues are also highly relevant to the structure of citizens' political preferences. Some relative importance is also attached to foreign policy and there was a range of support given to the constitutional schema, although these two issues could basically be included on the left–right ideological dimension. The limited data available on the distribution of preferences among Portuguese citizens show less consensus than in the Spanish case. While the strongest trend is again centrist, and the mean appears to be located very near the centre, there are other lower modes or poles of attraction to left and right.

Stabilising electoral rules

Certain basic criteria of electoral representation were established in Spain even prior to the first election in 1977, and these were mostly consolidated later on. As has been mentioned, a generic criterion of proportional representation was adopted for the lower chamber. But the wish on the part of the reformists in power at the time to use their advantageous position in favour of the government candidacies of the Union of the Democratic Centre (UCD) led to the over-representation of rural areas and strong correctives to the principle of proportionality.

The first election in 1977 was subject to a decree law which, in the designers' intention, was conceived as able to produce an absolute majority of seats for a party with one-third of the popular vote. In fact, it favoured the two most voted for electoral lists, at the time the UCD centre-right and the centre-left Spanish Workers' Socialist

Party (PSOE). The 1978 constitution, drawn up by a wide consensus among the parliamentary parties, confirmed the criterion of proportional representation for the Congress and extended it to the regional parliaments. In 1985, when the PSOE had an absolute parliamentary majority, an organic law was approved which confirmed many of the elements of the decree law of 1977, with the corresponding advantage in favour of the PSOE and the new larger party on the centre-right, eventually called People's Party (PP).

In accordance with these regulations the Congress of Deputies is relatively small in size: 350 seats (although the constitution allows up to 400). The seats are allocated according to the d'Hondt formula, with a threshold of 3 per cent of the votes (which is effective only in large districts). The element of the system which has the biggest political consequences is the magnitude of the electoral districts, which is determined by allocating a minimum of two seats to each province, with an additional number according to the population; the average is seven deputies per province, with wide variation, plus 2 single-member districts in Africa. In fact, among the total of 52 electoral districts a dual system operates: on the one hand there are 34 districts with fewer than 7 seats, which function as in a plurality system and which elect over 40 per cent of all deputies; on the other, there are just 18 districts with 7 or more seats, which elect the remaining 60 per cent of deputies, which permits a degree of multipartism. This duality nearly coincides with rural districts and predominantly urban districts, whose numbers of seats are respectively over-represented and under-represented in comparison with their populations. As a result, one can have such extreme cases, for example, as the district of Barcelona having four times as many electors per deputy as the district of Soria. Thus a party well established in the rural districts could gain a greater number of deputies than another more urban-based party which might receive more popular votes.

Fear of introducing instability into the democratic system acted as a disincentive to repeating certain elements of the electoral model of the republic of the 1930s, such as open lists. For this reason, personal relations between the voters and their representatives are very weak, and in fact Spain and Portugal are among the very few European countries with proportional representation in which the lists of candidates are closed.

These rules reward the two biggest parties and penalise, above all, the small and medium-sized Spain-wide parties. On the other hand, since the rules operate fairly neutrally as regards the big regional parties, they allow the electorate to express itself at the nationalist dimension and also promote the issue of decentralisation on the political agenda. In the 9 democratic elections in the period 1977–2004, the electoral systems has produced 4 single-party absolute majorities in Parliament, always based upon a minority of popular votes. The electoral deviation from proportionality averaged 13 per cent, the highest among all countries with proportional representation and very close to the deviation produced by the plurality system in Great Britain. The number of effective parties, which is below average for Europe, has decreased over time; in the 2004 election there were 3 effective parties in terms of votes, but this figure was reduced to 2.5 in terms of seats.

In most districts only two parties achieve representation; these were the centrist UCD and the Socialist PSOE in the 1977 and 1979 elections, and the PSOE and the People's Party AP/PP since 1982. The advantage share of these parties (their proportion of seats compared with their proportion of the votes cast) was 136 per cent for the UCD (1977–9), 116 per cent for the PP (1982–2000) and between 104 per cent and 126 per cent for the PSOE (in each of the two periods mentioned). By contrast, the shares of the Communist Party of Spain (PCE) and its successor the United Left (IU), and other minority Spain-wide parties, such as the former Democratic and Social Centre (CDS), have been around 50 per cent. The proportionality profile shows that a party can only achieve over-representation in seats if it obtains at least 20 per cent of the vote.

In addition to their mechanical effects upon proportionality and the number of parties, the electoral rules have important psychological effects, particularly favouring the strategic vote – commonly known in Spain as the 'useful vote' – on behalf of the big parties. According to a number of surveys, over 70 per cent of the voters who said they were 'near' to the PSOE and the PP – that is, to one of the two major parties – said that they had actually voted for them, whereas fewer than 40 per cent of those who considered themselves 'near' to the PCE/IU and CDS actually voted for their favourite party. It would seem, therefore, that voters learned to anticipate the consequences of the electoral rules and adapt their behaviour accordingly. This perceptiveness also expresses itself in different behaviour in the two kinds of district indicated previously; the adherents of the smaller parties tend to vote more sincerely – that is, in accordance with their preferences – in twice as big a proportion in the large electoral districts as in the small ones.

Besides those already mentioned there are other entry barriers to electoral competition, especially funding for the parties from the state budget, and access to the mass media, which are distributed according to the proportion of seats allocated by the rules and not on the basis of the proportion of votes bestowed by the electors. All these elements act as self-reinforcing mechanisms of the restrictive aspects of the electoral system. They have favoured high and increasing levels of polarisation of electoral competition between the two larger Spain-wide parties at the expense of political pluralism.

The initial reform of the authoritarian regime led to the creation of a second chamber, called the Senate, which was initially intended largely as a place of rest for elderly members of the Franco regime. The current Senate is elected with rules that tend to reduce the political supply even more than the Congress. A fixed number of senators are elected in each province, independently of population size (4 in the peninsular provinces, 3 in each of the three big islands, 1 in each of the 7 small islands, 2 in Ceuta and 2 in Melilla), giving a total of 208, to which are added 50 senators representing the Autonomous Communities (normally elected by their parliaments); that is, 258 altogether. The over-representation of rural areas is reflected in this case in the fact that the number of electors per senator is forty-five times greater in Barcelona than in Soria. It would thus be possible to obtain a majority of senators with only one-sixth of the popular vote.

The Senate ballot gives each elector a limited vote, that is, less than the number of seats up for election in the constituency. However, the voter is not obliged to elect a fixed number of candidates but can choose between one and three in the districts with four seats, between one and two in the districts with three seats, and one in those with one or two seats, so that this procedure might be called a limited approval vote.

This rule would incline each party to present the same number of candidates as the maximum number of votes at the disposal of each elector (for example three in the districts with four senators). If the big parties were to present as many candidates as seats up for election, they could run the risk of their followers dispersing their votes among these candidates, so that each might win fewer votes than the party. Likewise, if the small parties were to present only one or two candidates, they would be encouraging their followers to cast some of their votes for other parties' candidates. Because of these risk-averse party strategies, very few individual candidates have managed to get elected by calling upon their followers to vote for them alone.

As a result of the rules and the strategies they induce, local two-party systems are formed in the Senate elections. Usually the two parties share the seats out, three for one party and one for the other, or two each if the result is nearly a draw. Altogether, greater deviation from proportionality results than in the case of the Congress, and also different possibilities of winning parliamentary coalitions than in the lower chamber.

The rules for the election of the Autonomous Community parliaments vary, since they have been established autonomously, but they are very homogeneous. The electoral districts are usually the provinces, with smaller areas in some single-province Autonomous Communities (Asturias and Murcia) and the islands in the Balearic and Canary archipelagos. In five Autonomous Communities the average size of the districts is less than seven seats. Here, too, one can see a disparity in representation in favour of the rural areas, with an extreme case in the Basque Country, where the number of inhabitants per seat is four times greater in the province of Biscay than in Alava. In every case the d'Hondt formula is used, lists are closed and there are thresholds (3 per cent in nine cases, 5 per cent in seven – although in some the limit is applied to each province – and 20 per cent in each of the Canary Islands).

In political terms the main difference between the Autonomous Communities is that between the four which were set up between 1980 and 1982, which hold their elections separately and which can dissolve their parliaments and call new elections (the Basque Country, Catalonia, Galicia and Andalusia), and the other thirteen communities which since 1983 held their elections on a fixed date and at the same time as the municipal elections, although most of them have reformed their statutes in order to be able to call anticipated elections. In the first four communities it is much easier for the regional parties to develop specific strategies, while in the second group the Spain-wide parties have more opportunity to apply a global strategy. Specifically, during the period 1980–2007 the winner was different from the party in central government in 82 per cent of the 22 regional elections held separately, but only in 38 per cent of the 65 regional elections held simultaneously.

Municipal elections are held in single local districts, using the d'Hondt formula, with a threshold of 5 per cent, and closed lists (except in municipalities with under 250 inhabitants, where the limited approval vote is used, with a maximum of four individual votes for five seats). These rules foster a sincere vote among the citizens to a greater extent than in the parliamentary elections and have allowed greater pluralism on the town councils than in the other institutions referred to above.

Table 6.1 Elections to the Spanish Congress of Deputies, 1977–2008

Year	Turnout %	Communist PCE/IU	Socialist PSOE	Catalans CiU	Catalans ERC	Basque PNV	Centre UCD	Centre CDS	People AP/PP	Other
1977	79	9	29	3	–	2	35	–	8	14
1979	68	11	31	3	–	2	35	–	6	12
1982	80	4	48	4	–	2	3	7	26	6
1986	70	5	44	5	–	2	–	9	26	9
1989	70	9	40	5	–	1	–	8	25	12
1993	77	10	39	5	–	1	–	–	35	10
1996	78	11	35	5	–	1	–	–	38	10
2000	70	6	35	4	–	2	–	–	45	8
2004	77	5	43	3	3	2	–	–	38	6
2008	75	4	44	3	1	1			40	7

Note:

Communist: PCE/IU: Communist Party of Spain/United Left (Partido Communista de España/Izquierda Unida).

Socialist: PSOE: Spanish Workers' Socialist Party (Partido Socialista Obrero Español).

Basque: PNV: Basque Nationalist Party (Partido Nacionalista Vasco).

Catalans: CiU: Convergence and Union (Convergència i Unió); Republican Left of Catalonia (Esquerra Republicana de Catalunya).

Centre: UCD: Union of Democratic Centre (Unión de Centro Democrático); CDS: Democratic and Social Centre (Centro Democrático y Social).

People: AP: Popular Alliance (Alianza Popular); PP: Popular Party (Partido Popular).

In Portugal, too, the electoral rules have remained basically unchanged from the first election in 1975 to the constitution of 1976, the electoral law of 1979 and the later revisions of the constitution. In fact the constitution expressly excludes the possibility of revising the criterion of proportional representation.

Only the single-chamber Assembly, elected for a period of four years, has seen its size reduced, from 263 seats in 1975 and 250 in 1979 to 230 since 1991. As in Spain, the seats are allocated according to the d'Hondt formula, but without a threshold and with a distribution of districts which advantages the more populous and urban areas.

These rules have given the two biggest parties, the centre-left Socialist Party (PS) and the centre-right Social Democratic Party (previously the People's Democratic Party, PPD/PSD), over-representation in terms of number of seats in comparison with proportion of votes cast, while being fairly neutral towards the two smaller parties, the leftist Communist Party of Portugal (PCP, which usually presents itself in coalition with other leftist groups) and the right-wing People's Party (previously Democratic and Social Centre, CDS/PP). Only the smallest parties have regularly suffered, and they have hardly achieved representation.

As a consequence of the electoral rules and of the learning experience of the Portuguese voters themselves, successive and frequent elections have seen a growing concentration of votes on just a few candidates. In other words, the effective number of parties, measured in votes, has been reduced from 4.2 in 1975 to 3.4 in 2005; in the latter year there was a difference in relation to the effective number of parties

Table 6.2 Elections to the Portuguese Assembly, 1975–2005

Year	Turnout %	Communist BE	Communist PCP	Socialist PS	Renewal PRD	Social Democratic PPD/PSD		People CDS/PP	Other
1975	92	–	17	38	–	26		8	11
1976	83	–	15	35	–	24		16	10
1979	87	–	19	27	–		42	–	12
1980	84	–	17	28	–		48	–	7
1983	78	–	18	36	–	27		13	6
1985	75	–	15	21	18	30		10	6
1987	73	–	12	21	5	50		5	7
1991	70	–	9	29	–	51		4	7
1995	67	–	9	44	–	34		9	4
1999	62	–	9	44	–	32		9	6
2002	61	3	7	38	–	40		9	3
2005	64	6	8	45	–	29		7	5

Note:

Communist: BE: Leftwing Bloc (Bloco de Esquerda); PCP: Portuguese Communist Party (Partido Comunista Português), usually running in electoral coalitions with minor parties, such as Portuguese Democratic Movement (MDP) and Unitary Democratic Coalition (CDU) (with the Greens).

Socialist: PS: Socialist Party (Partido Socialista).

Social Democrat: PSD: Social Democratic Party (Partido Social Democrata).

People: CDS: Democratic and Social Centre (Centro Democrático Socia); PP: People's Party (Partido Popular).

measured in seats of 1.0 (that is to say, a relative reduction in the number of parties of 30 per cent). In general the electoral deviation has been around 9 per cent.

By contrast, electing the President of the Republic directly introduced an element of higher institutional pluralism. The President is elected every five years by absolute majority in two rounds. Both the distinct electoral procedure, which allows multiparty activity in the Assembly while inducing bipolarisation in the presidential polls, and the fact that the temporal mandates of the two institutions do not coincide mean that the parliamentary and governing majority has been different from the coalition of parties which has supported the winning presidential candidate most of the time. There has been single-party control of both the presidency and the parliamentary government only during the periods of Socialist dominance in 1999–2002 and 2005–6, four years in total over more than thirty years.

Spanish and Portuguese voters, respectively, elect 54 and 24 deputies to the European Parliament. Given the relatively small number of seats up for election, in 1987 Spain established a single electoral district for this kind of election, at the same time reproducing the criteria of the d'Hondt formula and closed lists. The single constituency encourages the formation of 'federal' candidacies between regional parties. It also results in greater proportionality than the Congress and Senate elections. Nevertheless, the low visibility and complex mediations associated with representation in the European Parliament have incited expressive and protest votes, especially against the party in domestic government.

Finally, both Spanish and Portuguese citizens can manifest their preferences through referendums on matters of special importance, although the results are not binding. The referendum mechanism was used in Spain during the transition to initiate political reform in 1976, to approve the constitution in 1978, to approve the first four regional Statutes of Autonomy, already mentioned, in 1979–81, and to give support to the project of European constitution in 2006. In the post-constituent framework, the consultative process has to be called on the initiative of the President of the government and authorised by a majority of the Congress, as happened in the referendum which confirmed Spain's membership of the North Atlantic Treaty Organisation (NATO) in 1986. In Portugal, two 1998 referendums to introduce legislative reforms on abortion and regionalisation failed, but the first issue was successfully reintroduced in 2007.

POLITICAL PARTIES

Political parties in Spain have a very low membership and a highly centralised organisation, which concentrates a lot of decision power in the hands of the party leadership. Two factors, above all, explain this situation. In the first place, the political transition and the drawing up of the democratic constitution were marked by negotiation between the political elites, which gave rise to a high degree of person-alisation of the political options. This high decision power of the leaders in the political process helped them to strongly control the parties' internal decisions, including the centralised nomination of electoral candidates. Second, as we have seen, the institutional rules erect strong entry barriers to electoral competition and at the same time inhibit intra-party competition for the electors' votes by establishing closed lists of candidates. As a result, membership of political parties is very low, less than 5 per cent of all voters.

All the Spanish parties possess important characteristics in common which distinguish them from the big European mass parties. First of all, holders and seekers of public office make up a large proportion of the membership. Second, the elected office holders who work in the various state representative institutions usually have to submit to tight discipline from party headquarters.

The public financing of the parties reinforces these tendencies. On the one hand it reduces the subjective value attached by the leadership to the members' con-tributions (which in fact account for less than 5 per cent of the parties' resources). On the other hand the prohibition of private financing, the weak judicial control of party finances and the lack of publicity about many aspects of the parties' internal affairs have given rise to irregularities which have been the focus of numerous corruption scandals. Among these one may single out large debts in respect of bank loans obtained on pre-election expectations of later public financing; the tendency to inflate spending, especially during election campaigns; the informal agreements between parties and business which have provided hidden funds in exchange for concessions, contracts and licences granted by the public adminis-trations under party government control; and the setting up of fictitious companies as party instruments for collecting contributions.

These Spanish traits of social isolation and organisational rigidity are replicated, although not to such a high degree, in Portugal's political parties. The sudden disappearance of the authoritarian regime in 1974 and the consequent institutional void gave enormous opportunities to the party leaderships, which they used to create new institutional rules in their own favour – such as the closed electoral lists – and to establish an overwhelming party presence in public offices, state enterprises, social institutions, including the trade union movement, and the media. The Portuguese parties are basically financed out of public funds, although in this case the sums depend on the number of votes obtained. The fact is that they have increased their membership since 1975 to nearly 10 per cent of the voters. Internally they too are restrained by a highly centralised discipline, which reaches its highest level in the case of the Communists.

Two parties with regional multipartism

The Spanish party system has evolved, over more than thirty years of democratic elections, from moderate multipartism to high polarisation between the two larger Spain-wide parties, which is supplemented only by a number of regional parties. In the first stage of democracy, after the elections of 1977 and 1979, the multi-party system which was created was coherent enough to arouse expectations that it might be consolidated. It was made up of two big parties, the centre-right UCD and the centre-left PSOE, both competing for the centre-ground. There were two other parties on the flanks, the right-wing AP and the left-wing PCE (with less than 10 per cent of the votes each), which acted as supporters of the big two parties while at the same time pulling them towards the extremes and maintaining some distance between them. Each of the two blocs, the UCD and AP on the right and the PCE and PSOE on the left, won an almost identical number of votes, while various regional parties were also represented. Under this system the centre-right UCD could form a minority government, under the presidency first of Adolfo Suárez and then of Leopoldo Calvo-Sotelo, seeking parliamentary support alternately from the conservative AP, the Catalan nationalists of the CiU and other regional groups, and even from the socialist PSOE on questions of the constitution and regional autonomy.

This situation came to an end after an attempted coup d'état in 1981 and the subsequent 1982 election, which provoked the destruction of the UCD – which went from being the party of government to complete dissolution in just a few months. There followed, first, a long period of governments by the socialist PSOE, led by Felipe González, after its victories in four elections in 1982, 1986, 1989 and 1993 (on the first three occasions with an absolute majority of seats in Parliament). Eventually, there was alternation in favour of the PP, which won the elections of 1996 and 2000, after a long process to absorb and concentrate the votes of the centre-right and the right on one single candidate. The recovery of the right included the withdrawal of its leader during the transition, Manuel Fraga (still remembered by many voters as one of Franco's ministers), his replacement by the younger José M. Aznar, 'refounding' of the party, various pre-election coalitions with small centrist and regionalist parties, affiliation to the Christian Democratic International (lately relabelled, at the Spaniards' initiative, Centre Democratic International), and a new array of priority campaign issues with special emphasis on the previous governments' 'corruption' and 'dirty war' against terrorism. More recently, a new alternation of parties in government was produced, in favour of the Socialist Party, led by José-Luis Rodríguez-Zapatero, in 2004, renewed in 2008.

The party configuration has thus moved from one organised very symmetrically around two larger parties, the centre-left PSOE and the centre-right UCD, and two smaller more extreme parties at the corresponding flanks, the left PCE and the right AP, to an asymmetrical configuration with a single party on the right of the spectrum. This has produced the unexpected consequence that the centre-right position has been partly occupied by regional nationalist parties. In particular, the Catalan nationalists of the CiU have played a crucial pivotal position in Parliament, first supporting a minority government of the socialist PSOE in 1993–95, and then supporting (together with the Canary Island nationalists and the Basque nationalists for a while) an alternative minority government of the conservative PP in 1996–2000. A smaller Catalan radical party, Left Republican of Catalonia (ERC), together with the post-communist United Left (IU), also supported a minority government of the Socialists in 2004–7.

Actually, the proliferation of regional parties is the main factor in deciding that a multi-party rather than a bi-party system exists. In point of fact the Spain-wide party system interrelates with different arrangements in the Autonomous Communities. In eleven of the communities there are just imperfect bi-party systems, since the two major parties, the PSOE and the PP, together always account for over 80 per cent of the vote, although there are always small or regional parties which gain some representation, at least in the autonomous parliaments.

But in another four communities there are moderate multi-party systems including prominent regional parties. In Catalonia, in particular, the two main groups are the Socialists' Party of Catalonia (PSC, federated to the PSOE) and the centre-right nationalist coalition CiU, flanked on one side by the radical Catalan ERC and the left-wing Initiative-Greens (federated to the IU) and on the other side by the conservative PP. This two-dimensional characteristic of the Catalan ideological space can be seen above all in the practice of shifting votes in favour of the nationalist CiU in regional elections and in favour of the Spanish government party, whether the PSOE or the PP, in Spain-wide elections. In the other three communities alluded to above there is a system of basically three parties: PSOE, PP and a regional party, which is rightist in Aragon, leftist in Galicia and centrist in the Canary Islands.

It is only in the Autonomous Communities of the Basque Country and Navarre, where the national dimension is the most relevant one, no less in general than in regional elections, that one can observe a greater degree of multipartism, fractionalisation and bi-polarisation. The two parties with the biggest vote generally collect only some 50 per cent of the vote. On the nationalist dimension there are ideological contiguities between the Socialist Party of the Basque Country (federated to the PSOE) and the conservative PP, on the one hand, and the Nationalists of the PNV and the Basque Nationalists (EA) on the other, To this scenario must be added an anti-system party, the radical nationalist Unity (Batasuna), which is considered to support the terrorist organisation ETA (Basque Motherland and Liberty). The strategies employed to form coalitions show a latent two-dimensional relationship.

Table 6.3 Left–right placement of parties in Spain

Communists IU	Socialist PSOE		Catalans ERC, CiU	Basque PNV	People PP	
Left	Centre-left		Centre		Centre-right	Right

Party names:
IU: United Left (Izquierda Unida).
PSOE: Spanish Workers' Socialist Party (Partido Socialista Obrero Español).
ERC: Republican Left of Catalonia (Esquerra Republicana de Catalunya).
CiU: Convergence and Union (Convergència i Unió).
PNV: Basque Nationalist Party (Partido Nacionalista Vasco).
PP: People's Party (Partido Popular).

A moderate multi-party system

In the initial phase of Portuguese democracy, too, a four-party system appeared to be establishing itself, but subsequently there has been an increasing concentration of votes. In 1975 and 1976 the centre-left PS obtained the greatest number of votes, followed by the centre-right PPD. This later changed its name to Social Democratic Party (PSD), although at the time it was a member of the Liberal International and eventually became a partner of the centre-right European People's Party. These two parties, the centre-left PS and the centre-right PPD/PSD, were flanked by two smaller but influential parties, the left-wing PCP and the right-wing Democratic and Social Centre (CDS), later called People's Party (PP). In this situation each party seemed to occupy the ideological space attributed to it in the voters' range of preferences, leaving the two largest parties to engage in a degree of competition for the centre-ground.

Higher polarisation was introduced for the elections in 1979 and 1980 when the PPD and the CDS, as well as the small monarchist party, PPM, joined in a single candidacy as the Democratic Alliance (AD), headed by Francisco Sa Carneiro and, after his death in an apparent accident, by Francisco Pinto Balsemâo. The AD coalition was the most voted-for list in the two elections and, thanks to the electoral rules, was rewarded with two absolute parliamentary majorities. In the later elections of 1987 and 1991 the PSD, led by Aníbal Cavaco Silva, obtained over 50 per cent of the vote and was easily able to form single-party governments with a parliamentary majority. Later on, José-Manuel Durâo Barroso from the PSD also became Prime Minister with the support of the PP.

This unifying strategy of the centre-right contrasted with the divisions and confrontation on the left side of the spectrum. The Communist Party, in collaboration with the Armed Forces Movement, had been the driving force in the plan for the revolutionary transformation of the country, which was in part reflected in the 1976 constitution. Subsequently the PCP has never been a party of government, nor has it accepted the later amendments of the constitution. In addition, a new Democratic Renewal Party (PRD), led by former President General Ramalho Eanes, who was opposed to the constitutional reduction of presidential powers, entered the competition in the mid-1980s.

Finding it impossible to enter into a coalition with other left parties in parliament, the PS, led by Mario Soares, undertook an erratic policy of pacts. In 1978 the PS formed a government with the right-wing CDS (in a coalition with no connection on the left–right dimension, since it left out the centre-right PSD) at the same time as it confronted President Eanes; yet in 1980 the PS broke with the CDS and allied itself with the Communists in supporting the presidential re-election of Eanes; but in 1983 the PS again confronted Eanes and this time formed a government with the centre-right PSD, the so-called 'central bloc' coalition; Mario Soares could only compete for the presidency of the republic by distancing himself even from the PS. The Socialists didn't recover until the PRD disappeared and the Communists and the extreme left weakened and split. Under the new leadership of António Guterres, the Socialist Party won the elections of 1995 and 1999 and, led by José Sócrates, again in 2005. The Socialists controlled both the government and the presidency for a few years, in 1999–2002 and in 2005–6, the only periods of unified government in democratic Portugal.

Thus the institutional conflict and frequency of elections which characterised the first period of Portuguese democracy, when there were several alternations of parties and government coalitions, seem to have served as a learning experience for the voters and some party leaders, eventually consolidating the system of representation, to some extent, by concentrating votes on the two central parties. Although the party system was initially polarised by the existence of an anti-system party, the unifying and centripetal strategy of the liberal-conservative PSD and the socialist PS helped to consolidate political equilibrium around the moderate centre. Party fragmentation is relatively low in Portugal (70 per cent in votes and 60 per cent in seats, less than the European average), with 3.4 effective parties in votes and 2.4 in seats in 2005.

Table 6.4 Left–right placement of parties in Portugal

Communists BE, PCP	Socialist PS		Social Democrat PSD	People CDS/PP
Left	Centre-left	Centre	Centre-right	Right

Party names:
BE: Left Bloc (Bloco de Esquerda).
PCP: Portuguese Communist Party (Partido Comunista Português).
PS: Socialist Party (Partido Socialista).
PSD: Social Democratic Party (Partido Social Democrata).
CDS/PP: Democratic and Social Centre/People's Party (Centro Democrático Social/Partido Popular).

PARLIAMENT

In Spain the two-chamber structure of the parliament, the General Courts, which are made up of the Congress of Deputies and the Senate, dates from the political reform of the Franco regime, carried out in 1976–7, by which the incumbent rulers tried to secure positions for themselves in the second chamber and ensure varied representation. The two-chamber system was consolidated in the 1978 constitution, but it is strongly weighted in favour of the Congress.

Although there is a widespread consensus about the inefficiency of the Senate in the present institutional structure, there has not been enough agreement between the political parties to turn it into a federal chamber, as in other federal or decentralised European states. Some senators, as mentioned, are nominated by the Autonomous Communities, but the upper chamber plays no formal role in the relationship between central state institutions and the regional governments. Only on a few occasions have there been general debates in the Senate Commission of Autonomous Communities with the participation of the President of the central governments and the Presidents of the regions (except the Basque Country). In practice, negotiations between the central and autonomous governments proceed along extra-parliamentary paths, above all through the heads of the governing parties. In the legislative field the Senate reproduces the work of the Congress. The two chambers can introduce and modify Bills, but if there is disagreement between the Congress and the Senate the former has the last word, so that in fact the Senate has scarcely ever exercised legislative initiative.

In the post-constitution periods in government of both the centrist UCD, the socialist PSOE and the conservative PP decisions taken in the parliament have largely been determined by the agenda of the government and, in practice, that of the leadership of the governing party. The parliamentary rules further restrict the role of parliament, penalising any group indiscipline on the part of individual deputies and also any fragmentation of parliamentary groups, while at the same time favouring government stability. In fact the frequency of single-party absolute parliamentary majorities has impaired the pluralism which had been envisaged in setting up the constitution and strengthened the restrictive aspects of the parliamentary rules. This relationship can be seen in detail in the way that parliamentary groups function, in the work of the commissions and boards, and in the reduced role of individual representatives.

To form a parliamentary group in the Congress of Deputies requires fifteen deputies elected on the same platform, or a smaller number if they have been elected on a Spain-wide candidacy list and have gained at least 5 per cent of the votes cast, or have been elected on a regional list which has obtained at least 15 per cent of the votes and five deputies in the area concerned. The remaining deputies who are not included in these groups, although they may have competed with them in various lists, make up the 'Mixed Parliamentary Group', which is usually large, heterogeneous and inoperative. Parties which have established an electoral coalition can form only a single parliamentary group. Consequently, only four parties have ever been able consistently to form their own parliamentary group, namely the socialist PSOE, the conservative PP, the Catalan CiU and the Basque PNV. There have been about five parliamentary groups in each legislature, while in the Mixed Group there have been deputies from four to eight different electoral lists, most of them regional. The leaders of the main lists and parties are also the leaders of the principal parliamentary groups in the Congress.

As regards the Senate, ten senators are required to form a group. This is a figure which only the same four parties already mentioned – the PSOE, the PP, the CiU and the PNV – have achieved since 1986. No Autonomous Community can promote the formation of a regional group composed of senators returned by its own electorate. Only regional sub-groups of parliamentary groups are permitted, and only if they are formed by at least three senators of the same Autonomous Community, a figure which has been reached only by the PSOE and the PP. This has allowed these Spain-wide parties to appear as regional counterparts of the regional parties.

The principal parliamentary organisations are the boards (*mesas*), the commissions and the Committee of Spokesmen (*Junta de portavoces*). Each of the Congress and Senate boards is composed of a president, elected by absolute majority in the first round or by plurality in a second round, several vice-presidents (four in the Congress and two in the Senate) and four secretaries; in these elections every member of parliament has a vote limited to one candidate for vice-president and one candidate for secretary. Through these procedures a parliamentary plurality can elect a majority of the boards. The commissions, which are made up of around one-tenth of the total number of members of parliament, carry out the greater part of legislative discussion and control the work of the house. They are composed of representatives of the various parliamentary groups and are nominated by the heads of the groups, so that the possible winning coalitions are the same as in the full chamber. The Committee of Spokesmen sets up the agenda and calendar of parliamentary work and is formed by one representative from each of the parliamentary groups, which have a vote weighted according to the number of deputies in them.

Given this rigid organisational structure, the activities of individual members of parliament are very limited. Only the parliamentary groups are authorised to introduce Bills, while any amendment proposed by an individual member has to be endorsed by the spokesman of his or her group. There is strong voting discipline at the heart of each group, maintained through instructions and controls. Furthermore, there is little continuity among the individual members of any single commission, which prevents them from acquiring specialist expertise in any field and keeps them dependent on the decisions of the group leaders. The great majority of members have neither assistants nor advisers (except in technical and juridical matters). Altogether, the real parliamentary business of discussion, negotiation and the drawing up of alternatives is monopolised by the chairmen and women and spokespeople of the groups. For most members their presence in parliament is above all an opportunity to be recruited for other posts, and the main qualification for attaining such promotion is usually adherence to the discipline of the party. The leaderships of the major parties thus control the deputies and through them dominate the parliament.

Comparatively speaking, the Spanish parliament has produced a relatively small number of laws. Most legislative initiatives, especially the laws which receive final approval, are the work of the government, which intervenes markedly in the agenda and calendar of the parliament. As regards the subjects of the legislation, most laws have been about regulating the government's own institutions, and public finances. Among the remainder there are more general regulations than public policies or regulation of private interests. The laws are usually approved by oversized legislative coalitions – larger, that is, than is numerically necessary in order to win. At first, this was due to the broad negotiations and consensual agreements which characterised the drawing up of the constitution and the institutionalisation of democracy. In the second phase, the large majorities have been occasioned by the scant relevance of many of the laws approved, which incites the parties to behave and vote more for electoral reasons, and to take up generic positions on the ideological spectrum, than for any reason to do with the foreseeable limited effects of the legislation.

The Spanish political system is a parliamentary monarchy, but the rules of executive appointment and control concede only a limited role to the parliament. The President of the Government is nominated by the Crown, after having been elected by an absolute majority of the deputies in the first round or by a plurality in the second round, which means that an early dissolution of the chambers can be avoided if no candidate gets majority support.

The parliamentary constituents of 1977–8, worried by the danger of democratic instability, chose to limit the possibility of censure to only 'constructive' censure motions. This followed the model of the Federal Republic of Germany established in the post-war period in reaction to the governmental instability of the Weimar Republic, which has been compared to the Second Spanish Republic in studies of the breakdown of democratic regimes in the 1930s. In accordance with this system, the President of the Government can be deposed only by a motion which includes an alternative candidate, is sponsored by 10 per cent of the deputies (a figure which has been available only to the leading opposition party) and has obtained the approval of an absolute majority of the members of the two chambers. The presidential candidate is not obliged to present the members of the government to the parliament, nor can the latter move motions of censure against particular ministers.

As a result of these rules, it is possible for governments in a parliamentary minority to survive if the adversaries of the party with most votes are sufficiently divided on both left and right. In this way a high level of governmental stability has been achieved; if we exclude the constituent legislature which began in 1977, the seven subsequent legislatures have lasted on average more than forty-three months (against a legal maximum of forty-eight), the highest average in Europe. In practice the censure motions which have been moved (by the PSOE in 1980 and by the PP in 1987) have been mere denunciations of the government and party propaganda exercises in front of the electorate.

The powers of the Portuguese Assembly are even more limited than those of the Spanish Cortes, since, besides the dominance of the executive and the tendency for decisions to be made by the parties, the Assembly has to share its placing or withdrawal of confidence in the Prime Minister with the President of the Republic. Nevertheless, parliamentary powers have been increased since the revisions of the constitution in the 1980s and 1990s, involving diminution of the President's powers, reinforcement of the role of parliamentary committees, majority control over the agenda and widening of the Assembly's budgetary procedures.

Individual Portuguese members of parliament are also subject to strong party discipline and can act only through their groups, whose existence is actually envisaged in the constitution. No deputy may change group. Nevertheless the various parties which have formed the same electoral coalition can set up different groupings (*agrupamientos*), which have similar powers to those of the groups, except in moving government censure motions. The parliamentary agenda is established by the Leaders' Conference, which in practice means that parliamentary life is dominated by the party leaderships. There are frequent extra-parliamentary negotiations between the leaderships, and these have been decisive in promoting and approving such decisive laws as those on agrarian reform, national defence, the Constitutional Court and the amendments of the constitution, especially for allowing the re-privatisation of companies and banks.

The Portuguese Assembly elects by two-thirds qualified majority nine judges of the Constitutional Court, seven members of the Superior Council of the Judiciary, the Ombudsman, and the President of the Economic and Social Council. As regards the government, given its twofold dependence on both the Assembly and the President, there is no proper parliamentary election of a Prime Minister; however, in practice the person designated submits himself to a vote of confidence in the chamber. In 1977 the Socialist Mario Soares failed to obtain such a vote to form a government, and resigned. On the other hand, 25 per cent of the members of the Assembly can present a censure motion against the Prime Minister, which has to be approved by simple absolute majority, without having to put forward an alternative candidate. The first censure motion was presented by the Communists against the 'presidential' Prime Minister Mota Pinto in 1978; it was followed by the motions of the Socialists against Sa Carneiro in 1980, of the Conservatives against Soares in 1983 and of the Socialists against Cavaco Silva in 1989 – all of them more for propaganda than effective purposes, since the governments of all the censured Prime Ministers had majority backing in the chamber. Exceptionally, in 1987 a motion presented by the 'Eanist' PRD and supported by the Socialists and the Communists managed to overthrow the Prime Minister, Cavaco Silva, who at that time was in a minority position, but he obtained an absolute majority in the subsequent elections.

GOVERNMENT

The Portuguese dual executive

Under the Portuguese constitution of 1976 the President of the Republic possessed strong powers, which were later reduced. In the first place, he presided over the Council of the Revolution, a military organisation which claimed to be the guarantor of the revolutionary process and with which he shared the political direction of the state. The Council of the Revolution, besides advising the President and having the power of veto in military matters, acted as a constitutional court. For his part the President of the Republic nominated and could remove the Prime Minister and the government, could dissolve the Assembly, exercise a legislative veto which could be overriden only by a parliamentary qualified majority of two-thirds, and postpone the approval of legislation.

This power structure, characteristic of the 'semi-presidential' model more or less inspired by the French Fifth Republic, was modified by a series of constitutional revisions carried out by the Assembly, without reference to – and in the face of opposition from – the President. In the first place, the Council of the Revolution was abolished and replaced by a Council of State composed of the President of the Assembly, the Prime Minister, the President of the Constitutional Court and representatives of other institutions, with the task of advising the President of the Republic. The President's legislative veto became inoperative if it was opposed by a parliamentary simple majority, whilst he lost his power to delay legislation. The President also ceased to have the right to nominate ministers and was submitted to strong limitations regarding his intervention in the designation and removal of the Prime Minister and the dissolution of the Assembly. The President of the Republic remained head of the armed forces and guarantor of national unity, whilst with his authority to refer laws and government decisions to the Constitutional Court, he rather became a referee between institutions.

For its part the government was converted into the organisation in charge of the general direction of the country's policies, as well as being the highest organ of public administration. At times when a single party has had an absolute majority the government has held considerable legislative power, able in practice to dominate the Assembly through the governing party.

The structure of the government revolves around the Council of Ministers and is complemented by the secretaries and under-secretaries of state. As in the French model of relations with the bureaucracy (which has also been adopted in Spain), the private personal assistants of the ministers, who in practice are recruited from the ranks of the governing party, stand between them and the directors-general and other high officials.

As mentioned already, the executive dualism of the Portuguese system was initially regarded by scholars as a 'semi-presidential regime'. It fitted the model in the way the President is directly elected and keeps some powers in defence and foreign policy, but the President's powers have been significantly limited regarding both legislative influence and appointment of the government. The diminution of the President's powers and the shift in the balance of power between the parties have provoked different interpretations of and labels for the institutional structure, including 'semi-parliamentary' system and even 'prime ministerial presidentialism', but the Portuguese institutional system can be classified along with most parliamentary regimes in Europe.

The legal scope of government intervention in society has changed considerably since the beginning of the democratic period. While the 1976 constitution prescribed a transition to socialism through the collectivisation of the principal means of production and pronounced the nationalisation process irreversible, the further revisions took away constitutional obstacles to the development of a market economy which, in fact, had never ceased to exist. More significant is the survival of the former authoritarian corporatism, which have been partly reconverted into a democratic neo-corporatism. Together with the government, the main actors in the consensus are, on the one hand, the industrial, agricultural and commercial employers' federations which have been grouped together in the National Council of Portuguese Entrepreneurs (CNEP). In competition with the CNEP are the industrial associations which combined in the National Council of Entrepreneurs' Associations (CNAE) with the intention of speaking to the government directly without getting involved in social negotiations. The main agricultural and industrial trade unions, on the other hand, which have grown up from the strongly Communist-influenced *Inter-sindical* of the early years of the transition, go by the name of the General Confederation of Portuguese Workers (CGTP). Alongside the CGTP is the General Union of Workers (UGT), supported by Socialists and Conservatives, and mainly concentrated in the service sector.

The principal neo-corporate institution for negotiating economic policy is the Permanent Council of Social Negotiation, set up in 1984. It brings together, under the chairmanship of the Prime Minister, six trade union representatives (three from the UGT and three from the CGTP, the latter having refused to occupy seats for several years because they regarded membership as incompatible with the class struggle), six from the employers' confederations, and six ministers with economic and social portfolios. However, there have also been direct agreements between the industrial associations and the UGT on matters affecting incomes policy and vocational training.

Table 6.5 Governments of Portugal, 1976–2005

No.	Year	Prime Minister	Party composition
1	1976	M. Soares	Socialist
	1978	M. Soares	Socialist, People
	1978	A. Nobre da Costa	'Presidential'
	1978	C. Mota Pinto	'Presidential'
	1979	M. L. Pintassilgo	'Presidential'
2	1980	F. Sa Carneiro	Social Democrat, People, Monarchist
3	1981	F. Pinto Balsemâo	Social Democrat, People, Monarchist
4	1983	M. Soares	Socialist, Social Democrat
5	1985	A. Cavaco Silva	Social Democrat
6	1987	A. Cavaco Silva	Social Democrat
7	1991	A. Cavaco Silva	Social Democrat
8	1995	A. Guterres	Socialist
9	1999	A. Guterres	Socialist
10	2002	J. M. Durao Barroso	Social Democrat
	2004	P. Santana Lopes	Social Democrat
11	2005	J. Sócrates	Socialist

Note: The first party indicates the Prime Minister's affiliation.

Table 6.6 Presidents of Portugal, 1976–2006

No.	Year	President	Party support
1	1976	R. Eanes	Socialist, Social Democrat, People
2	1980	R. Eanes	Communist, Socialist
3	1986	M. Soares	Socialist
4	1991	M. Soares	Socialist, Social Democrat
5	1996	J. Sampaio	Socialist, Communist
6	2001	J. Sampaio	Socialist, Communist
7	2006	A. Cavaco Silva	Social Democrat

With a view to the coming European single market, the government implemented drastic economic reforms, privatising state-owned industries and promoting free enterprise. This economic plan was opposed by the trade unions, which held a general strike in 1988 and subsequent strikes and protests (very much in line with the attitude of the Spanish trade unions in the same period). While the agrarian and fiscal reforms were carried through, other measures approved by the government and the Assembly, such as those making it easier to dismiss workers, were later annulled by the Constitutional Court.

The Spanish government

Among the most important powers assigned by the Spanish constitution to the Crown are: representing the country abroad, leadership of the armed forces and the right of pardon. However, activities of the government are in fact directed by its President, who (with the approval of the Crown, which is merely a matter of protocol) can nominate ministers, call elections, dissolve the parliament, call consultative referendums, declare war or peace and sign international treaties.

Spain is the only country in continental Europe where only single-party governments have been formed, always with minority-voting support. At four of nine elections, a single party achieved a majority of seats in Congress thanks to over-representation produced by the electoral system (and in 1989 with the help of the expulsion of a few Basque independent deputies from parliament). In all other instances, minority governments have been formed under the protection of the restrictive parliamentary rules mentioned above. All the governments, including those supported by an absolute majority of parliamentary seats, have been based on a minority share of the popular vote – the average electoral support being 40 per cent.

From 1982 on, each President of the Government, whether Socialist Felipe González until 1996, Popular José M. Aznar until 2004 or Socialist José L. Rodríguez-Zapatero since then, added to his position as head of a single-party executive the roles of maximum leader of his party and President of the corresponding parliamentary group. The President leads the Council of Ministers, which meets with pre-established regularity. The government's delegated commissions, inter-ministerial commissions and under-secretaries' commissions work in parallel, adopting many agreements and decisions which are put before the council for ratification.

The government also directs the public administration, the traditional structure of which was inspired by the French model of a centralised bureaucracy relatively independent of the interest groups in society. Nevertheless, this model has undergone some modifications in the democratic period: political control of the higher levels of administration has increased, especially through ministers nominating people to politically responsible posts – such as directors-general and deputy directors-general – to carry out assignments which in other countries would be the responsibility of senior civil servants; some administrative corps have been heavily decentralised with the creation and consolidation of the Autonomous Communities; and some administrative agencies have been put more directly in touch with the social groups most affected by their powers and responsibilities.

The size of the public bureaucracy has grown rapidly since the second half of the 1970s, reaching proportions comparable with the EU average. The growth of the bureaucracy since the introduction of democracy can be attributed to two factors. First, particular interest groups and citizens in general have both had greater opportunity to express their demands for public intervention. Such demands are especially great in a society such as Spain's, which had traditionally embraced a 'subject' culture, disposed towards protectionism and state assistance. Second, the efficiency of the bureaucracy has increased, thanks to better education among civil servants and improved technical and organisational capacity. Thus, there has been a reduction in the number of juridical regulations and in the corps and scales of civil servants, and the salary and incentives systems have been clarified, all of which has increased productivity. But the well-known paradox has manifested itself whereby greater efficiency has allowed certain sectors of the administration wider margins to expand by themselves absorbing the public benefits of their activities. Also, since the traditionally low turnover of civil servants in their postings has scarcely been modified, any attempt to channel personnel appointments to different activities or services has tended to lead to an increase in staff.

Quantitatively, public spending has risen from 20 per cent of GDP in 1960 and 25 per cent in 1975 to 46 per cent in 2007 (compared with an EU average of 50 per cent), while the number of civil servants, which was around 10 per cent of the active population in 1980, is approaching 15 per cent (as against an average 17.5 per cent in the EU).

The Spanish constitutional norms, which, as we have seen, were drawn up by consensus between the various political tendencies, lay down varied criteria for government intervention. On the one hand, they make formal allowance for planning and for a high degree of regulation of economic activity; on the other, they establish a free-enterprise system within the framework of a market economy – stating specifically, for instance, that taxes shall not be confiscatory and that public spending will be guided by criteria of efficiency and economy.

There are certain institutional mechanisms for negotiation between the government and groups in society, especially as regards the direction and execution of economic policy, although in practice they have had a very limited effect. To understand the basic features of relations between the government and social groups in economic and social matters, it has to be borne in mind that while the Spanish Confederation of Entrepreneurs' Organisations (CEOE) groups together over 90 per cent of employers, albeit in a very decentralised structure, the trade unions – mainly the UGT and the Workers' Commissions (CCOO) – have an official membership of fewer than 15 per cent of wage earners (barely half of whom are up to date with their subscriptions).

The trade unions have based their negotiating power on the existence of committees elected by all the company's workers irrespective of their trade union affiliation, and on the legally binding nature of the agreements between social organisations and government for all firms and employees, whatever their links or independence. This 'inclusive' model of trade union negotiation is distinct from other traditions (for example the British), in which only their members are bound by the deals agreed by the unions. While the British 'exclusive' model gives the unions a strong incentive to increase their membership, in Spain the automatic binding of all workers to the terms of an agreement is a disincentive to active participation and union membership, which to workers seems an unnecessary expense. While their bases of organised support are increasingly concentrated among civil servants, the low level of membership causes the unions to give priority to action by their organising leaderships, which gives rise to a vicious circle.

Social negotiation, then, is poorly institutionalised. Although a certain amount of literature on neo-corporatism, based on experience in Central and Northern Europe, was imported during the 1980s, it was not until 1992 that Spain set up an Economic and Social Council, composed of a Chairman, twenty employers' representatives, twenty trade union representatives, and twenty experts representing other groups (farmers, consumers, fishermen, co-operatives), and which has a purely consultative status.

Up to that time, at least, three stages can be distinguished in relations between the government and social organisations. In the first period, 1977–84, in the midst of economic crisis and mostly with minority centre-right governments in power, the key was consensus and agreement. The first agreements on economic and social matters, known as the 'Moncloa pacts', were signed in late 1977, after the first political election. These pacts, aimed at stabilising the economy and institutionalising labour relations, were conceived of as a contribution to consolidating democracy and were signed, in fact, by the government and the parliamentary political parties, since entrepreneurs and trade unions were still in the first stages of getting themselves organised. Later on, most of the agreements between employers and trade unions, although they concentrated on fixing rates of wage increases, also had a markedly political character. The trade unions, on the one hand, undertook to moderate claims and strikes, while the government, on the other, legislated on workers' rights and provided public funding for the unions. In line with this generic orientation, the CEOE and the UGT signed the Inter-confederal Basic Agreement in 1979, the Inter-confederal Framework Agreement (AMI) in 1980, the AMI-2 and the Employment National Agreement (ANE) in 1981, the Inter-confederal Agreement (AI) in 1983, and the Economic and Social Agreement in 1984. For its part, the CCOO trade union joined the ANE, known as the 'pact of fear', only because it was signed shortly after the attempted coup d'état of 1981, and the AI, a few weeks after the formation of the first PSOE government.

The second stage began in 1985, initially in a period of economic growth and then, after 1991, in recession, and under governments of the centre-left. The keys of this stage were conflict and the absence of agreement, to a point where the unions have called several general strikes since 1988 against government economic policy.

Finally, social negotiations and agreements between workers' unions, employers' organisations and the government were resumed in 1996, immediately after the arrival of the People's Party in government. The explanation of this paradox – social conflict with centre-left governments and social pacts with centre-right governments – can be found in some aspects of the political game which have been outlined in previous sections. The PSOE governments, in particular, found themselves facing a major contradiction between the need for social negotiation, on the one hand, and the requirements of electoral popularity and medium- and long-term economic

Table 6.7 Governments of Spain, 1977–2008

No.	Year	President of Government	Party composition
1	1977	A. Suárez	Centre
2	1979	A. Suárez	Centre
	1981	L. Calvo-Sotelo	Centre
3	1982	F. González	Socialist
4	1986	F. González	Socialist
5	1989	F. González	Socialist
6	1993	F. González	Socialist
7	1996	J. M. Aznar	People
8	2000	J. M. Aznar	People
9	2004	J. L. Rodríguez-Zapatero	Socialist
10	2008	J. L. Rodríguez-Zapatero	Socialist

rationality, on the other. The remarkable social independence of the Socialist Party leadership and its fusion with the government leadership, plus command of an absolute parliamentary majority, allowed the PSOE to give the electoral game priority; that is, the PSOE tried to maintain the positions which made it attractive to a significant band of centrist voters, recruited from wide sections of the middle class, and showed a preference for economic policies aimed at growth, in defiance of protests from the less competitive sections of society and the trade unions' demands for redistribution. In comparison with other European socialist parties, the PSOE had the advantage that, due to its previous absence from power, it did not have to contradict any of its own previous policies.

INTERGOVERNMENTAL RELATIONS

Decentralisation

The biggest institutional innovation of the 1978 Spanish constitution was the decentralisation of public powers. In the context, outlined above, of bipolar electoral competition and high concentration of central power in single-party governments, local and regional governments have become the main instances of political pluralism in Spanish democracy.

Since 1979 this has included the democratisation of over 8,000 town councils (a larger figure than in other European countries, in relation to population), 50 provincial councils (some of which were later abolished when they became single-province Autonomous Communities) and the councils of the islands, as well as the creation of 17 Autonomous Communities between 1980 and 1983. This decentralisation is the principal element of pluralism and the devolution of power in the Spanish institutional structure, while at the same time being a notable stage for competition and negotiation between the political parties governing the various institutions.

In contrast, in Portugal only two rather remote islands in the Atlantic Ocean, the Azores and Madeira, were organised as autonomous regions with legislative assemblies and governments. Other provisions for establishing regional decentralisation were later abandoned and Portugal remained constitutionally defined as a unitary state. However, with Portugal's entry into the European Union pressures for regionalisation have increased.

In Spain, mayors are elected indirectly by an absolute majority of councillors supporting the person heading one of the lists of election candidates, and if no single candidate obtains such a majority the name at the head of the list which has attracted the most popular votes is designated. (Only the mayors of small municipalities with open councils, and the mayors of districts smaller than municipalities, are directly elected by plurality.) While a single party has won an absolute majority of councillors in more than one-third of the elections held for the biggest town councils, in many other cases the rules have allowed winning coalitions to be formed which have elected a different candidate from the one who attracted most votes.

Initially, two paths were laid down for forming the Autonomous Communities in Spain. On the one hand, there were the so-called 'historical' communities (those which had held plebiscites on autonomy in the 1930s), which held referendums to approve their statutes of autonomy, which secured greater powers from the very beginning, and which hold separate autonomous elections. These communities are the Basque Country, Catalonia and Galicia, to which was added Andalusia via a referendum promoted by its town councils. The other thirteen Autonomous Communities hold their elections jointly and at the same time as the municipal elections.

Every Autonomous Community has a parliamentary system. Its President is elected by the autonomous parliament through a two (or more) round procedure, with an absolute and relative majority, respectively, very similar to that for the election of the President of the central government by the Congress of Deputies. In most communities, the party system is more pluralistic than in the Spanish parliament, frequently producing multi-party coalition governments.

The constitution established two lists of areas (rather than legislative and executive powers properly speaking) which delimit the minimum activities of the central and autonomous institutions, respectively. Among the latter are urban policy, public works, transport, agriculture, the environment and culture. Although the first group of Autonomous Communities – the Basque Country, Catalonia, Galicia and Andalusia – initially received greater powers (specifically including linguistic and cultural responsibilities in the case of the first three), some of the second group of communities, such as Valencia, the Canary Islands and Navarre, soon obtained powers over similar areas, including education and health care. There has also been a transfer of powers in other areas from the central government to the Autonomous Communities, outstanding among which is security in the Basque Country, including the creation of an autonomous police force with responsibility for combating terrorism. As a result of 'autonomous pacts' between the two major political parties, the PSOE and the PP, in 1992 and 1997 additional powers were transferred to all the Autonomous Communities so that they were almost on a par with the first group. Successive fiscal agreements for the periods 1984–6, 1986–91 (prolonged further), 1997–2001 and 2002–6 have given increasing financial resources to the Autonomous Communities. The Catalan government initially asked for the collection of 15 per cent of income taxes, but 33 per cent was finally transferred to all regional governments, together with 35 per cent of value-added tax and full special taxes. Initially, most powers and responsibilities were shared or concurrent between the central government and the Autonomous Communities. But, as there has been a tendency for the central government to reserve basic legislation to itself, even in fields attributed to the Autonomous Communities, leaving to the latter the development and execution of the legislation, the autonomous governments have kept up constant pressure for the central government to transfer further powers. Since 2004, most Communities began to elaborate new Statutes of Autonomy to enlarge their capacity for self-government, following the initiative of the Basque Country and Catalonia. The project approved by the Basque parliament was rejected by a two-party majority in the Spanish parliament. But during the period 2006–7 new statutes have actually been approved for Catalonia, Aragon, the Balearic Islands, Valencia and Andalusia.

When decentralisation began in 1979 the distribution of public spending was 90 per cent by central government and 10 per cent by the town councils. In 2007 it was less than 50 per cent by central government (most of it for retirement pensions and debt interests), about one-third by the Autonomous Communities and one-sixth by town councils. The present level of regional decentralisation of public expenditure in Spain is comparable to that in Germany and Switzerland (but also to locally decentralised Denmark and Sweden). It should be borne in mind that this decentralisation has been accompanied by a notable growth in overall public spending, the resources available to the Autonomous Communities representing more than 15 per cent of GDP. However, the level of decentralisation of taxes is significantly lower in Spain, since the central government still collects 75 per cent of tax revenue. Only the Basque Country and Navarre have their own funding formulas, which give them more resources per inhabitant. The distribution of civil servants was slightly more than proportional in favour of the Autonomous Communities and town councils, since these institutions provide many labour-intensive public services.

Financial and administrative decentralisation go together with political decentralisation, that is, the degree of disparity between the governing party at the centre and those governing in the regions. On average in the period 1980–2007, a majority of 9 of the 17 regional presidents belonged to parties which were not in central government at the time, as shown in Table 6.8. In the Basque Country, the Nationalist party has held the presidency without interruption since 1980. In Catalonia, President Jordi Pujol, of Convergence and Union, with 23 years in office, held one of the longest tenures at either regional or state level in the European democracies, from 1980 to 2003; only when he retired a new left coalition government was formed for the first time.

In contrast to the model of co-operative federalism, in which the governing parties of the federation and in the territories negotiate all the important decisions, in Spain the Autonomous Communities have developed steady competition for further decentralisation of powers. Intergovernmental relations have largely been replaced

Table 6.8 Political decentralisation in Spain

Period	Central government	Regional presidents			% regional presidents' party not in central government
		Socialist	People	Nationalist	
1980–2	Centre	1	1	2	
1983–7	Socialist	12	3	2	29
1987–91	Socialist	8	5	2	53
1991–5	Socialist	9	5	5	47
1995–6	Socialist	4	10	3	76
1996–9	People	6	8	3	53
1999–2003	People	6	7	4	59
2004–7	Socialist	7	7	3	59

Note: The right-hand column indicates the percentage of regional presidents whose party is different from the central government's party.
Source: Author's calculations, with 123 presidents elected immediately after every regional parliamentary elections (four further motions of censure and one change by turn are not counted).

by direct relations between the parties, in a framework of low institutionalisation. Typically the nationalist parties which govern in some Autonomous Communities employ a double-edged weapon – more or less veiled threats of secession or independence accompanying negotiation and cooperation – and are met, in turn, with restrictions, concessions and reprisals by the central government.

There are very few institutional bodies to negotiate and arbitrate between the central government and the Autonomous Communities. Unlike truly federal states, as we have seen, the Senate in Spain is not organised in such a way as to enable it to contribute decisively in this role. In law the Autonomous Communities have the power to initiate legislation before the Spanish parliament but in practice they never exercise it. The central government has a delegate in each Autonomous Community, but he is usually busier trying to safeguard central powers than coordinating the activities of the various administrations. The main instruments of cooperation between the central government and the Autonomous Communities are the Fiscal and Financial Policy Council and the sectoral conferences which some ministers hold periodically with the corresponding autonomous councillors in the same areas of responsibility.

There have been a significant number of conflicts over powers between the central government and the Autonomous Communities which have been referred to the Constitutional Court, most of them involving the Basque Country or Catalonia. Nevertheless, there has been a downward trend, suggesting that there was more controversy over laws on institutional matters in the first period, when the Autonomous Community was being set up, and that later on the legislators benefited from the learning experience and tended to settle their disputes by direct negotiations.

As with the rivalries and disputes, the greater part of such negotiations and agreements as there have been between the centre and the periphery have been the work of the leaderships of the parties governing in each sphere. Thus in 1982 the main negotiations over decentralisation took place between the UCD and the PSOE, which drew up an agreement on the 'harmonisation of the autonomy process' intended to work to the detriment of the nationalist parties (which was largely annulled by the Constitutional Court); in the 1990s the PSOE and the PP agreed on greater uniformity of the Autonomous Communities' powers; and there have been bilateral agreements between either the PSOE or the PP, on the one hand, governing the country at large, and the nationalist CiU, ERC, PNV and Canary Coalition, on the other, governing in their respective Autonomous Communities, resulting in concessions to the autonomous governments, including the approval of new Statutes of Autonomy and transfers of resources, in exchange for nationalist support to minority central governments in parliament. Likewise, the central government negotiated on municipal finances with the Federation of Municipalities and Provinces, led by the mayors of the biggest cities, belonging to various parties.

The hottest focus of conflict lies in the Basque Country, where the interplay between the central government party, whether Socialist or Popular, the Basque government presided over by the Nationalists, and the pro-independence terrorist group ETA and its political branch has not reached a political equilibrium. The attacks by ETA caused more than 800 deaths in a period of thirty years, but it has dramatically decreased its lethal activity since 2003. This was partly a consequence of the broad popular rejection of violent practices as developed by international Islamist terrorist groups – especially with the bombs attack in a Madrid train station on 11 March 2004, which caused almost 200 deaths.

The Basque Country was the only community in which the 1978 referendum on the Spanish constitution did not obtain majority popular support. But the Basques were the first to obtain their Statute of Autonomy and to hold elections for the corresponding autonomous parliament, having appeared since as the model of self-government to which most of the other regional governments aspire. The Basque parliament approved a new project of statute in 2004, which envisaged a confederal relation with the Spanish state 'in the absence of violence', which was rejected by the Spanish parliament. Thus, the Basque Nationalists have found themselves increasingly close to favouring independence, as well as in open confrontation with the Spanish government.

Justice

Spanish administration of justice is among the slowest in Europe. When sentences are pronounced years after the facts have been submitted for consideration – as often happens – it is very difficult to remedy the injury, establish adequate compensation or impose an effective or exemplary sentence. As a result, the justice system finds it hard to fulfil its role of guaranteeing impartially the rights of citizens in their relationships and disputes; instead it contributes to social inefficiency. In many lawsuits between individuals, between members of the public and institutions, and even between institutions themselves, there are often incentives for some of the parties to adopt fraudulent or abusive attitudes, since there is little likelihood of receiving a punishment proportionate to the harm inflicted and, above all, judgement is so far off that it is likely to involve a sanction significantly less than the unilateral benefit deriving from such conduct.

In Spain the independent body responsible for the administration of justice is the General Council of Judicial Power (CGPJ), an institution based on the French and Italian models. The council nominates the presidents of the Supreme Court and its lower courts, as well as the high courts of the Autonomous Communities, and is charged with the training and discipline of judges. In this context the Ministry of Justice has very little power of decision, except in providing finance for the service. Nevertheless the institutional procedure for designating the main organ of judicial governance does not guarantee its real political independence. Under a 1980 regulation, twelve of the twenty members of the CGPJ were to be elected by the judges and magistrates themselves, and the other eight by parliament (half by the Congress and half by the Senate). But, given that this meant that the justice administration was almost bound to give rise to a conservative majority, in 1985 a new regulation promoted by the PSOE parliamentary majority established that the twenty members of the council would be elected by the parliament (again, half by each chamber). According to its promoters, this new regulation sought to achieve 'political coherence' between the judicial power and the governing parliamentary majority, although – as the Constitutional Court subsequently reasoned – the partisan logic of distributing posts in proportion to the parliamentary force of each party has tended to frustrate the constitutional objective of pluralism.

One of the institutions which exists in both the Spanish and the Portuguese democracies, and which follows the example of the Federal Republic of Germany and other recent democracies, is the Constitutional Court. This is charged with hearing appeals on *habeas corpus*, rights and liberties, laws which contravene the constitution, and conflicts between state institutions – especially, in the case of Spain, between the central government and the Autonomous Communities and, in the case of Portugal, between the President and the Assembly. The Spanish Constitutional Court is composed of eight members elected by the parliament, two by the government and two by the CGPJ, a procedure which has also produced partisan majorities in favour of either UCD or PSOE or PP governments in different periods. Analogously, the Portuguese Constitutional Court is formed of ten members elected by the Assembly and three co-opted members.

The European Union

Like all the political relations analysed so far, those between the Spanish and Portuguese states and the institutions of the European Union suffer from a lack of appropriate institutionalisation. The two Iberian countries joined the European Community in 1986, since when their governments have maintained permanent representatives in Brussels and participated in the European Council, the Council of Ministers, the Commission, the European Parliament and the other EU bodies.

Nevertheless, most relations between each of the two states and the EU are articulated through their governments. In Spain, although coordinating organisations exist, such as that of the Secretary of State for the EU, part of the Ministry of Foreign Affairs, and the Inter-ministerial Commission on Economic Affairs relating to the EU, almost all decisions touching the European Union are taken by the Council of Ministers or by its Delegated Commission on Economic Affairs. A joint commission of the Congress and Senate, charged with bringing public policies and state legislation into line with EU provisions, has achieved little importance.

Since 1990, regional governments of Spain participate in the governmental conference for European Affairs, later enlarged to sectoral conferences. After the parliamentary agreement of the Catalan Nationalists to give support to the People's Party government in 1996, an observer from the regional governments was appointed to the Spanish permanent representation in the Council of Ministers of the EU and in working groups. Nevertheless, several communities such as the Basque Country, Catalonia, Galicia, the Canary Islands, Valencia and Murcia have permanent delegations in Brussels, with the task of advising their economic agents. The autonomous governments are also represented in the EU Committee of Regions, and several of them have subscribed to inter-regional agreements with regional governments in other European countries.

TWO-PARTY DEMOCRACIES

The principal institutional features of the Spanish and Portuguese democracies stem from the choices made during the transition from authoritarian regimes in the mid-1970s. Among these were the parliamentary monarchy in Spain and the semi-presidential republic in Portugal, as well as electoral systems based in both cases on criteria of proportional representation.

The transition and the constituent period in Spain were dominated by the fear of civil confrontation, which induced the adoption of various precautions to avoid the pluralism of society generating an excessive degree of electoral fragmentation and political conflict. Outstanding among these precautions were:

1   the 'corrective' measures included in the electoral rules, which tended to produce a marked deviation of actual representation from proportionality in votes and a great reduction in the number of parliamentary parties;
2   electoral candidates presented in the form of closed lists;
3   public financing of the parties;
4   rigidity of parliamentary rules;
5   the 'constructive' censure motion.

All were intended to confirm the political parties as the main actors in the decision-making process and to favour governmental stability. But the long periods with one party commanding an absolute majority in Parliament, far from contributing to institutionalising pluralism, instead concentrated power and increased the 'monist' aspects and interpretations of Spanish constitutional arrangements. As mentioned, Spain is the only country in continental Europe where no multi-party coalition governments have ever been formed. No government has been based on majority support by popular vote. Parliament is subordinated to the government, and the latter in turn to its President and to the leadership of the majority party; the Senate or upper chamber plays a junior role to the Congress and has not functioned as a federal chamber for negotiations between the central and autonomous governments; the judicial system has found it difficult to establish itself as an independent force; and, in general, political relations, whether in dispute or negotiation, have been monopolised by the party leaderships. 'Monist' features, that is, the actual concentration of power, have prevailed over the pluralist elements in the institutional arrangements of Spanish democracy. Long periods of single-party dominance have not helped institutional procedures for decision-making to function better or provide an apprenticeship for a new style of political relations which would be both representative of social variety and sufficiently effective.

The main institutional factor of pluralism, and the principal novelty of the 1978 Spanish constitution, was the introduction of widespread decentralisation, especially the creation of the so-called 'State of the Autonomies'. In the rather restrictive context above outlined, features such as the emergence of regional parties, high frequency of regional executives not controlled by the party in central government, and negotiations between them are major elements of political pluralism. However, they develop in a very weakly institutionalised framework and produce permanent competition rather than inter-institutional cooperation. The 'State of the Autonomies' has not been an institutional equilibrium, that is, a stable solution, but rather a framework for competition among regional Autonomous Communities demanding increasing self-government and inducing steady decentralisation of the state.

In Portugal, too, one can see the parties playing a strong leading role, often acquiring or discharging responsibilities which, under the constitution, ought to be the concern of independent institutions. Political and governmental stability in Portugal was not attained until more than ten years after the change of regime, with a period of serious conflict between 1975 and 1987 largely provoked by the existence of an anti-system Communist Party, and by inter-institutional conflicts between independent Presidents and parliamentary governments. Further revisions of the constitution submitted the military to civil control, moderated its original socialist and revolutionary tenor, and reduced the powers of the President of the Republic (as well as accommodating a European treaty, and introducing autonomy for the Azores and Madeira, new forms of participation and ratification of the International Criminal Court). (Constitutional revisions were approved in 1982, 1989, 1992, 1997, 2001 and 2004.) These reforms were agreed and supported by the major political parties, which facilitated the consolidation of a moderate multi-party system, with the consequent stabilisation of the democratic regime. This path of evolution, however, served also to reinforce the decisive role of the party leaders, who were the authors of the constitutional reforms and the new equilibrium of electoral representation.

In both countries, then, we have a situation in which democracy has been consolidated, in the sense that there are no major internal or external enemies to endanger the system of political freedoms and elected governments established after long periods of authoritarianism. Only the Basque pro-independence group ETA, which practised sustained terrorist activities, has appeared as a significant anti-system movement in Spain. Nevertheless, it seems clear that the two countries of the Iberian peninsula share a certain weakness in their democratic institutions, in the sense that their institutional capacity to regulate and coordinate the various interests and groups of society depends strongly upon the cohesion and stability of the political parties in government at the time. Despite important differences in their institutional structures, Spain and Portugal thus reflect common features of their contemporary history and of their still recent adoption of democratic regimes.

BIBLIOGRAPHY

Democratisation

Colomer, J. M. (1991) 'Transitions by Agreement: Modelling the Spanish Way', *American Political Science Review* 85 (4): 1,283–302.

—— (1995) *Game Theory and the Transition to Democracy: The Spanish Model*, Aldershot: Edward Elgar.

Costa Pinto, A. C. (ed.) (2005) *Contemporary Portugal*, New York: Columbia University Press.

Gunther, R. (ed.) (1993) *Politics, Society, and Democracy: The Case of Spain*, Boulder: Westview.

Linz, J. J. (1978) *The Breakdown of Democratic Regimes*, Baltimore: Johns Hopkins University Press.

Maxwell, K. (1995) *The Making of Portuguese Democracy*, Cambridge: Cambridge University Press.

Oppello, W. C., Jr (1991) *From Monarchy to Pluralist Democracy*, Boulder: Westview Press.

Preston, P. (2001) *The Triumph of Democracy in Spain*, London: Routledge.

Tusell, J. (2007) *Spain: From Dictatorship to Democracy*, London: Blackwell.

Elections

Colomer, J. M. (2004) 'Spain: From Civil War to Proportional Representation', in J. M. Colomer (ed.) *Handbook of Electoral System Choice*, Basingstoke and New York: Palgrave Macmillan.

Gunther, R. (1989) 'Electoral Laws, Party Systems, and Elites: The Case of Spain', *American Political Science Review* 83(3): 835–58.

Gunther, R., J. R. Montero and J. Botella (2004) *Democracy in Modern Spain*, New Haven and London: Yale University Press.

Lijphart, A., R. López Pintor and Y. Sone (1986) 'The Limited Vote and the Single Non-transferable Vote: Lessons from the Japanese and Spanish Examples', in B. Grofman and A. Lijphart (eds) *Electoral Laws and their Political Consequences*, New York: Agathon.

Magalhaes, P. C. (2005) 'Elections, Parties, and Policy-making Institutions in Democratic Portugal', in A. Costa Pinto (ed.) *Contemporary Portugal*, New York: Columbia University Press.

Oppello, W. C., Jr (1985) *Portugal's Political Development. A Comparative Approach*, Boulder: Westview Press.

Political parties

Balfour, S. (ed.) (2005) *The Politics of Contemporary Spain*, London: Routledge.

Bruneau, T. C. and A. MacLeod (1986) *Politics in Contemporary Portugal. Parties and the Consolidation of Democracy*, Boulder: Lynne Rienner.

Gillespie, R. (1989) *The Spanish Socialist Party: A History of Factionalism*, Oxford: Oxford University Press.

Gunther, R., G. Sani and G. Shabad (1988) *Spain after Franco. The Making of a Competitive Party System*, revised edition, Berkeley, Los Angeles and London: University of California Press.

Hopkin, J. (1999) *Party Formation and Democratic Transition in Spain: The Creation and Collapse of the Union of Democratic Center*, New York: St Martin's Press.

Mujal-Leon, E. (1983) *Communism and Political Change in Spain*, Bloomington: Indiana University Press.

Parliament and government

Brennan, G. and Casas J. Pardo (1991) 'A Reading of the Spanish Constitution (1978)', *Constitutional Political Economy* 2(1): 53–79.

Capo, J. (2003) 'The Spanish Parliament in a Triangular Relationship, 1982–2000', *Journal of Legislative Studies* 9 (2): 107–29.

Colomer, J. M. (1994) 'Development Policy Decision-making in Democratic Spain', in A. Bagchi (ed.) *Democracy and Development*, London: Macmillan.

Heywood, P. (1995) *The Politics and Government of Spain*, Basingstoke and New York: Palgrave Macmillan.

—— (ed.) (1999) *Politics and Policy in Democratic Spain: No Longer Different?*, London: Frank Cass.

Leston-Bandeira, C. (2004) *From Legislation to Legitimation: The Role of the Portuguese Parliament*, London: Routledge.

Lijphart, A., T. C. Bruneau, P. N. Diamandouros and R. Gunther (1988) 'A Mediterranean Model of Democracy? The Southern European Democracies in Comparative Perspective', *West European Politics* 11(1): 7–25.

Newton, M. and Donaghy, P. (1997) *Institutions of Modern Spain. A Political and Economic Guide*, Cambridge and New York: Cambridge University Press.

Decentralisation

Colomer, J. M. (1999) 'The Spanish State of Autonomies: Non-institutional Federalism', *West European Politics* 21, 44: 40–52.

—— (2007) *Great Empires, Small Nations. The Uncertain Future of the Sovereign State*, London: Routledge.

Colomer, J. M. and F. Martínez (1995) 'The Paradox of Coalition Trading', *Journal of Theoretical Politics* 7 (1): 41–63.

Douglas, W., C. Urza, L. White and J. Zulaika (eds) (2000) *Basque Politics and Nationalism on the Eve of the Millennium*, Reno: University of Nevada Press.

Guibernau, M. (2004) *Catalan Nationalism: Francoism, Transition and Democracy*, London: Routledge.

Muro, D. (2007) *Ethnicity and Violence: The Case of Radical Basque Nationalism*, London: Routledge.

CHAPTER 7

The Low Countries

Confrontation and Coalition in Segmented Societies

Hans Keman

Both national and international events have had serious ramifications for the conduct of politics in the Low Countries since the late 1980s. Internationally this concerned the (re-)democratisation of Central and Eastern Europe after the fall of the Berlin Wall and the further development of the European Community into a political union and the rapid enlargements since 1995. In particular, the introduction of the Euro and the involvement of Belgium, Luxembourg and the Netherlands through the EU and NATO in the Yugoslav internal conflict meant that foreign affairs and Europeanisation became contested in national politics and related policy formation. At the same time, national political developments have left their marks. It appears that the erstwhile politics of accommodation and policy concertation are definitively over: confrontation and competition are – so it seems – the name of the political game at present in the Low Countries.

Yet these signs of change were already noticeable before the 1990s. Between 1960 and 1970 a watershed in the political development of the Benelux countries was emerging, in particular in Belgium and the Netherlands. There is a *communis opinio* among most observers that the existing political institutions appeared less able to cope with the developing problems. Instead of *coalescence* as the main pattern of political behaviour, the name of the game appeared to be developing into political *confrontation* at elections, leading to change in the party system and within government.

In the Netherlands this process was reflected in a change in the informal rules of the game which, in turn, gradually changed the working of the political system. In

Belgium, however, adjusting to this new situation within the existing formal body of political institutions appeared impossible and eventually led to a radical overhaul of the polity. The consequences of the shift in politics surfaced most dramatically during the 1990s: in 1993 the Belgian polity became genuinely federalised and saw a further demise of Christian Democratic dominance. This latter effect also occurred in the Netherlands in 1994, when for the first time since 1917 a coalition government was formed without the Christian Democrats participating. In Belgium the same event took place in 1999. Furthermore, due to the emergence of (successful) 'new' parties between the 1970s and the 1990s the political landscape has indeed changed in the Benelux countries.

In this chapter I shall argue that the institutional configurations of both countries have profoundly changed and this has had ramifications for the behaviour of the political actors involved. These developments may well explain the different patterns of politics in Belgium and the Netherlands, which have led to different outcomes in terms of political performance and related processes of institutional change. In Luxembourg business remained more or less as usual, but for the slow fading of Christian Democratic dominance in parliament and the emergence of new parties.

In the comparative and national literature, the pursuit of political order in the Benelux countries has been labelled, more often than not, under Lijphart's denominator: 'consociationalism', or as it is currently considered as part of the broader type: 'consensus democracy'. This change in terminology as introduced by Arend Lijphart (1999) should not go unnoticed, since it implies that the focus of explanation has also shifted: the former concept focuses mainly on the societal structure that necessitates coalescent behaviour for effective political decision-making; the latter concept places greater emphasis on the political institutions *per se* which facilitate effective decision-making under adversarial societal conditions. In this chapter I shall employ the concept of consensus democracy, asking in what way existing political institutions and their workings have changed over time and to what extent these changes can explain the political behaviour in these countries, in particular since 1990.

Answering these questions not only implies the analysis of institutions and the way in which they have helped to solve societal conflict by including socio-political actors, but also the extent to which socio-economic actors have access to the political system. For one of the major characteristics of the politics of decision-making in Belgium and the Netherlands has been the inclusion of societal interests by means of political organisations, representing them on the basis of cultural divisions. Yet one of the features of the political history of the Low Countries has been that these organisational links have become weaker or even faded away. Instead of one, albeit complex, system of intermediation a second came into being: corporatism or policy control by diverse socio-economic actors.

This development has been noted by various observers of Dutch and Belgian politics and, more often than not, differently interpreted. Luc Huyse, for instance, sees corporatism as a successor to polarised politics; Daalder describes it as 'old wine in new bottles'; whereas Lijphart recently claimed that corporatism is merely a dimension of consensus democracy. In my view this development implies a fundamental institutional shift. Before 1970 the 'pillarised' political organisations represented almost all societal interests and dominated the decision-making process. After that time, societal actors acted more independently and gained selective access to the political and administrative system, leading to new institutional arrangements. The 'segmentation' of politics shifted slowly from its socio-cultural origins and foundations to socio-economic ones, although it did not mean that the old style of politics disappeared altogether. Yet what should be noticed is that in Belgium, Luxembourg and the Netherlands these gradual shifts resulted in other types of government and new forms of negotiation between organised interest and the body politic. In particular, in the course of the 1990s this change became clear in the Netherlands and eventually in Belgium and Luxembourg.

The most remarkable features of this change have been the sudden and high levels of electoral volatility, indicating a growing mistrust of the political elites, and conducive to the emergence of new parties on both the left and right of the political spectrum. Additionally, this electoral shift led to new coalitions, in which parties participated that had never been in government before, and which were also conducive to a change in the policy agendas in the Low Countries. Although the socio-economic issues remained salient, new issues arose: immigration and welfare retrenchment and crime and law and order. Furthermore, the EU became a contested issue because of the financial implications and the EU constitution. The combined effect of the changes has been a more polarised political climate in which the established parties (and their elites) have seemingly lost their erstwhile dominance in steering the ship of state in the past decade.

To a large extent the changing political landscape is still an unfinished journey. However, whatever the eventual result is, the politics and policies in the Low Countries will be different from in the heyday of consociationalism. All three countries are experiencing a development towards executive dominance. In Belgium, in particular, this development is a complex process in relation to its federalised structure of the state that is shaping up.

Below, we shall first focus on the relationship between the electoral system and new parties as well as on its consequences for the division of the respective party systems, particularly after 1970 and 1990. In the following section we shall elaborate the institutional development in relation to the decision-making process, which is characterised by adversarial and coalescent behaviour simultaneously. The following section is devoted to the formation and functioning of party government, in particular in terms of its potential to play a mediating role between societal conflict and political co-operation. Whether or not this still results in feasible and effective policy formation will be discussed in this context. Both the roles of bureaucracy and corporatism will be examined from this perspective. Attention will also be paid to the so-called tendency towards 'diffusion of politics', which appears to develop as a result of the political changes and is seen as an outcome of intra-national developments as well as of the process of European integration. Finally we shall pull together the main findings with respect to institutional developments in the Low Countries and assess to what extent these changes have been important and can explain the contemporary interaction of institutions, political actors and policy performance.

ELECTIONS

Electoral system

The right to vote was introduced and enshrined in the constitution of the Royal Kingdom of the Netherlands in 1814. In the Netherlands and Belgium a bicameral system exists (First and Second Chamber in the Netherlands; Senate and Chamber of Representatives in Belgium, since 1831). The Dutch Second Chamber (100 seats until 1956, thereafter 150 seats) and the Chamber of Representatives in Belgium (212 seats until 1995, since then 150) are directly elected by the electorate (at least) every four years. In both countries this occurs on the basis of proportional representation, using the d'Hondt formula. In Luxembourg there exists a unicameral system (Chamber of Deputies, 60 seats) and the electoral system is based on multiple limited constituencies employing the Hagenbach–Bischoff formula. This chamber is elected directly every five years. In terms of proportionality these electoral systems are quite 'true' and access for new parties is relatively easy, since there is barely any electoral threshold.

The Senate of the Netherlands, as the First Chamber is also called, is indirectly chosen through the provincial legislatures. In practice, however, this indirect type of voting has been abolished, since the outcomes of the regional elections (based on the PR principle) are conducive to the allocation of seats. In the Belgian Senate 106 members are elected directly, the remaining 75 seats are allocated by the nine provinces (50 seats) and by co-optation (25 seats).

The electoral systems of the Low Countries therefore resemble one another, although there are some significant differences between them. The Netherlands – the only country in Europe with a nationwide constituency – provides the maximum proportionality between votes and the party seats. In Luxembourg the voter has a bigger influence in selecting a candidate through an open ballot or '*panachage*'. Generally, the electoral systems in the Benelux countries rank high in terms of proportionality and reflect the preferences of the population at large. Additionally, it implies that the emergence of new parties and high electoral volatility are likely. These effects have indeed taken place since the 1990s and have affected both the development of the party system and the party composition of government in Belgium and the Netherlands.

The development of the electoral system of a country, and hence of the institutional choices made, to a large extent reflects the ruling ideas about the principal goals of representative democracy. In Belgium, the Netherlands and Luxembourg, the majoritarian electoral system based on plurality was replaced around the turn of the century in conjunction with the granting of universal male suffrage, which took place during or shortly after the First World War. Female suffrage was established in Luxembourg and the Netherlands in 1919, whereas Belgian women had to wait until 1948 to gain full voting rights. It was half conceded in 1921 as being a possible reform in the future, but since a two-thirds majority was needed to implement it, it took a long time. At present the rate of female participation in the respective parliaments is 37 per cent (the Netherlands), 35 per cent (Belgium) and 23 per cent (Luxembourg).

All in all, one could say that the process of democratisation by means of the enfranchisement, or the extension of voting rights to the population, took shape around the First World War and was laid down in an electoral system that enables minorities to be represented on the national level in parliament, to which governments were responsible. The type of electoral system chosen reflected not only the extant division of power in these countries, but also to some extent the historical roots of these countries: it assisted in a new form, i.e. parliamentary democracy, the idea of a 'republican monarchy'. In these polities the rights as well as the influence of minorities were respected, and in turn, these gained political room for manoeuvre. To ensure this representative distribution the compulsory vote was originally introduced. In the Netherlands alone this was abolished in 1971. Hence, the institutionalisation of democracy in the Netherlands, Belgium and Luxembourg took a specific trajectory and – as they were partially designed as political institutions to match societal divisions – it is worthwhile to examine the consequences.

The most frequently mentioned effect of a PR electoral system with low thresholds concerns the fractionalisation of the electorate and parliament, producing unstable voting behaviour and a fragmented party system in which the major parties are weak. The degree of fractionalisation among voters and parliamentarians is indeed comparatively high in the Benelux countries. Electoral fragmentation in the period 1945–90 was on average 0.84 in the Netherlands, 0.74 in Belgium and 0.71 in Luxembourg, whereas parliamentary fragmentation is slightly less. In Luxembourg and the Netherlands the degree of fractionalisation decreased somewhat after 1970, but increased in Belgium. Henceforth the number of political parties in parliament was relatively high. Belgium had 6 parliamentary parties before 1970 and 11 afterwards. The Netherlands is quite stable in this respect; on average 10 parties were represented throughout the post-war period, whereas in Luxembourg the number rises from 4 to 5 after 1970. More often than not this rise was associated with the emergence of new parties.

A comparison of the Benelux countries with other European countries with a PR system shows that the average number of parties in parliament in Luxembourg is by and large similar to the cross-European average, and in Belgium and the Netherlands slightly higher (Gallagher *et al.* (2005) report a European average of 3.9 parties before 1975 and 4.8 in the 1990s). Taking into account the relative strength of the first and second largest parties in parliament, however, it appears that the fractionalisation has dramatically changed: around 1970 these parties polled 49 per cent of the legislative vote in Belgium, 69 per cent in Luxembourg and 61 per cent in the Netherlands. At present these figures are 46 per cent, 60 per cent and 48 per cent, respectively. This development implies that the hold of the originally dominant parties is clearly vanishing in the Netherlands, but not in Luxembourg. The change in terms of fractionalisation of electoral support and subsequent fragmentation of the legislature in Belgium is in large part due to the process of federalisation of the polity.

The Belgian constitution requires that a qualified majority must pass legislation on territorial matters concerning socio-cultural issues and that it must be reaffirmed by a new parliament. In particular, after the 'Egmont pact' in 1970, this institutional requirement had an effect on parliamentary decision-making, which was, more often than not, postponed or delayed, and has been politicised during elections since then. By means of the political room for manoeuvre – available through the Belgian electoral system – 'communal/territorial' issues cut across the existing party divisions. It led to a separation of the parties (Socialists, Christians and Liberals) on the basis of language, and to the rise of territorial parties, exclusively representing Flanders, Wallonia and Brussels, since the 1970s.

In conclusion: the electoral systems of the Low Countries yield particularly dramatic differences regarding the number of parties. For example, the effective number of parties is, comparatively speaking, quite high. Over time (1950–2006) electoral volatility in Benelux has been around 12 per cent on average. After 1989 a steep rise in electoral volatility and successful new parties can be observed. From this survey it is obvious that electoral changes have occurred in the Benelux. The extent of this change in the Low Countries will be analysed in more depth by examining the relation between elections and parties regarding the changing divisions of the respective party systems.

New parties and party system change

Electoral systems based on the PR principle are not so susceptible to manufacturing majorities, but in such systems it is also difficult to earn a majority for a single party. This happened only once in Belgium, in 1950 (CVP: 108 of the 212 seats), almost happened in Luxembourg in 1984 (CSP: 26 of the, then, 52 available seats) and has never happened in the Netherlands. Hence, although Christian Democratic parties have been quite dominant electorally, until the 1990s their electoral fortunes dwindled.

Proportional representation supposedly mirrors societal differences, if not change, better than majority or plurality electoral systems. Hence it can be expected that the cleavage structure is reflected in electoral results. The literature on the relation between parties and elections suggests three aspects of this process: (1) the cleavage structures of society; (2) the ideological roots of parties; and (3) the type of policy issue saliency. Whereas a cleavage is a sociological concept, the ideological and policy dimensions are directly related to politics. The main ideological differences, however, appear after the cleavages in society are politicised and only partially assimilated into the political movements. Parties in Belgium and the Netherlands are based on societal differences and are at the same time differentiated according to well-known ideological 'blocs': Christian Democracy, social democracy and (conservative) liberalism. Historically two cleavages have been prominent in Belgium and the Netherlands:

1   *Religious or moral dimension*: In the north this division was based partly on rivalry between Protestantism (which was by many considered as an informal 'State Church') and Catholicism (which saw itself as an emancipating minority), but they both shared an interest against the ('liberal') state regulation of social life, which was expressed, particularly, in the issue of education. In the south this division was shaped much more by the process of secularisation of social life,

acquisition of individual rights and opposition to the overwhelming influence of Catholicism and its clerical organisation (although the principal issue also centred on the educational system).

2   *Left–right dimension*: In Belgium and the Netherlands the socio-economic division emerged in the wake of the concurrent processes of industrialisation and urbanisation. It was based on 'class consciousness', which developed more strongly and rapidly in the south than in the north, owing to its earlier and more encompassing pattern of industrial activities. In both countries the major socialist party was reformist and preceded the formation of a nationwide trade union federation. Hence the political party led the way, mainly through its campaign for universal suffrage and a wish to enter government. Together with the fact that other cleavages played an important role in the Low Countries, this meant that the sheer 'class' division was not strong and faded after the Second World War.

Up to 1970 these two cleavages and related ideologies dominated political life and to a large extent electoral developments. It was only then that in Belgium a third cleavage became politicised: the language–territorial or 'communal' cleavage, which tended to overshadow the other ones. The existing ideological differences remained, but were now organised within a territorial party system.

In the Netherlands the religious cleavage became less prominent and since the 1970s electoral campaigns have focused more on new issues in combination with the socio-economic conflict dimension. The so-called 'post-material' dimension appears to capture the 'moral' high ground. The new party combination 'Green Left', formed in 1989, can be considered as the representative of this development. Similarly the flourishing of genuine ecological parties can also be observed after 1990 in Belgium (Agalev and Ecolo) and Luxembourg (Greng).

Until the late 1980s electoral politics was largely influenced by a two-dimensional space of voters – religious–moral and socio-economic – and the emerging party system is characterised by three distinctive party 'families' or blocs: Christian Democrats (religious and capitalist), Liberals (secular and capitalist) and Social Democrats (secular and labour). Until the 1970s these three party families dominated political and social life in Belgium, Luxembourg and the Netherlands. As has been widely discussed and well documented, the main parties politically representing the cleavage structure in Benelux have had a tight relationship with their grass roots. Their differences concern their ideological homogeneity and strategic behaviour regarding elections and participation in government. It seems that under similar conditions each system allows different patterns of behaviour.

Several parties in the Netherlands represented the Christian Democratic bloc, whereas in Luxembourg this has never been the case. In Belgium the preponderance of the Flanders versus Walloon conflict after 1960 has produced an organisational and electoral division, whereas in the Netherlands the process of secularisation and depolarisation led to the unification of the Christian Democratic Party family into one party: the Christian Democratic Appeal (CDA).

Both the Social Democratic and Liberal Party families remained roughly the same throughout the post-war history of Luxembourg and the Netherlands. Although there have been splits within these blocs, these have mostly been temporary. The major shift that can be observed in all three party systems is the rise of green parties, in particular in the 1990s (8 per cent on average). Yet this new party family has not been able to distance itself in a clear way from the left–right dimension. Other new parties that have emerged have not either, but rather distinguish themselves by means of two features: (1) radical political views as regards left and right; and (2) populist tactics to make inroads into the heartland of both the left and right.

In Belgium this became visible with the Flemish Bloc and the National Front. The former has been most successful, whereas in the Netherlands various 'radical-right' parties attempted to gain electoral ground. It was only the ill-fated List Pim Fortuyn that caused a landslide electoral victory in 2002 (and to a lesser extent the Party of Freedom achieved the same in 2006). However, in the Netherlands a radical left-wing party also emerged in the 1980s, the Socialist Party, which slowly but

Table 7.1 Elections to the Belgian Chamber of Representatives, 1946–2007

Year	Turnout %	Communist KPB	Green Ecolo	Socialist PS/SP	Languages RW,	FDF,	VU	Christian CDH/CDV	Liberal MR/VLD	Flemish Vl.B	Other
1946	90	13	–	32	–	–	–	43	10	–	3
1949	94	8	–	30	–	–	2	44	15	–	2
1950	93	5	–	35	–	–	–	48	12	–	0
1954	93	4	–	39	–	–	2	41	13	–	2
1958	94	2	–	37	–	–	2	47	12	–	1
1961	92	3	–	37	–	–	3	42	12	–	3
1965	92	5	–	28	1	1	7	35	22	–	2
1968	90	3	–	28	3	3	10	9/22	21	–	0
1971	92	3	–	27	7	5	11	8/22	6/10	–	1
1974	90	3	–	27	6	4	10	9/23	5/10	–	2
1977	95	3	1	27	3	4	10	10/26	6/9	–	1
1978	95	3	1	13/12	3	4	7	10/26	5/10	1	3
1981	95	2	5	13/12	2	2	10	7/19	9/13	1	5
1985	94	1	6	14/15	0	1	8	8/21	10/11	1	3
1987	93	1	7	16/15	0	1	8	8/20	9/12	2	2
1991	93	0	10	14/12	0	2	6	8/17	8/12	7	6
1995	89	–	8	12/13	–	–	5	8/17	10/13	6	8
1999	91	–	14	10/10	–	–	6	6/14	10/14	10	6
2003	92	–	6	13/15	–	–	–	6/13	11/15	14	7
2007	91	–	7	11/10	–	–	–	6/19	13/12	18	4

Notes:

Communist: KPB: Communist Party.

Green: Ecologists (Ecolo/Agalev).

Socialist: PS: Walloon Socialist Party (Parti Socialiste); SP: Flemish Socialist Party (SP.A-Spirit/Cartel Social Progressief Alternatief).

Languages: RW: Walloon Assembly (Rassemblement Wallon); FDF: Francophone Democratic Front (Front Democratique Francophone); VU: Flemish Union (Vlaamse Unie).

Christian: CDH: Democratic and Humanist Centre (Centre Démocratique and Humaniste); CDV: Flemish Christian Democrat (Christen-Democratisch & Vlaams).

Liberal: MR: Reform Movement (Mouvement Réformateur); VLD: Flemish Liberal Democrats (Vlaamse Liberalen en Democraten).

Flemish: Vl.B: Flemish Bloc (Vlaams Belang).

consistently attracted more votes until it became the third-largest party in parliament, with fifteen seats.

In Belgium a fundamental and lasting change has taken place, which upset the party blocs which existed before 1965. Until then there were four parties in parliament representing the left (social democracy and the Communist Party), the centre (Christian democracy) and the right (Liberals). However, territorially based parties exclusively representing the language–territorial or 'communal' cleavage received more and more electoral support. Around the mid-1970s the traditional parties followed suit and organised themselves along this cleavage. The result has been that the Belgian party system had fourteen parties in which each territory – Flanders, Walloon and Brussels – was represented by the common ideological party families and by parties representing the language–territorial issue. After 1985 the latter parties gradually lost support (apart from the Flemish Bloc) and at present there are ten parties in parliament: a Flemish and Walloon party for each of the traditional ideological blocs, one large and one small language–territorial party, and, since the 1980s, two Green parties. All in all, it appears that the Belgian party system has drastically changed over time and is still in flux: not only because new parties have gained weight, but also because the main parties representing the Christian Democrats and the Liberals are changing their labels in an attempt to realign their voters, and – due to the federalist developments – are less similar to their brethren across the language communities.

Table 7.2 Elections to the Luxembourg Chamber of Deputies, 1945–2004

Year	Turnout %	Communist KPL/DL	Green G	Socialist LSAP	Christian CSV	Democrat DP	Others
1945	nd	11	–	23	45	18	3
1948	92	14	–	38	36	12	0
1951	91	3	–	34	42	21	0
1954	93	7	–	33	45	12	2
1959	92	7	–	33	39	20	1
1964	91	10	–	36	36	12	6
1968	89	13	–	31	38	18	0
1974	90	9	–	27	30	23	11
1979	89	5	–	23	36	22	14
1984	89	4	4	32	37	20	3
1989	87	4	8	26	32	17	11
1994	87	2	10	25	30	19	14
1999	87	2	9	24	30	23	13
2004	86	2	12	23	36	24	3

Notes:

Communist: KPL: Communist Party of Luxembourg (Kommunistesch Partei Lëtzebuerg). DL: The Left (Déi Lénk).

Green: G: The Greens (Déi Greng).

Socialist: LSAP: Socialist Labour (Lëtzebuerger Arbechterpartei).

Christian: CSV: Christian Social Union (Chrëstlich-Sozial Vollekspartei).

Democrat: DP: Democratic Party (Demokratesch Partei).

In Luxembourg the party system has remained remarkably stable and only during the 1980s were the Green movement and a radical left-wing party able to gain access to parliament. The total number of parties has risen from four during the 1950s to six since the 1980s. This growth is directly related to one issue: the reform of the welfare state, in particular pension reform. However, most of the new parties did not flourish for long.

In the Netherlands the first change occurred during the late 1960s, when a number of splits came about among the Social Democrats and the Christian Democrats. However, the most important change at that time was the foundation of Democrats '66 – a progressive liberal party – which gained a lasting, albeit volatile, position within the Dutch party system. During the 1980s the situation again changed through a number of mergers (resulting in the CDA and the Green left). An additional change has been the electoral growth of the conservative liberal VVD.

Table 7.3 Elections to the First Chamber in the Netherlands, 1946–2006

Year	Turnout %	Socialist SP	Green CPN,	PSP,	PPR	Labour PvdA	Democrat D'66	Christian KVP,	ARP,	CHU,	Oth	People VVD	Freedom PVV	Other
1946	93	–	11	–	–	28	–	31	13	8	2	6	–	1
1948	94	–	8	–	–	26	–	31	13	9	2	8	–	4
1952	95	–	6	–	–	30	–	29	11	8	6	9	–	1
1956	96	–	5	–	–	33	–	32	10	8	3	9	–	1
1959	96	–	2	2	–	31	–	32	9	8	3	12	1	0
1963	95	–	3	3	–	29	–	32	9	9	3	10	2	2
1967	95	–	4	3	–	24	5	27	10	8	3	11	5	2
1971*	79	–	4	1	2	25	7	22	9	6	4	10	1	9
1972	84	–	5	2	5	27	4	18	9	5	5	14	2	5
1977	88	–	2	1	2	34	5	CDA:	32		4	18	1	1
1981	87	–	2	2	2	28	11		31		5	17	0	2
1982	81	1	2	2	2	30	4		30		3	23	1	2
1986	86	0	1	1	1	33	6		35		3	17	0	2
1989	80	0	GL:	4		32	8		35		4	15	1	1
1994	78	1		4		24	16		22		5	20	3	5
1998	73	4		7		29	9		18		5	25	1	2
2002	79	6		7		15	5		28		4	16	19	0
2003	80	6		5		27	4		29		4	18	6	1
2006	80	17		5		21	2		27		6	15	6	1

Notes:

*Compulsory vote abolished.

Socialist: SP: Socialist Party (Socialistische Partij).

Green: CPN: Communist Party; PSP: Pacifist Socialist; PPR: Radicals; since 1989, merged into GL: Green Left (Groen Links).

Labour: PvdA: Labour Party (Partij van der Arbeid).

Democrat: D'66: Democrats (Democraten '66).

Christian: KVP: Catholics; ARP: Anti-Revolutionary Party; CHU: Christian Historical Union; since 1977, merged into CDA: Christian Democratic Appeal (Christen Democratisch Appel); Oth: Orthodox Catholic and Protestant parties.

People: VVD: Freedom People's Democratic Party (Volkspartij voor Vrijheid en Democratie).

Freedom: PVV: Freedom Party (Partij voor de Vrijheid).

Yet the most striking feature of Dutch electoral politics has been the soaring levels of electoral volatility: 21 per cent in 1994, 31 per cent in 2002 and 13 per cent in 2006.

It is clear from this overview that the Dutch and, to some extent, the Luxembourg party systems have gone through a period of transition. In Belgium the dominant cleavage is not in as much left–right but instead the 'communal' or 'federal' one. Since the 1970s, the overall number of parties has doubled and the original party blocs are split according to this cleavage. Instead of one, *two* party systems exist in Belgium, representing the party families in separate ideological blocs in Walloon and Flanders. The extent to which these developments in the respective party systems have influenced the behaviour of parties will be scrutinised below.

PARTY SYSTEMS. TURBULENCE AND TURMOIL

Before discussing the ideological differences between parties as well as their issue-guided behaviour, we will briefly describe the development of the major parties. Among the Benelux countries, Belgium has the longest history of a full parliamentary democracy in terms of a directly elected parliament to which government is responsible. It took until 1868 to reach this stage in Luxembourg and the Netherlands, when the principle of responsible government was introduced *de facto*. Hence parties emerged first as parliamentary groups as well as electoral organisations between 1846 and 1885 in Belgium, whereas in Luxembourg and the Netherlands the process of party formation took a different course.

Most present parties, except the Social Democratic ones (which were founded between 1893 and 1902), came into being after the Second World War. Although the Protestant parties of the Netherlands (Anti-Revolutionary Party, ARP, and Christian Historical Union, CHU) were also formed before or around the turn of the century, they have now ceased to exist after their mergers with the Catholic KVP into CDA (1977). The Catholic parties re-emerged as genuine people's parties after the war. The current liberal parties were founded between 1944 and 1950 in all three countries as a result of the regrouping of previously separate parties. The main difference between the pre-war and post-war liberal parties is due to populist tendencies. Although the ideological and organisational roots of the main parties in Benelux go back to the nineteenth century, their behaviour can be better analysed since the Second World War.

As has been noted already in the introduction to this chapter, after 1970 parties had to transform themselves in order to maintain their electoral support and at the same time they had to find the means to achieve optimal outcomes in terms of decision-making. To some extent both aims were contradictory or at least seem to have been inversely related. In order to remain viable political parties, the main parties of the Dutch and Belgian systems had to cope with societal developments and new political issues, as well as to re-establish links with the population. This led them consequently to rearrange the mode of interaction with other parties. This line of reasoning not only explains the transformation of the party system as an institution of collective decision-making, but also sheds light on the changing style of the politics of accommodation in the Low Countries. In order to understand this process of adjustment, we shall now focus upon party differences in terms of issues and ideology before and after 1970, i.e. the development of the party systems and parties in a consociational environment towards a situation of adversarial conditions during the 1990s. In addition, we shall focus on the changes after 1989 in particular which aptly illustrate the changing political behaviour in the Benelux from coalescence to adversarial party politics.

Adversarial politics and coalescent party behaviour

Political parties in Benelux are required to develop a dual strategy. On the one hand, parties must convince the electorate that they are the best choice for realising the voters' desires individually. On the other hand, parties must take into account the feasibility of future government participation. Hence parties must seek an optimal strategic position by means of an adversarial type of electoral competition and a coalescent attitude towards coalition formation. In other words, each party's problem is to reconcile its strategy concerning electoral competition and eventual co-operation in government coalitions that allows for decision-making with an eye to effective policy pursuit.

Originally, vote-organising, rather than vote-seeking, as an electoral strategy of parties was based primarily on societal cleavages, but since the late 1960s this option is no longer feasible. Parties must direct themselves in campaigning on the basis of issue salience. That is to say, parties compete on those policy-related issues on which they will be distinguished from other parties without making co-operation impossible. The relevant parties have to solve the paradox of ideological distance and policy connection in gaining access to government at a later stage.

A way of looking into this problem is to examine the extent to which parties differ in terms of their election programmes. To that end we here use a comparative left versus right scale, which shows the ideological differences between the three party blocs-cum-families and the new parties that have emerged on both the right and left of the respective party systems. First of all, it can be noted that after 1989 the pattern changes. The new parties on the left and the right are 'wing' parties, whereas the programmatic differences between Christian democracy and social democracy decrease. A glance at the range of each party system reveals that the party differences are strongly reduced. All in all, this implies a convergent movement with less space for competition.

In comparative perspective the party differences are not very great and tend to decrease. Furthermore, it can be noted that it is difficult to locate an obvious party at the centre of any of the party systems in the Benelux countries. The centre used to be occupied by the Christian Democrats (CDA in the Netherlands and CVP/PSV in Belgium). In Luxembourg the centre is not really occupied by any party, although the Social Democrats are close to the median. In short, the movements of parties in the Low Countries are less straightforward than before 1990. The overall movement is convergent for the established parties, with some divergence on the 'wings' of each party system as a result of the rise of new parties.

Since the late 1960s new parties definitely have entered the electoral arena in the Netherlands: Democrats '66 (D'66), the Green Left (a merger of small left parties in 1989) and the Socialist Party (SP). In particular D'66 and the SP have significantly changed the electoral game in the Netherlands, since the former competes with both the Freedom People's Democrats (VVD) and the Labour Party (PvdA); whereas the Green Left has been for some time a threat to the PvdA. However, the SP is the more serious threat by organising a homogeneous party bloc on the left of that party. In Belgium the party differences were well organised by the parties, in particular Social Democrats and Christian Democrats. After 1970 the language–territory or 'communal' cleavage gained real weight. This development is less reflected in the left–right distance than in the reorganisation of the main parties into Flemish and Walloon blocs. This was typically a strategy to limit the electoral room for manoeuvre of territorially based parties in Flanders (originally the Flemish Union, VU, and during the 1990s the right-wing Flemish Bloc, VB) and in Wallonia (the Reform Movement, MR) in order to maintain their electoral share and thus uphold their own position within the changing party system. In Luxembourg the main parties retain their electorate and are only marginally affected by the Greens and protest parties.

All in all, party system change has occurred in the Benelux. The general shift within each system has been towards the centre, where the party differences decrease, with a simultaneous development at the right and the left. Whereas the moral-religious dimension appears to fade, the socio-economic issues tend to become more important. The main change is the emergence of successful new parties on the left and right of the political spectrum that have a considerable share of the vote (12 per cent in Luxemburg in 2004, 24 per cent in the Netherlands in 2006, 27 per cent in Belgium in 2007). The room for electoral competition appears to be smaller than before and the programmatic differences between the established party families are diminishing. Traditional cleavages and related ideologies are less relevant nowadays. At the same time the saliency of issues is becoming more important for understanding the politics of policy-making in the Low Countries.

Table 7.4 Left–right placement of parties in Belgium

Greens Eco, Ag	Socialists PS, SP	Christians CDH, CDV	Liberals MR, VLD	Flemish VB
Left	Centre-left	Centre	Centre-right	Right

Party names:
Eco, Ag: Ecologist (Ecolo/Agalev).
PS: Walloon Socialist Party (Parti Socialiste).
SP: Flemish Socialist Party (SP.A-Spirit/Cartel Social Progressief Alternatief).
CDH: Democratic and Humanist Centre (Centre Démocratique and Humaniste).
CDV: Flemish Christian Democrats (Christen-Democratisch & Vlaams).
MR: Reform Movement (Mouvement Réformateur).
VLD: Flemish Liberal Democrats (Vlaamse Liberalen en Democraten).
VB: Flemish Bloc (Vlaams Belang).

Source: De Winter *et al.* (2006), Keman (2007).

Table 7.5 Left–right placement of parties in Luxembourg

Communist	Green	Socialist		Christian	Democrat	Justice
DL	G	LSAP		CSV	DP	ADR
Left		Centre-left	Centre	Centre-right		Right

Party names:
DL: The Left (Déi Lénk).
G: The Greens (Déi Greng).
LSAP: Socialist Labour (Lëtzebuerger Arbechterpartei).
CSV: Christian-Social Union (Chrëstlich-Sozial Vollekspartei).
DP: Democratic Party (Demokratesch Partei).
ADR: Action Committee for Democracy and Justice (Aktionskomitee fir Demokratie a Rentegerechtegkeet).

Table 7.6 Left–right placement of parties in the Netherlands

Socialist	Green	Labour		Democrat	Christian	People	Freedom
SP	GL	PvdA		D'66	CDA	VVD	PVV
Left		Centre-left		Centre	Centre-right		Right

Party names:
SP: Socialist party (Socialistische Partij).
GL: Green Left (Groen Links).
PvdA: Labour Party. (Partij van der Arbeid).
D'66: Democrats (Democraten '66).
CDA: Christian Democratic Appeal (Christen Democratisch Appel).
VVD: Freedom Democratic People's Party (Volkspartij voor Vrijheid en Democratie).
PVV: Freedom Party (Partij voor de Vrijheid).

Source: Keman (2007).

Salient issues

Party systems in the Benelux countries have changed over time in terms of party differences and this also implies a change in the way parties interact with each other. An important feature of party interaction is not only how far apart they are ideologically, but also what this means in terms of issue salience. As we stated before, issue salience is, in addition to ideology, an important feature of the working of the party system as an institution of parliamentary democracy. Party differences with respect to issues are a more direct indicator of the extent to which parties are capable of cooperative behaviour, which is central to the process of government formation. What parties stress as their salient issues may also be expected to shape their agenda if and when they enter government.

Keman (2007) and Klingemann *et al.* (1994) have shown by means of European cross-national comparisons that the programmatic contents of the three party 'families' – Social Democrats, Christian Democrats and Liberals – show considerable overlap. It demonstrates that there is indeed limited room for manoeuvre for each party to compete and also that a lot of common ground is covered by each party family. Hence, it is the actual saliency of issues that influences adversarial and cooperative behaviour in parliament and government.

Christian Democrats strongly emphasise the provision of social welfare. However, it should also be pointed out that within the Christian Democratic family values related to societal permissiveness or traditional morality are more strongly emphasised in Luxembourg and the Netherlands than in Belgium. A policy priority is prominent in Benelux Christian Democratic and Social Democratic parties: social justice (indicating the importance of solidarity and egalitarianism), i.e. the 'welfare state'.

The European pattern of social-democracy fits the national profiles of the Benelux countries. Yet in this case it is noteworthy that issues relating to economic goals (e.g. full employment) appear to be a lower priority. This is paradoxical if one takes into account the process of de-industrialisation in these countries since the 1980s. All Social Democratic parties in Benelux stress the development of the social welfare state, a policy concern they share with Christian-democracy.

The liberal parties of the Low Countries are more different from the European pattern than the other two party families. It appears that the Democratic Party of Luxembourg shows much more concern regarding the development of the welfare state than its counterparts in Belgium and the Netherlands. These liberal parties (the Flemish Liberal Democrats (VLD) and MR in Belgium and the VVD in the Netherlands) have an issue profile that is much more oriented towards values and goals regarding the market economy. In fact their profile better resembles the ideological priorities of the European conservative parties, in which economic orthodoxy is a prominent feature.

It can be concluded, therefore, that the main party differences, expressed in terms of issue salience in the Low Countries, to a large degree match the European pattern, with the exception of the Liberals, which are more inclined to a conservative ideology. This is an important conclusion, for it points to the fact that the degree of co-operation and conflict within each of the party systems can be viewed as taking place basically within a two-dimensional space with two main issues: the economy and social welfare. This pattern enables each party representing these issues considerable room for manoeuvre in building coalitions within parliament and with respect to government formation. It is essential to understand this, since it shapes the process of collective decision-making in these multi-party systems and thus helps us understand why politics in the Low Countries can be characterised as a pendulum between cooperation and confrontation in order to compete successfully for a maximum share of the vote, without losing sight of the other aim of parties, which is linked to government participation.

PARLIAMENT AND COALITION FORMATION

Given the structure of party politics in the Benelux countries, it goes almost without saying that in terms of collective decision-making party government is the paramount institution. Whatever description of politics in the Low Countries one examines, the formation and functioning of government are considered to be vital in explaining politics in those countries. Most important of all is that most writers focus on the role of parties with respect to the formation and subsequent behaviour of government in terms of policy pursuit and performance. Hence within this context of policy-seeking behaviour the policy space within the respective party systems is crucial for understanding the process of government formation.

Below I shall first describe the process of government formation in Belgium, Luxembourg and the Netherlands. This description revolves around three elements: (1) the main rules of the 'formation game'; (2) the primary objectives of those parties; (3) the outcomes of the government formation process. After that, we shall focus on the decision-making process of the coalition governments in Belgium and the Netherlands. This is important for it is there that the paradox of the politics of confrontation and cooperation comes to the fore. Cabinet decision-making seeks to solve adversarial policy issues, thereby shaping the executive–legislature relationship and, of course, to a large extent determining the policy performance.

Features of coalition formation

Party governments in the Benelux countries have almost always been coalitions. Unlike in Scandinavian countries, for example, governments must rely on a parliamentary majority. The exceptions to this rule are the so-called caretaker governments, which, however, function with clipped wings regarding policy-making. Caretaker governments are meant to pave the way for new fully fledged coalitions, mostly by preparing for new, often anticipated elections.

The Netherlands and Luxembourg fit the European average duration of governments quite well (786 days), and the composition of government is almost always a multi-party coalition. Since the 1970s the prevalent type of coalition government in Luxembourg and the Netherlands is the minimum winning coalition (MWC, with no superfluous members to form a majority). Over time the major change is that Christian Democrats are becoming less powerful after 1970, yet still holding the premiership more often than not. Another feature of party governance is that the parliamentary action of withdrawing legislative support from government is not often utilised. This suggests a diminishing role of parliamentary politics and a shift in the executive–legislature relation. From this overview of the features of party government in the Benelux countries it appears that, particularly in Luxembourg and the Netherlands, they are quite stable, tend to be minimum winning and have developed a relatively dominant position with respect to parliament.

However, it must be noticed that there is a striking contrast between Belgium on the one hand and Luxembourg and the Netherlands on the other as far as the features of coalition government are concerned. In virtually all respects Belgian governments

Table 7.7 Governments of Belgium, 1945–2007

No.	Year	Prime Minister	Party composition
1	1945	A. van Acker	Christian, Socialist, Liberal, Communist
		A. van Acker	Socialist, Liberal, Communist, Independent
2	1946	P. H. Spaak	Socialist, Liberal
		A. van Acker	Socialist, Liberal, Communist
		C. Huysmans	Socialist, Liberal, Communist
	1947	P. H. Spaak	Socialist, Christian
3	1949	G. Eyskens	Christian, Liberal
4	1950	J. Duvieusart	Christian
		J. Pholien	Christian
	1952	J. van Houtte	Christian
5	1954	A. van Acker	Socialist, Liberal
6	1958	G. Eyskens	Christian
	1958	G. Eyskens	Christian, Liberal
7	1961	T. Lefevre	Christian, Socialist
8	1965	P. Hamel	Christian, Socialist
	1966	P. Vandenboeynants	Christian, Liberal
9	1968	G. Eyskens	Christian, Liberal
10	1972	G. Eyskens	Christian, Socialist
	1973	E. Leburton	Socialist, Christian, Liberal
11	1974	L. Tindemans	Christian, Liberal
	1974	L. Tindemans	Christian, Liberal, Walloon
12	1977	L. Tindemans	Christian, Socialist, Francophone, Flemish
13	1978	P. Vandenboeynants	Christian, Socialist, Francophone, Flemish
	1979	W. Martens	Christian, Socialist, Francophone
	1980	W. Martens	Christian, Socialist
	1980	W. Martens	Christian, Socialist, Liberal
	1980	G. Eyskens	Christian, Socialist
14	1981	G. Eyskens	Christian, Socialist
	1981	W. Martens	Christian, Liberal
15	1985	W. Martens	Christian, Liberal
16	1987	W. Martens	Christian, Liberal
	1988	W. Martens	Christian, Socialist, Flemish
17	1992	J.-L. Dehaene	Christian, Socialist
18	1995	J.-L. Dehaene	Christian, Socialist
19	1999	G. Verhofstadt	Liberal, Socialist, Francophone, Green
20	2003	G. Verhofstadt	Liberal, Socialist
21	2007	G. Verhofstadt	Caretaker

Note: The first party indicates the Prime Minister's affiliation.

differ from the Dutch and Luxembourg ones: they are not minimal winning, they have not lasted as long and tend to be terminated for reasons that either have to do with internal dissent within the coalition or with losing parliamentary support. All these features of Belgian party government point to a lower degree of governmental stability.

In Belgium and to some extent in the Netherlands one should note that the internal cohesion of coalition government is fading. It is apparent that conflicts between parties tend to be fought out within the government, rather than in parliament. This may indicate a decline in traditional politics of accommodation.

Table 7.8 Governments of Luxembourg, 1945–2004

No.	Year	Prime Minister	Party composition
1	1945	P. Dupong	Christian, Socialist, Democrat, Communist
	1947	P. Dupong	Christian, Democrat
2	1948	P. Dupong	Christian, Democrat
3	1951	P. Dupong	Christian, Socialist
	1953	J. Bech	Christian, Socialist
4	1954	J. Bech	Christian, Socialist
	1958	P. Frieden	Christian, Socialist
5	1959	P. Werner	Christian, Democrat
6	1964	P. Werner	Christian, Socialist
7	1969	P. Werner	Christian, Democrat
8	1974	G. Thorn	Democrat, Socialist
9	1979	P. Werner	Christian, Democrat
10	1984	J. Santer	Christian, Socialist
11	1989	J. Santer	Christian, Socialist
12	1995	J.-C. Juncker	Christian, Socialist
13	1999	J.-C. Juncker	Christian, Democrat
14	2004	J.-C. Junker	Christian, Socialist

Note: The first party indicates the Prime Minister's affiliation.

Table 7.9 Governments of the Netherlands, 1945–2007

No.	Year	Prime Minister	Party composition
1	1945	W. Schermerhorn	Socialist, Christian
2	1946	L. J. M. Beel	Christian, Socialist
3	1948	W. Drees	Socialist, Christian, People
	1951	W. Drees	Socialist, Christian
4	1952	W. Drees	Socialist, Christian
5	1956	W. Drees	Socialist, Christian
	1958	L. J. M. Beel	Christian
6	1959	J. de Quay	Christian, People
7	1963	V. G. M. Marijnen	Christian, People
	1965	J. M. L. Th. Cals	Christian, Socialist
	1966	J. Zijlstra	Christian
8	1967	P. S. de Jong	Christian, People
9	1971	B. W. Biesheuvel	Christian, People, Social Democrat
10	1972	B. W. Biesheuvel	Christian, People
	1973	J. M. den Uyl	Socialist, Christian, Democrat
11	1977	A. A. M. van Agt	Christian, People
12	1981	A. A. M. van Agt	Christian, Socialist, Democrat
13	1982	A. A. M. van Agt	Christian, Democrat
	1982	R. F. M. Lubbers	Christian, People
14	1986	R. F. M. Lubbers	Christian, People
15	1989	R. F. M. Lubbers	Christian, Socialist
16	1994	W. Kok	Socialist, People, Democrat
17	1998	W. Kok	Socialist, People, Democrat
18	2002	J. P. Balkenende	Christian, People, Freedom
19	2003	J. P. Balkenende	Christian, People, Democrat
20	2007	J. P. Balkenende	Christian, Socialist

Note: The first party indicates the Prime Minister's affiliation.

Whichever way one looks at it, it seems that the structure and behaviour of governments have changed over time. Let us therefore turn to the process of government formation in the Benelux countries.

The process of government formation: a long and winding road

The formal and informal rules are structured in more or less the same way in Belgium and the Netherlands. Apart from short clauses/articles in the constitution pointing to the right of the Crown to appoint and dismiss ministers, there are few differences in a formal sense. The basic procedure is as follows: after the termination of government for whatever reason the monarch decides whether or not he or she will accept the resignation. Prior to the 1970s it was habitual to delay this decision in order to look into the possibility of restoring the old government by means of a reshuffle of either ministers or parties. It has been suggested, particularly in the Netherlands, that a new informal rule has been introduced: when a government is terminated, elections are anticipated in order to record the legislative distribution among parties before actually forming a new government.

The next step of the head of state is to appoint an *informateur*, or mediator, whose task is to find a viable combination of parties to form the next government. This is an important stage in the process, since he or she clearly steers the process of forming a government by laying the foundations for the basis of a policy agreement among the potential parties of government.

On the basis of this agreement the monarch appoints a *formateur*, an organiser, who is in fact nowadays the Prime Minister designate. It is the *formateur*'s task to find the proper candidates and to finalise between them and the parties involved the policy programme of the new government. This protracted process has become more time-consuming in the last two decades for two reasons: first, the inter-party bargaining used to be secretive and among party leaders only, while today the media receive more information about what is going on; second, parties themselves state more clearly what they want out of the negotiations and have preserved the right to have the policy agreement ratified by their party decision-making bodies.

Again, most of these procedures are not formal rules, but they are nevertheless adhered to. These informal rules explain why the process of government formation in Benelux countries can take quite some time (it took, on average, 52 days in the period 1946–70, and 85 days afterwards). These rules have, of course, a certain meaning: they are intended to bring about a stable government and a party combination that is primarily founded upon policy-seeking behaviour rather than on office-seeking motivations alone.

From the preceding section it is clear that the formation of coalition governments is a game in which two motives drive the actors or parties involved: office-seeking and policy-seeking. Second, it must be noticed that the number of relevant parties is limited and that the government-formation game in the Benelux countries is strongly influenced by both the initiating and the mediating role of the head of state and the *informateur*. They are in a position to include and exclude parties, albeit restrained by certain 'habits' or informal rules. However, the parties themselves decide the outcome of the negotiation process, and particularly the party elites representing and controlling the parties.

Another aspect of government formation, particularly since policy agreements are a crucial feature of this process, is the extent to which parties and their leaders stress policy pursuit. Again in Luxembourg and the Netherlands this is considered as a prime motive of behaviour, whereas in Belgium this has been less the case. The party leadership has a strong influence on building governments and, in Luxembourg and the Netherlands in particular, policy is traded off against office. It is therefore relevant to know what policies are considered important to the respective parties, for with such knowledge it is also possible to understand and to appreciate the final outcome of the coalition that is formed.

Earlier we found already that two issue dimensions appear to be important in each of the party systems: socio-economic left–right and matters regarding welfare-state development. Social Democratic and liberal parties are divided with respect to socio-economic issues, and Christian democracy takes up a position in between these two party families. Morality is clearly a core policy concern of the centre party in most governments: Christian Democrats. In addition, the development of the federal state *vis-à-vis* the language communities is an issue particularly relevant to the Belgian case. It can be concluded therefore that each party bloc (left, centre and right) is in pursuit of a salient issue, and it may be expected that this multidimensional division will spill over into the bargaining game.

A number of formal and informal rules figure in each system and define the room for manoeuvre, partly independently of their priorities. The following rules apply in Benelux:

1   Small parties and 'radical' parties are often discarded.
2   No minority governments are formed.
3   Without a policy agreement between parties, no government is formed.
4   Without the approval of the representative bodies of each party involved, there is no participation.
5   Parties have preferences for policy and related ministries.
6   Distribution of offices in government should be proportional to the share of seats of participating parties in parliament.

In addition to these general rules, there are a few specific ones, particularly in Belgium. First of all, faced with the need to find solutions with respect to the reform of the unitary state into a federalised polity, governments were wise to look for two-thirds support in both legislative bodies, making constitutional changes possible. Second, since 1971 linguistic parity of ministers in government is constitutionally required. Third, until 1993 it was felt necessary to have a corresponding political majority in the regional councils, which reinforces the fact that in Belgium federalisation is an important issue. At present this process is becoming even more difficult since the electoral differences across the three territorial communities is diverging.

Examining the eventual outcomes of this process we can assess the working of the six informal rules. Rules 1 and 2 have been relevant in all Benelux countries since the beginning of the cold war. In the Netherlands small parties were included in government during the hectic period of the early 1970s and after 2002. The reformist Social Democrats (DS70) were part of a centre-right coalition because the 'normal' parties of government had lost their majority after the elections in 1971. In 1973 both the radical PPR and D'66 participated in Government. D'66 returned to government in 1981, 1994 and 2003. In 2006 the Christian Union (CU) – an orthodox party – took office.

In Belgium the situation has been similar. Since 1974, mainly owing to the constitutional changes we referred to earlier, it is essential to have linguistic parity within the cabinet and to form oversized cabinets to be able to introduce new constitutional arrangements. This led to the forced inclusion of territorially based parties (the Flemish Union, VU, the Walloon Assembly, RW, and the Francophone Democratic Front, FDF, later the Reform Movement, MR). Yet, more recently, owing to the organisational splitting of the parties representing the main party families and the constitutional resolutions of the 1990s, this has no longer really been necessary and the original rule appears to be once more in operation. It can be concluded, apart from caretaker governments and the temporary inclusion of small parties in the 1970s, that Rules 1 and 2 have generally been followed in Belgium, the Netherlands and Luxembourg.

According to Rules 3 and 4, policy agreements are vital, for two reasons. The first is to ensure a majority in parliament in order to find approval. In Luxembourg and the Netherlands there is no formal rule of investiture, as there is in Belgium. Yet a legislative vote is always held on the contents of the Government Declaration, and this procedure is functionally equivalent. The second reason is that in Belgium and Luxembourg parties participating in government are obliged to get the approval of their representative bodies. *De facto* this is merely a 'rubber-stamping' procedure and shows, *inter alia*, the powerful position of the extra-parliamentary leadership. In the Netherlands this latter procedure is not obligatory, but most if not all parties follow this practice. On only two occasions has the outcome of the procedure led to eventual failure to round off the intended formation of government. In 1969 the socialist Luxembourg LSAP blocked the formation of government, and in 1977 the Labour Dutch PvdA did the same.

In respect to Rules 5 and 6, we have pointed out that policy-seeking and office-seeking are related motives in the countries under review. Recall also that policy pursuit is particularly emphasised in Luxembourg and the Netherlands, and that in Belgium office-seeking is on a par with policy pursuit (which can be understood from its requirements regarding the representation of linguistic communities). In addition, until the 1980s there were two conflict dimensions in terms of policy priorities in all three countries: social welfare and societal permissiveness. In particular the Christian Democratic parties had a pivotal position in this respect: in terms of left versus right they almost always controlled the median legislator, and they almost always were the largest party in parliament. Christian Democrats have benefited most from Rules 5 and 6. First of all they have almost always been in government as well as having a leading role by taking the premiership. Second, more often than not these politicians have controlled those ministries that are relevant to their policy aims, i.e. Education, Justice and Social Welfare. Third, the ratio between legislative size and ministerial representation has been maintained in all three countries.

The other partners in government could be considered as junior partners. In Belgium Social Democrats participated in 60 per cent of post-war governments, and the Liberals participated only in 30 per cent of all cabinets. In the Netherlands the left and right were both equally represented: both the Labour Party (PvdA) and the Freedom Party (VVD) participated in half the total number of governments formed. Yet these parties quite often held the ministries relevant to their policy concerns, representing the left–right dimension. Hence Rule 5 appears to work quite well, whereas Rule 6 used to be more beneficial to the Christian Democrats. Yet, during the 1990s the actual situation seemed to be changing, although the six rules are *still* in operation. Recall that Christian Democratic issues appear to be less effective in vote-seeking terms and that socio-economic issues have become even more salient. The result has been that Christian democracy eventually lost its 'pivotal' position in the respective party systems. This has led to a dramatic change in the composition of coalitions in the Netherlands since 1994 and in Belgium since 1999. In the former case it led to the formation of the 'purple coalition' with the Social Democrats together with the 'progressive' and 'conservative' Liberals, i.e. D'66 and VVD. In Belgium the Liberals (VLD/PRL) formed a coalition without the Christian Democratic parties. Luxembourg maintained its familiar process of forming governments of the two electorally strongest parties and therefore always has experienced a minimum winning coalition.

It can be concluded that the actual process of coalition formation in the Benelux countries is the result of the working of the party system and the existing procedures or rules of the game. It appears that many rules have been developed to facilitate a government formation process in which parties play a crucial rule. Until recently the Christian Democratic Party family gained most from this game (especially in holding the premiership). The interaction between the actors involved and the institutions results in viable and often lasting governments in Luxembourg and the Netherlands.

Party government and cabinet decision-making

The vital link between government and parliament with respect to decision-making lies in the policy agreement between the parties in government. Over time this document has acquired almost sacrosanct status in the Netherlands and binds parties of government in parliament. In Belgium the government programme is equally binding on the participating parties, but here the party leaders have more room to manoeuvre to deviate from it. In contrast to the Netherlands, the party Chairman has a strong influence on cabinet decision-making, as he regularly meets every week with the most prominent government ministers in the party. All this means that in both countries the balance between the executive and legislature is tilted in favour of the cabinet. Yet, at the same time, there are important differences between the countries regarding how decision-making takes place and thus how effective partisan control of government is in terms of policy pursuit.

In the Netherlands ministers are constitutionally part of the Queen's government and bear responsibilities that go beyond party. Of course, ministers are answerable to parliament, which, in practice, can dismiss them. There is no separation of powers as, for instance, in the United States, nor are the powers fused, as in Great Britain. Ministers cannot be members of parliament, nor can they assume other public offices at other levels of the state. Both members of parliament and ministers can introduce legislation but most if not all initiatives come from the government. Hence government is clearly the most powerful policy-making agent in the Netherlands. Until the 1970s ministers and supporting parties remained quite independent of each other, since, for instance, the parliamentary leaders rarely took up a post in government. After 1970 this situation changed, and instead of 'specialist and technocrats' more and more generalist politicians have become ministers in the Netherlands. This development has led to a reduced role for the party leadership outside government. This gradual change in the recruitment of ministers may explain, together with the increased status of the policy agreement, why termination of Dutch governments is less often the result of parliamentary action than of internal dissent. Political co-operation and conflict over policy is by and large a matter of politics within the cabinet.

Another feature of Dutch cabinet government that has changed over time is the position and role of the Premier. Until the 1970s his position can best be described as *primus inter pares*. Yet today, although he or she still has few formal powers, he or she is influential in the decision-making process. The Premier draws up the agenda and chairs all the meetings of the cabinet and its committees. He or she casts the deciding vote when there is a tie, and is increasingly regarded as the referee concerning disputes within the cabinet. A final characteristic of the decision-making of Dutch cabinets is that all members are collectively bound by the final outcome. From this description it is clear that party government is not only dominant in the Netherlands with respect to policy-making but also appears to be well organised as a result of a number of formal and informal rules. Only recently this 'practice' of running government has been under pressure. This was mainly due to the electoral success of List Pim Fortuyn, which entered government, and the inability of the parliamentary party to act as a governing party. However, after the elections of 2003 (caused by the ministers representing List Pim Fortuyn) the new coalition returned to business as usual.

The formal institutionalisation of cabinet decision-making in Belgium is similar to the Dutch system. Ministers are in principle appointed by the Crown and are responsible to parliament. Yet there are a number of differences, which are important for understanding Belgian cabinet decision-making and the related policy performance. The major differences concern the position and role of the individual minister in relation to the government as a ruling body. In addition the role and power of the Premier is somewhat different. Each minister holds an individual responsibility and is not bound by definition by the collective decision-making of the Council of Ministers. In actual fact, no such council exists in the constitution; nor is it organised by means of Standing Orders (as the Dutch cabinet has developed over time). Dewachter (1992: 165) remarks that the Belgian government is in fact a political body in which decision-making is dependent on consensus rather than on majorities (i.e. ministers have a kind of veto power). Another difference is the role of central government *vis-à-vis* the autonomous territorial communities. Almost half of the spending by government is sub-nationally decided and therefore central government must negotiate its policies in concert with the regional communities. This only reinforces the urge for consensus politics as regards policy pursuit.

In short, the ministers have a stronger position individually and each party has a strong influence, owing to the rule of consensus decision-making. In part, this explains the greater number of governments, and also the higher degree of government termination due to parliamentary action and internal dissent than in the Netherlands.

It can be concluded that Belgian cabinet government is the apex of the political arena, in which parties *per se* play a dominant role with respect to decision-making. The Belgian government can be considered as a party government and its system of decision-making as a continuous process of intra-national bargaining. The style of decision-making of Belgian governments is therefore different from the Dutch style. Although every government is also formed on the basis of a policy agreement between the participating parties, it is less binding. Parties (i.e. their chairmen) and their individual ministers feel freer to deviate from this agreement. Moreover, not all government actions need to be sanctioned by the cabinet. The role of the Premier can therefore be considered as less powerful than that of his or her Dutch counterpart and more dependent on his or her personal and political skills than on his or her formal position. The Dutch Premier (and also his or her Luxembourg colleague) has developed into a 'supreme referee', whereas his or her Belgian counterpart remains a 'co-ordinator-mediator'. Furthermore, the federalisation of the Belgium nation-state has led to an even more complex process of decision-making. The devolution of a growing number of competences to the regions and communities – in particular after 1993 – has been conducive to this. Finally, given the coalitional type of central and regional governments, policy-making in Belgium is at present affected by the fact that the eventual decision-making is a compromise between parties and the different governing bodies which tends to be conducive to non-decisions and to incremental policy-making.

Government and parliament: emerging osmosis

In Belgium and the Netherlands parliamentary activism has increased over time, in particular since the 1970s. This is a paradoxical development. First, the number of governmental law-making initiatives in Belgium increased from 100 before 1970 to 500 per year in 1990, whilst in the Netherlands the average was 300 after 1970. The number of parliamentary initiatives was relatively low: 11 per cent in Belgium, 5 per cent of the total initiatives in the Netherlands for the same period. Second, the success rate of initiatives by the government is quite high, namely 90 per cent in Belgium and 95 per cent in the Netherlands. This implies that parliament is increasingly a rubber stamp with very little policy-making capacity. Yet it shows a lot of activity, although limited to its controlling functions. One may speak of an emerging osmosis between governmental parties in parliament and governmental action in parliament. As a consequence, parliament has shifted its activities from policy-making to controlling and adjusting governmental initiatives. These parliamentary activities have, however, decreased the speed of the decision-making process.

Another proposition discussed concerns the extent to which government policy reflects the party's preferences in terms of policy pursuit, i.e. 'accountability'. Research has investigated this relationship by relating the content of electoral programmes to patterns of budgetary allocations (Klingemann *et al.* 1994: 206–39). The result of this analysis has been that in the Netherlands the relationship is positive and thus more or less accountable. In Belgium, however, the relationship is weak. Moreover, it appeared from the analysis that in the Dutch system the left–right distinction was a relevant indicator, meaning that centre-left coalitions showed a distinctive pattern of policy-making compared with centre-right coalitions. Therefore in the Netherlands alternating party combinations do matter regarding policy-making, whereas in Belgium the language–territorial cleavage and its federal structure have affected policy formation.

Looking at the budgetary developments in both countries, it appears that the decision-making costs related to finding co-operation and consensus are high as well as difficult to alter. In Belgium government total outlays were 50 per cent of GDP, of which almost 50 per cent was devoted to social welfare in 2005. In the Netherlands government spending is slightly lower: 46 per cent of total outlays, of which 40 per cent was on social welfare in 2005. Until the mid-1990s these ratios had hardly changed, but under the influence of the EMU agreement and economic pressures the levels of public expenditure, particularly concerning the welfare state and public debt, have been curbed (in particular in the Netherlands).

It can be concluded that in reality governmental power in Benelux is stronger than that of parliament, regardless of the latter's formal powers. Second, government decision-making can be characterised by cumbersome procedures. This seems inevitable, owing to the fact that multi-party coalitions are necessary to form viable governments. Yet governments do govern, albeit constrained by policy agreements in the Netherlands and hampered by federalised power sharing in Belgium. Finally, although these factors appear to arrest policy-making, it is clear that, in so far as decisions on policies are made, the Netherlands shows a positive record in terms of accountability (the relation between a party's policy stance and policies made) by comparison with Belgium.

Governments in Belgium and the Netherlands tend to make policy on the basis of political co-operation and by finding societal consensus. Such a process can often induce higher levels of spending, as well as incrementalism and policy immobility. In Belgium the situation is aggravated by the complex federal structure, whereas in the Netherlands the major parties seem to have been captured by various organised interests, which did not allow much policy change either.

The role of bureaucracy and corporatism

Policy-making in Belgium and the Netherlands is politically a complex process, but to make a policy work is equally complex. Two institutional *modi operandi* play an important role in the process of policy implementation: on the one hand, bureaucracy; on the other, corporatism. Particularly interesting is the extent to which these institutional *modi operandi* have a bearing on political decision-making and facilitate policy implementation. One could assert that although the formal structure of bureaucracy in both countries is by and large identical, the way it works is not similar: in Belgium, so it seems, the bureaucrats are captured by politicians, whereas in the Netherlands the bureaucracy appears to be more or less captured by interest groups. The extent to which this is a tenable proposition may well explain differences in policy performance of these countries.

Belgium and the Netherlands had in common the fact that their state structures can be described as being unitary and decentralised. Like labelling their political system 'republican monarchies', this denotes a paradox. From the constitutions of Luxembourg and the Netherlands it is obvious that the ultimate regulating powers rest with the central authorities. This was also the case with Belgium. However, since 1993 the Belgian state has been federalised. Yet as regards the organisation of its bureaucracy little change has taken place. Hence, both Belgium and the Netherlands (but not Luxembourg) have constitutionally organised their state apparatus as 'decentralised and unitary'. This formal aspect of the unitary state is reinforced by the fact that, for instance, the main source of state income, tax revenue, is collected by the central state. In Belgium (still) 90 per cent of all tax revenue is organised through central government and in the Netherlands the figure is 95 per cent, whereas this figure is 84 per cent in Luxembourg. Hence the central state allocates funds and regulates public policy from the centre, in which, of course, the bureaucracy has an important role to fulfil. Why then should the term 'unitary decentralised' state be used instead of simply depicting both countries as unitary and centralised?

Three reasons can be noted. First of all, the organisation of the public administration is a three-tier system: central state, provinces and municipalities. Much of the policy organisation is both functionally and, particularly in Belgium, territorially decentralised. In the Netherlands the countervailing power lies predominantly at the level of the municipalities, whereas in Belgium, until the 1990s, the provincial tier was quite important. From then on the countervailing powers *vis-à-vis* the central, now federal, state were devolved to the three *communities*: French- Flemish- and German-speaking and responsible for cultural matters; as well as the three *regions*: Flanders, Wallonia and Brussels-Capital, responsible for the socio-economic and infrastructural matters. Hence policy *implementation* is by and large decentralised in both Belgium and the Netherlands, whereas decision-making and allocation remain to a large extent centralised in the latter country. Second, the size of the bureaucracy is relatively small in both countries. The number of central civil servants in Belgium and the Netherlands does not exceed 6–7 per cent of the working population. In many other European countries the figures are higher. Hence in terms of manpower the bureaucratic state in the Benelux is not huge. Third, apart from territorial decentralisation and the concomitant delegation of authority and co-determination of policies, both bureaucracies are to a large degree functionally decentralised (e.g. by means of 'parastatals' in Belgium and by departmental autonomy in the Netherlands) or, with regard to implementing policies, are dependent on other agencies (e.g. trade unions, employers' organisations, professional associations, etc.). One could say therefore that there has been a development towards policy networks that have been institutionalised over time and in due course have gained a certain institutional autonomy *vis-à-vis* the central state.

Bureaucratic autonomy of the central state is thus in practice limited, owing to the decentralisation of its organisation of implementation, the relatively small size of the central civil service and the emergence and structural growth of policy networks. Bureaucratic power is further limited because of its 'culture' or, to put it differently, the way it operates. In this respect the Belgian and Dutch bureaucracies differ considerably: in Belgium the civil service is captured by politics, whereas in the Netherlands this is not the case. Here the top civil servants are considered quite influential with regard to policy-making and implementation. Another difference is the fact that in the Netherlands appointments are by and large non-political; in Belgium they are more politicised. Unlike Belgium, Dutch ministers hardly have a political cabinet, let alone a separate political staff. Apart from tensions between the departments, the loyalty and continuity of the bureaucracy are not questioned in the Netherlands. In Belgium, the opposite developments have occurred and, in consequence, the bureaucracy is merely an apparatus for technocratic implementation and has little influence on the making and shaping of substantial public policy.

In contrast to the bureaucratic style, within the concept of corporatism the emphasis is placed on the informal procedures that have developed over time and have led to the institutionalisation of relations between the state and organised interests.

Two types of corporatism can be distinguished: centralised and sectoral corporatism, which depict the organisational level of interactions, respectively between state agencies and actors representing nationwide organised interests and between public and private agents on the level of sectoral interests and specific departments (e.g. Health Care, Housing, Infrastructure etc.). These differences have much to do with the types of interest represented and what is to be achieved by concerted policy action. For instance, in Belgium and the Netherlands social and economic policy formation, as well as industrial relations, used to be organised at the level of the central state. This type of corporatist intermediation is intended to find co-operation by means of bargaining between the state, employers' organisations and trade unions. In general, if a bargain is struck, it leads to a set of arrangements, which are binding for all concerned, i.e. policy-making is by concertation. Conversely, sectoral corporatism is based less on antagonistic than on shared interests. Here the function of corporatist intermediation is co-determination in policy formation and delegation of implementation. An example is the Dutch social security system, which is organised, composed and controlled by public and private agents. In Belgium one can observe the same development – for instance in the organisation of health insurance. Instead of devolution of authority, as is the case in the decentralised state, one might denote this type of policy implementation as 'contracting out' on the basis of shared interests and mutual responsibility.

In contrast to Belgium, where after the Second World War the foundations of corporatist policy-making were laid in the so-called 'social pact' which bound the social partners voluntarily, corporatism in the Netherlands was slowly institutionalised by means of formal regulations and the creation of three-party bodies (e.g. the Social Economic Council in 1950). It can be put forward, somewhat exaggeratedly, that Dutch corporatism can be characterised as 'statist', whereas the Belgian type could be labelled 'societal' corporatism. However, at present – so it seems – this distinction is fading. According to many observers Dutch corporatism was transformed during the late 1980s and early 1990s into a '*Poldermodel*'. This phenomenon can be characterised as a system of interlocking (public and private) interests, whose agents share collective goals, instead of negotiating conflicting ones.

Summarising our discussion of corporatism as an institutional design, it appears that this type and style of policy-making and implementation not only exist in both countries, but also amplify the notion of 'unitary decentralisation', as both central and decentralised types of corporatism exist simultaneously. The central system of corporatism regarding public–private concertation is seen as facilitating socio-economic policy-making at the national level, whereas the decentralised type occurs regularly on the intermediate level in order to facilitate sectoral or functional policy implementation by means of semi-public agencies (in the Netherlands) or contracting out the implementation of policies (in Belgium). This decentralised style of corporatism can be considered an institutionalised part of both polities. Yet, in the same period, it appeared that attempts at concerted policy-making remained ineffective, owing to lack of regulating potential, and were quite often burdened by negotiation costs (e.g. in the form of tax exemptions, wage indexation, and allocations by means of transfer payments). Decentralised corporatism, however, appears by and large to be operating effectively but at a high cost. The institutionalisation of organised interests by means of corporatism has led to a situation in which existing arrangements, particularly in the realm of the welfare state, are difficult to change, let alone reverse. However, during the 1990s this situation changed for the better. This cannot, however, be attributed solely to the changing modus operandi of corporatism, but should also be considered as an effect of a changing political climate. The convergence of the party systems and the solving of longstanding conflicting issues shaped the room to manoeuvre of both the political actors and the private interests.

To conclude: what is remarkable is the observation that in Belgium and the Netherlands institutional change appeared possible and feasible. In Belgium, it took a long period and needed a thorough constitutional change of the polity. In the Netherlands, the break with the past was the result of a dramatic shift in the political coalitions: the combination of conservative liberals and Social Democrats paved the way for the institutional regeneration of corporatism.

THE DIFFUSION OF POLITICS: INTRA-NATIONAL AND TRANS-NATIONAL DEVOLUTION OF AUTHORITY

Today national sovereignty, as well as the institutional autonomy of the central state, has become more and more questioned. Again, there is a paradox. On the one hand, political life is still enshrined in constitutional rules, which define the autonomy and authority of the democratic state. On the other, public regulation by law appears to be reduced in practice. This is not just due to decreasing legitimacy, but also a result of change in the actual use and scope of rule from the centre. The Benelux countries are no exception to this general trend. On the contrary, the devolution of power, as well as the ruling behaviour of local authorities and the judiciary, is increasingly mentioned as a factor limiting the assumed and historically defined powers of the central state. The extent to which this is the case (no less if it is only believed to be so!) implies a tendency towards the diffusion of politics. This process assumes a changing relationship between state and society, public and private, and a different meaning of the political chain of command (and delegation). In other words the loci of power tend to become dispersed and hierarchical relations within these polities seem to become less effective.

In this section we shall discuss the decentralisation of political administration, in particular the development of federalism in Belgium. In addition, the changing role of the judiciary, which is considered to have become more important in co-determining formal legislation, will be investigated. Finally, we shall discuss the role of the European Union as a trans-national actor influencing the room for manoeuvre of the nation-state in terms of subsidiarity. These developments can be considered as indicators of institutional change, manifesting a tendency towards a diffusion of politics.

Regional autonomy and local authority

In legal terms the organisation of public administration in the Benelux countries is defined according to the principles of a nation-state. Budgetary autonomy is some-what restricted in Luxembourg and the Netherlands, as is the regulatory potential of regions and municipalities. Belgium differs, of course, from the other Benelux countries in that its regional governments and communities possess more institutional autonomy than Dutch provinces and Luxembourg districts. Constitutionally, these entities have since the early 1990s more room for manoeuvre in Belgium, because these bodies have the constitutional right to deal with cultural and socio-economic affairs as well as with everything that is of interest solely to the territory and not already covered by the central state. Hence, apart from the transformation of the Belgian unitary state into a federal one during the 1980s and 1990s, local and regional government in Belgium is more autonomous and able to self-regulate on the basis of the rule of 'subsidiarity'.

Local politics, and in particular its democratic quality, is a contested notion in Benelux. The main issue is the contradictory situation in which local and regional representatives are elected by the citizens of a territory but local government is held responsible by (or it is dependent on) central government and public administrative rules. Hence the electoral chain of command and control is short and weak. Without doubt this situation impairs democratic quality at the sub-national level.

The Netherlands can serve here as an illustration: since compulsory voting was abolished in 1971 the participation rate in local and regional elections has steadily declined by comparison with general elections. Between 1971 and 2004 on average nearly 80 per cent of the electorate participated in the elections to the upper chamber, whereas in the municipal elections the participation rate dropped from 76 per cent to almost 50 per cent in 1998 (on average; in the larger cities the rate is close to 45 per cent). This situation has led to many proposals for institutional reform in the Netherlands. On one hand, these initiatives focus on increasing the institutional autonomy of provinces and municipalities by means of devolution (enabling independent policy formation); on the other, an attempt has been made to create smaller units of local government and to hold referendums at the municipal level. So far, the devolution of central powers has not gone very far and attempts to involve the electorate have not improved the participation rate.

In Belgium and Luxembourg local democracy is less an issue. Given the size of Luxembourg, this is hardly surprising. But why not in Belgium? First of all, because local politics has been the foundation of many a political career. Success in local or regional politics is a stepping-stone to a national career. Second, more offices (e.g. mayor and alderman) are contested in elections. Third, national parties are well organised at the levels of local and regional politics, and consider it important to have a balance of power at all intra-national levels of decision-making. Together with the rule on compulsory voting, these reasons can explain a higher level of party activism at the regional and local level, albeit perhaps not always motivated by interest in local politics and government *per se*.

In conclusion: local authority in terms of institutional autonomy is somewhat limited in Luxembourg and the Netherlands in particular. The central state defines the room for manoeuvre, and devolved policy-making is responsive to the central public administration in most of its activities. This implies that political authority and democratic legitimacy are weak, particularly in the Netherlands (most initiatives to modernise local and provincial democracy have not been introduced because parliament could not find consensus). In Belgium the situation is different, owing to the role of the 'party-cracy', and because local and regional politics have been part of the evolution towards a federal state. A process of transition in which the devolution of political and administrative power was instrumental to language–territory issues or 'communalism' has led to a complex institutional structure of regions and communities.

The federal organisation of Belgium has in fact been the last stage in a long process. The institutional transition to a federal polity can be seen as a compromise between the 'unionists' and the 'independentists'. Instead of the development of a clear division and devolution of political authority, the federalisation of Belgium has been the result of centrifugal tendencies in and between the language territories. The main difference between Belgium and other federal states is that there exist three conflict dimensions which have made political solutions so difficult to achieve: economic structure and development; closed linguistic communities; territorial 'bones of contention' (i.e. the language boundary and the geographical position of the capital, Brussels). These differences have led to political compromises that reflect the asymmetries inherent in each conflict dimension. As a consequence, the federalisation of Belgium is shaped to institutionalise divergence, rather than to unite diversity within one state.

The resulting complexity, laid down constitutionally between 1980 and 1993, clearly favours the 'federalists' (and not the 'unitarians'). A system has been developed with compromises on a huge variety of institutions, in which congruence is difficult to establish. The division into three regions with competence in social affairs and economic matters and four communities with competence in cultural matters and individual rights forms the structure of the federal state. The fundamental disparity is that Flanders is homogeneous and economically prosperous whereas in Wallonia this is not the case. Hence, there is an inherent asymmetry between the regions which hinders fiscal equalisation and leads to political differences within the Belgian party families.

In sum, the role and position of local and regional government and the extent of decentralised institutional autonomy are somewhat limited in Luxembourg and the Netherlands. This also applies to the Belgian case only, if one regards the regions and communities as functionally equivalent to states within the federal state. In fact a trend towards diffusion and decentralisation appears to be prevalent in the Benelux as a whole. Recent developments with regard to European integration and the role of international treaties (if ratified by national legislatures) appear also to have affected the role of politics within these nation-states.

The limits of the nation-state: judicial review and subsidiarity

Judicial review is a major and important institution of any liberal democracy. It defines the way the separation of powers works in a democratic society and the extent to which state power is limited. This separation serves the purpose of safeguarding the constitutional rights of the citizen.

Two recent developments make the role of judicial review in the Benelux countries particularly interesting. First, unlike countries such as the United States, Germany and France, there is no separate and superordinate judicial institution with the power to review ordinary laws in the light of the constitution. Instead, the only option open to a citizen is to contest the procedures embodied in the law or related to the law-making process. However – and this is the new development – with the ratification of, for example, the Universal Declaration of Human Rights (1945) and the Treaty of Rome (1957) the legal opportunity exists to review national regulations and laws on the basis of these international treaties.

Second, legal observers suggest that the role of the judiciary is tending to become a more active one. There appears to be a shift from a strictly formal type of review to a more normative and material type of judicial review. Changing societal values and norms of social justice have become part of judicial deliberations and have resulted in judgements that affect legislative practice. In addition, it can be observed that, particularly in the Netherlands, there is a tendency to bring forward test cases representing political issues (e.g. the right to abortion or euthanasia; the exercise of the right to strike; the admissibility of organisations like fascist or radical movements). Some see this as wrongful interference by the judiciary; others see it as a positive development enhancing the position of the citizen *vis-à-vis* the state. It can be concluded, then, that the ratification of international treaties and a change in the attitude of the judiciary both appear to challenge the institutional autonomy of the nation-state.

The Benelux countries were among the 'founding fathers' of the European Community in 1957. This represents the common point of view of these small nations, held since the Second World War, that upholding their sovereignty is by and large dependent on international integration and military co-operation. Hence international co-operation and integration have become the key words for the Benelux countries in the post-war world. The paradox of this attitude is, of course, that the aim of national sovereignty was to be achieved by means of subsidiarity to international politics. However, unlike those of other member states of the EU, both the politicians and the population did not appear to view this as jeopardising their status as a nation-state until the early 1990s. However, since this time the 'permissive consensus' of the public at large has dropped dramatically in Belgium and the Netherlands. For example, opinion polls revealed that between 1982 and 2003 there was a drop of 14 per cent in Belgium and 18 per cent in the Netherlands in the number of those in favour of a European government (only 3 per cent in Luxembourg), and 55 per cent of the population think that their country benefits from the EU (but only 44 per cent in Belgium!).

It can be argued that the development of the European Union, in particular towards a single market and as a political union, has severe implications for national institutions in relation to political decision-making of the member states. Moreover, this development is not yet matched by a simultaneous development of democratic control of EU decision-making processes. Europeanisation implies a decrease in political control as well as a decline in autonomous policy-making by the member states. In particular the agreement on European Monetary Union has made this clear since fiscal policy is in part directed by the EU.

These developments can be observed further in the working of EU regulations and the role of the European Court, as well as in the creation of a single market since 1987 and the introduction of the Euro currency. Member states are obliged to follow and enforce at the national level all regulations accepted by the Council of Ministers. As we saw above, this implies a change in state–society relations: citizens, as well as associations and interest groups, may use the national judicial system to enforce the implementation of EU regulations (as, for instance, is regularly the case in the Netherlands with regard to environmental matters and labour-market regulations). Conversely, both the EU administration and citizens can appeal to the European Court to enforce EU regulations at the national level. As the court's decisions are binding, and override those of domestic courts, this means that the scope and range of national and sub-national decision-making are constrained as far as they concern matters dealt with at the European level. It should be added, however, that judgements of the European Court are merely declaratory and do not (yet) have executive force, other than by sanctions eventually mediated through domestic courts. Hence EU regulations do confine the scope for national policy formulation, but it takes complex and often lengthy procedures before it takes effect, if and when national and sub-national governments do not co-operate.

With the move towards a single market and the adoption of a single currency in 2001, it appears inevitable that political decision-making within the member states will be affected and to a certain extent subjected to EU policy formation. It has been calculated, for instance, that measures emanating from the Single Market Act affect that around 75 per cent of national legislation will be directly or indirectly because national legislation is in conflict with them, or because the policy directive simply does not exist.

Apart from the direct consequences of European integration within the context of the EU, what is of interest here is that this will inevitably lead to institutional changes in the Benelux countries. Although 'federalisation' is perhaps too strong a word, it is obvious that the trend towards subsidiarity implies a shift towards a European government, i.e. the idea that policy issues which either are taken up by the EU or concern issues that cannot adequately be dealt with by national authorities should be organised at the level of the community. This trend is strongly supported by Christian Democrats, as well as by Social Democrats, albeit more hesitantly.

Along with the effects on national legislation and related institutional procedures that have already been mentioned, this development also affects the modes of interest representation and may well lead to the sectoralisation of policy-making. Hence a diffusion of politics and policy formation appears inevitable. Agriculture and the environment are good examples of this process of diffusion. Interest groups have changed their strategy for influencing policy-making away from the national level (e.g. lobbying in parliament) to Brussels. Simultaneously, departments responsible for these policy areas are more concerned to comply with directives and measures emanating from Brussels. In short, the development of a single market heralds an increase in trans-national policy-making, which has consequences for the organisation of national decision-making and processes of implementation. At the same time it also has strong implications for the relation between societal interest aggregation and representation and national political decision-making. The loci of power are shifting and with them the legitimacy of national institutions.

In this section we have discussed the relation between local and regional government and national politics, the role of the judiciary and the impact of Europeanisation on the national state. It is argued that the independent role of the judiciary, as well as the development of the European Union, can be considered as changing the nature of the institutional autonomy of the state and tends to reduce its capacity for solving societal problems independently.

SIMILAR POLITIES, DIFFERENT TRAJECTORIES

In this chapter we have described the political institutions of the Low Countries and have analysed the way in which they shape political life. As was set out in the Introduction to this book (pp. 1–16), institutions can be viewed as the 'building blocks' of political life. Institutions are, so to speak, the rules of the game which mould and direct the behaviour of the players, and conversely the players make use of these institutions to attain their ends. The outcome of this 'game' is conceptualised in the Introduction as a 'structure-induced equilibrium'. It is pursued by the main political players (i.e. political parties and organised interests) of the Benelux countries by means of two simultaneous strategies: adversarial or confrontational politics, on the one hand, and bargaining on consensual decision-making, on the other. This structure-induced equilibrium is a potential outcome of either political strategy and can be conceived of as a pendulum between societal conflict and political consensus.

Throughout history, social conditions prone to instability appear to have dominated Belgian and Dutch politics, but at the same time it has appeared possible to develop relatively stable systems. That is, until the 1990s. Since then, so it seems from the analysis, things have – sometimes dramatically – changed. It may be suggested, therefore, that the nature of politics in these countries has changed: from co-operation between political elites, based on the support of passive social segments, towards an open model of adversarial party politics in which coalescence has become a final consideration instead of a point of departure. There has been a shift from a coalescent to a competitive style of politics. This change in the style of, for instance, electoral politics has taken place under the same institutions, which made it possible to play the original game, labelled by Lijphart the 'consociational' type of politics. Remarkably, this means that the existing electoral formula did not prevent a drastic change of politics and apparently allows old and new players room for manoeuvre.

In Belgium this process has been manifested in the development of two and a half party systems since 1970 – one Flemish, one Walloon and Brussels in between – and this was accompanied by constitutional changes during the 1990s. In the Netherlands one can observe a reorganisation of the parties after 1970, as well as reorientation of their ideologies and salient issues. As a consequence not only the faces of parties changed, but also the political exchange between the parties. In addition, new parties secured a position within the party system. This change occurred within the existing electoral system and has resulted in relatively high levels of electoral volatility from the 1990s onwards. In Luxembourg political change was restricted to the emergence of a Green party family and short-lived protest parties. Yet, its pattern of party government did not change and Christian democracy is still dominant.

It can be concluded, therefore, that political change has taken place in both countries, yet in Belgium it led eventually to constitutional change (i.e. federalisation of the unitary state), whereas in the Netherlands the institutional structure has persisted. In other words, societal change is and can be manifested in differential political behaviour under similar conditions, but has led to divergent trajectories in terms of institutional change. Despite strong popular support for political reform in the Netherlands, very little has actually taken place. Conversely, in Belgium institutional reform appeared inevitable, but why?

The answer to this question must be sought in the nature and effects of the political change that took place since the 1970s and intensified during the 1990s. In Belgium the original 'structure-induced equilibrium' was based on co-operation across party-political elites which shared a common interest, namely a 'unitary' Belgian state, but this became increasingly difficult. Instead of facilitating decision-making, the existing institutions appeared to function as instruments forestalling that process. Several minor adaptations of political institutions, introduced to meet demands related to the language–territory or 'communal' conflict, turned out to induce highly unstable outcomes in terms of decision-making and negotiation costs, which in the end led to persistent stalemates. The nature of the game has shifted from co-operation across the language segments in society to non-co-operation, which was made possible precisely through these institutional changes, as, for example, the requirement of bilingual parity in government composition and the constitutional requirements of parliamentary consent to solve political problems by the regions and communities. Additionally, the emergence of territorial parties and the asymmetry of electoral strength across the regions induced diverging party systems conducive to confrontation instead of coalescent party behaviour.

In the Netherlands a new equilibrium could be established within the existing institutional structures. Yet the nature of the game has also changed. Instead of 'depoliticising', the new trends were political decision-making by means of behind-the-scenes bargaining by party elites and leaving the implementation of the resultant agreements to government. Hence in the Netherlands a mixed game developed: the confrontation and coalescence game. On the one hand, this was due to a shift from a two-dimensional type of party competition based on religious and socialist ideas to a division of the party system where increasingly social permissiveness was considered a negative asset and left-wing ideas on 'big government' as detrimental to the Dutch economy. On the other, government formation became the central political arena, where, by means of seemingly endless negotiations, policy agreements were struck and spelled out for implementation by government. Through this development the Cabinet became a pivotal force in the Dutch political system based on co-operation. This has led to new informal rules concerning the legislature–executive relationship: the government governs – although strongly bound to its predetermined policy agreement – and, throughout its electoral period, is supported by its parties. The 'purple coalition' can serve as an illustration of this. However, this situation has been, in retrospect, as exceptional as the emergence of the 'radical right': adversarial electoral politics creates short-lived successes, but party government remains the same after all. At the same time the 'corporatist' game was played in a different way: instead of a centralised tri-partite structure it slowly transformed into a bi-partite one with strong decentralist features. These changes within the Dutch polity mean that the 'structure-induced equilibrium' was adjusted in the 1990s.

It can be asserted therefore that societal change has transformed politics in Belgium and the Netherlands, but the difference between the two polities is clear: in the former, institutional reform appeared the only option, whereas in the latter the rules of the game could be changed within the existing institutional framework. These institutional changes were in part, then, as we observed, a consequence of societal change, which in turn was reflected in the changing behaviour of the political players involved in the game. These changes have clearly affected the process, the efficacy and the quality of decision-making by multi-party coalition government in the Low Countries.

In Belgium the threat of withdrawal by parties or individual ministers (i.e. veto power) and the predominance of the issue of 'communalism' have induced very high negotiation costs and have led to new coalitions, both on the federal and the regional level. In the Netherlands policy-making appears to have become more effective, but has in turn reduced the influence of the parliament and limited the influence of organised interests that are not represented at the negotiation table. Hence, like in Belgium, the present equilibrium is quite sensitive to the quality of the players and the resulting policy performance in terms of public welfare. Yet at the same time it is difficult to see whether other scenarios could have been developed in the Benelux after the 1970s.

Perhaps this counterfactual question will be answered in the near future as a result of the institutional changes that are taking place in view of the Europeanisation of national politics and policy-making. We have labelled this progression towards the political integration of Europe a part of the 'diffusion of politics'. The reason for this is that one can observe a dual development in the 'vertical' organisation of the Belgian and Dutch polities: a trend, on the one hand, towards decentralisation and policy segmentation; on the other, towards trans-nationalisation of politics and of policy co-ordination. Both developments may well imply further institutional changes through which the democratic chain of command and control is becoming less dominated by *national* political actors and peak interest organisations, reducing the option of regulating matters concerning the *res publica* autonomously by these actors alone.

It appears that the advent of the European Union in particular is the foremost force to challenge the institutional autonomy of national politics. On the one hand, political and legal regulation affects the room for manoeuvre in domestic policy-making; on the other, the binding force of EU regulations enables political actors, especially sectoral and regionally organised ones, to defy or to hold up implementation of policy by national authorities. Although political power appears more dispersed, political support within such nations for Europeanisation becomes diffuse – as the Dutch referendum on the EU constitution illustrates – and affects the legitimacy of national politics.

Perhaps the lesson that can be drawn from political and institutional developments in the Low Countries is that institutions matter with regard to politics. However, the way they do so also depends on the extent to which societal interests and related problems become politicised. Both the recent electoral developments and changing patterns of party government have shown that this tends to become more complex than before 1990. The way in which societal problems are transferred to the political scene and the extent to which the extant institutions allow political actors to contribute to societal problem-solving is then crucial. In the final analysis, the answer will be dependent on the question of whether or not the institutionalisation of political life in Benelux on every level can be considered to contribute to an optimal structure-induced equilibrium.

BIBLIOGRAPHY

General

Andeweg, R. B. and G. Irwin (2005) *Governance and Politics of the Netherlands*, Basingstoke: Macmillan.

Daalder, H. and G. Irwin (eds) (1989) *Politics in the Netherlands: How Much Change?*, London: Frank Cass.

Dewachter, W. (1992) *Besluitvorming in Politiek België*, Amersfoort/Leuven: Acco.

Huyse, L. (1987) *De Gewapende Vrede. Politiek in België na 1945*, Amersfoort/Leuven: Kritak.

Kossmann, E. H. (1994) *The Low Countries: History of the Northern and the Southern Netherlands*, Rekken: Stichting Ons Erfdeel.

Lijphart, A. (1999) *Patterns of Democracy: Government Form and Performance in Thirty-six Countries*, New Haven: Yale University Press.

Elections

Brug, W. van der and H. Pellikaan (2003) 'Electoral Revolt or Continuity? The Dutch Parliamentary Elections 2002 and 2003', special issue, *Acta Politica* 38 (1): 1–106.

Deschouwer, K. (2001) 'Symmetrie, Kongruenz und Finanzausgleich: die regionale Ebene in Belgien seit den Wahlen von 1999', *Jahrbuch des Föderalismus 2001*, Baden-Baden: Nomos.

Gallagher, Michael, Michael Laver and Peter Mair (2005) *Representative Government in Modern Europe*, New York: McGraw-Hill.

Political parties

Budge, I., H.-D. Klingemann, A. Volkens and J. Bara (2001) *Mapping Policy Preferences. Estimates for Parties, Electors and Government*, Oxford: Oxford University Press.

De Winter, L., M. Swyngedouw and P. Dumont (2006) 'Party System(s) and Electoral Behaviour in Belgium: From Stability to Balkanization', *West European Politics* 29 (5): 933–56.

Keman, H. (2007) 'Experts and Manifestos: Different Sources, Same Results for Comparative Research?', special issue, *Electoral Studies* 26 (1): 1–14.

Klingemann, H.-D., R. I. Hofferbert, I. Budge, with H. Keman, F. Petry, T. Bergman and K. Strom (1994) *Parties, Policies, and Democracy*, Boulder: Westview Press.

Laver, M. and I. Budge (1992) *Party Policy and Government Programmes*, Basingstoke: Macmillan.

Parliament

Keman, H. (2006) 'Party Government Formation and Policy Preferences: An Encompassing Approach?', in A. Weale and J. Bara (eds) *Democracy, Parties and Elections*, London: Routledge.

Laver, M. and K. Shepsle (1996) *Making and Breaking Governments*, Cambridge: Cambridge University Press.

Government

Budge, I. and H. Keman (1990) *Parties and Democracy, Coalition Formation and Government Functioning in Twenty States*, Oxford: Oxford University Press.

Woldendorp, J., H. Keman and I. Budge (2000) *Party Government in 48 Democracies (1945–1998). Composition – Duration – Personnel*, Dordrecht: Kluwer.

Inter-institutional relations

Keman, H. (2000) 'The Policy-making Capacities of a Decentralised Unitary State', in D. Braun (ed.) *Public Policy and Federalism*, Aldershot: Ashgate.

Kersbergen, K. Van and B. J. Verbeek (2004) 'Subsidiarity as a Principle of Governance in the European Union', *Comparative European Politics* 2 (2): 142–62.

Swenden, W., M. Brans and L. De Winter (2006) 'Politics of Belgium: Institutions and Policy under Bipolar and Centrifugal Federalism', special issue, *West European Politics* 29 (5): 863–1,092.

Visser, J. and A. Hemerijck (1997) *A Dutch Miracle. Job Growth, Welfare Reform, and Corporatism in the Netherlands*, Amsterdam: Amsterdam University Press.

Witte, E. (1992) 'Belgian Federalism: Towards Complexity and Asymmetry', *West European Politics* 15 (4): 95–111.

CHAPTER 8

The Nordic Countries

Compromise and Corporatism in the Welfare State

Jan-Erik Lane and Svante Ersson

'Norden' is the label for the five countries situated in northern Europe comprising Denmark (5.4 million people in 2005), Finland (5.2 million), Iceland (0.3 million), Norway (4.6 million) and Sweden (9.0 million). The land area covered by these five nation-states is quite extensive, especially if one adds Greenland (2,166,000 sq. km) and the Faroe Islands (1,393 sq. km), which are autonomous areas within the Kingdom of Denmark.

The Nordic countries have strong links with each other, economically and politically. They co-ordinate their policies by means of the Nordic Council, formed in 1952, which has resulted in the harmonisation of regulations and a free labour market. They also to some extent act in a collective fashion in international bodies, although their membership of various supranational bodies varies. Thus Denmark, Iceland and Norway have been members of NATO since 1949. Norway and Iceland are not members of the EU, though they are in the European Economic Area (EEA) with the EU.

Relationships between the Nordic countries and Europe have not been entirely smooth. A number of referenda have been conducted on this issue and the result is that only Finland is a member of both the EU and the Eurozone. Denmark but not Norway became a member of the European Community in 1973, while Sweden and Finland entered the EU in 1995. The Danish 'No' in 2000 in the referendum on joining the European Monetary Union (EMU) as well as a similar referendum in Sweden in 2003 indicate that Norden is far from endorsing full participation in all aspects of the European project. Table 8.1 displays the outcomes of the most important referenda on this issue between 1972 and 2003.

Thus, three Nordic countries are members of the EU, while the other two countries are part of the EEA. Only Finland has decided to endorse the European Union completely as it has entered the EMU, accepting the Euro. Both Denmark and Sweden have opted out of the EMU. All the Nordic countries have been part of the Schengen Accord since 2001 – Norway and Iceland on an associated basis. This partial integration has, however, opened up a so-called 'Europeanisation' of the Nordic states: public administration and policies.

The Danish, Norwegian and Swedish languages are quite similar, whereas Finnish belongs to an entirely different language family, although to some extent Icelandic is also distinct. All the Nordic countries have been ethnically homogeneous, although there exist substantial and growing minorities, in particular immigrants but also small Sami populations. Multiculturalism has been fostered by globalisation and a firm but quick naturalisation policy. Thus, all the Scandinavian capitals and Helsinki have today sizeable groups with foreign ethnic origins. They all have advanced economies mixing a market economy with large welfare state programmes.

'Scandia' was the old Latin name for the three countries of northern Europe: Denmark, Norway and Sweden (the 'Scandinavian countries') had already formed states or kingdoms during the high medieval period. Finland was ruled by Sweden up to 1809, then came under Russian rule but declared its independence in 1917. Iceland remained under Denmark up to 1944. It should be pointed out that Denmark ruled Norway from 1385 to 1814, when Sweden conquered the country. It became independent again in 1905.

The standard model for the interpretation of Nordic politics is the so-called Scandinavian model. In the international literature it has been pointed out that Nordic politics does not fit conventional democracy models such as the Anglo-Saxon Westminster model or the Continental consensus model. The Scandinavian model comprises a distinct set of institutions, covering the state and local government, the party system, interest groups and the economy.

Table 8.1 Referendums on relations with the European Union, 1972–2003

Country	Year	Question	Turnout %	Yes %
Denmark	1972	Entry to the EC	90	63
	1992	Maastricht	83	49
	1993	Edinburgh	87	57
	2000	Euro	88	47
Finland	1994	Entry to the EU	74	57
Norway	1972	Entry to the EC	79	47
	1994	Entry to the EU	89	48
Sweden	1994	Entry to the EU	83	52
	2003	Euro	83	42

It is not easy to unpack the concept of a specific governance model in Norden, as its features vary somewhat from one country to another. The Scandinavian model emerged out of the Great Depression of the inter-war years around 1935, became hegemonic after the Second World War but has run into increasing difficulties since the early 1980s, particularly in Sweden. Its core is a blend of compromise politics, local government autonomy and corporatism, where party competition is nested together with political and social co-operation. Scandinavian-model politics was initiated by red–green cooperation in Denmark and Sweden in 1933, in Norway in 1935 and in Finland in 1937.

The Scandinavian model developed from small-scale political co-operation across the deep cleavages between the socialist and the non-socialist camps and the urban and rural opposition into a large-scale institutional blueprint combining a universal welfare state with an efficient capitalist economy. The Scandinavian model involves a substantial policy commitment dating back to the 1930s, when a social pact was agreed upon by the major players, replacing the conflict between capital and labour as well as between city dwellers and rural farmers with a compromise that protected the institutions of the market economy but allowed for large-scale government activity in relation to unemployment, protection of peasants and social security. What distinguishes the Nordic welfare state is the generality and comprehensiveness of the programmes. The outcome has been the characteristic feature of a model with a large public sector involving a strong emphasis on more equal distribution of income as well as promoting gender equality. It is also striking that the economies of Nordic countries have done exceptionally well, especially Norway and Denmark, both having oil, as all of them tend to rank high with respect to achievements within the information technology sector, such as internet access.

Politically speaking, the institutions of the Scandinavian model express compromise politics while at the same time the overall constitutional frame remains the Westminster type of adversarial competition. The exact balance of adversarial and compromise politics may vary from one country to another in Norden, as well as shifting with time. Resort to compromise politics is evident in the use of special institutional mechanisms such as the system of public investigations with broad-based participation, bargaining in the parliamentary committees, as well as a variety of corporatist practices in both policy-making and policy implementation. Institutionally speaking, the Nordic state is a unitary state with a parliamentary system of government. Nordic politics is party government on the basis of a multi-party system expressing a multi-dimensional cleavage structure, to which must be added a strong dose of corporatism. The Nordic state has an ambition to score high on rule of law, and its most prominent institution to that effect is the Ombudsman Office.

It should be pointed out that Finnish politics has been somewhat different, as it has housed so-called consociational devices, or grand coalitions. Not only is there a strong tendency towards oversized government coalitions, but specific constitutional rules have called for qualified majority decisions on a regular basis. Up to 1992 one-third of the MPs in the Finnish Parliament (67 out of 200) could delay the passage of a Bill adopted by parliament until parliament assembled again the next year. This extraordinary consociational device was paralleled by the requirement of a two-thirds majority for tax decisions. Both these institutions were abolished in 1992.

In addition, Finland cannot be described as a strictly parliamentary system of government, owing to the strong formal position of the President. The Finnish constitution is based upon a separation of powers between the executive, with real presidential prerogatives, and the legislature, 'dualistic parliamentarianism'. The strong power of President Kekkonen has been reduced in the advantage of the Premier since the 1980s. This ongoing trend implies a change from a presidential regime through a semi-presidential one to a parliamentarian regime, which was codified with the new constitution enacted in 1999 and enforced from March 2000. Iceland is also led by a President, but political power is concentrated in the Premier. The Scandinavian countries have maintained their royal families.

All the Nordic countries have written constitutions. As the Norwegian constitution is the oldest, dating back to 1814, it comprises the obsolete rules of a constitutional monarchy and lacks formal recognition of the principle of parliamentarianism. Iceland's Basic Law of 1944 outlines a republic based upon parliamentarianism. The Danish constitution of 1953 contains a strong referendum institution, which requires a referendum for constitutional changes, whereas the Norwegian Basic Law stipulates a two-thirds majority in the Parliament for such decisions. The old 1919 Finnish constitution demanded a majority, then a two-thirds majority, with an election in between, or a five-sixths majority followed by a two-thirds majority decision confirmation; the present constitution from year 2000 has not been changed in this respect. In Sweden the 1974 Basic Law states that constitutional changes may be brought about by two majority decisions by the Parliament with an election in between.

The referendum institution undoubtedly plays a prominent role in Danish politics. Whereas in Norway, Sweden and Iceland the referendum is only consultative and facultative, it is on many issues obligatory and decisive in Denmark. Thus far, in the post-Second World War period Sweden has had 5 referendums, Norway 2, Finland 1 and Iceland no referendum, while Denmark has had 16 during this period.

The judicial branch of government in Norden is framed around the conception of the sovereignty of parliament. There is room for some independent legal review by the ordinary courts in Norway only. No country has a Constitutional Court, though human rights have constitutional protection. The five countries have unicameral National Assemblies. All forms of public power derive ultimately from Acts of parliament, which principle of legislative supremacy has not prohibited a fairly extensive system of local government autonomy, especially in Sweden, Denmark and Finland.

The chief characteristic of Nordic politics – the combination of Westminster politics with consensus politics – does not involve a once-and-for-all fixed structure of political institutions. The actual working out of the combination of adversarial and compromise politics shifts over time and differs from one country to another in Norden, the adversarial atmosphere sometimes dominating, at other times compromise. Changes do occur, as we have noted with Finland, but it is also true that there is a clear ambition to move away from the minority-government framework to minimum winning governments in Scandinavia, while at the same time restraining corporatism or the political power of organised interests.

ELECTIONS

Scandinavian democracy rests upon an election system strongly geared to proportional representation, underlining both extensive citizen participation in elections and the capacity of minorities to organise and gain representation. The Scandinavian model does not accept any form of majoritarian electoral formula, as all the states attempt to achieve as high a level of correlation between votes and seats as possible. The minimum voting age is eighteen years. The mechanism of adversarial politics, the plurality formula, has not attracted much attention in the five Nordic countries – Iceland being an exception up to 1959. Although discussed somewhat at the time of the introduction of democracy around the end of the First World War, the electoral system has recognised the typical feature of the party systems: the large degree of fractionalisation. The general emphasis is upon strict proportionality, as a system of regional mandates is used to correct for lack of proportionality in the election results. Only Sweden employs a rather high 4 per cent threshold to counteract excessive fractionalisation, with the Danish Parliament using a 2 per cent threshold. As it had been argued that the political parties dominate the elections to the exclusion of personal choice, the Finnish system has a strong element of personal choice for the voter, which is also true for the Danish system, while an element of personal choice was introduced in the Swedish system at the election in 1998. Yet Nordic politics adhere to the model of party governance, as party discipline tends to be high.

The process of translating social cleavages into political life is closely tied up with the development of the political institutions constituting Nordic democracy. Rokkan identified three thresholds that were crucial to the establishment of a democratic regime: extension of the franchise (male and female), proportionality in representation and executive control. The timing of these three thresholds in Norden was:

1   Male suffrage: 1898 Norway, 1906 Finland, 1909 Sweden, 1915 Denmark and Iceland.
2   Female suffrage: 1906 Finland, 1913 Norway, 1915 Denmark and Iceland, 1921 Sweden.
3   Proportional representation: 1906 Finland, 1909 Sweden, 1915 Denmark, 1959 Iceland.
4   Parliamentarianism: 1884 Norway, 1901 Denmark, 1904 Iceland, 1917 Sweden, 1919 Finland.

The electoral systems in Norden really result in proportional outcomes. For Denmark we have 98 per cent proportionality, for Finland 93 per cent, for Iceland 97 per cent, for Norway 94 per cent, and finally for Sweden 96 per cent in the elections held during the period 1993–2007. Since Iceland introduced proportional representation (PR) in 1959 there have been very minor differences in the degree of proportionality between the various electoral systems. The overall impression is that the Scandinavian systems display a high degree of proportionality, employing the Sainte-Laguë formula, with Finland scoring marginally lower, as it uses the d'Hondt formula, which Iceland also employs.

There can be little doubt that the strong institutionalisation of proportionality in Nordic election rules has been conducive to multipartism as well as a high level of electoral participation. The average turnout for the post-war period has hovered around 85 per cent in Denmark and Sweden, with Norway at about 80 per cent, whereas Finland has a lower average score of about 77 per cent and Iceland almost reaches 90 per cent. There is a downward trend in electoral participation in the most recent years. The decline in participation in Finland has been interpreted as a manifestation of increasing apathy. It may be pointed out that the turnout for European Parliament elections is extremely low; in the 2004 election the turnout in Sweden was less than 38 per cent and in Finland 41 per cent, while Denmark came close to 48 per cent turnout.

Table 8.2 Elections to parliament in Denmark, 1945–2005

Year	Turnout %	Communists DKP/EL	Socialists SF	SD	Liberals RV	CD	V	Christian KrF	Conservatives KF	People DF	Progress FrP	Other
1945	86	13	−	33	8	−	23	−	18	−	−	5
1947	86	7	−	40	7	−	28	−	12	−	−	6
1950	82	5	−	40	8	−	21	−	18	−	−	8
1953	81	5	−	40	9	−	22	−	17	−	−	6
1953	81	4	−	41	8	−	23	−	17	−	−	6
1957	84	3	−	39	8	−	25	−	17	−	−	8
1960	86	1	6	42	6	−	21	−	18	−	−	6
1964	86	1	6	42	5	−	21	−	20	−	−	5
1966	89	1	11	38	7	−	19	−	19	−	−	5
1968	89	1	6	34	15	−	19	−	20	−	−	5
1971	87	1	9	37	14	−	16	2	16	−	−	4
1973	89	4	6	26	11	8	12	4	9	−	16	4
1975	88	4	5	30	7	2	23	5	6	−	14	4
1977	89	4	4	37	4	6	12	3	9	−	15	7
1979	86	2	6	38	5	3	13	3	13	−	11	7
1981	83	1	11	33	5	8	11	2	15	−	9	4
1984	88	1	12	32	6	5	12	3	23	−	4	4
1987	87	1	15	29	6	5	11	2	21	−	5	4
1988	86	1	13	30	6	5	12	2	19	−	9	3
1990	83	2	8	37	4	5	16	2	16	−	6	2
1994	84	3	7	35	5	3	23	2	15	−	6	1
1998	86	3	8	36	4	4	24	3	9	7	2	0
2001	87	2	6	29	5	2	31	2	9	12	1	0
2005	84	3	6	26	9	1	29	2	10	13	−	0

Note:

Communist: DKP: Communist Party (Danmarks Kommunistiske Parti); EL: Unity List (Enhedslisten).

Socialists: SF: Socialist People's Party (Socialistisk Folkeparti); SD: Social Democrats (Socialdemokratiet).

Liberals: RV: Radical Left (Radikale Venstre); CD: Centre Democrats (Centrumdemokraterne); V: Agrarian Liberal (Venstre).

Christian: KrF: Christian People's Party (Kristeligt Folkeparti).

Conservative: KF: Conservative People's Party (Konservativt Folkeparti).

People: DF: Danish People's Party (Dansk Folkeparti).

Progress: FrP: Progress Party (Fremskridtspartiet).

From the introduction of democratic regimes around the First World War the typical feature has been the five-party system, with some variations between nations and over time. On the left there were the social democratic and the communist parties, while the non-socialist parties typically comprised conservative, liberal and agrarian parties. Considering the mere number of political parties represented in parliament the average figure for the years 1945–2007 is higher for Denmark and Finland, 7.8 and 8.0 respectively, than for Norway, with 6.6, Sweden, with 5.6 and Iceland with 4.8. There is a clear trend towards an increase in fractionalisation.

Typical of Nordic politics is moderate fractionalisation, which can be measured by the effective number of parties, which hovers around 5.0. Thus, Sweden has the lowest average score, with 3.7 for 1945–2007, and Iceland and Norway come close with 3.9 and 4.2, respectively, as the average score. Denmark and Finland score

Table 8.3 Elections to parliament in Finland, 1945–2007

Year	Turnout %	Communist SKDL/VAS	Green VIHR	Socialist SDP	Swede SFP	Liberals LKP	Centre KESK	Christian SKL	Conservatives KOK	Rural SMP	Other
1945	75	24	–	25	8	5	21	–	15	–	2
1948	78	20	–	26	8	4	24	–	17	–	1
1951	75	22	–	27	8	6	23	–	15	–	1
1954	80	22	–	26	7	8	24	–	13	–	0
1958	75	23	–	23	7	6	23	0	15	–	3
1962	85	22	–	20	6	6	23	1	15	2	4
1966	85	21	–	27	6	7	21	1	14	1	3
1970	82	17	–	23	5	6	17	1	18	11	2
1972	81	17	–	26	5	5	16	3	18	9	1
1975	78(74)	19	–	25	4	4	18	3	18	4	4
1979	81(75)	18	–	24	4	4	17	5	22	5	2
1983	81(76)	14	1	27	5	–	18	3	22	10	1
1987	76(72)	9	4	24	5	1	18	3	23	6	7
1991	72(68)	10	7	22	6	1	25	3	19	5	3
1995	72(69)	11	7	28	5	1	20	3	18	1	6
1999	68(65)	11	7	23	5	0	22	4	21	1	5
2003	70(67)	10	8	25	5	0	25	5	19	2	2
2007	68(65)	9	9	21	5	0	23	5	22	4	2

Note:

Turnout: Figures in parenthesis include Finnish citizens living abroad.

Communists: SKDL: Finnish People's Democratic League (Suomen Kansan Demokraattinen Liitto); VAS: Left Alliance (Vasemmeistoliitto).

Green: VIHR: Green League (Vihreä Liitto).

Socialist: SDP: Social Democratic Party of Finland (Suomen Sosialidemokraattinen Puolue).

Swede: SFP: Swedish People's Party (Svenska Folkpartiet).

Liberals: LKP: Liberal People's Party (Liberaalinen Kansanpuolui).

Centre: KESK: Centre Party (Agrarian) (Keskustapuoiue).

Christian: SKL: Finnish Christian League (Suomen Kristillinen Liitto).

Conservative: KOK: National Coalition Party (Kansallinen Kokoomus).

Rural: SMP: Finnish Rural Party (Suomen Maaseudun Puolue).

higher, 4.8 and 5.6 respectively. Again we note the trend towards more fractionalisation. All the Nordic countries fall outside the Westminster two-party model, which has not prevented the occurrence of both adversarial tactics and catch-all strategies as well as an ambition to form minimum-winning majority coalition governments.

The Nordic political cultures have an activist civic orientation as expressed in relatively high, although decreasing, levels of electoral participation and in the strong backing for several political parties.

Table 8.4 Elections to parliament in Norway, 1945–2005

Year	Turnout %	Communist NKP	Socialist SV	Labour DNA	Centre SP	Christian KRF	Liberal V	Progress FRP	Conservative H	Other
1945	76	12	–	41	8	8	14	–	17	0
1949	82	6	–	46	8	9	14	–	18	1
1953	79	5	–	47	9	11	10	–	19	0
1957	78	3	–	48	9	10	10	–	19	0
1961	79	3	2	47	9	10	9	–	20	0
1965	85	1	6	43	10	8	10	–	21	0
1969	84	1	3	47	11	9	9	–	20	0
1973	80	–	11	35	11	12	4	5	17	4
1977	83	0	4	42	9	12	3	2	25	2
1981	82	0	5	37	7	9	4	5	32	1
1985	84	0	6	41	7	8	3	4	30	1
1989	83	–	10	34	7	9	3	13	22	2
1993	76	0	8	37	17	8	4	6	17	4
1997	78	0	6	35	8	14	5	15	14	3
2001	75	0	13	24	6	12	4	15	21	5
2005	77	0	9	33	7	7	6	22	14	2

Note:

Communist: NKP: Norwegian Communist Party (Norges Kommunistiske Parti).

Socialist: SV: Socialist Left Party (Sosialistik Venstrepartei).

Labour: DNA: Norwegian Labour Party (Det Norske Arbeiderparti).

Centre: SP: Centre Party (Agrarian) (Senterpartiet).

Christian: KRF: Christian People's Party (Kristelig Folkepartei).

Liberal: V: Liberals (Venstre).

Progress: FRP: Progress Party (Fremskrittspartiet).

Conservative: H: Conservative Party (Høyre).

Table 8.5 Elections to parliament in Sweden, 1944–2006

Year	Turnout %	Communist VPK/V	Green MP	Socialist SAP	Centre CP	Liberal FP	Christian KD	Moderate M	Other
1944	72	10	–	47	14	13	–	16	1
1948	83	6	–	46	12	23	–	12	0
1952	79	4	–	46	11	24	–	14	0
1956	80	5	–	45	10	24	–	17	0
1958	77	3	–	46	13	18	–	20	0
1960	86	5	–	48	14	18	–	17	0
1964	84	5	–	47	14	18	2	14	0
1968	89	3	–	50	16	16	2	14	0
1970	88	5	–	45	20	16	2	12	1
1973	91	5	–	44	25	9	2	14	1
1976	92	5	–	43	24	11	1	16	0
1979	91	6	–	43	18	11	1	20	1
1982	91	6	2	46	16	6	2	24	0
1985	90	5	2	45	10	14	3	21	1
1988	86	6	6	43	11	12	3	18	1
1991	87	5	3	38	9	9	7	22	8
1994	87	6	5	45	8	7	4	22	2
1998	81	12	5	36	5	5	12	23	3
2002	80	8	5	40	6	13	9	15	3
2006	82	6	5	35	8	8	7	26	6

Note:

Communist: V: Left Party (Vänsterpartiet).

Green: MP: Environmental Party – the Greens (Miljöpartiet De Gröna).

Socialist: SAP: Swedish Social Democratic Workers' Party (Sveriges Socialdemokratistika Arbetarparti).

Centre: CP: Centre Party (Agrarian) (Centerpartiet).

Liberal: FP: People's Party – the Liberals (Folkpartiet-Liberalerna).

Christian: KD: Christian Democrats (Kristdemokraterna).

Moderate: M: Moderate Unity Party (Moderata Samlingspartiet).

PARTIES AND PARTY STRATEGIES

From the very beginning of the democratic regime the socio-economic cleavage or left–right division has been dominant in Scandinavian politics. Political parties have been formed according to this dimension and several of the political issues developed around this cleavage. Against the socialist bloc comprising a large Social Democratic party plus one more left-wing party, whether a left-Socialist party or a Communist party, has stood a non-socialist bloc consisting of a Conservative party plus a few centre parties. Only in Finland has polarisation been high, reflecting the fact that the Communist Party scored over 20 per cent support here up to the 1960s.

The size of the Social Democratic parties varies from the very large ones in Sweden and Norway to smaller ones in Denmark, Finland and Iceland. The left-Socialist parties in Denmark and Norway are not insignificant. The non-socialist spectrum covers a Conservative party, a Liberal party and an Agrarian party (Centre party), complemented recently by Populist and Green parties in the 1980s. The electoral outcomes of the various so-called bourgeois or non-socialist parties have fluctuated considerably over time.

The left–right dimension still has an impact on Scandinavian politics, although there are indications that its relevance has decreased over time. One major post-Second World War trend is the striking decline in class voting. It may be measured by the proportion voting for the left, i.e. Socialist or Communist parties, among the working classes. In Denmark the decline is from 73 per cent (1957) to 42 per cent (2001), in Finland from 81 per cent (1958) to 50 per cent (2003), in Norway from 78 per cent (1957) to 40 per cent (2001) and in Sweden from 76 per cent (1956) to 66 per cent (1998). If one employs the Alford class voting index the same trend is found, as class voting is down from 48 to 6 in Denmark, from 64 to 22 in Finland, from 44 to 2 in Norway and from 51 to 26 in Sweden.

That class voting is on the retreat is a long-run tendency that admits short-term fluctuations. Thus one may expect a rise in class voting in periods of economic crisis, as in the early 1990s. Still, it is a fact that the socio-economic cleavage, based upon material foundations, tends to be replaced in Norden by another kind of cleavage, summarised in the theme of post-materialism or *new politics*. Data indicate that post-materialist values have an anchor, especially among the post-war generations. However, the other major trend since 1945, besides de-alignment along the class cleavage, has been the realignment of the electorate according to the logic of new politics.

Party government is institutionalised in Norden, political action being over-whelmingly dominated by political parties, which channel electoral participation by means of list voting. All states have generous systems for the public funding of political parties. The Nordic party systems express multi-dimensional issues, involv-ing one strong alignment between the left and the right and less strong additional alignments expressed partly by the parties in the non-socialist bloc but also by the Green party.

A majority of the parties operating on the Nordic political scene date back to the 1920s and earlier, including the Liberal and Conservative parties as well as the Social Democratic parties. The Norwegian Venstre and Høyre were formed back in the 1880s, while the Danish Venstre goes back to 1871. The Swedish and Finnish non-socialist parties were built up in the years around 1900. The Social Democratic parties were founded around the same time, with the Danish party the oldest (1871) and the Finnish party the youngest (1899). The Agrarian and the Communist parties made their appearance shortly before and after the First World War, respectively. The Finnish Agrarian party is the oldest (1907) and the Norwegian Agrarian party the youngest (1920), while the Swedish Communist Party is the oldest (1917) and the Norwegian Communist Party the youngest (1923).

The political parties in Iceland differ somewhat from the prevailing Scandinavian model. They include a large conservative party – the Independence Party, formed in 1929 as a reaction to Danish rule. Its share of the electorate has hovered around 35–40 per cent. The second party is the Progress Party, which is a rural party with average support of around 20 per cent. The Social Democratic Party has never equalled the

Nordic Social Democratic parties in size, hovering at about 15 per cent. As a matter of fact the Left-Socialist Party in Iceland has received slightly more support than the Social Democrats. The most conspicuous party may have been the Women's Alliance, its highest share of vote 10.1 per cent in 1987, and with a 5 per cent share at the 1995 election. In the 1999 election some merged with the Social Democratic Alliance while others joined the Left-Green Movement.

Size of traditional parties

These parties, representing six different party types if the ethnic Swedish-language People's Party in Finland is added, have played a dominant role since the early 1920s. Looking at electoral support for these parties, here called the 'traditional' parties, from the 1940s to the 2000s one may establish that these parties totally dominated the political scene until the phenomenon of new politics arrived in Norden in the 1970s.

In the 1940s the traditional parties reached very high levels of support, roughly 94 per cent in Denmark and 99 per cent in Finland, Norway and Sweden. They more or less managed to retain that level of support until the 1970s, when the overall pattern started to change. The average scores for these parties were already much lower in the 1970s in Denmark and Norway, at 70 per cent and 73 per cent, but it was not until the early 1990s that their share of the vote was also down in Finland and Sweden, at 83 per cent and 82 per cent. And this pattern holds true also for the early 2000s, when the traditional parties had a stronger standing in Finland and Sweden than was the case in Denmark and Norway. One of the most conspicuous aspects of recent Nordic politics is the dealignment as well as the realignment of the electorate around new parties. The process of increasing instability manifested itself in a few major changes in the party systems up to the early 2000s: (1) the decline of the Social Democratic parties; (2) the introduction of new political parties; (3) the emergence of left-wing Socialist parties, partly as a transformation of the Communist parties. As a result, voter volatility is up sharply, both gross and net volatility.

The average support for Social Democratic parties between 1945 and 2007 was as high as 44 per cent in Sweden and 40 per cent in Norway, whereas the average scores were clearly lower in Denmark, at 35 per cent, and in particular in Finland, at 25 per cent, and Iceland, at 15 per cent. The Finnish exception depends upon the high level of support for the Communist Party, as high as 17 per cent on average. In the Scandinavian countries the Communist parties rallied far less support, at 2 per cent in Denmark, 3 per cent in Norway and 6 per cent in Sweden during the period 1945–2007. In the early 1990s the former Communist parties transformed themselves into left-wing parties. The Danish party has no real successor, while the experience of the Finnish and Swedish parties varies. The Finnish successor party is supported by some 10 per cent of the electorate, whereas the Swedish Left party temporarily received an increased support, to some extent due to its EU-negative standing, but this went down in the early 2000s.

Among the non-socialist parties, the Conservative parties have managed to attract considerable support from one election to another, amounting to almost one-fifth of the electorate. Between 1945 and 2007 the average outcome was 15 per cent in

Denmark, 18 per cent in Finland, 20 per cent in Norway and 18 per cent in Sweden, where the Conservative party reached 26 per cent in 2006. With increasing voter volatility, the fortunes of the Conservative party have, however, varied significantly, with a low of 9 per cent support in Denmark in 1998 and the Norwegian Conservative party suffering a setback from 32 per cent in 1981 to 14 per cent in 2005. The overall trend for the Liberal parties in Norden is downward. Average support in 1945–2007 was much lower in Denmark, with 7 per cent, Finland, with 4 per cent, and Norway, with 7 per cent; Sweden was the only exception, with an average of 14 per cent support for the Liberal party. The trend for the last elections indicates a further strong reduction in electoral support for the Liberal parties.

One of the distinctive traits of Nordic politics is the strong political institutionalisation of an agrarian movement. Not only were special Agrarian parties organised early in the process of introducing mass politics, but they have been successful in retaining considerable electoral support, especially since they identified themselves as centre parties. The strongest centre party is to be found in Finland, where the average level of support between 1945 and 2007 was 21 per cent. In 2003 and 2007, it received around a high 24 per cent. Also the Danish Agrarian party (Venstre) is large, relatively speaking, with 19 per cent support on average but scoring a high 29 per cent in 2005. Yet with increasing voter volatility the fortunes of the Centre parties vary. Thus, the Swedish Centre party, with 13 per cent on average, shrank considerably in the late 1980s and early 1990s, only to stabilise at around 8 per cent in 2006. In the 1990s, the Centre party was also standing strong in Norway, where it had risen from 7 per cent in 1981 to 17 per cent in 1993, leading the opposition to Norwegian entry to the European Union, but it declined in 1997 and again in 2005. The Agrarians (Centre party) are thus standing strong in Denmark and Finland in the early 2000s.

Introduction of new parties

The transformation of Nordic politics started with setbacks for the traditional parties, beginning with the 1973 'earthquake' elections in Denmark and Norway, and continued in the 1991 election in Sweden. The first new parties on the political scene were the religious parties (beginning with the Christian People's Party, KRF, in Norway) and the left-socialist parties (starting with the Socialist People's Party, SF, in Denmark). The other new parties entering the political arena were populist parties on the one hand and Green parties on the other. The amount of support given to populist parties in Norway (22 per cent in 2005) and Denmark (13 per cent in 2005) has shocked international observers, as these parties challenge the Scandinavian model.

Religious parties were created in all the four major Nordic countries. They are now somewhat larger in Norway and Sweden than in Denmark and Finland, with support of around 7 per cent in Norway and Sweden in the early 2000s, against 2 per cent and 5 per cent in Denmark and Finland, respectively.

The relatively large left-socialist parties in Denmark and Norway, with support of 6 per cent and 11 per cent in the 2000s, respectively, have not suffered from the decline of communism, as they had already marked their distance from the Communist parties in the 1960s; the Norwegian SV was thus able to enter government for the first time in 2005 in coalition with the Social Democrats and the Agrarians.

The populist parties started to receive support in the early 1970s in Finland, Denmark and Norway, while it was only in 1991 that a populist party entered parliament in Sweden; however, it lost its mandate in the 1994 election and has since disappeared. Only in Denmark and Norway have populist parties gained strong electoral support. The Norwegian Progress Party was in fact the strongest non-socialist party in the 1997 and 2005 elections. The Danish Progress Party suffered a split in 1995 and the leading populist party in Denmark is now the Danish People's Party, led by Pia Kjærsgaard and clearly outflanking the Progress Party from its first election in 1998.

The Green parties have met with limited success, where most support was provided in Finland in 2007, at 9 per cent, with the party being part of the government between 1995–2002 and 2007. In Sweden the ecologists entered the Parliament in 1988, did not reach the threshold in the 1991 election, then returned to the Parliament in 1994. In the 2006 election, the Swedish Greens scored 5 per cent. There are also Green parties in Denmark and Norway, but they have so far only received very limited support from the voters.

Nordic politics has been very much focused on the major changes taking place within the party systems from the early 1970s onwards. The rise of new parties and the decline of the traditional parties indicate increasing instability in the party systems, making elections more unpredictable as the electorate is more prone to change its allegiance from one election to another.

Rise in volatility, both gross and net

Looking at data on net as well as gross volatility gives support to such a conclusion, gross volatility measuring how the voters move from one party to another and net volatility measuring the resultant changes in overall support for a party. One aspect of Scandinavian exceptionalism by comparison with the Continental countries in Europe was a long period of low volatility scores, beginning in the late 1940s and ending in the early 1970s in Denmark and Norway and in the 1980s in Finland and Sweden. Each country has its particular election year when instability surfaced.

In the 1950s net volatility amounted to 6 per cent in Denmark and 4 per cent in Norway, but during the 1970s it rose to 16 per cent in both countries, gross volatility reaching 31 per cent in Denmark and 25 per cent in Norway. For Sweden and Finland net volatility was very low in the 1950s, at 5 per cent and 4 per cent, respectively. However, in the early 1990s the picture changed dramatically, as net volatility was up to 15 per cent and 13 per cent, respectively. Gross volatility has increased from 7 per cent in the 1950s to 20 per cent in the 1980s and to 34 per cent in 2006 among the Swedish electorate. The gross volatility scores remain high for both Denmark and Norway, with scores around 34 and 40 per cent, respectively, in the recent elections of 2001 and 2005, meaning that almost 1 voter in 3 changed his or her allegiance. In general, measures of net and gross volatility go together, but the rise in net volatility is portrayed in a more straightforward way in the data than gross volatility.

The tendency towards party system instability has induced a reassessment of the pros and cons of party government. There is more scepticism today about political parties, which is expressed among other things in a clear decline in party membership. There is a general downward trend in the four larger Nordic countries. Looking at data comparing membership as a percentage of voters in 1980 and the early 2000s, this trend is most marked in Norway, where the ratio in 1980 was 15 but 6 in 2003, while this ratio is higher in Norway than in both Denmark and Sweden.

Although there have been important changes in the party systems during the last decades, it should be emphasised that the traditional parties still have a rather strong standing. The general ability of these parties to adapt to changing circumstances is of major importance, as, for instance, one crucial institutional factor was the introduction of public funding of political parties. Legislation allowing state funding of political parties was introduced first in Sweden in 1965, followed by Finland in 1967, Norway in 1970 and Denmark only in 1986. It holds true that the smaller the party the more it is dependent upon public funds. With regard to small parties, 80 or 90 per cent of their budget is covered by public funds, while overall dependence on public funding ranges between 50 and 60 per cent.

Party strategies: ideology and issues

The strategies followed by the political parties may be characterised in terms of the distinction between ideology (reliance on the party programme) and tactics (maximisation of parliamentary influence and impact on the executive). Important for the choice of strategy has been, on the one hand, the size of the party in parliament and, on the other, the political relevance of the party, i.e. its position on the left–right political scale. Parties stressing tactics are to be found among the traditional parties, with the exception of the Communist parties. The new parties underline ideology more, although the religious parties have recently mixed tactics with ideological purity, as secularisation appears unstoppable in Norden. Looking at some major issues during the post-war era, it is evident that the ideological dimension has played a minor role while the tactical component has played the decisive role in deciding the party orientation to these issues. The Social Democratic parties and the Conservatives have adopted catch-all strategies.

Yet data on party policy alignment show that the right–left dimension is still the prevailing mode for the voters to position themselves in relation to the political parties. Tables 8.6–8.9 show how voters placed themselves in the four major Nordic countries during the early 2000s. It is also the case that this pattern is quite similar for the four countries: on the left the leftist or the former Communist parties and on the right the populist and the Conservative parties, while the Social Democrats, Christians, Liberals and Centre parties tend to occupy the political centre, and the Greens are left of centre.

Table 8.6 Left–right placement of parties in Denmark

Communist EL	Socialists SF, SD	Radical RV	Centre CD	Christian KrF	Liberal V	Conservative KF	People DF	Progress FrP
Left	Centre-left		Centre			Centre-right		Right

Party names:
EL: Unity List (Enhedslisten).
SF: Socialist People's Party (Socialistisk Folkeparti).
SD: Social Democrats (Socialdemokratiet).
RV: Radical Left (Radikale Venstre).
CD: Centre Democrats (Centrumdemokraterne).
KrF: Christian People's Party (Kristeligt Folkeparti).
V: Agrarian Liberal (Venstre).
KF: Conservative People's Party (Konservativt Folkeparti).
DF: Danish People's Party (Dansk Folkeparti).
FrP: Progress Party (Fremskridtspartiet).

Source: As for Table 2.4; Grendstad (2003).

Table 8.7 Left–right placement of parties in Finland

Communist VAS	Green VIHR	Socialist SDP	Swede SFP	Centre KESK	Christian SKL	National KOK	Rural SMP
Left	Centre-left		Centre		Centre-right		Right

Party names:
VAS: Left Alliance (Vasemmeistoliitto).
VIHR: Green League (Vihreä Liitto).
SDP: Social Democratic Party of Finland (Suomen Sosialidemokraattinen Puolue).
SFP: Swedish People's Party (Svenska Folkpartiet).
KESK: Centre Party (Agrarian) (Keskustapuoiue).
SKL: Finnish Christian League (Suomen Kristillinen Liitto).
KOK: National Coalition Party (Kansallinen Kokoomus).
SMP: Finnish Rural Party (Suomen Maaseudun Puolue).

Source: As for Table 2.4; Grendstad (2003).

Issue voting may be on the rise due to the fact that social heterogeneity has both increased and decreased. As the Nordic countries are facing a larger number of foreign residents entering their countries, this has added cultural heterogeneity to the social structure. Foreign residents as a percentage of the entire population have increased relatively rapidly during the last decades. Around 2000, they amount to 5 per cent in Denmark, Norway and Sweden, but only 2 per cent in Finland. At the same time the Nordic countries have extended citizenship to large proportions of the immigrants, so that the share of the populations who are of foreign descent is much larger than these figures suggest. The metropolitan areas of the Nordic countries have today substantial proportions of people from non-European countries, who are either first- or second-generation immigrants. How relevant the immigration issue may be can be

Table 8.8 Left–right placement of parties in Norway

Socialist	Labour		Centre	Christian	Liberal	Progress	Conservative
SV	DNA		SP	KRF	V	FRP	H
Left	Centre-left		Centre		Centre-right		Right

Party names:
SV: Socialist Left Party (Sosialistik Venstrepartei).
DNA: Norwegian Labour Party (Det Norske Arbeiderparti).
SP: Centre Party (Agrarian) (Senterpartiet).
KRF: Christian People's Party (Kristelig Folkepartei).
V: Liberals (Venstre).
FRP: Progress Party (Fremskrittspartiet).
H: Conservative Party (Høyre).

Source: As for Table 2.4.

Table 8.9 Left–right placement of parties in Sweden

Communist	Green	Socialist	Centre		Liberal	Christian	Moderate
V	MP	SAP	CP		FP	KD	M
Left	Centre-left		Centre		Centre-right		Right

Party names:
V: Left Party (Vänsterpartiet).
MP: Environmental Party–the Greens (Miljöpartiet De Gröna).
SAP: Swedish Social Democratic Workers' Party (Sveriges Socialdemokratistika Arbetarparti).
CP: Centre Party (Agrarian) (Centrepartiet).
FP: People's Party–the Liberals (Folkpartiet–Liberalerna).
KD: Christian Democrats (Kristdemokraterna).
M: Moderate Unity Party (Moderata Samlingspartiet).

Source: As for Table 2.4; Grendstad (2003).

seen from the electoral success of the populist parties, in particular in Denmark and Norway.

On the other hand, what has decreased social heterogeneity is the social transformation of the class system, increasing the middle classes at the expense of the working classes and the high bourgeoisie. The attendant outcome of social mobility and reduction of social barriers is an immense increase in voter volatility, as people are no longer loyal towards their social background. This has forced the political parties to change their appeal from a cleavage-oriented message to issue-based platforms with a strong media appeal that change from one election to another. This has especially hurt the working-class parties, whose voters sometimes desert them for other parties, including populist ones to some extent.

The Nordic countries have been seen as prototypes for the Lipset and Rokkan (1967) theory of frozen party systems in Western Europe. Nordic politics used to be channelled through a stable and persisting pattern of social cleavages. Thus, the party system was based upon proportional representation techniques, which expressed the social cleavages in the agrarian-industrial society. The working classes had their political parties, the agrarian group its party, the middle classes their parties and the wealthy their party. Ethnicity was expressed in the Finnish party system through the Swedish People's Party as well as in Norway in the issue of Norwegian language ('*nynorsk*'), whereas the aboriginal groups of Sami and Eskimos were too small or dispersed to be politically organised.

Although the Nordic party systems remain multi-party systems they are no longer based upon these traditional cleavages. Profound developments both among the political parties and in the social structure have resulted in processes of dealignment as well as realignment. New parties have been formed, such as left-Socialist parties, religious parties, Green parties and populist parties. And some of the old parties dating back to the introduction of mass politics in a democratic polity have been transformed considerably, such as the Agrarian and Communist parties, becoming Centre and Socialist parties respectively. These conspicuous developments have cut the links between party support and position in the social structure, entailing a sharp rise in gross volatility in elections in the early 2000s.

PARLIAMENTS

The Nordic countries have strong parliaments both on paper and in reality. Today all Nordic countries have unicameral parliaments. Denmark moved to a one-chamber system in 1953 and Sweden in 1970. The Norwegian Parliament (Stortinget) divides into two sections (Lagtinget and Odelstinget) on legislative matters. Explicitly, their constitutions provide the National Assemblies with exclusive legislative powers and formally or informally with the power to dismiss governments that lose their confidence. The political systems of the Nordic countries embrace the principle of the sovereignty of parliament, meaning that all exercise of public power must go back to law enacted in the representative assembly, which is a Westminster-model feature of Norden.

Finnish constitutionalism departs somewhat from the Scandinavian practice. It includes a presidential system of government where the powers of the President used to be truly impressive. However, it is another matter whether the presidents have managed to employ those powers. Whereas Kekkonen was stronger than both the Premier and the cabinet over a very long period of time (1956–82), developments under Koivisto (1982–94) and Ahtisaari (1994–2000) strengthened Finnish parliamentarianism at the expense of presidential rule, at the same time as a procedure for directly electing the President was introduced in 1994. Recent constitutional changes have further reinforced the power of the Premier, as, for instance, the President can no longer dissolve parliament without a proposal from the Premier. The first female Finnish President, Tarja Halonen, elected in 2000, thus has less formal power than her male predecessors. Therefore it is appropriate to classify the Finnish regime today as more parliamentarian than semi-presidential.

The amount of parliamentary activity, as well as the political significance of such activity, has increased considerably since the Second World War with all the legislation necessary for building the Nordic welfare state. As minority governments came to prevail in Denmark, Norway and Sweden, there was a major shift towards so-called committee parliamentarianism, i.e. policy-making has been negotiated in the standing committees of parliament. More and more the government needs to bargain with different parties from one policy area to the other, where the crucial decisions are hammered out in parliamentary committees. The standing committees number 25 in Denmark, 14 in Finland, 12 in Iceland and Norway and 15 in Sweden; the EU advisory committee in Sweden is not formally considered to be a standing committee. It remains to be seen whether the bare-majority coalition governments which came to power in the 2005 and 2006 elections in Norway and Sweden will lead to a stronger position for the government in relation to the National Assembly.

Real parliamentary political power is heavily dependent upon the nature of government formation, majority governments being conducive to 'Minister Caesarism', whereas in 'committee parliamentarianism' the standing committees of the National Assembly have the final responsibility for drafting the policies that parliament will vote upon. During periods of majority government, the national assemblies in reality constitute rubber-stamp bodies, approving policies that have been drawn up elsewhere, e.g. in iron triangles comprising the Cabinet, the bureaucracy and the interest groups, where corporatist practices loom large.

Clearly, the typical feature of Scandianvian politics has been committee parliamentarianism, except for the periods of Social Democratic hegemony. This trend is strengthened by the tradition of strong party cohesion at roll-call votes in Parliament. An index measuring the degree of cohesion in the mid-1990s (the Rice index, ranging from 0 to 100) shows scores over 96 in four of the countries, with Finland slightly deviating with a score of 88.6. Yet the ambition to form majority governments has never been relinquished despite the many minority cabinets in Denmark, Norway and Sweden.

In the Nordic National Assemblies, policy-making has become more or less formalised into a semi-rational policy-making structure involving the creation of a commission of inquiry whose reports are sent out for review by all concerned and then end up in parliament for committee scrutiny and final legislation. The attempt at comprehensive policy-making is combined with consultation procedures, resulting in opportunities for expressing various opinions as well as for compromise among interested parties. An inquiry into legislative matters may also be initiated by the opposition parties in parliament, by calling on the government to appoint a commission with broadly-based representation.

The Nordic parliaments have been a vehicle for deprived groups ascending to political power to employ public policies to change society. One aspect of this is how well the opinions and the social background of the voters are represented by MPs. Comparative data on opinion – or issue – agreement indicate that there is a variation between the Nordic countries, but with regard to the basic left–right issue dimension then there is more of agreement between voters and MPs. Two basic patterns may be identified: one elite polarised pattern where MPs on the left and on the right are more radical than their voters (Denmark); and one left-leaning elite where the MPs tend to be more left-leaning than their voters from the left to the right (Finland).

The gender dimension in the representative assembly may now be regarded as the major indicator of social representation. There has been a substantial growth in the number of female MPs in all Nordic countries. As a matter of fact, in 2005 the Nordic countries ranked among the highest with regard to female parliamentary representation worldwide. In 1950 the relative share of female representatives was 8 per cent in Denmark, 9 per cent in Finland, 3.5 per cent in Iceland, 4.5 per cent in Norway and 9.5 per cent in Sweden. Around 2005 the corresponding figures had climbed to 37 per cent in Denmark, 42 per cent in Finland, 32 per cent in Iceland, 38 per cent in Norway and 47 per cent in Sweden. Since 1970 there has been steady growth in female representation, so that in 2005 slightly more than one in three MPs was a woman. The situation of women in Iceland has been different, and the low representation of women may have been one factor of major importance in the foundation of the Women's Party in Iceland in the early 1980s.

GOVERNMENTS

Although the political culture in Nordic countries emphasises compromise, the goal of forming a one-party majority government has in no way lost its relevance. In Finland there is frequent resort to oversized coalitions, but in the Scandinavian states both the left and the right aim to achieve a simple majority government either by means of a minimum-winning coalition among the non-socialist parties or by means of a real majority situation in parliament for the Social Democratic parties, supported tacitly by other left-wing parties, such as the former Communist Party in Sweden. Only in Finland are there the typical so-called consociational devices like consensus governments and minority protection, whereas government formation in Scandinavia involves much adversarial politics between the socialists and the non-socialists. Icelandic governments tend to be majoritarian.

Information about government formation in the four major Nordic countries is presented in Tables 8.10–8.13. Looking at the composition of governments between 1945 and 2007, different kinds of government have been formed in the various Nordic states. Majority single-party governments can only be found in Norway (27 per cent of the time) and in Sweden (3 per cent). As a matter of fact, it has become impossible to form this kind of government today, due to the heavy party fractionalisation and multidimensional nature of the political issues. The classic examples of single-party dominance include the long period in power of the Gerhardsen Social Democratic majority government in Norway and the many years in government for the Swedish Social Democrats, ruling with a minority government, supported tacitly by one or more parties.

Majority coalitions have been formed in all the Nordic countries, but they occur often only in Finland (82 per cent) and in Iceland (95 per cent). It must be emphasised, though, that oversized majority or 'surplus' governments are formed almost exclusively in Finland. In the other countries, the majority government coalitions tend to be minimal winning. In Norway the non-socialist parties have formed majority coalition governments a couple of times (13 per cent), which is also true of Denmark (6 per cent) and Sweden (6 per cent). The other major type of government is a Social Democratic single-party minority government, as in Sweden (74 per cent), in Norway (45 per cent) and Denmark (37 per cent). Over time, it has become increasingly difficult to form majority governments in Scandinavia, especially in Denmark, where there are more and more minority coalition governments (48 per cent).

One institution of major importance for the frequent use of minority governments in Nordic politics is negative parliamentarianism. Its basic rule is that governments may be formed without the explicit and positive support of a political majority in parliament. A government survives as long as it is at least tacitly tolerated, because it has to step down only when there is an intentional vote of no confidence. Actually the Schlüter government in Denmark survived several parliamentary defeats during the 1980s and remained in power.

The overall pattern of government formation differs between the various countries, reflecting the variation in voter support for the largest party, the Social Democrats.

Table 8.10 Governments of Denmark, 1945–2005

No.	Year	Prime Minister	Party composition
1	1945	K. Kristensen	Agrarian
2	1947	H. Hedtoft	Social Democrat
3	1950	H. Hedtoft	Social Democrat
	1950	E. Eriksen	Conservative, Agrarian
4	1953	E. Eriksen	Conservative, Agrarian
5	1953	H. Hedtoft	Social Democrat
	1955	H. C. Hansen	Social Democrat
6	1957	H. C. Hansen	Social Democrat, Radical
	1960	V. Kampmann	Social Democrat, Radical
7	1960	V. Kampmann	Social Democrat, Radical
	1962	J. O. Krag	Social Democrat, Radical
8	1964	J. O. Krag	Social Democrat
9	1966	J. O. Krag	Social Democrat
10	1968	H. Baunsgaard	Radical, Agrarian, Conservative
11	1971	J. O. Krag	Social Democrat
	1972	A. Jørgensen	Social Democrat
12	1973	P. Hartling	Agrarian
13	1975	A. Jørgensen	Social Democrat
14	1977	A. Jørgensen	Social Democrat
	1978	A. Jørgensen	Social Democrat, Agrarian
15	1979	A. Jørgensen	Social Democrat
16	1981	A. Jørgensen	Social Democrat
	1982	P. Schlüter	Conservative, Agrarian, Centre, Christian
17	1984	P. Schlüter	Conservative, Agrarian, Centre, Christian
18	1987	P. Schlüter	Conservative, Agrarian, Centre, Christian
19	1988	P. Schlüter	Conservative, Agrarian, Radical
20	1990	P. Schlüter	Conservative, Agrarian
	1993	P. Nyrup Rasmussen	Social Democrat, Radical, Centre, Christian
21	1994	P. Nyrup Rasmussen	Social Democrat, Radical, Centre
	1996	P. Nyrup Rasmussen	Social Democrat, Radical
22	1998	P. Nyrup Rasmussen	Social Democrat, Radical
23	2001	A. Fogh Rasmussen	Agrarian, Conservative, Centre
24	2005	A. Fogh Rasmussen	Agrarian, Conservative, Centre

Note: The first party indicates the Prime Minister's affiliation.

Table 8.11 Governments of Finland, 1945–2007

No.	Year	Prime Minister	Party composition
1	1945	J. A. Paasikivi	Agrarian, Social Democrat, Swedish, Liberal, Communist
	1946	M. Pekkala	Communist, Agrarian, Social Democrat, Swedish
2	1948	K. A. Fagerholm	Social Democrat
	1950	U. Kekkonen	Agrarian, Swedish, Liberal
	1951	U. Kekkonen	Agrarian, Social Democrat, Swedish, Liberal
	1951	U. Kekkonen	Agrarian, Swedish, Liberal
3	1951	U. Kekkonen	Agrarian, Swedish, SFID
	1953	U. Kekkonen	Agrarian, Swedish
	1953	S. Tuomija	Caretaker
4	1954	R. Törngren	Agrarian, Social Democrat, Swedish, Social Democrat
	1954	U. Kekkonen	Agrarian, SDID
5	1956	K. A. Fagerholm	Social Democrat, Agrarian, Swedish, Liberal
	1957	V. Sukselainen	Agrarian, Swedish, Liberal
	1957	V. Sukselainen	Agrarian, Swedish
	1957	V. Sukselainen	Agrarian, Workers', Liberal
	1957	R. Von Fieandt	Caretaker
	1958	R. Kuuskoski	Caretaker
6	1958	K. A. Fagerholm	Social Democrat, Agrarian, Conservative, Swedish, Liberal
	1959	V. Sukselainen	Agrarian
	1961	M. Miettunen	Agrarian
7	1962	A. Karjalainen	Agrarian, Conservative, Swedish, Liberal
	1963	R. R. Lehto	Caretaker
	1964	J. Virolainen	Agrarian, Conservative, Swedish, Liberal
8	1966	R. Paasio	Social Democrat, Agrarian, Communist, Workers'
	1968	M. Koivisto	Social Democrat, Agrarian, Swedish, Communist, Workers'
9	1970	T. Aura	Caretaker
	1970	A. Karjalainen	Agrarian, Social Democrat, Swedish, Liberal, Communist
	1971	A. Karjalainen	Agrarian, Social Democrat, Swedish, Liberal
	1971	T. Aura	Caretaker
10	1972	R. Paasio	Social Democrat
	1972	K. Sorsa	Social Democrat, Agrarian, Swedish, Liberal
	1975	K. Linanmaa	Caretaker
	1975	M. Miettunen	Agrarian, Social Democrat, Swedish, Liberal, Communist
	1976	M. Miettunen	Agrarian, Swedish, Liberal
	1977	K. Sorsa	Social Democrat, Agrarian, Swedish, Liberal, Communist
	1978	K. Sorsa	Agrarian, Liberal, Communist
12	1979	M. Koivisto	Social Democrat, Agrarian, Swedish, Communist
	1982	K. Sorsa	Social Democrat, Agrarian, Swedish, Communist
	1982	K. Sorsa	Social Democrat, Agrarian, Swedish, Liberal
13	1983	K. Sorsa	Social Democrat, Agrarian, Swedish, Populist
14	1987	H. Holkeri	Conservative, Social Democrat, Swedish, Populist
	1990	H. Holkeri	Conservative, Social Democrat, Swedish
15	1991	E. Aho	Agrarian, Conservative, Swedish, Christian
	1994	E. Aho	Agrarian, Conservative, Swedish
16	1995	P. Lipponen	Social Democrat, Conservative, Swedish, Green, Communist
17	1999	P. Lipponen	Social Democrat, Conservative, Swedish, Green, Communist
18	2003	A. Jäätteenmäki	Agrarian, Social Democrat, Swedish
	2003	M. Vanhanen	Agrarian, Social Democrat, Swedish
19	2007	M. Vanhanen	Agrarian, Conservative, Green, Swedish

Note: The first party indicates Prime Minister's affiliation.

Table 8.12 Governments of Norway, 1945–2005

No.	Year	Prime Minister	Party composition
1	1945	E. Gerhardsen	Labour
2	1949	E. Gerhardsen	Labour
	1951	O. Torp	Labour
3	1953	O. Torp	Labour
	1955	E. Gerhardsen	Labour
4	1957	E. Gerhardsen	Labour
5	1961	E. Gerhardsen	Labour
	1963	J. Lyng	Conservative, Agrarian, Christian, Liberal
	1963	E. Gerhardsen	Labour
6	1965	P. Borten	Agrarian, Christian, Conservative, Liberal
7	1969	P. Borten	Agrarian, Christian, Conservative, Liberal
	1971	T. Bratteli	Labour
	1972	L. Korvald	Christian, Agrarian, Liberal
8	1973	T. Bratteli	Labour
	1976	O. Nordli	Labour
9	1977	O. Nordli	Labour
	1981	G. Harlem Brundtland	Labour
10	1981	K. Willoch	Conservative
	1983	K. Willoch	Conservative, Agrarian, Christian
11	1985	K. Willoch	Conservative, Agrarian, Christian
	1986	G. Harlem Brundtland	Labour
12	1989	J. P. Syse	Conservative, Agrarian, Christian
	1990	G. Harlem Brundtland	Labour
13	1993	G. Harlem Brundtland	Labour
	1996	T. Jagland	Labour
14	1997	K. Bondevik	Christian, Agrarian, Liberal
	2000	J. Stoltenberg	Labour
15	2001	K. Bondevik	Christian, Conservative, Liberal
16	2005	J. Stoltenberg	Labour, Agrarian, Left Labour

Note: The first party indicates Prime Minister's affiliation.

Table 8.13 Governments of Sweden, 1946–2006

No.	Year	Prime Minister	Party composition
1	1946	T. Erlander	Social Democrat
2	1948	T. Erlander	Social Democrat
	1951	T. Erlander	Social Democrat, Agrarian
3	1952	T. Erlander	Social Democrat, Agrarian
4	1956	T. Erlander	Social Democrat, Agrarian
	1957	T. Erlander	Social Democrat
5	1958	T. Erlander	Social Democrat
6	1960	T. Erlander	Social Democrat
7	1964	T. Erlander	Social Democrat
	1968	T. Erlander	Social Democrat
	1969	O. Palme	Social Democrat
9	1970	O. Palme	Social Democrat
10	1973	O. Palme	Social Democrat

Table 8.13 (continued)

No.	Year	Prime Minister	Party composition
11	1976	T. Fälldin	Agrarian, Liberal, Conservative
	1978	O. Ullsten	Agrarian
12	1979	T. Fälldin	Agrarian, Liberal, Conservative
	1981	T. Fälldin	Agrarian, Liberal
13	1982	O. Palme	Social Democrat
14	1985	O. Palme	Social Democrat
	1986	I. Carlsson	Social Democrat
15	1988	I. Carlsson	Social Democrat
16	1991	C. Bildt	Conservative, Agrarian, Liberal, Christian
17	1994	I. Carlsson	Social Democrat
	1996	G. Persson	Social Democrat
18	1998	G. Persson	Social Democrat
19	2002	G. Persson	Social Democrat
20	2006	F. Reinfeldt	Conservative, Agrarian, Liberal, Christian

Note: The first party indicates the Prime Minister's affiliation.

In Norway and Sweden, the Social Democratic Party has had such a strong hold on government that people sometimes spoke of a 'statist' political party. The Norwegian Social Democrats enjoyed majority support in the Stortinget in the period 1945–61, whereas the Swedish Social Democratic Party was able to rule as if it was a majority government from 1945 to 1976, first on the basis of government co-operation with the Agrarian Party up to 1957 and then in a minority government with the tacit support of the Communist Party, and more recently during the 1990s and the 2000s supported by either the Centre Party (1994–8) or the Left Party and the Green Party (1998–2006). In Denmark, Finland and Iceland the labour movement never achieved such a hegemonic position.

Government stability has been lower in Denmark and Finland, where the number of governments between 1945 and 2007 is 34 and 39, respectively, with an average duration of 21 months and 15 months. Finland had very unstable governments in the 1950s before turning to oversized cabinets. The number of governments is lower in Sweden (28), Norway (29) and Iceland (28), and the average duration is longer, i.e. some 25 months. The degree of parliamentary support and the number of parties participating in government is consistently higher in Finland than in Scandinavia, owing to the occurrence of oversized coalitions. Average support is as high as 59 per cent in Finland and the number of parties included is three, whereas in the Scandinavian countries parliamentary support hovers between 41 per cent (Denmark) and 46 per cent (Sweden, Norway). The chief developing trend, however, is that government life spans have decreased in the Scandinavian countries but increased in Finland. Minority governments are frequent in Scandinavia, although the non-socialist parties in Sweden managed once more to form a majority coalition Cabinet in 2006 at the same time as the Norwegian Social Democrats put together a majority government with support from the Left-Wing Socialists (SV) and the Centre Party (SP).

The pattern of ideological composition varies between the nations. Sweden and Norway have had a long tradition of single-party Social Democratic governments, covering 75 per cent and 69 per cent of the time between 1945 and 2007. The Danish pattern includes both social-democratic single-party governments (31 per cent) and right-wing-led governments (40 per cent), while in Finland governments tend to be formed that balance the right and the left in the same cabinet (65 per cent). In Iceland coalition governments are formed by parties of the centre, often taking the form of a coalition between the dominant conservative Independent Party and the Social Democrats or the Agrarians.

Corporatist patterns

It is impossible to talk about Nordic party government without bringing up the question of corporatism. On the one hand, inherent in the compromise culture is the fact that strong interest organisations are afforded a number of opportunities to exercise influence over policy initiation and legislative decision-making as well as policy implementation. On the other hand, since the Nordic countries are characterised by the hierarchical and encompassing nature of the interest organisations among both employees and employers, there is also strong pressure for interest consultation and interest intermediation.

Trade union density rose between 1950 and 2003, from 53 per cent to 70 per cent in Denmark, from 34 per cent to 74 per cent in Finland, from 48 per cent to 53 per cent in Norway and from 68 per cent to 78 per cent in Sweden. The Scandinavian countries and Finland constitute the most typically corporatist countries in Western Europe apart from Austria. Although it is true that the relevance of corporatist interest intermediation and interest concertation tends to swing back and forth with time, corporatist patterns of policy-making and policy implementation make for important elements of political institutions in Norden.

Corporatism in Nordic politics emerged from the Great Depression, when crucial system choices, or compromises, were made combining a capitalist economy with extensive state regulation and trade union involvement. The existence of strong trade unions was accepted by the employers' associations, where industrial relations were to be managed by means of broad agreements between the interest organisations. A tripartite system of policy interaction was introduced covering the trade unions, the employers' associations and the state.

Corporatism acquired its most characteristic features after the Second World War, when it became a cornerstone of the Scandinavian model. It involved the notion of an industrial pact between employers and employees in order to enhance economic growth by means of low wage increases resulting in low inflation. As Mancur Olson (1990) has emphasised, the Scandinavian model achieved considerable growth rates first in Sweden and Finland and later in Norway and Denmark in the 1980s.

Each Nordic country has its own version of corporatism. Perhaps the Swedish model took social corporatism to its limits. The Swedish interest organisations were to some extent integrated with the state. Not only were they given a prominent role in the policy-making process, having the right to state their view on almost any reform proposal, but they were also partly integrated in policy implementation by virtue of their capacity to nominate members of state agencies as well as to execute public functions.

In Norway the interest groups played a large role in the promotion of an 'organised democracy', to use the words of Johan P. Olsen (1983). In Finland 'structural corporatism' grew strong in the 1960s, which resulted in a political role for the interest groups. In Denmark the interest groups play a large role in various administrative regimes, including straightforward implementation of policies. Nordic corporatism has been institutionalised in the following five policy and implementation procedures:

1   involvement of interest groups in the hearings process concerning major policy reforms ('*remiss*');
2   interest groups' participation in major policy investigations;
3   board representation of interest groups in central government agencies;
4   schemes for employee representation on various boards as well as for co-determination;
5   the delegation of administrative tasks to the interest group.

A conspicuous case of the last-mentioned institution was the construction of the unemployment insurance funds, where Denmark, Finland and Sweden have had union-run unemployment insurance schemes, funded with public money but operating in accordance with public law. Yet since the late 1980s and in the 1990s different assessments of corporatism have surfaced, including negative ones. Patterns of corporatist interaction are no longer sacrosanct, as they have been attacked for harbouring special interests promoting themselves at the expense of the public interest. In the wake of the economic depression of the 1990s, the Nordic countries have attempted to remove some of their institutional sclerosis, unpacking certain corporatist schemes. Still it may be too early to proclaim the end of corporatism in Scandinavia. During the 1990s there were even signs of a return of corporatism. Others have noted a shift from less corporatism to more lobbyism when characterising the relationships between the state and the interest groups.

BUREAUCRACY AND INTERGOVERNMENTAL RELATIONS

Although they are unitary states, the Scandinavian countries adopted a three-tier system of government, whereas Finland and Iceland have a two-tier framework. The principle of local government autonomy has of tradition a strong standing in the Nordic countries, although there is much state regulation and state funding.

In the local government sector amalgamations have been undertaken in every country, although in Finland, Norway and Iceland the number of municipalities remains very high, which means that many local governments are responsible for only a few thousand inhabitants, reflecting a political philosophy of strong support for peripheral communities and local participation in these countries. In Denmark a new local government reform will reduce the number of municipalities to ninety-eight. And in Sweden reforms at the regional level are yet to be decided – replacing counties with regions. The central government is made up of ministries and a large number of agencies and boards, which tend to enjoy a degree of autonomy not found in Continental Europe. The Swedish model of the autonomous agency (Ambetsverk) is the typical model, to which Finland and Norway come close, whereas the Danish model involves more ministerial rule. Administrative matters are delegated to these independent agencies and boards to a considerable extent. These central government authorities are run either by a chief director or a board that often includes corporatist representation. The structure of the central government bureaucracy may be interpreted as an institutional mechanism that moderates the amount of centralisation in the Nordic unitary state. The same applies to the institutionalisation of extensive autonomy granted the municipalities and county councils. Nordic politics puts a heavy emphasis upon administrative accountability and procedural predictability in the public sector, accomplished by an encompassing system of overview, offering the citizens the possibility of complaint and redress, ultimately safeguarded by the strong institutionalisation of the Ombudsman, who is accountable to Parliament.

During the post-war period the size of local government functions has increased tremendously, as the local government authorities are entrusted with the provision of many welfare services. Whereas the municipalities take care of education, social services and infrastructure, the county councils are responsible for health care. In Finland special associations set up between the municipalities provide health services, as Finland has a two-tier structure. In 2001 these health care services were taken over from the regional governments by the Norwegian state, setting up national hospitals. As the budgets of the local authorities have multiplied, the local government sector increasing more rapidly than GDP, the organisational framework of the local government authorities has been transformed, underlining their formal structure as well as their function as major employers. Only tiny Iceland diverges from the general decentralised pattern of public consumption.

Welfare programmes date back to the late nineteenth and early twentieth centuries as the national government took steps to protect workers against the consequences of the rapid process of industrialisation and urbanisation that swept through the Nordic countries during the second half of the nineteenth century. The economic crisis of the 1930s led to sustained expansion of various aspects of the public sector, involving both the provision of welfare services and transfer payments. The real expansion of the public sector began, however, after the Second World War.

The overall growth of the public sector has been dramatic in Norden. Measured as a percentage of GDP, the Danish figures climbed from 18 per cent in 1950 to 54 per cent in 2003, in Norway from 22 per cent to 46 per cent, in Sweden from 23.5 per cent to 57 per cent, whereas in Finland the expansion of the tax state started with a more moderate rise from 19.5 per cent to 42 per cent in 1990, but jumped to 51 per cent in 2003. Considering that overall resources as measured by GDP have more than doubled during the post-war period, the increase in the capacity of the Nordic states to embark on extensive public-sector programmes involves a major change in the relations between state and society in those countries, from a historical point of view, i.e. the establishment of a mixed economy.

The Scandinavian welfare state was gradually built up on the basis of a consensualist policy style that delivered broad reform proposals backed by all except the small extremist parties. When it worked, at its best, it combined high economic growth with low unemployment and much redistribution by means of public transfer programmes. However, in the late 1970s and early 1980s the Scandinavian model began to malfunction; inflation and unemployment increased, as did the number of working days lost to strikes. The strong increase in membership of several trade unions in the public sector created more difficulties in bringing about reforms to secure economic growth. The power of distributional coalitions was strengthened along with the expansion of the public sector. During the 1980s, institutional sclerosis increased in the sense that strong policy networks could mobilise special interests to a considerable extent. The economic crisis in the 1990s paved the way for welfare state reforms, as public sector expansion was halted and public budgets trimmed.

The Nordic welfare state comprises a set of three broad policies: extensive public resource allocation in education and health, universal transfer payments for social security and a heavy commitment to full employment, including extensive job retraining programmes. The state and the local government in particular are responsible for the provision of many goods and services, final government consumption standing in 2005 at 26 per cent in Denmark, 22 per cent in Finland, 20 per cent in Norway and 27 per cent in Sweden. However, the increases in social security or transfer payments between 1950 and 2003 were even more spectacular, from 6 per cent to 22 per cent in Denmark, from 4.5 per cent to 21 per cent in Finland, from 5 per cent to 22 per cent in Norway and from 6.5 per cent to 26 per cent in Sweden.

At first it was possible to combine high average growth in the overall economy with steadily expanding public spending, but from the 1970s on there has been a clear reduction in economic growth at the same time as the expansion of the public sector at all levels of government, but particularly the local government level, was far in excess of private-sector expansion. The Scandinavian model implies both substantial public resource allocation, providing a number of services almost free of charge, and huge social security programmes, redistributing income between various social groups. Such heavy reliance on public provision has led to a large increase in the number of public employees. Sweden especially suffered from a long period of reliance upon the public budget for resource allocation and income redistribution, with huge central government deficits and a large accumulated national debt as the most urgent problem in the early 1990s. At the beginning of the twenty-first century deficits have again changed into surpluses, and the Nordic macro economies show economic growth with low inflation rates. All Nordic countries have abandoned traditional Keynesian fiscal policy-making, emphasising today the importance of monetary stability. Economic stability in Norway and Denmark has been much promoted by the oil revenues in those countries.

The Nordic welfare state has cherished equality as its first and foremost goal, both equality of opportunities and equal results. Thus services were to be provided equally to all citizens, and regional and class disparities were to be equalised. When the Nordic welfare state was constructed and expanded, centralisation was the major tool, the national government laying down standards and using local government to provide the goods and services. This has had the effect that the traditional commitment ·to local government autonomy was weakened by the weight of state legislation and considerable allocation of central government grants to local government. However, since the beginning of the 1980s the trend has been reversed, as decentralisation has been in favour. Local governments have passed through comprehensive organisational growth processes, transforming them into huge formal organisations with large budgets and many employees.

Since the 1990s, the emphasis is upon improving efficiency in the state and local governments. Thus cutbacks in public spending and public employment have occurred, especially at the local level. New public management (WPM) was well received in Norden, where the state, the county councils and the local governments have been interested in replacing bureaucratic organisation with tendering/bidding and internal markets. In the health care sector, such NPM reforms have been fairly comprehensive. The Danish workfare-state programmes are well known. Almost all public enterprises with a considerable total workforce have been incorporated, and some privatised.

Whereas intergovernmental interaction was characterised by planning and the use of various control schemes such as detailed rule regulation in combination with earmarked grants, the strong decentralisation drive has involved a profound movement from a top-down perspective to a bottom-up approach. Framework legislation has been employed, together with block grants, augmenting discretion at the regional and local level of government, also within the state (deconcentration). The central government now only outlines the major objectives in the various policy sectors, refraining from the employment of policy instruments used earlier but underlining the relevance of the evaluation of outputs (productivity) and outcomes (effectiveness). The overall trend in intergovernmental relations is the replacement of *ex ante* steering mechanisms with *ex post* instruments such as performance evaluation in particular. The costly public health care sector especially has experienced a number of reforms, aiming at increasing competition and choice between alternative providers while containing costs without finding an optimal format. Thus in Denmark the running of hospitals lies with the fourteen counties. However, the hospitals in the local authorities of Copenhagen and Frederiksberg are run by a special administrative body: the Copenhagen Hospital Cooperation. Norwegian hospitals are run as state organisations, whereas some Swedish hospitals have been incorporated.

The process of Europeanisation has had a clear impact. Brussels is now an actor that all Nordic governments take into account, also in Oslo. Central government bureaucrats in the capitals now interact with central bureaucrats in Brussels. But there is also a growing interaction among regional or local actors participating in the many EU-inspired networks.

INSTITUTIONAL REFORM

Considering the size of the Scandinavian welfare state, it is scarcely surprising that most reform activity has focused upon the public sector. Two chief objectives may be identified: (1) enhancement of productivity and effectiveness within state agencies and local governments, and (2) initiation of cutback management in relation to several programmes in the social security systems. Major types of reform strategies attempted include: (1) decentralisation, (2) privatisation and (3) new public management.

The temporal sequence between these objectives and measures is that the political reforms, particularly decentralisation, came before the resort to cutback management and privatisation strategies. The decentralisation reform involved on the one hand deconcentration within the state, moving functions and resources from the central level to the regional and local levels of government. On the other hand, there was a strong emphasis on the values of the local government system, meaning that both the municipalities and the county councils were allowed to expand far more rapidly than the growth rate of the economy as a whole. The local governments are now the major employers of people in the Nordic countries. The reform of the Scandinavian welfare state has had a strong dose of decentralisation attempting to reduce the workload of the central government. The main exception to the emphasis upon local and regional decentralisation is the Norwegian state nationalising the hospitals in early 2000, where the central government maintains a firm grip upon events, partially due to its immense revenues in the state-controlled oil sector.

The basic tenor of the debate about the pros and cons of the Scandinavian welfare state has shifted. The increasing relevance of market values in these countries, with their earlier strong socialist ambitions, was at first reflected in various institutional attempts to reform the public sector, but as the financial pressure grew along with the depression of the early 1990s it became necessary to initiate various policies of retrenchment. This applies in particular to the Swedish context, where there have been substantial cutbacks both at the central government level in the transfer programmes and at the local government level, where people have been laid off. The public sector in Denmark and Norway were in better shape than in Sweden and Finland, where the economic depression hit hard, resulting in high unemployment figures. The economic development during the 2000s has, however, resulted in more convergence between the countries. Unemployment figures are again lower, but they have not reached the low levels of the early 1970s. Part of the reduction in unemployment is because of the increase in the number of people who have been given early retirement for various reasons.

The innovations in the economic reform of the public sector have comprised a number of different steps:

1   new budgetary and evaluation techniques, promoting efficiency;
2   contracting out or tendering/bidding;
3   incorporation of public enterprises, i.e. transforming them into public joint-stock companies, e.g. in infrastructures such as energy and telecommunications;
4   hiving off bureau functions to public joint-stock companies (health care);
5   user fees instead of taxation;
6   the introduction of market-type mechanisms such as internal markets as well as individual salary schemes into the state bureaucracy and especially at the local government level;
7   privatisation proper, meaning the selling off of public property.

The reforms of the Scandinavian model of a mixed economy with a blend of market economy and a large public sector that gives a high priority to distributional matters have been much inspired by the market philosophy that flows around the world with globalisation. Thus, new public management has been introduced on a large scale in some local and regional governments, especially in the healthcare sector. For instance, the Stockholm County Council and the '*Region Skane*' both employ internal markets in practically all healthcare supply. The transfer programmes – pensions, unemployment benefits, sickness compensation – have been restructured in accordance with ideas about incentive compatibility, as governments increasingly link future benefits with past contributions or differences in salaries. Finally, the private supply of services has been more accepted in the 2000s. The Scandinavian model has become less monolithic, more competitive and less egalitarian. More and more public services are contracted, either outsourcing or insourcing. And public enterprises have been fully incorporated, now active under schemes of deregulation with some private or international competition. What may be a successful scheme of this kind is the all-Nordic pool for the supply of electricity, although doubts have been raised about the long-term efficiency of its operations.

CONCLUSION

The Scandinavian model outlined a distinct set of political institutions that made Nordic politics different from both Anglo-Saxon practices and Continental European realities. It combined adversarial politics with consensus institutions, the latter including anything from patterns of consultation and negotiation in parliament to corporatist policy concertation. Compromise politics between socialists and non-socialists resulted in a strong policy commitment to the welfare state without parallel elsewhere.

Yet Scandinavian political institutions are not working as they used to when the reputation of this institutional model was at its peak, in the 1970s and 1980s. There is less consensus between the labour-market organisations. The public sector has been transformed by structural reform, underlining market incentives and contracting, at a time when the major process of public-sector growth was halted. Besides the drive for more efficiency in public services, cutback strategies have been implemented, particularly in Sweden and Finland. The Scandinavian model has been transformed in several ways: less corporatism, more choice and competition, as well as less collectivism and more personal freedom.

The reforms of the 1990s and early 2000s stemmed from a recognition that it is not easy to combine the two basic values of the Scandinavian welfare state – efficiency and equality. Some data indicated profound public-sector productivity problems, and the comprehensive and generous transfer programmes were hardly an incentive compatible with the presuppositions of an advanced open market economy. There has increasingly been a search for efficiency-enhancing reforms and retrenchment policies that trim the social security systems and workfare policies. The question of membership in the European Union and adherence to the Euro raised the same type of confrontation in Finland, Norway and Sweden, where adherents underlined the economic benefits whereas opponents feared the negative regional consequences.

A most conspicuous change in Nordic politics is the sharp increase in electoral volatility. The processes of dealignment and realignment have resulted in party system transformation, including the phenomenon of *new politics*, as well as in governmental instability, which makes policy-making more complicated. The typical compromise institutions now involve more unpredictability and strategic behaviour. Scandinavian exceptionalism is waning at the same time as Norden is becoming increasingly integrated into Western Europe, Denmark, Sweden and Finland being members of the EU, with Norway and Iceland having signed the EEA treaty and Finland having adopted the Euro. The impact of Europeanisation may not yet be that powerful, but there are indications suggesting convergences between the Nordic countries and the rest of Europe when it comes to law and economics. The legislative process and institutional reforms are increasingly influenced by European policies and European law.

Yet there remain in the early twenty-first century still some distinct features of a 'Nordic model' of politics. Nordic exceptionalism is to be found with respect to the following combination of traits: the electoral system of proportional representation; party systems with a multi-dimensional issue pattern; parliamentary behaviour supported by strong committees; the patterns of coalition formation prone to minority cabinets and oversized cabinets; a state structure including local government autonomy and the Ombudsman; as well as corporatist policy-making. Nevertheless, Westminster characteristics are in no way absent, and there is a clear ambition for minimum winning coalitions, decreased corporatism and increased new management in the public sector.

BIBLIOGRAPHY

General

Andersen, J. G. (2006) 'Political Power and Democracy in Denmark: Decline of Democracy or Change in Democracy?', *Journal of European Public Policy* 13: 569–86.

Andersen, J. G. and J. Hoff (2001) *Citizenship and Democracy in Scandinavia*, Basingstoke: Palgrave.

Arter, D. (2006) *Democracy in Scandinavia: Consensual, Majoritarian or Mixed?*, Manchester: Manchester University Press.

Bergqvist, C. (ed.) (1999) *Equal Democracies?: Gender and Politics in the Nordic Countries*, Oslo: Scandinavian University Press.

Einhorn, E. S. and J. A. Logue (2003) *Modern Welfare States: Scandinavian Politics and Policy in the Global Age*, 2nd edn, Westport, CT: Praeger.

Heidar, K. (2001) *Norway: Elites on Trial*, Boulder, CO: Westview Press.

—— (ed.) (2004) *Nordic Politics: Comparative Perspectives*, Oslo: Universitetsforlaget.

Ingebritsen, C. (2006) *Scandinavia in World Politics*, Lanham, MD: Rowman & Littlefield.

Jenssen, A. T. P. Pesonen and M. Gilljam (eds) (1998) *To Join or Not to Join: Three Nordic Referendums on Membership in the European Union*, Oslo: Scandinavian University Press.

Lewin, L. (1988) *Ideology and Strategy: A Century of Swedish Politics*, Cambridge: Cambridge University Press.

Lindwall, J. and B. Rothstein (2006) 'Sweden: The Fall of the Strong State', *Scandinavian Political Studies* 29: 47–63.

Lipset, S. M. and S. Rokkan (1967) 'Cleavage Structures, Party Systems and Voter Alignments: An Introduction', in S. M. Lipset and S. Rokkan (eds) *Party Systems and Voter Alignments: Cross-national Perspectives*, New York: Free Press.

Miller, K. E. (1991) *Denmark: A Troubled Welfare State*, Boulder, CO: Westview Press.

Olsen, J. P. (1983) *Organized Democracy: Political Institutions in a Welfare State: The Case of Norway*, Bergen: Universitetsforlaget.

Olson, M. (1990) *How Bright are the Northern Lights? Some Questions about Sweden*, Lund: Lund University Press.

Petersson, O. (1994) *The Government and Politics of the Nordic Countries*, Stockholm: Fritzes.

Raunio, T. and T. Tiilikainen (2003) *Finland in the European Union*, London: Frank Cass.

Østerud, Ø. and P. Selle (2006) 'Power and Democracy in Norway: The Transformation of Norwegian Politics', *Scandinavian Political Studies* 29: 25–46.

Elections

Aardal, B. (ed.) (2003) *Velgere i villrede . . .: En analyse av stortingsvalget 2001*, Oslo: Damm.

Andersen, J. G., J. Andersen, O. Borre, K. M. Hansen and H. J. Nielsen (eds) (2007) *Det nye politiske landskab: Folketingsvalget 2005 i perspektiv*, Copenhagen: Academica.

Grofman, B. and A. Lijphart (eds) (2002) *The Evolution of Electoral and Party Systems in the Nordic Countries*, New York: Agathon Press.

Holmberg, S. (2004) *Väljare: svenskt väljarbeteende under 50 år*, Stockholm: Norstedts.

Parties

Arter, D. (ed.) (2001) *From Farmyard to City Square?: The Electoral Adaptation of the Nordic Agrarian Parties*, Aldershot: Ashgate.

Berglund, S. and U. Lindström (1978) *The Scandinavian Party System(s)*, Lund: Studentlitteratur.

Gilljam, M. and H. Oscarsson (1996) 'Mapping the Nordic Party Space', *Scandinavian Political Studies* 19: 25–43.

Grendstad, G. (2003) 'Reconsidering Nordic Party Space', *Scandinavian Political Studies* 26: 193–217.

Heidar, K. and K. Pedersen (2006) 'Party Feminism: Gender Gaps within Nordic Political Parties', *Scandinavian Political Studies* 29: 192–218.

Karvonen, L. (1993) 'In from the Cold? Christian Parties in Scandinavia', *Scandinavian Political Studies* 16: 25–48.

Widfeldt, A. (2007) *The Extreme Right in Scandinavia*, London: Routledge.

Parliaments

Arter, D. (1984) *The Nordic Parliaments: A Comparative Analysis*, London: Hurst.

Bergman, T. and E. Damgaard (eds) (2000) *Delegation and Accountability in European Integration: The Nordic Parliamentary Democracies and the European Union*, London: Frank Cass.

Damgaard, E. (ed.) (1992) *Parliamentary Change in the Nordic Countries*, Oslo: Universitetsforlaget.

Esaiasson, P. and K. Heidar (eds) (2000) *Beyond Westminster and Congress: The Nordic Experience*, Columbus, OH: Ohio State University Press.

Raaum, N. C. (2005) 'Gender Equality and Political Representation: A Nordic Comparison', *West European Politics* 28: 872–97.

Governments

Arter, D. (2006) 'The Prime Minister in Scandinavia: "Superstar" or supervisor?', *Journal of Legislative Studies* 10: 109–27.

Bergman, T. (ed.) (2004) 'Special Issue: Parliamentary Democracy in Scandinavia: Shifting Dimensions of Citizen Control', *Scandinavian Political Studies* 27: 2.

Damgaard, E. and H. Jensen (2005) 'Europeanisation of Executive–Legislative Relations: Nordic Perspectives', *Journal of Legislative Studies* 11: 394–411.

Indridason, I. H. (2005) 'A Theory of Coalition and Clientelism: Coalition Politics in Iceland, 1945–2000', *European Journal of Political Research* 44: 439–64.

Mattila, M. (1997) 'From Qualified Majority to Simple Majority: The Effects of the 1992 Change in the Finnish Constitution', *Scandinavian Political Studies* 20: 331–45.

Mattila, M. and T. Raunio (2002) 'Government Formation in the Nordic Countries: The Electoral Connection', *Scandinavian Political Studies* 25: 259–80.

Miller, K. E. (1996) *Friends and Rivals: Coalition Politics in Denmark, 1901–1995*, Lanham, MD: University Press of America.

Müller, W. and K. Strøm (eds) (2000) *Coalition Governments in Western Europe*, Oxford: Oxford University Press.

Paloheimo, H. (2003) 'The Rising Power of the Prime Minister in Finland', *Scandinavian Political Studies* 26: 219–43.

Strøm, K. (1990) *Minority Government and Majority Rule*, Cambridge: Cambridge University Press.

Woldendorp, J., H. Keman and I. Budge (2000) *Party Government in 48 Democracies (1945–1998): Composition – Duration – Personnel*, Dordrecht: Kluwer.

Inter-institutional relations

Baldersheim, H. and K. Ståhlberg (2002) 'From Guided Democracy to Multi-level Governance: Trends in Central–Local Relations in the Nordic Countries', *Local Government Studies* 28 (3): 74–90.

Bjørnå, H. and S. Jenssen (2006) 'Prefectoral Systems and Central–Local Government Relations in Scandinavia', *Scandinavian Political Studies* 29: 308–32.

Blom-Hansen, J. (2000) 'Still Corporatism in Scandinavia? A Survey of Recent Empirical Findings', *Scandinavian Political Studies* 23: 157–81.

Elvander, N. (2002) 'The Labour Market Regimes in the Nordic Countries: A Comparative Analysis', *Scandinavian Political Studies* 25: 117–37.

Pallesen, T. (2006) 'Scandinavian Corporatism in a Trans-Atlantic Comparative Perspective', *Scandinavian Political Studies* 29: 131–45.

CHAPTER 9

The European Union
A Federal, Democratic Empire?

Josep M. Colomer

The aim of achieving an 'ever closer union' between European states, as is literally mentioned in the Treaty of Rome in 1957, evokes the aim of forming a 'more perfect union' included at the very beginning of the 1787 constitution of the United States of America. In a similar way to the American case the union was developed mainly as a self-protecting mechanism for newly independent states against the former colonial power and other foreign threats, that is, for reasons of war there were also some military reasons for the initial project of building the United States of Europe.

The union of Europe was promoted by some European leaders by mid-twentieth century mainly as a reaction to frequent military conflicts between European states, usually involving France and Germany, as well as domestic civil wars and political instability, culminating in the Second World War in 1939–45. The further expansionist policy of the Soviet Union, as demonstrated with the occupation and domination of Central Europe, and most dramatically with the division of Germany, also reinforced the incentives for Western European states to create a common defence, in addition to relying upon the military protection of the United States. Later on, Southern countries also sought membership as a guarantee against the re-emergence of past military dictatorships. Recent members in Eastern Europe had been victims of either the German expansion in the early 1940s or the further Soviet expansion at the end of the Second World War, or both.

The union of Europe began thus as a military enterprise. After the establishment of the North Atlantic Treaty Organisation (NATO) led by the United States in 1949, a first attempt was made to create a European Defence Community in 1952, which failed after being rejected by the French National Assembly. A second attempt, more

creation of the Western European Union

al economic agreements among several
reduce competition for strategic resources
auses of war. Six states – Belgium, France,
herlands – created the European Coal and
ll as the European Economic Community
Community (Euratom) with the Treaty of
nunities (ECSC, EEC and Euratom) even-
nity (EC), which formed a single Council
. Particularly influential political leaders in
onnet, as well as the French Minister Robert
rad Adenauer, the Italian Prime Minister
Democrats, and the Belgian Prime Minister,

oser' union has been driven by the aim of
an by direct military initiatives. So far, the
has been highly successful in diffusing the
, in this way preventing the emergence of
r states of the union. Building Europe-wide
asic consensus among its member states on
ay to prevent inter-state wars. Strengthening
naintenance and establishment of democratic
d among potential new candidates to join the

selves have been found to suffer from 'demo-
y, the political institutions of the European
ons corresponding to an international organ-
nion, but falling somewhere in between. First,
mid-1986, the institutional relations of the
nternational or diplomatic organisation shaped
according to the so-called intergovernmental
e Council of Ministers, which was formed by
f the member states. As they considered them-
ate had a power of veto over collective decisions,
made by unanimity. Actually, many important
by unanimity – at summit meetings of heads of
lised as the European Council in 1974.
l organisation the EEC was remarkably inno-
ial and agricultural common market by lowering
ers and to establish common external tariffs.
odel of decision-making significantly curbed
reaty established that by 1965 the Council of
Ministers would replace unanimity rule for decision-making with majority rule for
selected matters. But the French government reached to maintain the right of veto
of each member state in the Council 'when very important interests were at stake'

by the so-called 'Luxembourg compromise' in 1966. This proved to be highly ineffective, especially after successive enlargements of the EC from six to twelve member states, including the United Kingdom of Britain, Denmark and Ireland in 1973, Greece in 1981, and Portugal and Spain in 1986. A single member's veto was able to paralyse any initiative. The intergovernmental model led to a period of stagnation in the 1980s, also called 'Eurosclerosis' and 'Europessimism'.

In reaction, from the approval of the Single European Act in 1986 on, the EC accepted that certain decisions could be made by less than unanimity rules, typically qualified majorities, and subsequently enforced only by a subset of member states. This institutional model has been called 'reinforced', 'closer' or 'enhanced' cooperation, as well as 'asymmetry', 'variable geometry', 'concentric circles', 'strong core', 'two speeds', 'à la carte', 'flexible', and other metaphors. It has permitted much more effective decision-making than the previous intergovernmental model, especially on matters concerning completion of the single market programme. New decisions by these rules include the social chapter of the European Community, which does not encompass the United Kingdom, the Schengen agreement on border controls, which affects a different subset of countries, and the single currency, the euro, which was initially accepted by only 12 of the then 15 member states (although it was expanded later).

Since the creation of the EU by the Maastricht Treaty in 1992, more federal-oriented institutional relations have developed. These brought about an even further reduction of the fields in which unanimity decisions are required and a more significant role for the European Parliament, which is the only directly elected European institution. Different provisions were introduced in order to promote decision-making by a combination of a qualified majority of the Council of Ministers and a simple majority of the European Parliament. With these procedures, representatives of the territorial units share decision power with representatives of the people of the EU at large. The principle of territorial representation is made compatible with the possibility of making enforceable decisions for all countries – in contrast to the limits imposed by the 'asymmetry' model – as would correspond to the typical institutional formula of a democratic federation. Under this framework, new enlargements of the EU up to twenty-seven members were implemented with the accession, first, of Austria, Finland and Sweden in 1995, of Cyprus, the Czech Republic, Estonia, Hungary, Latvia, Lithuania, Malta, Poland, Slovakia and Slovenia in 2004, and of Bulgaria and Romania in 2007. (Norway remained out of the EU institutions after two failed referendums for membership, in 1972 and 1994, although it belongs to the European Economic Space, forming a common market, and cooperates with the European institutions on interior, defence and security policies.)

The processes of successive enlargements and internal institutionalisation of the European Union have not always matched well. The territorial expansion of the EU was accelerated: the first enlargement with three new members took almost twenty years; further enlargements of three members each were then approved in successive lapses of about ten years each; but on the latest occasion no less than twelve new members joined. In parallel, institutional instability was also increasing. The founding Treaty of Rome was modified only after almost thirty years by the Single European Act; but from that moment on a series of treaties were approved within increasingly short periods: Maastricht, Amsterdam, Nice. After a failed attempt to produce a single constitutional text, the Treaty of Lisbon was approved in 2007, but only to be enforced from 2014 on. Putting an end to the long process of unlimited territorial expansion appeared then as a necessary condition for the European Union to achieve internal institutional stability.

In certain journalistic and political literature one can hear that the institutional formulas of the European Union are 'unique', 'exceptional' or 'unprecedented'. However, an experience which is widely considered to be somewhere in between the models of international organisation and of federal state may fit the traditional notion of 'empire' quite well. Like other great empires in the past and the present, the European Union is indeed a very large political unit (currently with the third largest population in the world), it is organised with diverse institutional formulas across the territory, and has multiple, overlapping institutional levels of governance – including Europe-wide institutions, states, self-governed territories inside large states, Euroregions crossing state borders, counties, municipalities and metropolitan areas. Indeed the motto of the EU is 'unity in diversity'.

In contrast to critical self-assertions in traditional states, the European structure of multi-level governance implies that no unit is actually 'sovereign' in the sense of being a superior, exclusionary source of power. In contrast, separation of powers among institutions for different policy issues, as well as power sharing, is a crucial characteristic of the relations between the European Union and the other levels of government across the territory. According to the so-called principle of subsidiarity, which was adopted in the Treaty of the European Union, each policy issue should be allocated to the lowest possible institutional level able to fulfil the corresponding competence with sufficient effectiveness.

As is typical of empires, the European Union has expanded continuously outward, from the initial six to the current twenty-seven members, with no fixed territorial limits. There are still more than a dozen potential candidates for membership. The territorial limits for an empire are only those of another empire. In this case a logical limit should be Russia, which has been shrinking since the dissolution of the Soviet empire in 1991. It may seem logical to expect, in particular, that the region of the Balkans, which is completely circled by EU territory, would be liberalised, democratised and stably pacified if it were integrated in the Union. However, only one country out of seven in the region, Slovenia, is a member of the EU, and one more, Croatia, has been formally accepted as candidate. If the European Union stopped its fifty-year process of steady expansion short of the limits of Russia, it would produce frustrated expectations and perhaps significant discontent and instability among the excluded.

Only under conditions of stable membership and territorial stability may the European Union be able to design a relatively durable internal institutional frame-work. A similar dilemma between further enlargements and internal stabilisation was faced about one hundred years ago in the process of building the American union, after more than one hundred years of territorial expansion, diverse institutional formulas in different territories and weak federal coordination. As happened in the United States of America, only when the borders of the union will be established within the limits of moderate heterogeneity and capability of assimilation can well-proved formulas of federal union be applied also at the European level.

In the following pages, the main European Union institutions are analysed from the perspective here outlined. The EU can indeed be studied with standard analytical tools, approaching the legislative, the executive and the judiciary, as well as its multi-level governance. We will keep the same order for the presentation of the political institutions of each European state as is used in the previous chapters, so that comparisons can more easily be made, although it is not the most usual order found in other presentations of the European Union.

We start with the analysis of the institution organising the representation of the European people at large: the direct elections to the European Parliament and the formation of large political parties of increasingly Europe-wide scope. This helps to understand the increasing capability of the European Parliament to make decisions supported by multi-party majorities. Then, we turn to the main institution representing the member states: the Council of Ministers, which can be understood as a second chamber of territorial representation. Finally, we examine the European Commission, which can be considered to constitute the EU's executive, as well as the European Council, which acts as a kind of presidency in the summit.

Next, we examine how recent inter-institutional processes of decision-making involving the Parliament, the Council and the Commission have given relatively high effectiveness to such a complex institutional framework. Other institutions are also reviewed, including the Court of Justice and the European Central Bank, which have significant separate powers, as well as two advisory committees, the Economic and Social Committee and the Committee of the Regions. The chapter concludes with an assessment of past events and a bet on the future.

ELECTIONS

The largest member states of the European Union – Germany, Britain, France, Italy, Spain, Poland and Romania – are under-represented in the European Parliament in terms of seats per population, while the other twenty countries are over-represented. Over-representation of small unit members is a typical feature in federal unions, although the level of mal-apportionment of the European Parliament is relatively high when compared to that of lower chambers in democratic states. The number of inhabitants per seat is about twelve times higher in Germany, ten times in Britain, France and Italy, and so on, than in Luxembourg and Malta.

All countries use some formula of proportional representation for the direct popular election of the members of the European Parliament (EP). But there is no single European electoral system; each member state can adopt its own rules, which tend to be similar to the rules used in national elections. The most visible exceptions are Britain and France, which use majoritarian rules for state-wide elections but proportional representation for the European Parliament.

Most states use the d'Hondt formula of proportional representation, but Germany and Italy use the Hare formula, Sweden uses modified Sainte-Laguë, and Ireland and Northern Ireland, as well as Malta, use Droop. Candidates have to pass a threshold of 5 per cent of votes in the Czech Republic, France, Germany, Hungary, Lithuania, Poland and Slovakia, of 4 per cent in Austria and Sweden, and of 3 per cent in Greece to obtain representation. As every member state is allocated fewer seats in the European Parliament than seats in its national parliament, most states elect their Euro-deputies in a single, very large district, although some states have adopted a few, still large regional districts (Belgium, Britain, France, Germany, Ireland, Italy, Poland). The corresponding large district magnitudes allow all the variety of formulas just mentioned to produce significantly proportional allocations of seats to parties on the basis of the popular vote.

Regarding the individual selection of deputies, different procedures are used in different states. An open ballot allowing the voter to choose candidates from different lists is used in Luxembourg. Ireland, Northern Ireland and Malta use transferable ordinal votes. Most states use preferential ballots by which the voter can choose individual candidates within a list. Only a few use categorical ballots by which the voter cannot modify the order of candidates given in closed lists, including France, Germany, Greece, Portugal and Spain.

Turnout in European elections is always lower than in state-wide elections. This may correspond to the lower level of influential decisions per capita that the European institutions can make compared with state-wide institutions. If the potential benefits of decisions made at each institutional level for the average citizen were measured, for instance, by the corresponding proportions of per capita public expenditure under their jurisdiction, the 'importance' of states would still be about thirty times higher than that of the European Union. This admittedly rough measure is just a suggestion that the calculus of individual benefits and costs of voting should produce lower levels of turnout for European elections. This finding is also consistent with what usually happens at regional and local elections as compared to state-wide elections.

The average turnout in the elections to the European Parliament has slowly declined from the first election: it was 63 per cent in 1979, 61 per cent in 1984, 59 per cent in 1989, 57 per cent in 1994, 50 per cent in 1999 and 46 per cent in 2004. An important part of these variations can be explained by the fact that some European elections concurred with state or local elections, especially in the earliest periods, which increases the incentives to go to the polls, while separate elections tend to produce lower turnout. In the EP election of 2004, the most extreme values were produced, on the one hand, in countries with compulsory voting, such as Belgium and Luxembourg, with more than 90 per cent, and, on the other hand, in new members like the Czech Republic, with 28 per cent, and Poland, with 21 per cent. In spite of all this, the average turnout for the European Parliament elections is still higher than, for instance, that for the United States Congress in mid-term elections, that is, those not coinciding with presidential elections.

Although the European Parliament elections are held simultaneously in all member states over a period of four days, the formation of candidacies, the selection of issues and the campaign strategies are primarily conducted in a domestic framework. Only a handful of deputies in the European Parliament have been elected in countries other than their own (although a number of other members of the EP are dual nationals). The media usually offer citizens of any country more information on separate state campaigns and elections in other countries than on European election campaigns in other countries, since the latter overlap with the corresponding simultaneous domestic campaign. According to these characteristics, the European

Parliament's elections have been termed 'second-order national elections' for having more of a character of domestic 'midterms' than of true European events.

Just as in midterm congressional elections in the United States a significant number of voters choose to vote against the incumbent President's party, similarly in European elections some voters choose to vote against the incumbent government's party in their country. This behaviour helps to produce different party compositions in the European institutions based on representatives of the member states' governments and in the European Parliament.

PARTIES AND PARTY SYSTEM

Paralleling successive enlargements of the EC/EU with new member states, increasing numbers of different political parties have obtained representation in the European Parliament, up to about 170 in 2004. As mentioned, no Europe-wide significant aggregation is developed at the stages of forming candidacies, the electoral campaign and voting. Yet, interestingly, the increase in the number of state-wide or regional parties in the European Parliament has not caused a similar growth in the total number of European political groups, that is, the aggregative Europe-wide parties that parties form within the Parliament. On the contrary, the degree of concentration of deputies in a few groups has significantly increased over time.

The formation of increasingly large, aggregative Europe-wide political groups in the European Parliament during the late twentieth and early twenty-first centuries can be compared to certain processes of forming increasingly large, aggregative state-wide political parties in state parliaments of European countries during the late nineteenth and early twentieth centuries (as, for instance, in Britain, France, Germany and Spain). Many political representatives of the time were strongly rooted in local constituencies and promoted local interests with no clear priorities on large-scale issues, while holding vague ideological positions. The parallel with the present EU institutions can be extended to the fact that some state parliaments at the time were relatively weak in making the executive accountable (especially in the monarchies).

At that time, the aggregation of local representatives in state-wide parties created higher policy and ideology homogeneity among political representatives while contributing to reinforcing the role of parliaments, in a way comparable to that in which the aggregation of state representatives in European political groups is now promoting more effective decision-making and contributing to giving the European Parliament more institutional strength. To the extent that local parties are submitted to majority decisions within large European political groups and to the corresponding group's voting discipline in the Parliament, nationalistic positions against an ever closer union of Europe have lower prominence in the institutional process.

From state parties to European parties

Generally, state-wide or regional political parties face a dilemma with respect to their mode of representation in the European Parliament. They can choose either to try to lead a small European political group, and hence be highly influential within this group, or to join a larger European political group that is more influential in the Parliament, within which they may, however, have little influence.

The rules for forming European political groups are rather permissive. According to the Rules of Procedure for the European Parliament enforced in 2007, a European political group can be formed by twenty deputies if they come from at least six member states. Once the European political groups have formed, every group makes decisions on the basis of a majority of its members. State party members are submitted to the internal voting discipline of the European political group to which they belong. Under rather flexible requirements for forming European political groups, after the election in 2004 fewer than 2 per cent of the deputies were unable to become members of European political groups (and thus forced to join the group of 'Non-Attached').

As will be seen in more detail, the aggregative effort was developed at different paths on the centre-left, the centre-right and in the centre. Within the centre-left, a rather strong degree of concentration into the European Socialist Party can be observed from the first election in 1979. On its left, the European Communist Group was dominated by the Italian Communists (PCI), the largest party on the left of the political spectrum in Italy at the time, as it had more than 50 per cent of the seats of the group. Yet, when the Communist Group became decreasingly powerful within the European Parliament, the PCI made an initial somewhat costly move by creating its own group, the European United Left, together with a few minor partners, in 1989. This ended up being only an intermediate step, since at the following election, in 1994, the Italian Communists, already transformed into the Party of Democratic Left (PDS), entered the European Socialist Party. Pluralism within the centre-left increased with the creation of the Rainbow Group in 1984 and 1989 and the Radical Alliance in 1994, as well as the emerging Greens since 1989, but only the latter survived after the election of 1999.

The evolution of political parties was more intricate within the centre-right. Together with the larger European People's Party, three small European political groups in the centre-right space were initially created: the Democratic Group, the Democratic Alliance and Forza Europa. The Democratic Group was dominated by the British Conservatives, as they always had more than 50 per cent of the seats in the group. The Spanish Popular Party provisionally joined the Democratic Group after Spain entered the EC; then the Democratic Group became quite powerful, even holding the presidency of the European Parliament in 1986–9. Yet at the subsequent election in 1989 (the first one for the Spaniards), the Spanish Popular Party, faced with what still would be an absolute majority of Britons in the group, moved to the European People's Party. In 1992 the weakened British Conservatives, followed by their previous Danish minor partner, also moved into the European People's Party, in spite of significant policy and ideological differences in their traditional positions, including with regard to further EU union and enlargement.

The Group of Democratic Alliance was dominated by the French Gaullists (Assembly for the Republic, RPR), as they always had more than 50 per cent of the seats in the group. Most French Christian Democrats, Liberal and Republican candidates who were included in the Union of French Democracy (UDF) coalition in domestic politics and had run separately from the Gaullists in previous elections to the European Parliament, ran together with them in 1989 and in 1994. Yet after each election they split into different groups once in the Parliament: the Gaullist-dominated Democratic Alliance, the Liberal Group and, in increasing numbers, the People's Party. The Gaullists gained the temporary support of Let's Go Italy (Forza Italia, the new largest centre-right party in Italian domestic politics after the crisis of the Christian Democrats), which dissolved its own previous group, Forza Europa, and merged with the Gaullists in the new group Union for Europe. Yet, shortly before the end of the 1994 legislature, Let's Go Italy joined the European People's Party and, after the election of 1999, persuaded its Gaullist former partner to do the same. On the other hand, a minor Portuguese party, the Democratic and Social Centre (CDS), left the People's Party after the 1994 election on the basis of its anti-EU stand. Yet the major centre-right Portuguese party, the Social Democratic Party (PSD), previously in the Liberal Group, moved to the People's Party during the 1994 legislature, thus globally increasing the Portuguese membership in the group. Reflecting its pluralistic aggregation, the group was renamed the 'European People's Party (Christian Democrats) and European Democrats'.

The European People's Party has, thus, not only gathered together Christian Democratic parties from eight countries (Belgium, France, Germany, Greece, Ireland, Italy, Luxembourg, the Netherlands). It has gradually integrated other parties previously belonging to separate European groups and from countries without strong traditions of Christian democracy, including the Conservatives from Britain, Denmark and Spain, populist parties from France and Italy, and new conservative groups from the Czech Republic, Hungary, Poland and other Eastern countries. Most of the non-Christian Democratic centre-right parties have held nationalistic positions and rather reluctant stands on further advances towards a closer union of Europe. But on joining the European People's Party they expected to enhance the global power of the group within the European Parliament. The rationale of these moves is that each party can expect to have more global influence within the Parliament by being member of a large, powerful European political group, such as the People's Party, than by forming its own small, weak European political group.

A comparable evolution can be observed in the centre of the political spectrum around the Liberal Group. It not only included classical liberal parties from Belgium, Britain, Denmark, Finland, Germany, the Netherlands and Sweden, but other parties with radical or Christian Democratic precedents in France, Italy, the Netherlands, as well as new groups from Bulgaria, Estonia, Lithuania and Romania.

The European party system

As a result of the aggregative effort developed by political parties to form large Europe-wide parties, the effective number of European political groups (EPGs) has significantly decreased since the first election to the European Parliament in 1979. The 'effective number' takes into account the relative size of each party, in this way measuring the degree of concentration of individual representatives in large parties (according to the formula given in Table 9.1). In spite of representing twenty-seven

Table 9.1 Political pluralism in the European Union, 1979–2007

	Member states		Political parties	European political groups	
	Number	Effective no.	No.	No.	Effective no.
1979	9	6.0	41	8	5.2
1984	10	6.6	46	9	5.3
1989	12	8.2	70	11	5.0
1994	12	8.1	95	10	4.6
1999	15	9.5	110	8	4.0
2004/07	27	10.8	170	9	4.3

Note: Data correspond to the initial composition of the European Parliament after every election, plus the representatives from Bulgaria and Romania added in 2007. The 'effective number' (N) reflects the number and the relative size of the units represented; it is calculated according to the formula $N = 1/\Sigma p_i^2$, where p is the proportion of seats of member state, party or group i.

member states with their own political regimes and party systems, the European Parliament has a similar level of aggregation (as measured by the effective number of parties) than the parliaments of several European countries, such as Belgium, Denmark, Finland and the Netherlands.

More specifically, both the absolute number and the effective number of member states of the EC/EU considerably increased between 1979 and 2007: the absolute number of member states grew from 9 to 27, while the effective number of member states, weighting for their size, has increased accordingly from 6 to 10.8 (except for a small adjustment at the time of the German reunification, since it created a larger member state). The number of Eurodeputies has also increased at every enlargement, from 410 in 1979 to 785 in 2007. Logically, the number of political parties gaining representation in the European Parliament has also increased, from 41 in 1979 to 170 in the election of 2004 and further enlargement. Yet the absolute number of European political groups, which increased twice during the first period, from 8 to 11, decreased afterwards, from 11 to 9. (The numbers are from 6 to 10 and then to 8 if the Non-Attached and independents' Groups are not counted.) The effective number of European political groups, as weighted by their size and thus reflecting the degree of aggregation from an increasingly pluralistic setting of elected parties, has decreased from a value of 5.2 in 1979 to 4.3 in 2007.

The European political groups can be located on the left–right axis, consistent with most state parliaments. The relevance of the left–right dimension in the European Parliament and the location of the European political groups has been analysed with empirical data, finding that coalitions form on the basis of ideology, not nationality. Five major party positions of European political groups from left to right can be distinguished:

1   left: the Communists in 1979 and 1984, the Communist-dominated United and Nordic Left and the European United Left in 1989, and the European United Left/Nordic Green left since 1994;

2   centre-left: the groups formed by the Socialists in the six elections from 1979 to

2004, the Rainbow in 1984 and 1989, the Radicals in 1994 and the Greens since 1989;

3   centre: the Liberals in the six elections;

4   centre-right: the People's (mostly Christian Democrats) in the five elections, the Conservative Democrats in 1979, 1984 and 1989, the Gaullist Democratic Alliance in 1979, 1984, 1989 and 1994, Forza Europa in 1994 and Europe of Nations since 1994;

5   right: the Right in 1984 and 1989, Democracies and Diversities in 1999, and Independence and Democracy as well as Identity, Tradition, Sovereignty in 2004. The Non-Attached in 1994 can be included in this cluster due to it rightist and nationalist composition.

'Moderate' parties have tended to prevail in the European Parliament. The European Socialist Party has integrated parties from all the member states since the first election in 1979 (with the exception of Ireland in 1984, Cyprus and Latvia in 2004). The European People's Party included parties from only seven out of nine member states in 1979, but representatives from all member states are included since 1989. In all elections since 1979, the European Socialist Party and the European People's Party together have gathered more than 50 per cent of the total number of seats, from 54 per cent in 1979 to 63 per cent in 2007.

Table 9.2 The European Parliament: seats of European political groups, 1979–2007

	Left	Centre-left		Centre	Centre-right				Right			
	Communist UL	Green G	Ra	Socialist PS	Liberal LD	People PP	Conservatives DG	DA	EN	Right DD	IT	Others NA	Total
1979	44	–	–	113	40	107	64	22	–		–	9/11	410
1984	41	–	20	130	31	110	50	29	–	16	–	7	434
1989	14/28	29	14	180	49	121	34	22	–	17	–	10	518
1994	28	23	19	198	43	157	27	26	19	27	–	–	567
1999	42	48	–	180	50	233	–	–	30	16	–	27	626
2004/07	41	42	–	218	106	277	–	–	44	23	20	14	785

Note:

Communist: UL: Communist (1979, 1984), Left Unity (1989), United Left (1989), United and Nordic Left (1994, 1999, 2004).

Green: G: Green/Free Alliance (1989, 1994, 1999, 2004); Ra: Rainbow (1984, 1989), Radicals (1994).

Socialist: PS: Socialist Party (1979, 1984, 1989, 1994, 1999, 2004).

Liberal: LD: Liberal, Democrat and Reform (1979, 1984, 1989, 1994, 1999, 2004).

People: PP: People's Party (1979, 1984, 1989, 1994), People's (Christian Democrat) and Democrat (1999, 2004).

Conservatives: DG: Democratic Group (1979, 1984, 1989); FE: Forza Europa (1994); DA: Democratic Alliance (1979, 1984, 1989, 1994); EN: Europe of Nations (1994, 1999, 2004).

Right: DD: European Right (1984, 1989), Non-Attached (1994), Democracies and Diversities (1999), Independence and Democracy (2004); IT: Identity, Tradition, Sovereignty (2004).

Others: NA: Coordination Defence of Independents (1979), Non-Attached (1979, 1984, 1989, 1999, 2004).

The smaller group of the Liberals, always third in number of seats, is usually placed in an intermediate position between the Socialist and the People's Group when measured on a left–right ideological scale. Hence, a 'connected' winning coalition could always be formed with the Socialists, the Liberals and the People's Group. This scheme based on these three European political groups closely resembles the domestic party structure in Germany, and it is not dissimilar to the distribution of parties in Belgium, the Netherlands and Luxembourg, as examined in previous chapters of this book.

THE EUROPEAN PARLIAMENT

The European Parliament is popularly elected every five years. Its members can be re-elected indefinitely and often they are. Many of them have followed some previous political career at local, regional or state levels. The official seat of the European Parliament is in Strasbourg, France, but most of its committee meetings and an increasing number of plenary sessions are held in Brussels, Belgium.

In contrast to the state parliaments in parliamentary regimes, the European Parliament has no legislative initiative, although with some frequency it is able to put new issues on the EU agenda. The Parliament has significant decision powers, together with the Council, especially on single market issues and most economic, social, environmental, research and technology, and cultural policy areas. It also shares significant powers with the Council in the process of approving the budget of the EU. Disagreements between the Parliament and the Council regarding legislation are negotiated at the Conciliation Committee. The European Parliament also has significant powers in the appointment and dismissal of the European Commission and its President, as well as in approving appointments of independent institutions made by the Council. The Parliament appoints the EU Ombudsman.

The President of the Parliament is elected every two and a half years, which permits two-party agreements on turning between two candidates in a single legislature. Different two-party majorities have been formed to elect the President of the European Parliament: on the centre-left between the Socialists and the Liberals in 1979, on the right between the People's Group and the Conservatives in 1984, on the centre-right between the People's Group and the Liberals in 1999, and grand coalitions between the Socialists and the People's Group in 1989, 1994 and 2004. In total, since the first direct election of the Parliament in 1979, there have been five Popular, four Socialist, two Liberal and one Conservative presidents. The European Parliament is organised into twenty permanent committees (as well as a few temporary committees and subcommittees), which is a relatively high number in comparison with state parliaments – a sign of its ability to make decisions with relatively high effectiveness.

Available data show remarkably high and increasing degrees of parliamentarians' participation and internal cohesion of the European political groups in the European Parliament. Participation of individual members of the European Parliament in voting sessions increased from about 48 per cent in 1989–94 to 61 per cent in 1994–9 and to 72 per cent in 1999–2000. The highest levels of attendance correspond to the largest groups – the People's Group, the Socialists, the Liberals and the Greens – all of them above the average, with values between 73 and 77 per cent. Internal cohesion of the European political groups has also increased steadily during successive legislative periods. Calculations on the basis of roll-call votes show that the average proportions of individual members of the Parliament voting in accordance with their European political group rises over time: from 74 per cent in 1984–9, to 84 per cent in 1989–94, 88 per cent in 1994–9 and 90 per cent in 1999–2000. Specifically, the largest groups – the People's Group, the Socialists, the Liberals and the Greens – have reached the highest degrees of discipline in voting, at between 90 and 95 per cent. Internal cohesion of European political groups in the European Parliament is higher than that of political parties in the United States Congress.

The European political groups in the European Parliament tend to form connected winning coalitions (CWC), that is, coalitions between ideologically neighbour parties on the left–right axis, regardless of the size of the coalition. This behaviour corresponds to the specific set of institutional incentives provided by the role of the Parliament within the European Union framework. On the one hand, on the basis of the possibility of successive re-elections, the Euro-deputies develop significant electoral and policy motives, leading the European political groups to prefer close, 'connected' partners rather than more distant ones. On the other hand, since, in contrast to what happens in state parliaments in parliamentary regimes, they don't elect executive offices to be spoiled, they can agree to form surplus voting coalitions with numerically superfluous partners because this doesn't reduce the share of power that each party can obtain.

Within the set of viable CWCs, there is some variation depending on the subject matter, but always including the centre. A centre-left majority, including the Socialists and the Liberals as its core (with the Greens joining often), dominates on civil liberties, foreign affairs and the environment. The majority built around the centre by the Socialist, the Liberal and the People's groups dominated on constitutional, institutional and budgetary affairs. Centre-right coalitions based on the Liberal and the People's groups dominated on economic affairs, industry, budget control and employment. Although the largest numbers of seats are in the hands of the Socialist and the People's groups, the Liberals achieved relatively high influence in forming coalitions by bargaining and voting, due to their intermediate position always holding the decisive median seat. The other groups are relatively less influential than could be expected from their proportions of seats. (Figures on parliamentarians' participation, cohesion, voting and coalitions are the author's calculations using data from the European Parliament.)

◼ THE COUNCIL AS A SECOND CHAMBER

The Council of Ministers of the European Union is formed by representatives of the twenty-seven EU member states at 'ministerial level' (which means that not only members of the state government but also regional ministers can attend and even chair, as will be discussed below). Meetings of the Council at the highest level are held monthly, mostly in Brussels and sometimes in Luxembourg. They are chaired by the representative of the member state that holds the presidency for six-month turns.

As previously mentioned, the Council has important co-decision powers with the European Parliament, especially on legislation regarding economic, social and related policy issues, as well as on the EU budget. The Council, however, can adopt common positions and joint actions of the EU member states in the fields of Common Foreign and Security Policy and in Cooperation on Justice and Home Affairs, typically by unanimity and on the basis of the guidelines established by the European Council. In addition, the Council has a strong role in the appointment of the European Commission and its President, as well as in the nomination of the President and the Executive Board of the European Central Bank, the President of the European Monetary Institute and the members of the Court of Auditors.

The Council is organised in nine sectoral councils. Each council is formed by the corresponding branch ministers of all member states, who meet roughly once every month (so with a total of about 100 council meetings a year). The most important sectoral council is the General Affairs Council, which is formed by the member states' Ministers of Foreign Affairs and, in most cases, also the minister or secretary of state in charge of European Affairs. In 1999 the Council appointed a Secretary-General and High Representative of the EU for the Common Foreign and Security Policy, Javier Solana, a former Secretary-General of NATO, who also became Secretary-General of the Western European Union for a while. The High Representative in Foreign Affairs and Security Policy will also be vice-president of the European Commission.

Other prominent sectoral councils are the Economic and Financial Affairs Council (known as Ecofin) and the Agriculture and Fisheries Council. One of the most recently created councils is Justice and Home Affairs, which, in contrast to the others, was formed only by the ministers of those member states having agreed on developing a common policy on these issues. There are also informal meetings, including of several branch ministers together.

The Council of the EU is supported by the Committee of Permanent Representatives (Coreper), formed by career diplomats at the level of ambassadors, which meets weekly in Brussels. This structure is duplicated by a so-called Coreper-2, made up of the permanent representatives plus supporting staff, which also meets weekly. The Committee should prepare the work of the ministers in the Council, although usually it is considered to have a great influence on the decisions to be made.

According to the rules, which are expected to remain in force until 2014, each of the twenty-seven member states is given a number of weighted votes in the Council, from 29 votes to the four largest countries to 1 vote to the smallest ones, with a total of 345 votes, as shown in Table 9.3. The distribution of votes is significantly biased against the larger countries, in corresponding to the principle of territorial representation that would correspond to a federal upper chamber in a more structured institutional framework. Most decisions have to be made by a qualified majority of at least 255 votes out of 345 (about 74 per cent), which must include at least a majority of 14 out of the 27 member states. This rule creates the possibility of forming a 'blocking minority' able to prevent a new decision being made by three large member states together with any other state. An alternative, more demanding rule which is used for decisions not based on a proposal from the European Commission,

Table 9.3 Distribution of power in the European Union, 2009–14

	Population %	Parliament seats	%	Council votes	%	Commission members
Germany	17	99	13	29	8	1
United Kingdom	12	78	10	29	8	1
France	12	78	10	29	8	1
Italy	12	78	10	29	8	1
Spain	8	54	7	27	8	1
Poland	8	54	7	27	8	1
Romania	5	35	4	14	4	1
Netherlands	3	27	3	13	4	1
Greece	2	24	3	12	4	1
Czech Republic	2	24	3	12	4	1
Belgium	2	24	3	12	4	1
Hungary	2	24	3	12	4	1
Portugal	2	24	3	12	4	1
Sweden	2	19	2	10	4	1
Bulgaria	2	18	2	10	4	1
Austria	2	18	2	10	4	1
Slovakia	1	14	2	7	2	1
Finland	1	14	2	7	2	1
Denmark	1	13	2	7	2	1
Ireland	1	13	1	7	2	1
Lithuania	1	13	1	7	2	1
Latvia	1	9	1	4	1	1
Slovenia	1	7	1	4	1	1
Estonia	<1	6	1	4	1	1
Cyprus	<1	6	1	4	1	1
Luxembourg	<0.1	6	1	4	1	1
Malta	<0.1	5	1	3	1	1
Total	100	785	100	345	100	27
Qualified majority				255	74	

Note: Percentages are rounded by the method of the greatest remainders: the integers with the greatest remainders are rounded up until they sum 100, and then the other integers are rounded down.

requiring 255 out of 345 weighted votes and two-thirds (18 out of 27) of the member states. In all cases the votes must represent at least 62 per cent of the EU's total population.

With the new rules coming into force in the future, each member state will have a single vote in the Council, but decisions will be made by the so-called rule of 'double majority', which requires 55 per cent of the states (15 states with a membership of 27) to gather together 65 per cent of the EU's population. This rule is even more biased against the larger countries than the current formula, thus reinforcing the federal principle of territorial representation in the Council. By making decision-making in the Council more difficult, this rule may contribute to balancing inter-institutional relations in favour of the Parliament.

Qualified majorities in the Council are formed along several different dimensions by the member states. A major cleavage can be identified between rich Northern countries (including Britain, Germany, Sweden and Denmark), the intermediate Southerners (France, Italy, Spain, Portugal, Greece) and the relatively poorer Easterners (including Poland, Bulgaria, Romania and others). The first tend to support market-oriented policies, while the others favour, to different degrees, the regulation of certain aspects of market exchanges and subsidies for the production of certain crops. However, on some issues, territorial closeness tends to put together the so-called Franco-German axis, the Benelux countries, the Mediterranean 'late-comers' (Greece, Portugal and Spain) or the Nordic countries. Other subsets of countries are formed on different issues, such as environmental protection (usually including Austria, Denmark, Germany, Ireland, Luxembourg, Norway and Portugal), liberalisation of air transportation (including Belgium, Germany, Ireland, the Netherlands, Portugal and Spain) or security policy (with Belgium France, Germany, Luxembourg, the Netherlands and Spain forming the so-called Schengen group). The member states' policy positions on the left–right axis also vary with the political composition of governments at different moments, although most of them form multi-party coalitions.

At the same time, the size of winning coalitions formed by member states beyond the required voting thresholds does not seem to be very relevant. The rationale for this behaviour lies in the fact that the Council does not distribute significant offices among its members, which makes the expected benefits of decision-making inde-pendent of the number of coalition partners. Actually observers note that Council members usually attempt to make compromises in order to obtain the support of as many member states as possible for most decisions, instead of stopping negotiations when the necessary majority is reached, thus placing the Council on the side of consensual-style decision-making.

THE EXECUTIVE COMMISSION

Precedents for what would correspond to the European Union executive in a federal framework can be found in the High Authority of the European Coal and Steel Community, whose first president in 1952 was Jean Monnet, as well as in the presidencies of the European Economic Community and Euratom since 1958. With the merger of the three communities, the first European Commission was formed in 1967, although at that time with very limited powers and initiative.

The role of the Commission within the European Union institutional framework was crucially reshaped and enhanced during the presidency of Jacques Delors (1986–95), who had the longest tenure so far. Under Delors' presidency, the Commission played a very significant role in the completion of the European single market, in drawing up the blueprint for monetary union and the creation of the Euro, in introducing a new redistributive policy for higher 'cohesion' between the regions of Europe, and in coordinating the assistance to Eastern European countries undergoing democratisation which would become candidates for further EU enlargement.

In its present composition, the European Commission is formed by one member from each of the twenty-seven member states, but from 2014 it will have a rotating membership of only two-thirds of member states. Since the enforcement of the Treaty

Table 9.4 European Commission presidents, 1952–2009

E. Coal and Steel Community	E. Atomic Energy Community	E. Economic Community
1952–5 J. Monnet (France)		
1955–8 R. Mayer (France)		
1958–9 P. Finet (France)	1958–9 L. Armand (France)	
1959–63 P. Malvestiti (Italy)	1959–62 E. Hirsch (France)	
1963–67 R. Del Bo (Italy)	1962–7 P. Chatenet (France)	1958–67 W. Hallstein (Germany)

European Commission
1967–70   J. Rey (Belgium, Liberal)
1970–2   F. M. Malfatti (Italy, Christian Democrat)
1972–3   S. Mansholt (Netherlands, Labour)
1973–7   F.-X. Ortoli (France, Gaullist)
1977–81   R. Jenkins (Britain, Labour)
1981–5   G. Torn (Luxembourg, Liberal)
1986–95   J. Delors (France, Socialist)
1995–2000 J. Santer (Luxembourg, Christian Democrat)
2000–4   R. Prodi (Italy, Left)
2004–9   J.-M. D. Barroso (Portugal, Conservative)

of the EU, the Commissioners are appointed for a period of five years in order to coincide with the European Parliament's term. Within such a period, almost every member state holds elections that may change the party composition, the leadership or the personal composition of the corresponding state governments, as represented in the Council of the EU. This makes the European Commission quite independent from state governments and the political composition of the other EU institutions. The Commission meets weekly in Brussels.

The role of the Commission within the European Union institutional framework has evolved from an international secretariat, when intergovernmental relations prevailed, to some features corresponding to an EU executive. First, the Commission has the initiative to set the EU agenda, which corresponds to the usual role of the cabinet in a parliamentary regime. Formally, the founding Treaty of Rome already gave the Commission the responsibility to initiate legislation, although for a long period its proposals were usually consulted and even pre-negotiated with the member states as represented in the Council or the Coreper before being openly launched. Second, the Commission has an extended role throughout the legislative process to ensure that the treaties are applied, including the right to 'formulate recommendations and deliver opinions', a mediating role between the EU institutions and the member states, and the right to take a member state to the European Court of Justice. Third, the Commission has extensive executive powers, especially in areas delegated by the Council, such as Agriculture, as implemented by its management and administrative apparatus (about 25,000 people, roughly half of the total employed by the European institutions). Fourth, the Commission represents the European Union in other countries and in many international organisations.

Like the executive in a bicameral parliamentary regime, the Commission is appointed and can be dismissed by the decisive intervention of both the Council of the EU and the European Parliament. The process is as follows. First, the President of the Commission is nominated by the Council and must be approved by the Parliament. Second, the other commissioners are nominated by the Council (usually by the General Affairs Council), in consultation with the nominee for President, who can veto governments' nominees for commissioners and allocate portfolios to them. Then, the nominees for President and commissioners have to be approved or 'invested' by the Parliament, in practice since 1995 after a series of parliamentary hearings or interrogations. Also, the European Parliament can promote a motion of censure of the President of the European Commission or the Commission *en bloc*, leading to their dismissal if approved by a simple majority.

The internal organisation of the Commission increasingly resembles that of a state government. The Commissioners hold different portfolios roughly paralleling those of state ministers. Prominent portfolios within the Commission are Budget, Economic and Financial Affairs, Competition Policy, and Agriculture. The Commission is also organised in forty directorates-general (DGs) and specialised services, each reporting to a commissioner. However, the division of areas of competence among the DGs does not coincide with those of the Commissioners, most of whom have responsibility for more than one DG.

Decisions in the European Commission are made by an absolute majority of its members. The President does not control the agenda of meetings and, like the other commissioners, has only one vote. The members of the Commission, usually gathered around a round table, vote by a show of hands, but votes are recorded in the Commission minutes and can be widely known. However, the Commission members usually attempt to reach a broad consensus before proceeding to vote.

THE PRESIDENCY

The European Council is the institutionalisation of a previous tradition of informal but highly influential meetings of chief executives of the member states. At the initiative of French President Valéry Giscard D'Estaing, the European Council was formally created in 1974 and held its first meeting in 1975, in Dublin, Ireland. The European Council is formed by the twenty-seven heads of government or state – usually prime ministers, but also the Presidents of Bulgaria, Cyprus, France, Lithuania and Poland, all of them directly elected and with some executive powers – assisted by the ministers of Foreign Affairs, meeting together with the President of the European Commission, the President of the Parliament and the High Representative for Foreign Affairs and Security Policy, so more than thirty members in all. It usually meets at least twice and up to four times a year. With the new rules, the president of the European Council will be chosen for a period of two and a half years, renewable once, so up to five years in coincidence with the Parliament and the Commission terms.

Although the European Council has no formal decision powers, it is an important agenda setter, providing the European Union with both the impetus and the apathy of its uneven development and defining the general political guidelines thereof. Actually, the European Council sets the conditions and the timetable for accepting new European Union members and associates. Some of the most prominent members of the European Council were long-tenured member states' chief executives, such as Margaret Thatcher (1979–91) and Tony Blair (1997–2007) from Britain, Helmut Kohl (1983–98), Gerhard Schröder (1998–2006) and Angela Merkel (2006–10) from Germany, François Mitterrand (1981–95), Jacques Chirac (1995–2007) and Nicolas Sarkozy (2007–12) from France, and Felipe González (1982–96) and José M. Aznar (1996–2004) from Spain. The European Council was particularly decisive in the establishment of the conditions and timetable for the common currency, in promoting a Common Foreign and Security Policy, including the decision to integrate the Western European Union into the institutions of the European Union, in proceeding with eastward enlargement with former Communist-dominated countries and in launching the so-called Lisbon strategy for growth and jobs.

INTER-INSTITUTIONAL DECISION-MAKING

The intergovernmental model of decision-making, which was based on the unanimity principle within the European Council and the Council of Ministers, remains in force only for a few important matters, including the acceptance of new members and associates, as well as basic regulations of the European Central Bank and the European Parliament. More federalising inter-institutional relations combining the principle of territorial representation with the representation of the European people at large in the Parliament have been gradually adopted for most policy subjects.

The Council was required only to 'consult' at that time indirectly appointed European Assembly according to the Rome Treaty (1957). Significant changes began after the first direct elections of the European Parliament in 1979. Further stages in its reinforcement include the following: the introduction of new rules forcing the Council to share certain legislative powers with the Parliament or co-operation procedure, as embodied in the Single European Act (1986); the co-decision procedure for legislative Acts, as well as the formal requirement of the Parliament's support for the appointment of the Commission President, as introduced by the Maastricht Treaty on European Union (1992); and the replacement of the co-operation procedure with co-decision rules, as well as the requirement for a formal investiture of the Commission and its President by the Parliament prior to the commissioners taking office, as introduced by the Amsterdam Treaty (1997) and the Nice Treaty (2001).

Typically the initiative role of the Commission favours policy change, mostly in favour of further Europe-wide integration and harmonisation of legislation. Sometimes the Commission finds it expedient to propose radical innovation in the expectation that its proposals will be moderated during the ensuing negotiations in the Council and the Parliament. The co-decision procedure, which permits a decision to be made with the support of a qualified majority of the Council together with a simple majority of the Parliament, has increased the volume of legislation. An annual average of 55 legislative Acts were approved by the previous co-operation procedure, in an overwhelming proportion by the Council unanimity, during the period 1987–93. With the introduction of the co-decision procedure an annual average of twenty-four legislative Acts were approved by this procedure during the initial period

1993–2002, but this figure has almost doubled in the years up to 2006 (author's own calculation using data from the European Parliament).

The role of the European Parliament in the elaboration and approval of the EU budget has also become increasingly relevant. During the early years of the Community, from 1958 to 1974, the Parliament had no real budgetary powers. From 1975 on, the Council and the Parliament developed frequent conflicts regarding the classification of expenditures between 'compulsory' (as such expenditure necessarily derived from the EU treaties, according to the Council interpretation) and 'non-compulsory' (which initially concerned only administrative expenditure). In this way, the Council reserved for itself exclusive competences on agriculture and certain international agreements, which amounted to the bulk of the EU budget. At the requirement of the Parliament, the European Court of Justice judged the 1986 budget, calling upon the two institutions to reach an agreement. More cooperative decisions were fostered by the Inter-institutional Agreement on budgetary discipline and improvement of the procedure signed in 1988. In 1995, on the basis of the lack of agreement with the Council, the President of the European Parliament declared the final adoption of the EU budget unilaterally, although a new decision of the Court of Justice forced the resumption of the previous procedure. Inter-institutional cooperation between the Council and the Parliament led to the approval of the EU financial Agenda 2000–6.

Interestingly, successive motions of censure on the European Commission by the European Parliament, although all formally failed, obtained an increasing number of favourable votes: 16 in June 1990, 8 in July 1991, 96 in December 1992, 118 in February 1997 and 232 in January 1999. The latter was still short of a majority, but the credible threat that a new vote could obtain larger support precipitated the resignation of the whole European Commission, including its President, in March 1999. Similarly, votes of confidence on incoming Commissions have obtained increasing numbers of negative votes: 31 in February 1981 (Gaston Thorn Commission), 34 in January 1985, not recorded in January 1989, 84 in January 1993 (on the three Jacques Delors Commissions), 104 in January 1995 (Jacques Santer Commission), and 138 and 153 in September 1999 (Romano Prodi Commission).

When the Parliament and the Council disagree on an issue, the differences are settled within the Conciliation Committee, where representatives of the Commission are also present. The unity of action of the commissioners, together with their expertise on technical policy proposals, as well as the frequency of actual unanimous agreements within the Council, give these two institutions some bargaining advantage regarding the Parliament.

DIVISION OF POWERS

Other institutions with significant autonomy within the complex framework of division of powers in the EU are the Court of Justice and the European Central Bank. The Court of Justice was created in 1952, at that time in the framework of the European Coal and Steel Community. Currently, it is formed by twenty-seven judges, one per member state, and eight advocates-general. The judges are appointed for six-year terms and renewed by halves every three years. They are selected among law professionals, including a number of academics, in most cases by consensus between each state government and the corresponding opposition.

The Court of Justice is to ensure that the European Union legislation is equally interpreted and applied in all member states and it is given primacy over state and local laws. The Court has jurisdiction to hear disputes among EU institutions, member states and citizens. In particular, it can develop proceedings for failure to fulfil an obligation (usually brought by the Commission against some member state), for annulment of decisions made by the EU institutions (usually brought by some member states), or for failure to act, as well as for damages and appeals (to be brought by citizens). Thousands of cases have been brought before the European Court of Justice, including 2,860 actions for a member state to fulfil its obligations (Italy being the first, with 559). Since 1989, the Court has focused on the interpretation of EU legislation, while a newly created Court of First Instance makes judicial safeguards available to individual citizens. An important development is the so-called preliminary rulings by which state and local courts, which are usually more directly available to citizens, can ask the European Court to rule on the validity of EU acts. This reinforces cooperation between Europe-wide and state and local judicial institutions. Important judicial decisions have been made on common market issues, including free movement of goods, capital and persons, freedom to create companies and market competition, on environmental protection, and on individual rights, including the establishment of equal pay for men and women.

The so-called 'Eurosystem' of central banks is made up of the European Central Bank and the national central banks of the member states. The member states which do not participate in the Eurozone have a special status allowing them to conduct their own monetary policies. The Eurosystem defines and implements the monetary policy of the Eurozone, including the management of foreign reserves of the member states, with the intention of maintaining price stability. It also supervises private financial institutions. The European Central Bank is ruled by the Governing Council, which comprises the President, the Vice-President and four other members appointed by the member states, as well as the governors of the national central banks of the Eurozone. In order to enhance their independence from national governments, the members of the board of the European Central Bank are appointed for a minimum term of eight years, while the governors of national central banks have a minimum term of office of five years. The national banks subscribe and hold the capital of the European Central Bank on the basis of the member states' respective shares of gross domestic product and population. Most decisions in the Governing Council are made by simple majority, although some important decisions regarding capital are made by qualified majority with weighted votes based on each member state's capital share.

Finally, we review two advisory committees, the European and Social Committee and the Committee of Regions, which have no separate powers but work in collaboration with the Parliament, the Council and the Commission. In both cases, the representation of the member states in the Committee responds to the same numerical criteria, roughly similar to the distribution of votes in the Council. The two committees also share a common administrative apparatus.

The European Economic and Social Committee sketches a corporatist framework inspired by previous experiences developed in some of the EU member states. It is formed by 317 members, appointed by the member states for terms of four years. The Committee is organised in three groups, respectively representing the employers (as organised in the European Union of Industries), the workers' unions (as corresponding to the European Confederation), and others, including farmers, traders, artisans and professionals' representatives. The Committee is an advisory body of the Council of the EU and the European Commission on issues related to common economic and social policies.

The Committee of the Regions was established in 1994 to deal with the demands of regional and local governments. The initial impulse was given by the German *Länder* governments with the aim of preserving their decision powers within a federal framework. Most Autonomous Communities in Spain soon joined the demand for regional representation within the EU institutions.

There are at least two new sources of increasing regional and local demands within the European Union. The first is income disparities. Between member states of the EU, they are maintained up to a proportion of 4:1, Ireland being the highest and Bulgaria and Romania the lowest (double the proportion of, for instance, the United States). But income disparities among regions are much higher, up to 12:1, as between Inner London, Brussels and Luxembourg, on one side, and Severozapaden in North West Bulgaria and North East Romania, on the other. Although there is increasing emigration from relatively disadvantaged regions, their governments also compete for foreign investment, mostly on the basis of lower labour costs, at the same time as seeking redistribution through EU subsidies. The second economic source of increasing regionalism is developing in more advanced regions as Europe-wide free trade diminishes the previous advantages of large states protecting large markets for local producers. This creates new opportunities for relatively socially and culturally homogeneous regions to increase their own government's powers without significant economic loss.

The Committee of the Regions can channel and reconcile all these varied demands in a rather limited manner. The Committee is formed by 317 representatives of regional and local institutions, appointed for terms of four years. The Committee of the Regions is an advisory body of the European Commission on issues related to regional and local governments competences, including transport, telecommunications, energy, public health, education and culture, as well as the management of structural and development funds.

More interesting, the role of regional governments has also increased in the Council of the European Union. This is consistent with the role of territorial representation that would correspond to the Council as the upper chamber in a federal development of the EU institutions. Especially in highly decentralised member states, the principle of territorial representation in the EU institutions may be embodied by the state governments together with the regional and local governments. As a matter of fact, in Germany, Belgium, Austria and to minor extent in Britain and Spain, regional governments coordinate with the corresponding state government in permanent cooperation committees dealing with European policy. Since 1993 a member state can be represented in the Council of the EU by a regional minister.

Accordingly, the Belgian representation in the Council is made up of either a mix of state and regional governments or the latter on issues such as industry, research, education, culture, territorial planning and tourism. In 2001, for the first time a Council of Ministers of the EU, that on Research, was presided over by a regional minister, from Brussels-capital. The representation of Germany in the Council of the EU is negotiated in the upper chamber of the German parliament, the Bundesrat, which is made up of representatives of the *Länder* governments. The Austrian *Länder* and the governments of Scotland and Wales also participate in the Council of the EU.

FROM EMPIRE TO DEMOCRATIC FEDERATION

The future institutional structure and the formal decision-making rules of the European Union are designed in a 'reform treaty' launched by an intergovernmental Conference in 2007, but some of its innovative provisions will not come into force until 2017. Most of the new changes were previously intended to be included in a treaty establishing a constitution for Europe, which was elaborated by a European Convention and signed by the heads of state or government of the EU in 2004. The constitutional treaty, which aimed at replacing all the existing treaties with a single text, was approved by most member states by different internal procedures, including several referendums, but the planned process of ratification failed because it did not obtain sufficient support in referendums in France and the Netherlands in 2005.

The most prominent institutional changes put forward include the following: the Parliament would enlarge its legislative and budgetary powers; the Council should replace unanimity rule with double qualified majority rule in new fields (but not on justice and home affairs); the president of the Commission should be elected, as it is, by the Council and the Parliament, but 'taking into account the parliamentary elections'; and the presidency of the European Council, instead of rotating every six months, would be appointed for periods of two and a half years, renewable once, so up to five years, coinciding with the terms of the Parliament. All these changes would certainly favour a more federal working of the EU institutions. But they would not diminish the consensual mode of decision-making which has characterised fifty years of Europe-building in democracy, prosperity and peace.

Indeed political pluralism and consensus have been the rule in the European Union. The European Parliament and the Council usually have different political party majorities due to the tendency in elections to the former for the electorate to vote against the incumbent domestic government and to the latter's composition based on those governments. Only in 2004, for the first time, did a centre-right majority, which was basically made up of members of the People's and the Liberal groups, exist in the Parliament, the Council and the Commission. However, as seen in the previous pages, broad multi-party coalitions tend to be formed in the European Parliament, with different party compositions for different policy issues. In the Council, even if only a qualified majority is legally required, it is common to deliberately pursue attempts to obtain broader agreements, which produces many unanimous votes. In the whole process of inter-institutional decision-making in the European Union, certainly the most powerful actors – the largest member states and the largest European political groups – tend to attain high influence. But the interests of minorities are usually accommodated and all actors tend to be conciliated to some degree. Consensual decision-making favours citizens' and representatives' support of the existing institutional framework, that is, 'legitimacy'. Since the rules for decision-making are frequently judged by the way they work, that is, by the type of decisions they tend to produce, broadly distributed satisfaction with the outcomes creates broad support for the institutional regime.

Consensus and agreements among European states are fostered by the actors' sense of having a long past and an expected long future in common. Concessions can be made on some issues in the expectation of compensations on others. The long history of permanent conflicts and increasingly frequent and bloody inter-state wars, as well as the challenges derived from new technological changes and the subsequent enlargement of the scale of human interactions, make relevant European actors aware of the potentially very high costs of major disagreements within the European Union. 'Unity in diversity' is also strengthened by sanctioning mechanisms to enforce EU decisions, which have in fact been accepted as obligatory devices by the member states' representatives.

Regarding the future of the European democratic 'empire', again the comparison with the United States of America can be helpful. From its foundation in the late eighteenth century and for more than one hundred years, the founding states of the American union kept their 'sovereign' rights, very different institutions existed across the territory (including direct rule from Washington) and the territorial limits of the union were undefined. Only during a long period after the inter-state, intra-American Civil War were the limits of the steady expansion of the United States established (with borders around the Caribbean Sea). It was then, as late as the early twentieth century, that the union managed to organise all the territory in states with elected legislatures and governors, the federal Senate was elected with homogeneous rules in all the states, and the creation of the Federal Reserve forced monetary union.

Starting in the aftermath of the intra-European civil war called the Second World War, and during a period of more than fifty years, the European Union has followed a comparable path to eradicate war and establish security, create a great common market and set the institutional frame for the provision of large-scale public goods over an extended territory. As has been shown in this chapter, the outline of a potentially more democratic and efficient federal union in Europe is basically designed and positively tested. Probably the most crucial decision ahead of the EU is the establishment of clear borders of the union, which appears to be a condition for further stability, consolidation and progress.

BIBLIOGRAPHY

Origins and evolution

Colomer, J. M. (2007) *Great Empires, Small Nations: The Uncertain Future of the Sovereign State*, London: Routledge.

Hesse, J. J. and V. Wright (eds) (1996) *Federalizing Europe? The Costs, Benefits, and Preconditions of Federal Political Systems*, Oxford: Oxford University Press.

Hix, S. (2005) *The Political System of the European Union*, 2nd edn, Basingstoke: Palgrave Macmillan.

Nugent, N. (2006) *The Government and Politics of the European Union*, 6th edn, Basingstoke: Palgrave Macmillan; Durham: Duke University Press.

Peterson, J. and M. Shackleton (2006) *The Institutions of the European Union*, 2nd edn, Oxford: Oxford University Press.

Riker, W. H. (1996) 'European Federalism: The Lessons of Past Experience', in J. J. Hesse and V. Wright (eds) *Federalizing Europe? The Costs, Benefits, and Preconditions of Federal Political Systems*, Oxford: Oxford University Press.

Zielonka, J. (2006) *Europe as an Empire*, Oxford: Oxford University Press.

Elections

Marsh, M. (1998) 'Testing the Second-order Election Model after Four European Elections', *British Journal of Political Science* 28: 591–607.

Reif, K. (1997) 'European Elections as Member State Second-order Elections Revisited', *European Journal of Political Research* 31 (1): 115–24.

Van der Ejik, C. and M. Franklin (eds) (1996) *Choosing Europe? The European Electorate and National Politics in the Face of Union*, Ann Arbor: University of Michigan Press.

Parties

Bowler, S., D. M. Farrell and R. Katz (1999) *Party Discipline and Parliamentary Government*, Columbus: Ohio State University Press.

Colomer, J. M. (2002) 'How Political Parties, Rather than Member States, Are Building the European Union', in B. Steunenberg (ed.) *Widening the European Union*, London: Routledge.

Colomer, J. M. and M. O. Hosli (1997) 'Decision-making in the European Union: The Power of Political Parties', *Aussenwirtschaft* 52: 255–80.

Hix, S. and C. Lord (2004) *Political Parties in the European Union*, Basingstoke: Palgrave Macmillan.

Kreppel, A. (2001) *The European Parliament and Supranational Party System*, Cambridge: Cambridge University Press.

Laver, M. (1997) 'Government Formation in the European Parliament', *Aussenwirtschaft* 52: 223–48.

Parliament

Corbett, R., F. Jacobs and M. Shackleton (2000) *The European Parliament*, London: John Harper.

Judge, D. and D. Earnshaw (2003) *The European Parliament*, Basingstoke: Palgrave Macmillan.

Council

Bulmer, S. and W. Wessels (1987) *The European Council*, London: Macmillan.
Hayes-Renshaw, F. and H. Wallace (2006) *The Council of Ministers*, 2nd edn, Basingstoke: Palgrave Macmillan.
Westlake, M. (1995) *The Council of the European Union*, London: Cartermill.

Commission

Cini, M. (1996) *The European Commission: Leadership, Organisation and Culture in the EU Administration*, Manchester: Manchester University Press.
Donnelly, M. and E. Ritchie (1997) 'The College of Commissioners and their Cabinets', in G. Edwards and D. Spence (eds) *The European Commission*, London: Cartermill: 33–67.
Edwards, G. and D. Spence (eds) (1997) *The European Commission*, London: Cartermill.
Nugent, N. (2001) *The European Commission*, Basingstoke: Palgrave.

Decision-making

Albgaba, E., J. M. Bilbao and J. R. Fernandez (2007) 'The Distribution of Power in the European Constitution', *European Journal of Operational Research* 176: 1,752–66.
Crombez, C. (1996) 'Legislative Procedures in the European Community', *British Journal of Political Science* 26: 199–228.
Steunenberg, B. (ed.) (2002) *Widening the European Union*, London: Routledge.
Thomson, R., J. Boerefijn and F. Stokman (2004) 'Actor Alignments in European Union Decision-making', *European Journal of Political Research* 43: 237–61.
Thomson, R., F. S. Stokman, C. H. Achen and T. König (eds) (2006) *The European Union Decides*, Cambridge: Cambridge University Press.
Tsebelis, G., C. B. Jensen, A. Kalandrakis and A. Kreppel (2001) 'Legislative Procedures in the EU', *British Journal of Political Science* 31 (4): 573–99.

Court

Dehousse, R. (1998) *The European Court of Justice*, Basingstoke: Palgrave.
Hunnings, N. M. (1996) *The European Courts*, London: Cartermill.

Regions

Ansell, C. K. and G. di Palma (eds) (2004) *Restructuring Territoriality: Europe and the United States Compared*, Cambridge and New York: Cambridge University Press.

Jeffery, C. (ed.) (1997) *The Regional Dimension of the European Union. Towards a Third Level in Europe?*, London: Frank Cass.

Jones, B. and M. Keating (1995) *The European Union and the Regions*, Oxford: Clarendon Press.

INDEX

Adenauer, Konrad 281
adversarial politics 14, 37, 102, 103, 218–220, 250;
    see also majoritarian regimes
Agrarian parties, in Scandinavia 255, 266
Ahtisaari 262
Algeria 98, 103, 107, 126
Almond, Gabriel A. and Verba, Sidney 5
authoritarian regimes 174–175
Aznar, José M. 194

Balsemao, Francisco Pinto 187
Basque Nationalist Party (PNV) *see* Regional parties
Basque Nationalists (EA) *see* Regional parties
Bavarian Party *see* Regional parties
Bérégovoy, Pierre 123, 129
Berlusconi, Silvio 137, 140, 148, 150, 154, 161,
    164–166, 168, 170
Blair, Anthony 29, 42, 54
Blum, Leon 96
Bonino, Emma 162
Borsellino, Paolo 164
Bossi, Umberto 137, 148
Brossolette, Pierre 123
Brown, Gordon 29
bureaucracy *see* civil service; government
Burin des Roziers 123

Cabinet *see* government
Calvo-Sotelo, Leopoldo 185
Canary Coalition *see* Regional parties
Carneiro, Franciso Sa 191
Cavaco Silva, Anibal 186, 191
Chaban-Delmas, Jacques 105, 125
Chirac, Jacques 104, 116, 121, 125, 132
Christian Democratic Union (CDU) *see*
    Christian-democrats, in Germany
Christian-democrats: in Belgium (CVP/PSC)
    213–217, 219–221, 229–230; in France (MRP)
    105–106; in Germany (CDU/CSU) 59, 63,
    64–76, 79, 87; in Italy (CCD-CDU, DCI, ED,
    PPI, UDEUR) 136–147, 151, 153, 157, 159,
    166, 169; in Luxembourg 213, 217, 220,

229–230; in the Netherlands (KVP/CDA) 213,
    217–221, 229–230; *see also* European Political
    Groups: European People's Party
Christian Social Union (CSU) *see*
    Christian-democrats, in Germany
Ciampi, Carlo Azeglio 153
civil service: in Great Britain 41–42, 45–46, 54; in
    Ireland 42–43
'Clean Hands' investigation 136, 145, 158, 162
cleavages: class 18–20, 54, 62, 65; language, region,
    territory 22–23, 25, 60, 65, 216–218, 221, 227,
    233, 236–237; religion, moral 62, 64, 215, 217
coalitions: in Finland 258; in Germany 66–68; in
    Great Britain 25, 37; in Low Countries 224–229;
    in Scandinavia 264; *see also* government
co-decision procedure 299
Colomer, Josep M. 135
Communists: in Finland 255; in France (PCF) 102,
    103, 106–109; in Germany (PDS) 60–61, 64, 67;
    in Italy (PCI) 139, 146, 157–160, 169, (RC)
    138–140, 143, 145, 161; in Norway 255; in
    Portugal (PCP) 183, 192; in Spain (PCE, IU)
    178–179, 184–186, 188, 201; in Sweden 264,
    267; *see also* European Political Groups: United
    Left
Conservatives: in Great Britain 18–19, 25, 28,
    35–36, 45–46, 53–55, 287–288; in Portugal
    (CDS-PP) 187–188, 289; in Spain (AP-PP) 142,
    177–179, 185, 188–191, 194–197, 201, 288; *see
    also* European Political Groups: European
    Democratic Group, European People's Party
Constitutional Court: in France 97; in Germany 83;
    in Portugal 202; in Spain 203
Convergence and Union (CiU) *see* Regional parties
Council of Ministers (Europe) 282–284, 291,
    291–299, 302–305
Craxi, Bettino 138, 152, 158, 170

D'Alema, Massimo 139, 166
D'Antoni, Sergio 145
d'Hondt formula *see* electoral systems
Dahl, Robert 5